The Differentiated Network

Nitin Nohria
Sumantra Ghoshal

The Differentiated Network

Organizing Multinational Corporations
for Value Creation

Jossey-Bass Publishers • San Francisco

Substantial discounts on bulk quantities of Jossey-Bass books are available to corporations, professional associations, and other organizations. For details and discount information, contact the special sales department at Jossey-Bass Inc., Publishers (415) 433–1740; Fax (800) 605–2665.

For sales outside the United States, please contact your local Simon & Schuster International Office.

Jossey-Bass Web address: http://www.josseybass.com

(Copyright credits appear on page 253)

TCF Manufactured in the United States of America on Lyons Falls Turin Book. This paper is acid-free and 100 percent totally chlorine-free.

Library of Congress Cataloging-in-Publication Data

Nohria, Nitin, date.
    The differentiated network : organizing multinational corporations for value creation / Nitin Nohria, Sumantra Ghoshal.
       p.   cm. — (Jossey-Bass business & management series)
    Includes bibliographical references (p.   ) and index.
    ISBN 0–7879–0331–0 (alk. paper)
    1. International business enterprises—Management.
2. Technological innovations—Management. 3. Diffusion of innovations. I. Ghoshal, Sumantra. II. Title. III. Series.
HD62.4.N64 1997
658'.049—dc21   96-48257
                                           CIP

FIRST EDITION
HB Printing 10 9 8 7 6 5 4 3 2 1

The Jossey-Bass

Business & Management Series

To Monica and Susmita
with love and appreciation

Contents

Figures and Tables

Tables

Preface

This book represents the synthesis of a stream of research that began more than a decade ago when we were both at the Massachusetts Institute of Technology. It is based on a series of papers that we have written over this period, some together, others in collaboration with graduate students and colleagues who became interested in our research and joined us in advancing it further.

We decided to write this book because we felt that even though we had published many of the ideas in various outlets, the sum of these parts did not adequately capture all we had learned through our research. A major theme in this book is that to be truly effective, multinational corporations should be differentiated and integrated. Similarly, this book represents an attempt to integrate what might otherwise have remained differentiated parts.

The primary idea we wish to advance here is that the modern MNC must be organized as a differentiated network to tap the full value-creation potential of its globally distributed capabilities. This basic idea is not new. Indeed, it has been elaborated in some detail by Chris Bartlett and Sumantra Ghoshal in *Managing Across Borders: The Transnational Solution* (1989), a book that is the intellectual forebear of this one. What is new in this book is a more systematic examination of this core idea—especially an effort to ground the concept of a differentiated network more firmly in organization theory and to test its validity more rigorously using large-sample data.

Our aspirations in writing this book are twofold. First, we continue to believe that despite their increasing importance in the global economy, MNCs remain neglected in organization theory.

This neglect, we believe, stems in part from the practical difficulties of studying these complex organizations. We hope that the concepts and the pragmatic empirical strategies advanced in this book will stimulate more research on MNCs.

Second, we wish to revive interest in the topics of organization structure and design. The internal structures and processes of complex organizations was a subject of intense study in the 1970s, the heyday of contingency theory. However, since then, these topics have taken a backseat to an interest in the organization's environment. Indeed, in most of the currently popular strands of organization theory, such as population ecology, institutional theory, network analysis, and organizational economics, the internal organization of firms is almost completely neglected. Though much has been learned from these new perspectives, we feel that it is time to think about organization design again, especially because the concepts advanced in the 1970s do not always provide a good guide for designing organizations moving forward into the new millennium.

As these aspirations indicate, this book is written primarily for our academic colleagues. Yet we have tried to write in plain English. We hope that practitioners will thus be able to read and benefit from this book. To enhance their interest in doing so, we have explicitly spelled out the practical implications of our findings throughout the book.

This book's intellectual genesis lies in the work of Chris Bartlett. We owe him a great debt for having introduced us to the fascinating world of MNCs and for having been a mentor, friend, and research partner throughout the years. This book could never have been written without his contributions.

We also wish to thank Luis Almeida-Costa, Ranjay Gulati, Monica Higgins, Harry Korine, Peter Moran, and Gabriel Szulanski, our coauthors on some of the papers that we draw on in this book. Don Lessard, Michael Scott-Morton, and Eleanor Westney, our teachers at MIT, have had an intellectual influence on us that is evident throughout this book.

As we have all experienced, the final 20 percent of the work involved in writing a book seems to take 80 percent of the time. Ramin Toloui, our research associate, was a driving force for this project during this final stage. We are also grateful to Peter Amirault, Vanita Datta, Diana Line, and Misiek Piskorski for burning the midnight oil to help complete this book. Cedric Crocker and David Horne, our editors at Jossey-Bass, waited patiently and showed remarkably good cheer as we struggled to meet our deadlines. Their encouragement was instrumental in enabling us to get this book done.

We would also like to thank the Division of Research at the Harvard Business School and Booz, Allen, and Hamilton, the sponsors of the Strategic Leadership Research Program at the London Business School, for their generous support.

Finally, we reserve our last acknowledgment for the two people who have sacrificed the most for the cause. In recognition of the numerous occasions when we turned over to them at home work that we should have done ourselves, we dedicate this book to Monica Chandra and Susmita Ghoshal, our wives. We hope that they will deem the result worthy of all they have given up for it.

London
January 1997

Nitin Nohria
Sumantra Ghoshal

Chapter One

The Differentiated Network

It was about thirty years ago that Vernon (1966) proposed the product cycle theory that identified the ability to innovate as the *raison d'être* for multinational corporations. Over the past three decades, many new theories have been proposed to explain why MNCs exist, but innovation has continued to occupy center stage in these explanations (see Calvet, 1981). The multinational's facility to invest and manage its affairs in many different countries, it is argued, allows it to secure the benefits of innovations in multiple locations through its own internal organization more effectively than market-mediated mechanisms (Buckley and Casson, 1976; Rugman, 1981).

As this characterization suggests, the focus of traditional theories of innovation in the MNC has been on knowledge appropriation. The multinational is an organizational form that internalizes knowledge flows that would otherwise have to take place through market transactions among its diverse set of subsidiary organizations. Because the price mechanism fails to value knowledge properly in the marketplace, thus inhibiting socially beneficial transactions, the multinational creates value by internalizing knowledge flows. This account of the existence of the MNC is simply a version of the standard microeconomic transaction cost theory of the firm. It is in essence a *negative* theory of the firm: the reason for the existence of the firm is described in terms of its facility to avoid a stifling market failure.

Increasingly, however, the MNC's ability merely to enable the flow of knowledge from its headquarters to its national subsidiary units no longer represents a sufficient competitive advantage. The maximization of innovative activity and knowledge creation has become an imperative organizational challenge for today's multinational firms. Traditionally, many MNCs could compete successfully by exploiting scale economies or arbitraging imperfections in the world's goods, labor, and capital markets, but these advantages have tended to erode over time. In many industries, MNCs no longer compete primarily with national companies; nowadays they go head-to-head with a handful of other giants that tend to be comparable in size, international resource access, and worldwide market position. Under these circumstances, the ability to innovate prolifically (and to exploit those innovations rapidly and efficiently) across the globe has become crucial to a multinational's competitive advantage.

Moreover, the division of the global economy into a technologically advanced center that produces all innovation for a technologically backward periphery is rapidly becoming obsolete. Modern multinationals depend on innovations created not only in home-market units but also in a growing number of national subsidiaries. Furthermore, as markets outside the home market grow in importance, national subsidiary units command larger and larger shares of the firm's total resources. To remain competitive on a global scale, the firm must leverage all of these resources in the service of knowledge creation. The idea that the multinational organizational form can act to facilitate innovation throughout its network of national subsidiaries offers a rather different economic rationale for its existence than that espoused by the transaction cost approach. According to this argument, in addition to avoiding market pitfalls in knowledge appropriation, the MNC can create a shared social context that actively promotes knowledge creation—potentially, a *positive* theory of the multinational firm (Moran and Ghoshal, 1996).

These accounts of negative and positive conceptions of the existence of the multinational are not merely descriptive; they also have normative implications for the ideal structure of MNCs. If the central function of the multinational is knowledge appropriation, a hierarchical organization structure is sufficient for the task. With decision-making authority centralized in the headquarters unit, knowledge can be distributed from one subsidiary to others according to the will of central management. Subsidiary autonomy is not required for the avoidance of transaction costs associated with market-mediated knowledge transfer; indeed, such autonomy may actually inhibit knowledge dissemination if subsidiary managers disagree with the judgments of headquarters.

As knowledge creation becomes increasingly important for the MNC, a hierarchical structure may be inferior as an organizational form. For example, highly centralized management can suffocate the innovative energies of individuals in the subsidiary units. At the same time, a highly formal system in which internal processes are governed by a set of impersonal rules may discourage creativity. Indeed, Hedlund (1994) has argued that the logic of hierarchical organization must be reconsidered in light of the requirements for effective knowledge management. As contemporary MNCs mobilize firm assets worldwide to meet the innovation challenges of the global marketplace, business academics have identified a growing number of alternative organizational forms for the multinational. The traditional focus on hierarchical headquarters-subsidiary relations has given way to the recognition of a diverse set of intrafirm relations, whether "heterarchical" (Hedlund, 1986), "multi-focal" (Prahalad and Doz, 1987), or "transnational" (Bartlett and Ghoshal, 1989). All of these models describe in some way the structural responses of the modern MNC to meet the demands of innovation and knowledge creation in a dynamic global economy.

Two Themes

The imperative of knowledge or value creation and its structural requirements highlight the inadequacy of the hierarchical archetype as a preferred organizational form for MNCs today. The challenge for business academics and managers is to replace the hierarchical model with a theory of the MNC that acknowledges the new environmental conditions and the changes in the internal organization of MNCs that are needed to confront them. The purpose of this book is to offer a new theoretically and empirically useful model of the multinational. In the course of this investigation, two central themes will be visited and revisited. Concerning what pulls organizational units apart and what pulls them together, these themes, taken together, provide an incisive framework to enhance our understanding of the structure of the MNC. This framework holds relevance for managers seeking to implement changes in their administrative systems to boost firm performance and for academics attempting to explain the existence of prevailing administrative forms and, in the process, to discover organizational features best suited for future managerial challenges.

Our first theme is that the structure of the MNC must be conceptualized as a *differentiated network* rather than as a broad structural archetype, such as an area, a product, or a matrix structure. The MNC consists of diverse subsidiaries operating in distinct national environments. Each presents unique exigencies that cannot be adequately addressed by a uniform organizationwide structure. Thus a model that fails to differentiate the various organizational entities and linkages within an MNC does not accurately represent the realities of the business world, one in which internal differentiation is requisite to a firm's success. A greater elaboration on internal structural relations is necessary for a theoretically sound model to test interesting empirical propositions.

A model of the multinational is developed in this book that takes these considerations seriously. It is called the differentiated network to underline its network perspective. At its crux is the premise that the structure of the MNC can be understood as a differentiated network composed of distributed resources linked through different types of relations: (1) the "local" linkages within each national subsidiary, (2) the linkages between headquarters and the subsidiaries, and (3) the linkages between subsidiaries themselves.

In Part One of this book, we demonstrate that the differentiated network model is a powerful tool for analyzing knowledge flows and value creation through the generation and exploitation of innovations within the multinational. Chapter Two provides an overview of distributed innovation in the multinational. Chapter Three examines how the existence and distribution of slack resources affects knowledge creation in the national subsidiaries, and Chapter Four investigates the impact of a range of structural attributes on the creation, adoption, and diffusion of innovations throughout the MNC. The transaction cost view of the firm focuses primarily, if not exclusively, on the transfer of innovations from the headquarters to the subsidiaries, tasks that the hierarchical structure is particularly well suited to address. To the extent that the creation, adoption, and diffusion of innovations needs increasingly to be distributed throughout the MNC for the organization to perform well, a more complex model of the multinational is required. In Part One of this book, we demonstrate that MNCs organized as differentiated networks are most likely to tap their full global innovative capacity. In addition to its utility for academic empirical research, the differentiated network model is shown to offer prescriptive insights for managers seeking to organize their firms to enhance innovation.

Part Two generalizes the conclusions of Part One to the overall performance of the multinational. In Chapter Five, employing the differentiated network model, we find that overall subsidiary performance is positively correlated with a high degree of internal differentiation, in the same way that differentiation is required for enhancing innovation. These results illustrate the inadequacy of general structural archetypes, such as area, product, or matrix, used to characterize MNCs in the past. Such models obscure the important reality that diversity through internal differentiation is essential to optimal firm performance. By highlighting the degree of complexity with which internal relations in the firm can be structured, the differentiated network model offers a useful heuristic for managers seeking to adapt their organizations to the demands of the global business environment.

Chapter Six reveals that firm profitability is also positively correlated with high levels of shared values across the subsidiaries.

This conclusion is not particularly surprising. Multinationals are extremely diverse organizations, with far-flung subsidiaries all over the globe, operating in different regulatory environments, cultures, and time zones. Add to this diversity a highly differentiated system of internal organization, and it seems surprising that the MNC can hold itself together at all. Integrative mechanisms serve to foster an organizational cohesiveness and a shared social context that are conducive to firm success and profitability.

Though it is relatively easy to speak in abstract language about "integrative mechanisms," the practical meaning of that expression is not necessarily straightforward. In Chapters Seven and Eight, we conduct an empirical examination of two types of integrative mechanisms, interunit communication networks and interpersonal networks, both of which contribute to the creation of shared values and lead to "normative integration." We argue that normative integration is the glue that holds differentiated networks together as entities called firms. Ownership may distinguish between parts of the larger network outside the firm (customers, government regulators, upstream suppliers) and the components of the firm itself, but it is the distinctive codes of communication shared by the members of the multinational that truly demarcate the boundaries of the organization (Monteverde, 1995). Thus when describing the structure of the MNC in terms of a differentiated network, the model must include the overlying concept of normative integration, which can substantively affect how successfully the firm competes. Furthermore, the nature and extent of normative integration are key decision variables that may be manipulated by managers in the diverse environments in which they operate and in the goals they seek to achieve. The importance of integrative mechanisms that bind the differentiated parts of the MNC together is the second major theme of this book.

The overarching theoretical perspective we adopt throughout this book is contingency theory (Lawrence and Lorsch, 1967; J. D. Thompson, 1967; Galbraith, 1973). We share the view of Donaldson (1995) that contingency theory remains the most useful paradigm for studying organization design and effectiveness. Contingency theory provides a powerful lens through which we can examine the relationship between organizations and their environments. It is also a theory that leads to useful guidelines for practice. Even though this book is written primarily for an academic audience, we adopt a contingency perspective because we deeply subscribe to the value that theory must be relevant for practice. Throughout the book, we therefore spell out the practical implications of our findings.

Part Three discusses the limits and extensions of the differentiated network, and the contingency perspective we adopt is most starkly evident in the first chapter of this section, Chapter Nine, where we outline the environmental conditions for which the differentiated network structure outlined in this book is most suited. We argue that the differentiated network structure is most suited to environmental conditions that require MNCs to meet simultaneously the demands of national responsiveness and global integration. Indeed, as we discuss in Chapter Ten, our concluding chapter, meeting these demands requires the modern MNC to manage a network of relationships that extends beyond the internal boundaries of the firm to include external entities such as suppliers, competitors, customers, and regulators. We show how the network perspective we have advanced throughout this book can be readily extended to analyze this external network of relations and its implications for the internal organization of MNCs. In this final chapter, we also reiterate the importance of building a positive theory of the MNC—a theory that recognizes that the unique organizational advantage of the modern MNC lies in its ability to create a shared social context that enhances the value-creating capacity of its globally dispersed parts.

A Brief History of MNC Organization

As we noted at the outset, Vernon's life cycle model (1966) serves as the starting point of the theory of MNC organization and defines its early evolution. After developing and then exhausting the home market for its innovative products, a firm would expand abroad, first through export and later, once the market had developed sufficiently, through production facilities abroad. In time, the firm would attempt to supply all its markets through local or geographically proximate subsidiaries. Eventually, when the product matured and became fully standardized, the firm would reconcentrate production in the lowest-cost location and even export the product back to the home country.

In this early evolutionary phase, the key structural decision confronting these firms was the organization of their expanding international operations. Stopford and Wells (1972) proposed a "stages model" as a way to think about the structural evolution of MNCs during this phase (see Figure 1.1). They suggested that at the early stages of foreign expansion, defined by limitations in sales and product diversity, MNCs managed their international operations through an international division. Subsequently, those firms that expanded foreign sales without increasing product diversity typically adopted the "area division" structure. In contrast, firms that expanded by increasing product diversity adopted the "worldwide product division" structure.

Finally, when both foreign sales and foreign product diversity were high, firms adopted the "global matrix" structure.

The focus on different structural archetypes was in keeping with the issues most germane to the early period of the MNC's development (see Davis, 1979, for cases and readings that reflect the concerns of the time). But once MNCs spawned a significant number of subsidiaries, each a quasi-autonomous organization much like a division in a multidivisional firm, the focus shifted to the structure of the headquarters-subsidiary relationship. Born out of the legitimate fear that due to their remote location and host country pressures, subsidiaries might simply pursue their own local interests, the paramount issue was that of control: how the parent organization or headquarters could properly govern its various national subsidiaries (Prahalad and Doz, 1987; Doz and Prahalad, 1981).

Figure 1.1. Stopford and Wells's Model of MNC Organization.

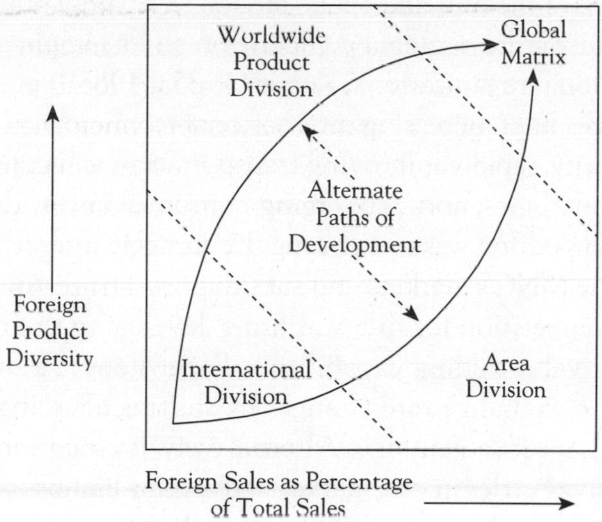

Source: Based on Stopford and Wells, 1972.

Scholars devoted a considerable amount of energy to questions arising from this focus on headquarters-subsidiary relations (see Otterbeck, 1981; Bartlett, 1986; and Egelhoff, 1988a). Specifically, what are the various mechanisms by which subsidiaries may be controlled? They concluded that there were a large number of formal and informal mechanisms by which subsidiaries could be governed (see Martinez and Jarillo, 1989). Given these choices, the structure of each headquarters-subsidiary relationship should be differentiated to fit its contextual circumstances (Gupta and Govindarajan, 1991; see also Chapter Six).

The literature on headquarters-subsidiary relations reflected a headquarters bias. It paid little attention to the structure of the subsidiary. However, in many cases, these subsidiaries were large multiunit organizations comparable in size and complexity to many global organizations. The structure of relations among the subsidiaries was also neglected. Each subsidiary was treated as independent of the other, and any connection was through a hub-and-spoke-like arrangement with a central-headquarters organization.

The rise of global competition dramatically illustrated the limitations of the hub-and-spoke model. In a pair of seminal articles on the nature of global competition and its implications for multinational organizations, Kogut (1985a, 1985b) pointed out that as a result of increasing international technological and economic parity, rapidly improving transportation and communication technologies, and converging consumer tastes, the key to global competition was recognizing the strategic interdependence among the MNC's markets and subsidiaries. The distinctive feature of competition for him was firms' leveraging their globally dispersed value-adding capabilities. For instance, a firm could respond to exchange rate changes by shifting sourcing to locations with a cost advantage. Alternatively, it could subsidize its competitive battles in one market with profits earned in another. These strategic choices required a great deal of operational flexibility, which in turn meant paying more attention to exactly how each subsidiary was structured and connected to the others. Indeed, subsidiaries needed be considered as parts of a global value-added chain.

Following Kogut, a substantial literature developed to describe the distinctive character of global competition and to explain its implications for the organization of the MNC (see Porter, 1986; Doz and Prahalad, 1981; and Ghoshal, 1987). Its theme was that global competition required simultaneous attention to multiple strategic drivers, including pressures for global integration, local responsiveness, and worldwide learning (Bartlett and Ghoshal, 1987a, 1987b). These strategic drivers profoundly affect the performance requirements that MNCs must now satisfy. For example, global integration opens up the potential for economies of scale and scope that a company must exploit to maximize static efficiency. Simultaneously, the need for worldwide learning makes it critical for national subsidiaries to create, adopt, and diffuse new innovations for the MNC's competitive advantage. And the need for local responsiveness implies that the MNC must remain sensitive to the differences across the various countries in which it operates. These strategic drivers can be expected to exert a powerful influence on the organization of the MNC.

It was to respond to these strategic drivers, scholars argued, that MNCs had to organize themselves more as a "heterarchy" (Hedlund, 1986), a "multi-focal organization" (Prahalad and Doz, 1987), or a "transnational corporation" (Bartlett and Ghoshal, 1989). In short, MNCs had to abandon the hub-and-spoke conception and adopt a more networklike perspective. This meant paying greater attention to the nodes of the network—the subsidiaries—and the linkages among them.

Although implicit in most contemporary work on MNC structure, the network perspective remains an evocative metaphor rather than a clear analytical framework. If continued to be used simply as metaphor, the network concept runs the risk of being trivialized or "applied so loosely that it ceases to mean anything" (Nohria, 1992, p. 3). The differentiated network model we offer in this book aims to prevent this from happening by providing a simple yet comprehensive framework for analyzing the structure of MNCs.

Characteristics of the Differentiated Network

The challenge for researchers interested in studying the organization of contemporary MNCs is vividly illustrated by Figure 1.2, which shows the simplest possible representation of the structure of Philips N.V., an MNC headquartered in the Netherlands. The company has its own operating units in sixty countries—lands as diverse as the United States, France, Japan, South Korea, Nigeria, Uruguay, and Bangladesh. Some of these units are large, fully integrated companies that develop, manufacture, and market a diverse range of products from lightbulbs to defense systems. Such subsidiaries might have five thousand or more employees and might be among the largest companies in their host countries. Others are small, single-function operations responsible for marketing or manufacturing one or more of the company's various products and services. Such units might employ as few as fifty people. In some cases, the units have been in operation for more than half a century; others are less than ten years old. Some units are tightly controlled from the headquarters; others enjoy relationships with the headquarters more akin to an equal partnership. Some units are at the center of dense inter-subsidiary relationships; others are relatively isolated.

With only minor alterations, Figure 1.2 could easily be a representation of an American MNC such as Procter & Gamble or a Japanese MNC such as Matsushita. The limitations of reducing such a complex structure to a simpler functional, product, area, or matrix structure are obvious. Equally problematic is describing them in terms of average levels of indicators such as degree of centralization or formalization because variations within such MNCs can be as great as variations across them.

To banish the complexity and heterogeneity inherent in these organizations is to fall into what Fisher (1970, p. 172) calls the "reductive fallacy"—the fallacy of reducing complexity to simplicity or diversity to uniformity. Instead, as Scott (1987, p. 22) recommends, we must "exhibit greater sensitivities to the complexities of organizational systems rather than treating the wider organizational structure as some kind of average of the characteristics of its work activities and work units. It would seem more appropriate to treat it as an overarching framework of relations linking subunits of considerable diversity, and to develop measures that capture the distinctive characteristics of this superstructure."

In keeping with Scott's recommendation, we suggest that the structure of modern MNCs, such as Philips, can be more appropriately conceptualized as a differentiated network. Viewing an MNC's structure as a differentiated network involves directing attention to the following key features.

First, the model, as shown in Figure 1.3, directs attention to the distribution of resources among the various national organizational units, each of which can be viewed as a node in this multinational network (Cook, 1977). Some national subsidiaries will be more resource rich than others. Depending on the resources and capabilities a subsidiary possesses, it may be assigned different roles and responsibilities and may need to be governed accordingly (Benson,

Figure 1.2. Structure of Philips.

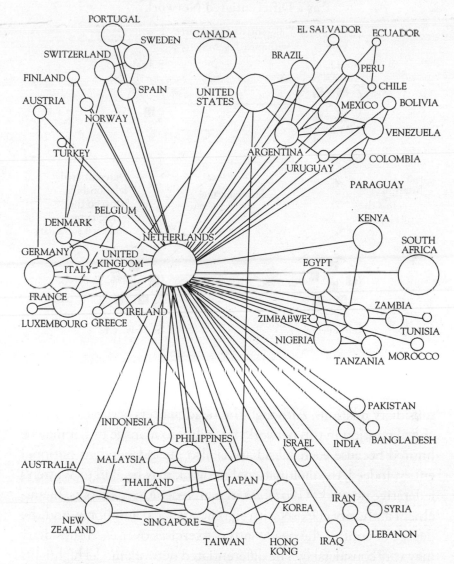

1975; Bartlett and Ghoshal, 1986). Similarly, the internal structure of subsidiaries may vary considerably. Some may be simple functional organizations, whereas others may themselves be large multidivisional organizations. In general, the differentiated network model suggests that the internal structure of each subsidiary be analyzed much as one would analyze the structure of any complex organization (see Pugh, Hickson, Hinings, and Turner, 1968).

**Figure 1.3. Reconceptualizing the Structure of an MNC
as a Differentiated Network.**

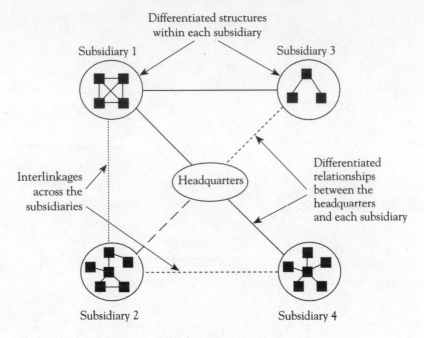

The second structural feature to which the differentiated network model draws attention is the nature of the various headquarters-subsidiary relations. Although the headquarters occupies a hierarchical position in this network, its ability to manage by fiat may be limited because each subsidiary is also an independent national entity. Indeed, the multinational network may be akin to Warren's federative networks (1967). As in such federative networks, hierarchical authority coexists with significant local autonomy, and the degree of control the headquarters exercises over each subsidiary may vary considerably. The differentiated network model highlights these internal differences in the structure of headquarters-subsidiary relations (for example, the degree to which different decision rights are centralized or formalized) and directs the researcher to explore both the antecedents and the consequences of such variations. The structure of different headquarters-subsidiary relations may vary, depending on the nature of interdependence in each situation, and can in turn influence outcomes such as a subsidiary's innovativeness (J. D. Thompson, 1967; Egelhoff, 1988a).

A third structural feature of the differentiated network is the extent to which the various subsidiaries are normatively integrated through various socialization mechanisms (Edstrom and Galbraith, 1977; Jaeger, 1983; Baliga and Jaeger, 1984). Put differently, this structural dimension focuses on the degree of organic solidarity and shared values that bind together the different organizational components of the network (Parsons, 1956).

The fourth important feature of the differentiated network is the communication flows that animate the network. These include lateral and vertical as well as formal and informal communication flows (Galbraith, 1973). The differentiated network highlights the importance of communication flows within the various subsidiaries, between the subsidiaries and the headquarters, and across the subsidiaries. The density, frequency, content, and structure of these communication flows are all seen as vital to the ongoing performance of the MNC. This is because communication patterns influence a variety of outcomes, including coordination costs, combinative capacity, intraorganizational trust, and shared values (see Arrow, 1974; Kogut and Zander, 1992; Ring and Van de Ven, 1992; and Edstrom and Galbraith, 1977).

Taken together, these various structural features, highlighted by the differentiated network model, provide a simple but complete conceptualization of the structure of modern MNCs. The model also provides a framework that researchers can employ to make better sense of substantive concerns. To the extent that reconceptualizing the structure of the MNC as a differentiated network provides a better understanding of the factors enhancing the performance of the MNC along the dimensions identified, the model provides academics with a theoretically simple yet empirically powerful instrument to investigate interesting questions about the operations of MNCs. In addition, the model offers managers a tool that they might employ to institute beneficial organizational changes made apparent by a better understanding of their firm's structure and its suitability for the prevailing environment.

Evaluating the Differentiated Network: An Empirical Approach

One of our primary objectives in this book is to offer a methodological contribution in the form of an empirical approach that can be used to investigate structure-performance relationships in MNCs. The substantive data used in the empirical sections of the book emerged from a research project consisting of three phases, each with a different methodological approach (see Figure 1.4)

The first phase of the project involved case studies of the organization structures, systems, and management processes in nine large multinational companies (Bartlett and Ghoshal, 1986).

In the second phase of the study, a detailed questionnaire survey of headquarters-subsidiary relations was administered in three of these nine companies (Ghoshal, 1986). Two different questionnaires were developed for the second phase of the project. The first was designed for response by headquarters' managers. In this questionnaire, all constructs were operationalized by single variables measured on centrally anchored five-point scales. The second questionnaire was designed for response by subsidiary managers and sought subsidiary responses for the same constructs used in the first instrument. In this instrument, however, the structural constructs were operationalized through multiple indicators.

In each of the three MNCs in which these questionnaires were implemented, two senior headquarters managers responded to the first questionnaire providing single indicators for the various constructs for at least five different national subsidiaries of the company. At the same time, between six and eight managers from each of those subsidiaries responded to the second questionnaire and provided multiple indicators for each of the constructs as applicable to their own subsidiary. Analysis of the data so obtained revealed that in each MNC, interrater convergence was high for

Figure 1.4. The Research Process.

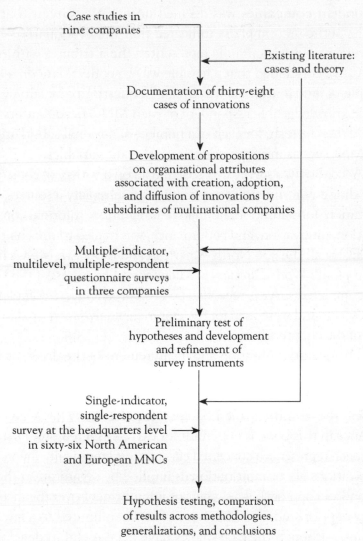

Case studies in
nine companies

Existing literature:
cases and theory

Documentation of thirty-eight
cases of innovations

Development of propositions
on organizational attributes
associated with creation, adoption,
and diffusion of innovations by
subsidiaries of multinational companies

Multiple-indicator,
multilevel, multiple-respondent
questionnaire surveys
in three companies

Preliminary test of
hypotheses and development
and refinement of
survey instruments

Single-indicator,
single-respondent
survey at the headquarters level
in sixty-six North American
and European MNCs

Hypothesis testing, comparison
of results across methodologies,
generalizations, and conclusions

the two headquarters-level respondents. Moreover, in each MNC, interrater convergence was also consistently high among head-quarters- and subsidiary-level respondents.

The three companies surveyed in the second phase had volunteered to undertake the burdensome logistical task of assuring the completion of the questionnaire by their corporate members.

Expecting such a high level of cooperation from a larger number of respondent companies was deemed unrealistic. Given that the results of the second phase indicated that the headquarters-level instrument quite accurately represented the attributes within the MNC, we concluded that a feasible way to collect data on a large sample of multinationals was to mail a questionnaire survey to a single knowledgeable respondent at each MNC headquarters who would then furnish, for each of a number of national subsidiaries of the MNC, measures for a number of relevant variables.

Accordingly, a survey that sought data on a variety of constructs, including environmental complexity, local subsidiary resources, centralization, formalization, normative integration, informal communication, innovation, and performance, was mailed to the chairman or CEO of all the 438 North American and European MNCs listed in Stopford's *World Directory of Multinational Enterprises* (1983). Of the completed surveys received, 66 (15 percent) were complete in all respects and were used for the empirical analysis reported in several of the chapters in this book.

The operationalization and measurement of the different variables used in our study are fully described in the Methodological Appendix of this book. While our measures no doubt have weaknesses, the empirical methodology for the study of MNCs we advance in this book is important for two central reasons. First, our approach represents a concerted effort to test empirically theoretical propositions about multinationals implied by organization theory. Second, our approach is a significant improvement over the methodology of prior studies, which have often been limited to a few case studies. Although the case studies have been useful in developing new models of the MNC, the generalizability of these models has not been systematically explored. The approach we have advanced here, by providing viable operationalizations of relevant constructs, allows for large-scale surveys and avoids the imprecision of anecdotal evidence, permitting, through the application of the differentiated network framework, more general and robust conclusions.

Beyond the Differentiated Network

The primary aim of this book is to demonstrate the theoretical utility and empirical applicability of the differentiated network model in describing and predicting the effects of the structure of relations within and among the various units of the MNC. But what about the firm's connections to outside entities? External relations include ties to customers, suppliers, regulators, and competitors with which different units of the MNC interact. Such interaction can take many forms: the national subsidiary of an MNC might engage in a vicious price war with one competitor while forming a strategic alliance with another; a subsidiary in one nation purchases inputs from a monopoly while its counterpart in another nation chooses from any number of competitive supplier firms. Different subsidiaries have differing amounts of market power, depending on the number of competitors and the size of the national market. There are endless variations.

In the most general sense, then, we can conceptualize the multinational as a network of exchange relationships among different organizational units, both inside and outside the MNC. That the differentiated network characterizing the MNC is embedded in another network is fully consistent, implied, indeed, by the characterization of the MNC as a differentiated network. The differentiated network model is motivated by the idea that structural relations within the MNC are not homogeneous but rather evince a considerable degree of variation. It follows that the same can be said about the complex set of relations the firm and its constituent parts have with the outside world.

To assert that the network somehow ends at the perimeter of the MNC seems dubious, although such an assumption may be necessary to facilitate empirical study. In the concluding chapter of this book, we explore this idea of an external network, which represents a plausible extension of the theoretical insights generated in this book and offers fertile ground for further research.

Part One

Distributed Innovation
in the Differentiated Network

Chapter Two

Distributed Innovation in Multinational Corporations (MNCs)

There has been a surge of interest in innovation in recent years. This rising interest is due, in part, to the increasing importance of innovation in an economic environment that is becoming more competitive, dynamic, and globally interlinked. With product life cycles becoming shorter and competitive advantage less sustainable, firms must continually innovate to maintain and enhance their performance. As Peters (1990) dramatically puts it, firms must "get innovative or get dead."

Traditional theories of the MNC have viewed the parent organization as the provider of innovations that are subsequently exploited abroad through the MNC's foreign subsidiaries (Vernon, 1966). In recent years, however, observers of large MNCs have proposed a rather different model (for example, Hedlund, 1994). In their view, the growing parity among industrial nations has resulted in technological expertise and lead users for specific products and services being increasingly dispersed among different countries (Vernon, 1979; Westney, 1993). As a result, MNCs must now create distributed innovations, with different national units using local resources to create innovative products, processes, and administrative practices that can be used locally as well as in other national markets in which the MNC operates (Ghoshal and Bartlett, 1988). Instead of relying exclusively on only the parent company or headquarters for innovations, the MNC must maximize what Kogut and Zander (1992) have called its "combinative capacity"—the ability to generate innovative combinations based on knowledge and capabilities distributed throughout the multinational system.

Based on case studies of thirty-eight innovations in nine large MNCs, we found that innovations are indeed no longer generated by the headquarters alone. Rather, they come about through four different organizational processes: center-for-global, local-for-local, local-for-global, and global-for-global. These processes differ in terms of the locations of different organizational capabilities brought to bear for creating and implementing the innovations and in the nature of interlinkages among the different parts of the organization.

Four Different Innovation Processes

The innovation process is one of the most complex of all organizational processes, and any stylized representation of this complexity can be guilty of oversimplification. However, past research has suggested a generic stages model (Figure 2.1) that views the innovation process as consisting of sequential but also interacting subprocesses of sensing, response, and implementation (Zaltman, Duncan, and Holbeck, 1973).[1]

To innovate, a firm must sense changes that may demand adaptation or allow exploitation of an internal capability. The acquired stimuli must then be addressed through the firm's response mechanisms: technologies and products developed, processes improved or adapted, or an available capability converted into a functional form that satisfies a latent, emerging, or existing demand. Finally, the innovation must be exploited through efficient and effective implementation.

As suggested earlier, this is a highly simplified representation of a complex organizational process. In practice, the different stages may be neither as discrete nor as neatly sequential (Gross, Giacquinta, and Bernstein, 1971; Ginzberg and Reilly, 1957). In any specific case, it may be extremely difficult to specify where the sensing process ends and the response process begins or at what point the implementation phase is said to have commenced. Similarly, the sequence suggested in the model, though logical, is not an invariant order of events. In reality, the process may be much more

Figure 2.1. A Model of the Innovation Process.

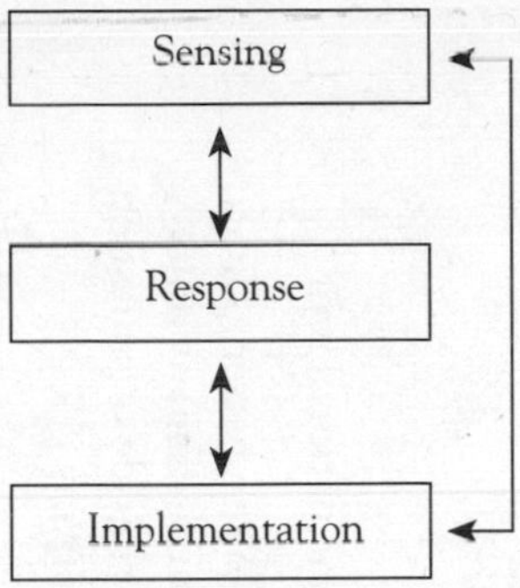

```
          ┌─────────────────┐
          │    Sensing      │ ◄──┐
          └─────────────────┘    │
                   ▲             │
                   │             │
                   ▼             │
          ┌─────────────────┐    │
          │    Response     │    │
          └─────────────────┘    │
                   ▲             │
                   │             │
                   ▼             │
          ┌─────────────────┐    │
          │ Implementation  │ ◄──┘
          └─────────────────┘
```

iterative or even circular, with a high degree of interaction among all three stages (Zaltman, Duncan, and Holbeck, 1973).

Despite its simplicity, the model provides, to use Roethlisberger's term (1977), a "walking stick" for analyzing the administrative tasks of organizing for innovation. To innovate, a firm must develop appropriate capabilities to sense, respond, and implement. But just these capabilities are not enough; the firm must also create appropriate linkages to tie these capabilities together so that they function in an integrative manner.

Based on this simple model, the thirty-eight cases of innovation we studied were categorized as shown in Table 2.1. For each case, the administrative units that carried out the sensing, response, and implementation tasks are identified. The analysis revealed four different patterns in terms of the locations of the three tasks and the organizational interlinkages required to create and implement the innovation. Each of these patterns represents a different organizational process; collectively, they suggest a scheme for classifying innovation processes in MNCs.

The Center-for-Global Innovation Process

Center-for-global innovations are those where the center—the parent company or a central facility such as the corporate R&D laboratory—creates a new product, process, or system for worldwide

Table 2.1. Innovation Processes in MNCs.

Innovation Process	Locations Where Different Tasks Are Carried Out			Number of Cases Observed
	Sensing	Response	Implementation	
Center-for-global	At the center (occasionally, some input may be provided by a particular national subsidiary)	Always at the center	In a number of organizational units worldwide	13
Local-for-local	In a particular national unit	In the same national unit	In the same national unit	11
Local-for-global	In a particular national unit	In the same national unit (possibly with some minor help from the center)	Initially, in the national unit; subsequently, in many units in the worldwide organization of the company	8
Global-for-global	In many organizational units, including the center and a number of national subsidiaries	In many organizational units, including the center and a number of national subsidiaries	In a number of organizational units worldwide	6

use. Most instances of center-for-global innovations we observed were technological innovations. Some were minor modifications, and others were substantial reorientations (Normann, 1971). Most involved no participation of the national subsidiaries except for routine tasks such as marketing support or nominal assembly at the implementation stage. In a few cases, one or more national organizations contributed in minor ways in the sensing process. However, in all cases the response task was entirely carried out at the center. The process by which L. M. Ericsson, a Swedish manufacturer of telecommunications switching and terminal equipment, created the AXE digital switch is one example of the center-for-global innovation process.

Impetus for the AXE digital switch came from an early sensing of both shifting market needs and emerging technological changes. The loss of an expected order from the Australian Post Office, combined with the excitement of a new digital switch developed by CIT-Alcatel, a small French competitor virtually unknown outside France, set in motion a formal review process within Ericsson's headquarters. The review resulted in a proposal for developing a radically new switching system based on new concepts and technology. The potential for the product was high, as were the costs and risks. The new product was estimated to cost over $50 million, to require two thousand worker-years of development effort, and to take at least five years before it could be introduced to the market. Even if the final design was spectacular, diverting all available development resources during the intervening period could irreparably erode the company's competitive position.

Rejecting almost all the "principles of innovation" proposed by Drucker (1985), Ericsson's managers decided to develop the new product, soon known as the AXE switch. The process they adopted was not "incremental" (Quinn, 1985). A detailed, event-by-event documentation of the history of the switch by a key participant in the development process (Meurling, 1985) shows little "controlled chaos" but rather the deliberateness and commitment of a programmed reorientation (Normann, 1971). The company provided full authority and all resources so that Ellemtel, the R&D joint venture of Ericsson and the Swedish telecommunications administration, could develop the product as quickly as possible. For over four years, the technological resources of the company were devoted exclusively to this task. The development was carried out entirely in Sweden. In 1976, the company had the first AXE switch in operation. By 1984, the system was installed in fifty-nine countries around the world.

Not all cases of center-for-global innovations were equally effective. NEC, for example, designed the NEAC 61 as a global digital switch and developed it through a traditional centralized development process. However, though engineers at the Japanese headquarters had excellent technical skills, they were unfamiliar with the highly sophisticated and complex software requirements of the telephone operating companies in the United States, a principal target market for the product. As a result, even though the switch was appreciated for its hardware capabilities, early U.S. sales suffered because the software did not meet some specific end-user needs that were significantly different from those of Japanese customers.

The Local-for-Local Innovation Process

In diametric contrast to center-for-global innovations, local-for-local innovations are created and implemented by a national subsidiary entirely at the local level. The sensing, response, and implementation tasks are all carried out within the subsidiary. Most of these innovations tend to be market led rather than technology driven and usually involve minor modifications of an existing technology, product, or administrative system.

The ability of local subsidiaries to sense and respond in innovative ways to local needs and opportunities has been an important corporate asset for Unilever. Advanced laundry detergents, a major product line of the company, were not appropriate for markets like India where much of the laundry was done by hand in neighboring streams rather than at home in washing machines. A local adaptation that allowed synthetic detergents to be compressed into solid tablet form gave Unilever's local subsidiary a product that could capture a significant share of the traditional bar soap market. Similarly, in Turkey, where the company's margarine products did not sell well, an innovative application of Unilever's expertise in edible fats allowed the local subsidiary to develop a product from vegetable oils that competed with the traditional local clarified-butter product, *ghee*.

As with center-for-global innovations, local-for-local innovations are not always effective. At Philips, for example, the British subsidiary spent considerable resources to create a new TV chassis for its local market that turned out to be indistinguishable from the parent company's standard European model. Consequently, for years Philips unnecessarily operated five instead of four television set factories in Europe.

The Local-for-Global Innovation Process

Local-for-global innovations are those that emerge as local-for-local innovations, are subsequently found to be applicable in multiple locations, and are diffused to those organizational units. In other words, the initial sensing, response, and implementation tasks are undertaken by a single subsidiary, but then other subsidiaries participate in subsequent implementations as the innovation is diffused within the company.

Such was the case when Philips's British subsidiary reorganized the structure of its consumer electronics marketing division based on an analysis of changes in its product line and a growing concentration in its distribution channels. The traditional marketing organization, which operated with a standard set of distribution, promotion, and sales policies applied uniformly to all product lines, was increasingly ineffective in dealing with the large-volume chains that dominated the retail market. Philips's undifferentiated marketing strategies were further constraining efforts in the differentiated and rapidly changing markets for its diverse products. To cope with these problems, the U.K. subsidiary abolished its uniform structure and organized the marketing department into three groups: an advanced-system group for technologically sophisticated, high-margin, image-building products such as Laservision and compact disc players; a mainstay group for high-volume mature products such as color TVs and VCRs; and a mass-merchandising group for older, declining products such as portable cassette players and black-and-white TV sets.

The new organization enabled the company to differentiate between the nature and intensity of marketing support it provided to different products according to their stages in the product life cycle. Different marketing elements—including promotion, pricing, and distribution—could now be deployed in a more selective and specialized manner. Within the first year of implementation, the new structure had reduced aggregate selling expenses from 18 to 12 percent. During this period, though overall market demand for consumer electronics products in the United Kingdom fell by 5 percent, the subsidiary's electronic sales rose by 49 percent, including a 400 percent sales increase to Dixons, the largest reseller chain.

Meanwhile, increasing concentration in the distribution channels and a growing need for distinct marketing approaches for different products became manifest throughout Europe. The new model of the marketing organization developed by the British subsidiary was clearly appropriate for other subsidiaries. Despite initial resistance, the innovation was soon transferred to most other national organizations.

Resistance to such transfers is widespread and strong in MNCs, and several attempted local-for-global innovations were never implemented outside the initiating subsidiary. For example, Unilever was unable to transfer a zero-phosphate detergent developed by its German subsidiary to other European locations. Contending that its market needs were different, the French subsidiary insisted on developing its own "zero-p" product.

The Global-for-Global Innovation Process

Instead of finding individual local solutions or imposing a central solution on different subsidiaries, global-for-global innovations are created by pooling the resources and capabilities of many different organizational units of the MNC to arrive at a jointly developed general solution to an emerging global opportunity. Global-for-global innovations best represent an MNC's combinative capacity (Kogut and Zander, 1992). Ideally, this category of innovations involves the participation of multiple organizational units in each of the three stages of sensing, response, and implementation. However, what distinguishes it from the other categories is that the response task is shared instead of being carried out by a single unit. One of the best examples of this mode of innovation was the way in which Procter & Gamble (P&G) developed a global liquid detergent.

Despite the success of liquid laundry detergents in the United States, all attempts to create a heavy-duty liquid detergent category in Europe had failed due to different washing practices and the superior performance of European powder detergents, which contained enzymes, bleach, and phosphates at levels not permitted in the United States. But P&G's European scientists were convinced that the liquid detergent's performance could be enhanced to match the local powders. After seven years of work, they developed a bleach substitute (a fatty acid with water-softening capabilities equivalent to phosphate) as well as a means to give enzymes stability in liquid form.

Meanwhile, researchers in the United States were working on a new liquid better able to deal with the high clay soil content in dirty clothes in the United States. This group developed improvements in builders (ingredients that prevent redeposit of dirt in the wash). Also during this period, the company's International Technology Coordination Group was working with P&G scientists in Japan to develop a more robust surfactant (the ingredient that removes greasy stains) to make the liquid more effective in the cold-water washes common in Japan. Thus the units in Europe, the United States, and Japan were each developing effective responses to local needs, yet none shared its breakthroughs.

When the head of R&D for P&G in Europe was promoted to the company's top research job, one of his primary objectives was to create more coordination and cooperation among the diverse local-for-local development efforts, and the world liquid detergent project became a test case. Plans to launch Omni, the new liquid developed in the United States, were shelved until the innovations from Europe and Japan could be incorporated. Similarly, the Japanese and the Europeans shared their developments with the Americans and each other. Joint effort on the part of all groups ultimately led to the launch of Liquid Tide in the United States, Liquid Cheer in Japan, and Liquid Ariel in Europe. Each product incorporated the best developments created in response to European, American, and Japanese market needs.

Organizational Attributes
That Influence Innovation Processes

As the foregoing examples show, innovation in MNCs is no longer simply the responsibility of the corporate center. Indeed, relative to domestic companies, it is the capacity for distributed innovation that represents the unique organizational advantage of the modern MNC. Thus the most salient question from the vantage point of both theory and practice becomes this: How should the MNC be organized to enhance its capacity for distributed innovation or value creation?

Our analysis of the thirty-eight innovation cases we studied suggests that an MNC's ability to foster these different types of innovation depends on (1) the configuration of organizational assets and slack resources, (2) the structure of headquarters-subsidiary relationships, (3) socialization processes, and (4) patterns of communication. Table 2.2 summarizes our findings.

Table 2.2. Organizational Factors Influencing Innovation Processes in MNCs.

Innovation Process	Configuration of Assets and Slack Resources	Structure of Headquarters-Subsidiary Relations	Socialization Patterns	Communication Patterns
Center-for-global	Centralized at headquarters	Subsidiaries dependent on headquarters	Formal and collective initial training; transfers of few people from headquarters to subsidiaries, infrequently and for long terms	High density of communication between headquarters and subsidiaries
Local-for-local	Dispersed to subsidiaries	Subsidiaries independent of headquarters	Informal and individual initial training; subsidiary-to-subsidiary transfers of an international cadre of managers	High density of communication within subsidiaries
Local-for-global	Dispersed to subsidiaries	Subsidiaries independent of headquarters but mutually dependent on one another	Informal but both collective and individual initial training; subsidiary-to-subsidiary transfers of an international cadre of managers	High density of communication within and among subsidiaries
Global-for-global	Distributed, specialized	Headquarters and subsidiaries mutually dependent on one another	Both collective and individual initial training; two-way transfers of large numbers of managers among headquarters and the different subsidiaries	High density of communication within subsidiaries, among subsidiaries, and between the headquarters and the subsidiaries

Configuration of Organizational Assets and Slack Resources

In some companies, such as Matsushita, most key organizational assets and slack resources were centralized at the headquarters. Even though 40 percent of Matsushita's sales were made abroad, only 10 percent of its products were manufactured outside Japan. The Japanese manufacturing facilities were also the most advanced and best-equipped plants of the company, producing almost all of its sophisticated products. Similarly, R&D was fully centralized in seven research laboratories in Japan. The center-for-global process contributed most of the significant innovations in companies with such centralized configurations of assets and resources. In Matsushita, for example, *all* new consumer electronics products introduced between 1983 and 1986 were developed by the parent company in Japan and were subsequently introduced in its foreign markets.

In contrast to Matsushita, manufacturing, marketing, and even R&D facilities were widely dispersed throughout the organization in companies like Philips, ITT, and Unilever. Not surprisingly, local-for-local (and to a lesser extent local-for-global) processes contributed a significant number of innovations in these companies. An extreme case of the dispersal of assets and resources was the telecommunications business of ITT. The company had practically no central research or manufacturing activity, and each major national subsidiary was fully integrated and self-sufficient in its ability to develop, manufacture, and market new products. Until the advent of digital switching, all major products, including the Metaconta and Pentaconta switches, were initially developed in one or the other subsidiary and were subsequently "redeveloped" by other subsidiaries, resulting in several varieties of the same product being sold in different markets. Similarly, Philips's list of local-for-local innovations was endless; some examples are the first stereo color TV set, developed by the Australian subsidiary; teletext TV sets, by the British subsidiary; "smart cards," by the French subsidiary; and the programmed word processing typewriter, by North American Philips.

Some companies were embracing a third system of asset and resource configuration. Instead of either a centralized or a decentralized system, they were building an interconnected network of specialized assets distributed around the world. Ericsson, NEC, and Procter & Gamble were the most advanced in building such a system. These companies were most successful in introducing global-for-global innovations.

In NEC, organizational assets were traditionally centralized, and most innovations were created through the center-for-global process. The NEAC 61 digital switch, for example, was developed entirely in the company's central facilities in Japan, even though the product was principally aimed at the North American market. Subsequently, however, the company developed specialized software capabilities in the United States, while hardware expertise remained at the center. Such a distribution of resources allowed NEC to approximate the global-for-global process in developing the NEAC 61E auxiliary switch; the headquarters took the lead in building the hardware while the subsidiary participated significantly in designing the software. Similarly, the global liquid detergent project of P&G that we described earlier was made possible and necessary because research units responsible for product development in Japan, Europe, and the United States had each developed specialized capabilities that the other did not possess.

Structure of Headquarters-Subsidiary Relationships

The relationships between the headquarters and each of the different subsidiaries varied considerably across the organizations we studied. In some companies such as Kao, the large Japanese manufacturer of soaps and detergents, these relationships were based primarily on the subsidiary's dependence on the headquarters. National subsidiaries of this company had neither the competence nor the legitimacy to initiate any new programs or even to modify any product or administrative system developed by the parent company. They had few decision rights and little autonomy. For example, a particular brand of liquid shampoo that was extremely successful in Japan failed to produce desired effects when introduced in Thailand. The product, aimed to suit the sophisticated needs of the Japanese market, could not compete effectively with simpler, less expensive local products; it developed only a marginal 7 percent market share despite considerable marketing investments. The nature of the problem could be identified and remedial measures taken only after marketing experts from the headquarters visited the subsidiary along with executives from Dentsu, Kao's Japanese advertising agents. The local manager affirmed that the "expertise, knowledge, and resources" of the Japanese "made it appropriate for them to make such decisions." In companies where subsidiaries developed such highly dependent relationships with the headquarters, innovations were usually restricted to the center-for-global variety.

In other companies, such as ITT and Philips, subsidiaries had considerable strategic and operational autonomy, though the headquarters exercised varying degrees of administrative control through the budgeting and financial reporting systems. In such companies, where subsidiaries were relatively independent of the headquarters, local-for-local innovations were far more prevalent.

Local-for-global and global-for-global innovations require the involvement of multiple organizational units, including a number of different national subsidiaries. They were thus most prevalent in companies with dense intersubsidiary exchange relationships, especially exchange relationships based on reciprocal interdependence (J. D. Thompson, 1967).

In Procter & Gamble, for example, teams consisting of representatives from different national organizations in Europe ("Eurobrand" teams) coordinated regional strategies for different products of the company. For each product group, the team was headed by the general manager of a particular subsidiary and included brand managers from other major subsidiaries. These teams provided one of the many mechanisms in the company to promote exchange relationships among the various national subsidiaries. Further, by ensuring that general managers from different subsidiaries headed each team, the company deliberately created reciprocal interdependence. Each general manager recognized that the level of cooperation he or she could expect from the brand managers of other subsidiaries depended on the level of cooperation extended by his or her brand managers to the general managers of other product teams.

ITT's attempt to develop the System 12 digital switch through a similar global-for-global process floundered precisely because of the absence of such interdependence. Recognizing that the technical resources required for developing the switch could not be assembled in any one location in its highly decentralized international organization, ITT management decided to adopt the global-for-global process of designing and building the switch through coordinated and joint action involving most of its major national operations. However, conditioned by a long history of local independence, the national subsidiaries resisted joint efforts and common standards; this resistance led to duplication of efforts, divergence of specifications, delays, and an enormous budget overrun.

Organizational Socialization Processes

The manner in which managers were socialized by the different companies also had a profound influence on the kinds of innovations they were most likely to create. For instance, managers at both Philips and Matsushita were highly socialized into the strong cultures of their respective organizations, but in different ways that had a significant influence on the nature of innovation in the two companies. When working collectively at the central headquarters, Matsushita managers were highly innovative and continually seeking change. However, when working individually, as expatriate managers in different national subsidiaries, they were more likely to take a "custodial" stance, resisting any change local managers wished to make to centrally designed products, processes, and administrative systems. Expatriate managers at Philips, in contrast, were generally more willing to champion local initiatives and thereby foster local-for-local innovations.

Van Maanen and Schein (1979) suggest that the nature of initial and ongoing organizational socialization processes significantly influences member attitudes toward change. Certain socialization processes lead to custodial behavior and resistance to change, while others facilitate both content and role innovations by socialized members. In the cases of Philips and Matsushita, differences in postrecruitment training and subsequent career structures help explain why their managers exhibited such different attitudes toward change.

At Matsushita, college graduates were recruited as managers in large batches at the center and then collectively socialized through a common training program lasting for a year or more. Philips, in contrast, recruited managers in small numbers from diverse locations and quickly posted them to different units to learn on the job. Although there were occasional classroom sessions for the entire cohort of new recruits, initial socialization depended much more on new members' forming personal relationships with existing organizational members (often their immediate senior colleagues) on a one-to-one basis.

Before being assigned overseas, Matsushita managers were provided another dose of intense formal training. The company's Overseas Training Center (OTC) prepared managers for assignments abroad by ensuring that they thoroughly understood Matsushita's practices and values. Expatriate managers were posted to a foreign location for relatively long periods—usually five to eight years—after which they returned to the headquarters. They could be posted abroad again, later in their careers, often to the same location, though at more senior levels. At Philips, given the relatively insignificant role of the headquarters in the global business, a large number of managers spent a significant part of their careers abroad, spending two or three years in one subsidiary before moving on to the next. Many of these managers retired abroad; some returned home toward the end of their careers to take up top-level corporate positions.

As suggested by Van Maanen and Schein (1979), collective socialization processes like Matsushita's result in stronger conformity to collective values. Thus when change is proposed within the collective (for example, in the headquarters, which is seen as the repository of collective values), it tends to be supported. However, local changes in national subsidiaries that attempt to modify values, systems, or processes designed by the collective tend to be resisted. In contrast, individual socialization, as at Philips, tends to produce less homogeneous views and greater willingness to change at local levels.

Similarly, differences in career systems across these two companies can also be expected to result in different attitudes toward local innovations. At Philips, expatriate managers followed each other into key management and technical positions in the company's national organizations around the world. They viewed themselves as a distinct subgroup within the organization and developed a shared identity. At Matsushita, by contrast, there was little interaction among the expatriate managers in different subsidiaries. They thus tended to view themselves as part of the parent company on temporary assignment to foreign locations. Consequently, Philips's managers tended to identify strongly with the national organization's point of view and to serve as champions of local changes, whereas Matsushita managers were more prone to implementing centrally designed products and policies.

Communication Patterns

Almost all studies on innovation have emphasized the facilitating role of communication (Allen, 1977; Mohr, 1982; Rogers, 1983). This body of theoretical and empirical literature has found consistent support for the view that internal communication patterns are one of the most important determinants of an organization's ability to innovate.

The internal communication patterns in the companies we studied could be broadly categorized into three groups. In the first group, of which ITT and Philips are examples, internal communication within each subunit (the headquarters or individual national subsidiaries) was intense, but the level of communication among subunits (between the headquarters and the subsidiaries or among the subsidiaries themselves) was relatively low. In the second group, represented by firms such as Matsushita, communication links between the headquarters and subsidiaries were especially strong, but communication links both within and across the subsidiaries were limited. In the third group, consisting of firms such as Procter & Gamble and Ericsson, both internal communication within subunits and communication across subunits tended to be relatively rich and frequent. Local-for-local innovations were most common in the first group of companies (although some of them, such as Philips, could also create innovations through the local-for-global process), center-for-global innovations were dominant in the second group, and the third group could create all four types of innovations.

By examining internal communication patterns at Philips, one can see how they support local-for-local innovations. Historically, top management in all of Philips's national subsidiaries consisted of a committee of the heads of technical, commercial, and financial functions, rather than an individual CEO. The system of three-headed management stemmed from the functional independence of the two founding Philips brothers, an engineer and a salesman. It subsequently endured as a tradition of intensive intraunit, cross-functional communication and joint decision making within each subsidiary.

In most Philips subsidiaries, these integration mechanisms existed at three organizational levels. At the product management level, teams prepared annual sales plans and budgets and developed product policies. A second tier of cross-functional coordination took place through the group management team, which met once a month to review results, suggest corrective actions, and resolve any interfunctional differences. The highest level of cross-functional coordination and communication within the subsidiary was the senior management committee (SMC), consisting of the top commercial, technical, and financial managers of the subsidiary. Acting as the local board, the SMC ensured overall unity of effort among the different local functional groups and protected the legitimacy and effectiveness of communication forums at lower levels of the organization. These multilevel, cross-functional, integrative mech-anisms within each subsidiary were at the heart of Philips's ability to create local innovations in its various operating environments.

If the challenge for improving the efficiency of local-for-local innovations lies in strengthening cross-functional communication within subsidiaries, the key task for enhancing the effectiveness of center-for-global innovations lies in building linkages between headquarters and the subsidiaries. The main problem of centrally created innovations is that the persons developing new products or processes may not understand different local market needs or that the parties who will be required to implement the new product introduction locally are not committed to it. Matsushita solved these problems by creating multilevel and multifunctional linkages between the headquarters and each of the subsidiaries. These link-ages facilitated both the communication of local market demands from the subsidiary to the center and also central coordination and control over the subsidiary's implementation of the company's strategies, plans, and innovations.

The communication links connecting different parts of the Matsushita organization in Japan with the video department of MESA, its U.S. subsidiary, are illustrative of headquarters-sub-sidiary communication systems in the company. The vice president in charge of this MESA department had his roots in Matsushita Electric Trading Company (METC), the central organization responsible for the company's overseas business. Although formally posted to the United States, he continued to be a member of the senior management committee of METC, spending about a third of his time in Japan. The general manager of this department had worked for fourteen years in the video product division of Mat-sushita Electric Industries (MEI), the central production and domestic marketing company in Japan. He maintained almost daily communication with the central product division in Japan and acted as its link to the local American market. The assistant manager in the department, the most junior expatriate in the organization, linked the local unit to the central factory in Japan, where he spent five years. He handled all day-to-day communication with factory personnel and served as its local representative.

None of these linkages were accidental—they were deliberately created and maintained. They reflected the company's desire to preserve the perspectives and priorities of its diverse groups worldwide and to ensure that these groups had linkages to those in headquarters who could represent and defend them. Unlike companies that tried to focus headquarters-subsidiary communication through a single channel for the sake of efficiency, the multilevel and multifunctional linkages created by companies like Matsushita helped forge a broad band of communication through which each central unit involved in creating center-for-global innovations had direct access to local market information, while each local unit involved in implementing those innovations also had the opportunity to influence the innovation process.

Finally, a few companies like Procter & Gamble and Ericsson were able to create organizational mechanisms that simultaneously facilitated intense intraunit communication, extensive headquarters-subsidiary communication, and also considerable information flow among the subsidiaries. As a result, these companies were able to create the broadest variety of innovations.

At Ericsson, for example, intrasubsidiary communication was facilitated by a culture and tradition of open communication and, more specifically, by extensive use of ad hoc teams and special liaisons with the express mandate of promoting intraunit integration. Headquarters-subsidiary communication was strengthened by deputing one or more senior corporate managers as members of subsidiary boards. Unlike many companies whose local boards are pro forma bodies aimed at satisfying national legal requirements, Ericsson used its local boards as legitimate forums for communicating objectives, resolving differences, and making decisions. Intersubsidiary communication was facilitated by a number of processes such as allocating global roles to subsidiaries for specific tasks (for example, Italy was the center for transmission system development, Finland for mobile telephones, and Australia for rural switches) that require them to establish communication links worldwide. However, the factor that had perhaps the strongest effect on furthering communication in the dispersed Ericsson organization was its long-standing policy of transferring large numbers of people back and forth between headquarters and subsidiaries.

Ericsson's pattern of executive transfers was uncommon compared to NEC's practices. Whereas NEC would use one or two key managers to transfer a new technology, Ericsson would send a team of fifty to one hundred engineers and managers for a year or two; whereas NEC's flows were primarily from headquarters to subsidiaries, Ericsson's was a balanced two-way flow with people coming to the parent not only to learn but also to teach; whereas NEC's transfers predominantly involved Japanese nationals, Ericsson's multidirectional process involved all nationalities.

Ericsson's practices yielded handsome payoffs. Australian technicians transferred to Stockholm in the mid-1970s to bring their experience with digital switching into the development of the AXE switch created enduring relationships that helped in the subsequent initiation of a rural switch in Australia through the global-for-global process. When an Italian team of forty spent eighteen months in Sweden to learn about electronic switching, they acquired the knowledge and confidence that facilitated the greater decentralization of AXE software development and a delegated responsibility for developing the switch's central transmission system through a local-for-global process.

Conclusions

In this chapter, four critical organizational attributes that influence innovation processes in MNCs were identified: (1) the configuration of organizational assets and slack resources, (2) the structure of headquarters-subsidiary relationships within the company, (3) the socialization mechanisms employed to integrate organizational members, and (4) the nature of intra- and interunit communication. Each of these has long been recognized as a key factor influencing an organization's ability to innovate. Cyert and March ([1963] 1992) have identified the importance of slack resources for innovation. Burns and Stalker (1961) and Lawrence and Lorsch (1967) have shown how an organization's structure influences its capacity to innovate. Kidder (1981) and Deal and Kennedy (1982) have highlighted the important role of socialization mechanisms. Allen (1977) and Rogers (1983), among others, have emphasized the importance of communication flows. And Kanter (1983), in her description of the "integrative organization," identified each of these elements as key requirements for promoting innovation in organizations. Our findings thus reinforce these classic insights on the factors that promote innovation in organizations.

At the same time, our findings provide a point of departure and an avenue for augmenting existing theory. The source of this enhancement lies in our explicit focus on multiunit organizations, such as MNCs, that require simultaneous consideration of organizational attributes both within individual and across multiple units. Most prior research has been limited to single organizational units. In the case of Burns and Stalker (1961), the level of analysis is stated quite explicitly: "The twenty concerns that were the subject of these studies were not all separately constituted business companies. This is why we have used concern as a generic term. . . . [Some of them] were only small parts of their parent organizations" (p. 77). Other researchers have similarly observed a district sales office of General Electric, a department in 3M's headquarters, and a divisional data processing office of Polaroid but not the overall organizational configuration in any of these physically dispersed organizations. Indeed, with few exceptions, there have been no studies of distributed innovation in complex multiunit organizations like MNCs (Ronstadt, 1977; Prahalad and Doz, 1987; De Meyer and Mizushima, 1989).

When innovation in the MNC was primarily the function of the corporate headquarters, extending the lessons learned from focusing on innovation in unitary organizations was not a serious limitation. But the complexity and diversity of the technological, competitive, and market environments confronting most MNCs today requires them to create organizational mechanisms that can simultaneously facilitate all the innovation processes we have described. As we have seen, these processes are facilitated by organizational attributes that are different and possibly contradictory. Factors that promote the creation of innovations by a subunit may not be the same as those that further the subunit's capacity to adopt innovations created elsewhere in the company or its participation in joint innovation projects. Although a few companies in our sample had begun to tap the full innovative potential of their multinational organizations, creating such a capability on a more general and more permanent basis may be a challenge of considerable magnitude, given the potential contradictions in organizational attributes that facilitate each of these innovation processes. A more systematic study can thus be valuable because it can generate more reliable suggestions on how these potential contradictions might be overcome. Our purpose in the next two chapters is to undertake such a systematic investigation. Building on the findings of the innovation case studies discussed here, in Chapter Three we investigate the optimal amount of slack resources necessary to promote innovation within an MNC's subsidiaries. In Chapter Four, we analyze the trade-offs among the factors that promote the creation versus the diffusion and adoption of innovations within MNCs.

Note

1. The sense-response-implement model has an extensive history in multiple fields. It is directly adapted from the unfreeze-change-refreeze framework proposed by Lewin (1951) in the

organization development field and subsequently enhanced by Bennis, Schein, Beckhard, and others. For a brief review of this literature, see Lorange, Scott-Morton, and Ghoshal (1986). The same model, with different labels, has been adopted in marketing theory to describe the new-product introduction process (see, for example, Urban and Hauser, 1980) and by many scholars who have studied the organizational innovation process (see Zaltman, Duncan, and Holbeck, 1973, for a review).

Chapter Three

Optimal Slack
for Distributed Innovation

If value appropriation—or the pursuit of efficiency—were the sole objective of organizations, all forms of organizational slack would be signs of inefficiency, to be discovered and eliminated. However, because value creation—or the pursuit of innovation—is an equally, if not more important, organizational objective, some amount of slack is desirable and indeed must be protected and maintained. As we saw in Chapter Two, the distribution of assets and slack resources within an MNC significantly influences its innovative potential. Our case research suggested that the more widely distributed the slack resources, the more likely it was that innovations would be created throughout the MNC. But slack resources are not unlimited and thus cannot be increased throughout the MNC without some loss of efficiency. In this chapter, we explore this fundamental trade-off between efficiency and innovation by asking the question, What is the optimal amount of distributed organizational slack?

Answering this question is not easy. On the one hand, organizations are being forced to become more innovative to keep pace with an increasingly dynamic global economy in which Schumpeterian competition prevails—the gales of creative destruction blow constantly. On the other hand, organizational slack has come under sharp scrutiny as organizations feel pressured to eliminate all forms of inefficiencies in the face of increasingly intense global competition. These two countervailing forces suggest a potential irony. Given that slack is recognized as a form of inefficiency but is also viewed by many theorists as essential for innovation, the risk organizations face is that they may eliminate slack to the point where their capacity to innovate is unintentionally undermined.

The prior literature provides no clear answers on how to resolve this dilemma because theorists stand divided on whether slack facilitates or inhibits innovation. Proponents of slack argue that it plays a crucial role in allowing organizations to innovate (Cyert and March, [1963] 1992; Knight, 1967; Mansfield, 1963). Slack resources, proponents contend, permit organizations to experiment more safely with new strategies and innovative projects that might not ordinarily be approved in a more resource constrained environment (Cyert and March, [1963] 1992). Opponents counter that slack simply promotes undisciplined investment in R&D activities that rarely yield economic benefits (Jensen, 1986, 1993; Antle and Fellingham, 1990). According to this view, slack simply encourages the pursuit of pet projects by agents (managers) who show little regard for the interests of the principals (shareholders) they serve.

We argue that one way to reconcile this theoretical debate is to recognize that the relationship between slack and innovation is curvilinear—too little slack is as bad for innovation as is too much. This idea, though intuitively compelling, has not been explicitly advanced in the past. The closest anyone has come to proposing a similar view is Bourgeois (1981, p. 31), who suggests that the "correlation between success and slack is positive, up to a point, then negative; in other words the relationship is curvilinear." However, he offers no clear answer to our central question here—Does a slack-rich organization innovate, or does it restrict its scanning?—leaving it as an "empirical question worthy of further research" (p. 36).

In this chapter, we elaborate on this simple intuition for an inverse U-shaped relationship between slack and innovation. Building on areas of agreement between both the proponents and the detractors of slack, we propose two underlying mechanisms—the impact of slack on experimentation and the discipline placed on these experiments—that lead to this hypothesized relationship. Too little slack inhibits innovation because it discourages any kind of experimentation where success is uncertain. Equally, too much slack inhibits innovation because it breeds complacency and a lack of discipline that makes it more likely that more bad projects will be pursued than good. Taken together, these ideas suggest that intermediate levels of slack are optimal for innovation in any given situation.

We provide empirical support for these arguments based on data obtained from the second phase of our research design wherein we surveyed managers at both the headquarters and subsidiaries of three different MNCs.

What Is Slack?

Notions of what constitutes slack vary widely (see Bourgeois, 1981, and Lant, 1985, for comprehensive reviews). For some analysts, it constitutes a valuable buffer of excess resources that permits an organization to maintain cooperation among competing coalitions and buffer itself from unforeseen contingencies (March, 1976). Others view slack as a form of inefficiency, reflecting wasted resources that are not being put to their optimal use, resulting in performance, given a set of inputs, that is lower than the maximum possible (Leibenstein, 1969; Williamson, 1964). To stem any controversies that may arise from such varied notions of slack, let us start by being explicit about how we define slack.

We define slack as the pool of resources within an organization that is in excess of the minimum necessary to produce a given level of organizational output. These slack resources include excess inputs such as extra personnel, unused capacity, and unnecessary capital expenditures. They also include unexploited opportunities to increase outputs such as additional margins and revenues that might be derived from customers or known innovations that might be implemented to push the firm closer to the efficiency frontier. In keeping with the prior literature (Bromiley, 1991; Lant, 1985), we expect slack to build up during good times (when the unit's performance exceeds target or aspiration levels) and to be consumed during bad times (when performance drops below target or aspiration levels). Our view of slack further recognizes that slack can be deployed in various ways. Slack resources can be used to respond to smooth performance (Kamin and Ronen, 1978) in the event of contingencies such as budget cuts or environmental jolts (Meyer, 1982), as well as to engage in slack search or "irresponsible experimentation" (Levinthal and March, 1981).

It is important, as Sharfman (1988) has urged, to remember that for resources to be considered slack, they must be recoverable or employable in the future. This condition forces us to distinguish between forms of slack that are more or less recoverable. Bourgeois and Singh (1983) propose a typology of slack based on its ease of recovery. They differentiate available slack (immediately recoverable resources such as excess liquidity) from recoverable slack (resources recoverable with some effort such as excess overhead costs) and from potential slack (capacity to raise additional resources). Singh (1986) offers a condensed version of this typology, distinguishing between unabsorbed slack (which is easy to recover) and absorbed slack (which is hard to recover). Similarly, Sharfman (1988) contrasts high-discretion from low-discretion slack. High-discretion forms of slack (such as cash equivalents, credit lines, inventory, and flexible unused capacity) are excess resources over which managers have great latitude and can thus be readily recovered. In contrast, low-discretion forms of slack (such as above-market wages and lumpy capacity) are excess resources over which managers have less discretion and are thus harder to recover.

The foregoing distinctions all focus on the types of slack resources—some being more easily recoverable than other. Implicit in these distinctions is the time frame over which slack resources can be redeployed. Using Singh's continuum (1986), for instance, we would expect unabsorbed slack to be recoverable in a shorter period of time than absorbed slack. Similarly, in Sharfman's typology (1988), we would expect high-discretion slack to be recoverable over a shorter time frame than low-discretion slack. In this chapter, we focus on slack resources that are recoverable in the short term. Given that budgets and performance reviews typically follow an annual cycle, we define short-term slack as excess resources that can be recovered within a year. We restrict our focus on short-term or recoverable slack because we expect such resources to be more easily deployable to support innovative activity than long-term or absorbed slack. Notice that our definition of slack applies across organizational levels because it captures the extent to which any unit (be it an individual, a department, a function, a division, or the firm as a whole) has excess resources that can be quickly marshaled to respond to internal or external contingencies.

The Case for Slack

Why is slack not zero? The seminal answer to this question was provided by Cyert and March ([1963] 1992) in their behavioral theory of the firm. They start from the premise that all organizations can be considered as political coalitions, consisting of subgroups with competing goals. Though these goals overlap to some extent, they are never perfectly aligned. Thus goal conflict is latent in any organization. Slack exists because it plays a vital role in resolving this latent goal conflict and preventing the organization from breaking apart.

In addition to maintaining the firm as a political coalition, Cyert and March dwell extensively on several other organizational benefits of slack. Slack creates buffers that reduce information processing and coordination costs across subunits (see also J. D. Thompson, 1967, and Galbraith, 1973). It allows for intertemporal adjustments to environmental fluctuations such as demand or supply fluctuations in various factor and product markets (for example, excess labor that can be used to offset changes in labor markets or excess capacity and inventory to smooth out changes in demand and supply). It creates an unexploited pool of refinements to meet changes in competitive intensity (see also Levinthal and March, 1981). And it represents capital and cash reserves to meet changing pressures from capital markets.

By representing a source of resources that may otherwise not be approved in the face of uncertainty, slack is also seen to facilitate another kind of adaptive response, and that is innovation. Slack allows innovative projects to be pursued because it buffers organizations from the uncertain success of these projects, fostering a culture of experimentation (Bourgeois, 1981). Slack resources permit firms to experiment more safely with new strategies by introducing new products, entering new markets, and so on (Moses, 1992; Hambrick and Snow, 1977; Bourgeois, 1981). In lean times, such projects might otherwise be killed. Moreover, slack facilitates innovation by allowing the pursuit of what has been termed "foolishness" or slack search in the form of projects that do not appear to be justifiable by internal financial controls but have strong internal champions (March, 1976, 1981; Levinthal and March, 1981). Though such projects often fail, they sometimes fortuitously yield positive results that can be of great benefit to the firm (Nelson and Winter, 1982). The literature on innovation is replete with such chance discoveries that resulted from slack search (Marquis, 1969; Mokyr, 1990). A good example is the much celebrated discovery of Post-It notes at 3M, an organization that explicitly provides employees with slack time to pursue innovative ideas (Roberts, 1980).

Following such logical arguments in favor of slack, in most empirical studies on the organizational determinants of innovation, slack is predicted and in some cases shown to have a positive effect (for some recent examples, see Majumdar and Venkataraman, 1993, and Zajac, Golden, and Shortell,1991).[1]

The Case Against Slack

Relative to behavioral theorists, others, especially organizational economists such as Leibenstein (1969) and Williamson (1964), adopt a more hostile view toward slack. They view slack as synonymous with waste, reflecting managerial self-interest, incompetence, and sloth rather than a buffer necessary for organizational adaptation. Like Cyert and March, these scholars start by characterizing the firm as a coalition of competing interests. However, they contend that the proper way of thinking about these competing interests is to view them as a system of nested principal-agent relationships (Jensen and Meckling, 1976). The top management of the firm can be thought of as agents acting on behalf of the shareholders or principals; subsidiary managers can be thought of as agents acting on behalf of top management; and so on.

Conflict in this model arises because agents do not always have incentives to act in the best interests of the principals. Accordingly, top managers do not always act to maximize shareholder value. Similarly, subsidiary managers do not always act to maximize corporate performance. This suboptimization (from the perspective of the principal) arises because principals must delegate decision rights to the agent so that they can benefit from their specific local knowledge, but they typically do not have all the information necessary to monitor their agent's performance accurately. Agents can take advantage of this information asymmetry and act in their own interests as opposed to the principal's. Indeed, Williamson (1964) argues, that left to their own devices, agents are primarily motivated to build their own empires. Unlike behavioral theorists such as Cyert and March ([1963] 1992), economists generally do not view slack as being a useful way of resolving the principal-agent conflict. They argue that the right way to resolve these conflicts is to structure incentives in ways that align the interests of principals and agents. Slack, in their view, is an unnecessary cost that should be eliminated.

Opponents of slack thus view it as a clear sign of inefficiency that detracts from the overall value of the firm. Leibenstein (1969) even coined the felicitous term X-inefficiency to highlight the discrepancy that slack creates between actual output and maximum output for a given set of inputs. Leibenstein's ideas have found strong support in recent years. The growing emphasis on responsiveness, timeliness, and productivity has overturned many of the classic beliefs on how much slack, in terms of time and buffer resources, is necessary to permit an organization to adapt comfortably to environmental changes. Proponents of new management practices such as total quality management, just-in-time logistics systems, lean production, and concurrent engineering have challenged the view that slack provides necessary buffers to adapt to intertemporal variations in demand and supply (Garvin, 1994). Similarly, proponents of cross-functional teams, reengineered business processes, horizontal organization designs, and new information technologies argue that slack is in fact unnecessary to permit coordination across subunits (Davenport, 1993; Hammer and Champy, 1993). A strong case has thus developed in recent years to oppose earlier claims that high-slack organizations may be more adaptive.

The recent hostility toward slack extends to its presumed role in facilitating innovation. Indeed, it has been suggested that innovation may actually be hurt by excess slack. Jensen (1986), for instance, has argued that firms that have a high amount of slack often invest this slack in a number of dubious projects, such as "pet" R&D projects or unrelated acquisitions. Drawing on evidence from the petroleum industry in the late 1970s and early 1980s, he shows that on average most companies gained only about 60 cents for every dollar invested in exploration and development. In an even more graphic illustration of the problems of slack, he shows that if General Motors, Kodak, and IBM had simply invested the money they spent on R&D and capital expenditures in the 1980s in risk-free government securities, the value of their investment by the beginning of the 1990s would have been enough for each of them to have bought out their principal competitor (Jensen, 1993).

In sum, these theorists suggest that although excess slack may undoubtedly spur R&D expenditures that lead to the pursuit of many new projects, very few of these projects actually translate into value-added innovations for the firm. This is because the controls placed on these projects are lax, thereby allowing decision makers to make choices that "accord better with their own preferences than with economic considerations" (Child, 1972, p. 11).

An Argument for Optimal Slack

As we have seen, a credible case can be made both for and against the innovation-enhancing benefits of slack. Rather than weigh in on one side of the debate or the other, we would like to propose a reconciliation of these perspectives. In short, we suggest that the relationship between innovation and slack is curvilinear or inverse U-shaped.

This proposition rests on the following series of interrelated observations and arguments. The first observation is that both the advocates and the opponents of slack agree that slack promotes experimentation and the pursuit of new projects. For innovation to occur, organizations must cope with the uncertainty associated with innovative projects (Mansfield, 1963). This intrinsic uncertainty makes it difficult to gauge *ex ante* the net present value (NPV) associated with such projects. Not only do persistence and "patient money" play a role in fostering innovation, they also provide the flexibility necessary to adapt resource levels as projects progress over time. Given the ambiguity surrounding such innovative activities, slack provides a pool of resources that can be an effective cushion to adapt to the ebbs and flows of the innovation process (Grossman and Shapiro, 1987). Slack also frees up managerial attention, another scarce resource (Cyert and March, [1963] 1992). In organizations that have little slack, managerial attention is likely to be focused first and foremost on short-term performance issues rather than on more uncertain innovative projects. For all the above-mentioned reasons, the number of new initiatives undertaken undoubtedly increases as slack increases. Of course, the relationship may not be linear over the entire range of slack. We should expect diminishing returns (in the form of experimentation) as slack increases because of diminishing availability of possibilities for innovation as well as diminishing incentives because excess slack promotes complacency. The positive relationship between slack and experimentation is thus one factor that determines the relationship between slack and innovation.

An opposing dynamic that needs to be simultaneously considered is the diminishing discipline that is placed on this increased experimentation as slack increases. As slack increases, the discipline that is exercised in the selection, ongoing support, and termination of projects becomes lax (see, for example, Leibenstein, 1969, and Jensen, 1993). With increasing slack, we can expect projects with high risk and negative NPV to be funded simply because the resources exist to indulge agents for whom these are pet projects. Not only would we expect "bad" projects to be initiated, but we are also more likely to observe continual or escalating commitment to these projects because the existence of slack makes it harder to justify termination of someone's pet project (Staw, Sandelands, and Dutton, 1981). As Cyert and March ([1963] 1992) have pointed out, in times of slack, negotiations are not as intense and managers tend to be less stringent in demanding that projects meet their forecasted milestones. The lax discipline around resource allocation that slack fosters not only increases the risk that poor projects will not be terminated (even in the face of negative information) but also increases the risk that projects will be abandoned simply because someone ran out of energy, got bored, or ran into a tough problem that needed some extra effort to resolve. Thus excess slack can result in both Type I (selecting projects that should not have been funded) and Type II (stopping projects that should have been continued) errors.

Just as too little discipline can cause problems, too much discipline can also be problematic because it can curtail legitimate innovative projects. To some extent, innovative projects are always uncertain, and positive-NPV projects cannot always be easily distinguished from negative-NPV projects. One thus has to be wary of the damaging effect of overly stringent discipline that may result from too little slack. Overly strict controls and very low levels of slack can lead to a diminished sense of self-efficacy and reduce the expectation that one can successfully propose and pursue an innovative project (Bandura, 1986). In the extreme, low levels of slack may engender a sense of futility regarding the prospect of pursuing any innovative project at all (Gecas, 1989). In sum, the relationship between discipline and innovation is curvilinear, positive for the most part but falling off beyond a certain level.

If we put the two countervailing forces of experimentation and discipline together, as shown in Figure 3.1, we can expect a curvilinear relationship between slack and innovation. This suggests that there is an intermediate level of slack in any given organizational setting that is optimal for innovation and leads to the main hypothesis of this chapter:

HYPOTHESIS 3.1: *The effect of organizational slack on innovation is inverse U-shaped.*

Empirical Analysis

Given our interest in the conditions that facilitate distributed innovation in MNCs, we decided that the most appropriate level at which to study the relationship between slack and innovation would be the smallest organizational subunit with clearly defined financial and administrative boundaries. We thus chose to focus at the departmental level in a number of different subsidiaries at two of the multinational corporations surveyed in the second phase of our research, Matsushita and Philips.[2] In both these firms, the department was an organizational subunit with an independent

Figure 3.1. The Predicted Relationship Between Slack and Innovation.

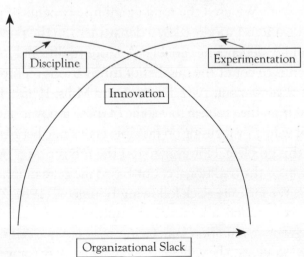

budget specifying performance objectives as well as available resources. From a theoretical standpoint, the managers in charge of the departments can be considered agents who must satisfy the performance demands placed on them by senior management, who thus act as principals. The setting is rife with classic problems of competing coalitions and agency costs. Departmental managers have better local knowledge and are more likely to distinguish good projects from bad. But their interests may not always be aligned with those of their principals. They may be motivated to accumulate slack, either to pursue pet projects or build a buffer for contingencies. However, their ability to garner slack resources depends on past performance and their negotiating leverage. It may also depend on the primary functional task of the subunit and the critical contingencies it controls (Pfeffer and Salancik, 1978). Thus we are likely to find considerable variance in the amount of slack across departments, making this a rich setting to explore the relationship between slack and innovation.

The main variables used in the empirical analysis reported in this chapter are listed in Table 3.1 and are briefly discussed here (for more details on how these were operationalized, see the Methodological Appendix).

Innovation. We used the total economic benefits of the three major innovations introduced by a department in the previous year as our primary dependent variable. A more traditional measure of innovation is to count the number of innovations reported by the focal unit (Damonpour, 1987; Delbecq and Mills, 1985). This measure suffers from the problem that some of these innovations may not create real value. By focusing on tangible economic benefits, we circumvent this problem. However, to test the robustness of our results, we also employ the traditional count-based measure of innovation.

Slack. We measure slack following Bourgeois (1981), who suggests that researchers ask organizational members such things as "'Suppose your organization were facing an economic crisis. By what percentage would you be willing to allow your salary (or wage) to be

**Table 3.1. Description of Variables
and Predicted Effect on Innovation.**

Description	Predicted Effect on Innovation
1. Dummy for company (Philips)	No prediction
2. Research and development	Positive
3. Manufacturing	Positive
4. Marketing	Positive
5. Centralization	Negative
6. Formalization	Negative
7. Socialization	Positive
8. Intrasubsidiary communication	Positive
9. Intersubsidiary communication	Positive
10. Slack resources	Positive
11. Slack resources (square term)	Negative

reduced before you would actively search for a position elsewhere?'
Or, alternately, 'How many perquisites . . . would you be willing to
give up?'" (p. 31). In the same spirit, we measured the degree of
slack by asking departmental managers how their output would be
affected by an unexpected reduction in their budgeted resources or
the time available to meet their goals. We reasoned that departments whose output would be significantly affected by such sudden
changes had less slack than those less likely to be affected.

Controls. So as reasonably to assess the relationship between
innovation and slack, it was essential to include as controls other
variables known or expected to affect innovation. It was especially important to control for the autonomy enjoyed by the
department, the extent to which the departmental managers had
been socialized, and the degree of intra- and interunit communication, all factors that we previously identified in Chapter Two,
in addition to slack resources, as being important determinants of
distributed innovation in MNCs. Table 3.1 identifies the controls
included in the analysis and the predicted signs for their effects
on innovation.

Standard ordinary least squares (OLS) regression models were used to estimate the effects of slack and the control variables on department-level innovation. Because the dependent variable is continuous (dollar value of innovations or number of innovations) and the data are cross-sectional, OLS models were considered adequate.

Table 3.2 shows the descriptive statistics and the correlation matrix for all the variables. The correlation matrix suggests that the collinearity among the variables is low. The exception is the squared term for slack, which was correlated with the corresponding linear effect of slack.[3]

The results of the OLS regression models explaining innovation are reported in Table 3.3. The first column reports the effects of the various control variables. This serves as a baseline from which the analysis proceeds.

The control variables generally have expected signs, though not all are significant. The first thing to notice is that the two companies did not differ significantly in the degree of innovation exhibited by the departments of their various national subsidiaries. Differences across departments within these companies were more significant than differences across them. In both companies, the R&D and marketing departments were more innovative. This might be expected because these departments have more opportunities to innovate in the realm of new-product introductions. The degree of control placed over the department had the expected negative effect on its innovativeness. The extent to which the department was constrained to follow formal rules and procedures had a significant negative impact. The degree to which the departmental manager had been socialized had the expected positive effect on innovation, though it was not statistically significant. Finally, the range of communication links the department had with other departments within the same subsidiary and across subsidiary boundaries had the expected positive effect, though again the effect was not significant.

From the perspective of this chapter, however, the most important results are those in column 2 of Table 3.3, in which the slack

Table 3.2. Means, Standard Deviations, and Correlation Matrix.

Description	Mean	SD	1	2	3	4	5	6	7	8	9	10	11	12	13
1. Dummy for company (Philips)	.31	.50	1.00												
2. Research and development	.05	.85	-.11	1.00											
3. Manufacturing	.19	.92	-.18*	-.11	1.00										
4. Marketing	.21	1.18	.11	-.11	-.25=	1.00									
5. Centralization	11.47	4.10	.28*	-.10	-.10	.09	1.00								
6. Formalization	14.06	2.71	-.14*	.03	.10	-.09	.11	1.00							
7. Socialization	1.52	.95	-.20*	.07	.09	-.01	-.16*	.01	1.00						
8. Intrasubsidiary communication	.48	.50	.05	-.04	.07	-.06	.01	.07	.24*	1.00					
9. Intersubsidiary communication	9.95	6.91	-.03	.04	-.12	.17*	-.04	.09	.20*	.09	1.00				
10. Slack resources	3.49	1.09	.30*	-.04	-.04	-.03	.17*	-.05	-.02	.15*	.03	1.00			
11. Slack resources (square term)	12.96	5.26	.22*	-.04	-.06	-.03	.13	-.04	-.02	.15*	.02	.93*	1.00		
12. Number of innovations	3.34	1.67	-.05	-.06	.09	-.09	-.05.	.02	.10	.10	.12	-.03	.08	1.00	
13. Scale of innovations	1.83	5.49	-.02	.07	.02	.20*	-.03	-.11	.07	.04	.09	-.05	.10	.10	1.00

*$p < .05$ ($N = 256$).

Table 3.3. Results of OLS Regression Analysis.

Independent Variables	Model 1	Model 2	Model 3
Constant	.85**	1.02	3.09***
	(.52)	(.84)	(.81)
Slack	—	.04***	.016***
		(.009)	(.003)
(Slack)	—	−.008***	−.003**
		(.0002)	(.0006)
Company	−.19	−1.02	−.33
	(.74)	(.79)	(.95)
Research and development	2.74**	2.65**	.17
	(1.57)	(1.56)	(.58)
Manufacturing	1.19	.98	.50*
	(.89)	(.90)	(.33)
Marketing	3.19***	3.24***	−.71***
	(.85)	(.86)	(.33)
Central	−.03	−.03	−.02
	(.10)	(.10)	(.03)
Formal	−.23**	−.25**	−.02
	(.14)	(.14)	(.05)
Social	.20	.05	.02
	(.41)	(.44)	(.14)
Intrasubsidiary communication	.49	.50	.19
	(.81)	(.82)	(.26)
Intersubsidiary communication	.01	.01	.01*
	(.01)	(.01)	(.005)
Adjusted R^2	.26	.31	.30

Note: The dependent variable in columns 1 and 2 is the dollar benefit from innovations and in column 3 is the number of innovations.

*$p < .10$; **$p < .05$; ***$p < .01$.

terms are added. The results are consistent with the predicted curvilinear effects of slack on innovation and are statistically significant.[4] As postulated, slack has an inverse U-shaped effect on innovation. Too little slack leaves no resources for experimentation, and too much slack allows wasteful and undisciplined experimentation that yields little benefit.

To test the robustness of our claims regarding the role of slack on innovation, we compared the results against an alternative measure for innovation, the number of innovations introduced by the department in the prior year. The results of this analysis, reported in column 3 of Table 3.3, clearly indicate that the effects of slack remain the same, even with this alternative measure of innovation. The inverse U-shaped relationship between innovation and slack is thus quite robust.[5]

It is worth noticing that the effects of some of the control variables are different, indicating that the factors that promote large-scale innovations (as measured in total dollar impact) are not necessarily the same as those that promote a large number of innovations. In particular, interunit communication densities have great significance in generating a larger number of innovations but do not play an equally important role in terms of the scale of innovations that result.

Conclusions

In this chapter, we tackled the question, What level of slack resources are optimal for promoting distributed innovation in MNCs? We propose a middle ground between scholars who argue that slack encourages innovation and those who suggest that slack inhibits innovation. We point out that the debate seems intractable only because both sides have not simultaneously considered two opposing effects of slack. One effect, which yields a positive relationship between slack and innovation, is that slack encourages experimentation and the initiation of projects that might potentially result in useful innovations. A second effect, which yields a negative relationship between slack and innovation, is that slack encourages complacency and discourages discipline. Increasing amounts of slack thus lead to diminished effort to seek value-added improvements or the pursuit of pet projects that are unlikely to yield useful innovation.

Rather than reconcile these opposing effects, the tendency in the past has been simply to weigh in on one side or the other. Our results suggest that the middle ground we have proposed offers a way out of this intractable debate. The issue is not whether organizational slack is universally good or bad for innovation but rather how much slack is optimal. Clearly, too little slack is likely to be inimical to innovation because a highly resource constrained and controlled environment discourages any experimentation. It is easy to agree that too much slack is apt to be equally inimical to innovation, breeding complacency and a lack of discipline that makes the pursuit of unfruitful projects more likely. The relationship between slack and innovation is thus properly viewed as being inverse U-shaped.

Though this general relationship between slack and innovation is intuitively compelling, answering the question of the optimal amount of slack is less straightforward. The optimal amount of slack may depend on a whole series of situational circumstances impossible to explore exhaustively in this book. For instance, one might argue that optimal levels of slack may be greater in a growing industry than in a declining one, due to the probability of more positive-NPV projects being available in the former than in the latter (Jensen, 1993). Similarly, subunit- and individual-level factors such as the characteristics of the leader of the subunit or the critical contingencies controlled by the subunit may influence the optimal amount of slack. One may, for instance, be willing to grant more slack to a manager with a track record of innovative accomplishments or to a subsidiary that can develop innovations that potentially benefit the firm as a whole.

These complexities notwithstanding, one thing is clear: to facilitate distributed innovation throughout the MNC, managers must carefully analyze and allocate slack resources throughout the organization. Assessing and managing the levels and distribution of organizational slack is critical in a world in which firms must confront simultaneous demands to be innovative and efficient. During the 1980s, firms invested heavily in cost-cutting programs that eliminated slack, often at the expense of investing in the future. We hope the results presented in this chapter add further warning to earlier cautions against such a shortsighted view (for example, Hamel and Prahalad, 1994). There is no doubt a pressing need to reduce slack in many organizations. But it is equally important to recognize that going too far can jeopardize a firm's capacity for innovation and renewal. For superior long-term performance, value creation can never be relegated to a secondary role, and so some amount of slack must always be maintained and distributed throughout the MNC.

Notes

1. For some earlier studies, see Damonpour, 1987; Singh, 1986; Lant, 1985; Delbecq and Mills, 1985; Downs and Mohr, 1976; Baldridge and Burnham, 1975; Zaltman, Duncan, and Holbeck, 1973; and Mohr, 1969.
2. NEC, the third company studied in this phase, was not used in this analysis because of limited data at the departmental level.
3. To address concerns of multicollinearity, we tried Cronbach's transformation, which recommends centering variables to their mean prior to forming the multiplicative term. However, there was no significant reduction in the correlation between the interaction terms and the main effects. As a result, we retained the original variables and introduced each of the interaction terms separately in the analysis to address concerns of multicollinearity.
4. Further evidence for the role of slack in explaining innovation is assessed by comparing adjusted R^2 terms across columns 1 and 2. Including slack and its squared term in column 2 leads to a

significant increase in the R^2 term over the baseline model, suggesting a better-specified model.

5. The results so far included a dummy variable to control for differences across the two companies. The insignificant coefficient for the company dummy variable suggests that there are no intrinsic differences across the companies in the innovativeness of their departments. However, it does not tell us whether the main effects hypothesized in this chapter differ across the two companies. More specifically, it is not clear if the relationship between slack and innovation holds for each of the companies. Accordingly, we estimated unrestricted models for each company. The signs of the coefficients indicated that the postulated main effects observed in the pooled sample hold true in each of the companies. We also estimated the models separately for each of the functional areas and again found consistent results. The results of these analyses are not reported here for the sake of brevity.

Chapter Four

Creation, Adoption, and Diffusion of Innovations Across the MNC

In Chapter Three, we investigated the role of organizational slack in enabling distributed innovation in multinationals. In this chapter, we develop a more complete model of the organizational factors that influence the innovative capacity of the MNC. We push for completeness in two directions. First, we highlight that the innovative capacity of an MNC is a function of each subsidiary's ability to foster innovation along three dimensions. (1) Subsidiaries can develop and adopt new products, processes, or administrative systems locally, using their own technical and managerial resources, to respond to local exigencies. We call this task *creation*, and the effectiveness of the various subsidiaries in creating such local innovations lies at the heart of an MNC's ability to be responsive to the unique opportunities in its different operating environments. (2) Subsidiaries may be required to adopt innovations developed by the parent company, a central R&D facility, or other national subsidiaries of the company. This is the task of *adoption*. The willingness of subsidiaries to adopt such innovations often plays a critical role in the MNC's ability to pursue an integrated global strategy. (3) Subsidiaries may also be required to diffuse their local innovations to the parent company or to other subsidiaries. The ability to facilitate such intraorganizational *diffusion* of subsidiary innovations allows an MNC to exploit the learning capacity inherent in its geographically diversified operations.[1] To tap their full value creation potential, MNCs must foster the capacity of their subsidiaries to create, adopt, and diffuse innovations.

The second direction in which we push for full comprehension is to apply the differentiated network framework to think systematically about the organizational factors that facilitate a subsidiary's ability to create, adopt, and diffuse innovations. Much of the literature on the organizational factors that promote innovation is based on the analysis of single organizational units and does not explicitly take into account that the focal unit is embedded in a network of other organizational linkages. As we discussed in Chapter One, conceptualizing the MNC as a differentiated network explicitly draws attention to this network of relationships. It directs attention to the distribution of slack resources across the MNC, the structure of the relationship between the headquarters and the subsidiaries, the socialization mechanisms used to bind together the members of the MNC, and the communication flows within each subsidiary, between the headquarters and each subsidiary, and across the various subsidiaries.

The benefits of adopting this more comprehensive framework are shown by bringing together insights obtained through each of the three phases of the research project—case research in nine companies, in-depth surveys in three companies, and a broader survey of sixty-six North American and European MNCs.

The Distribution of Slack Resources

In companies such as Matsushita and Kao, most key organizational assets and resources, including R&D, manufacturing, and even marketing capabilities, were centralized at headquarters, and the national subsidiaries operated with relatively low levels of slack. The national subsidiaries of companies such as ITT and Philips possessed relatively high levels of local resources, including development and manufacturing facilities. Subsidiaries of the first group of companies created relatively few innovations. There were thus few opportunities for diffusion. However, these subsidiaries also appeared to be extremely efficient in adopting and implementing central innovations both quickly and effectively. The subsidiaries of the second group of companies, by contrast, created a relatively higher number of innovations. However, they tended to be more resistant in adopting innovations from the parent company or from other subsidiaries, insisting often on developing their own responses to problems or opportunities or at least on significant modifications to others' innovations before adopting them.

These observations are consistent with the findings from Chapter Three that moderate levels of slack resources are necessary to enable organizations to engage in the search and trial-and-error activities necessary for innovation. Diffusion similarly requires slack because the major benefits of internal diffusion of innovations accrue to the recipients, and diffusing units are not expected to engage in this activity by withdrawing resources committed to maintaining current operational activities. However, local slack may impede adoption because of the "not invented here" (NIH) syndrome (Katz and Allen, 1982) and, in the specific context of MNCs, because local search activities promoted by slack may uncover valid reasons why direct adoption of innovations created in other environments is inappropriate (Poynter and White, 1984). Hence we hypothesize:

HYPOTHESIS 4.1: *Local slack resources will facilitate creation and diffusion but impede adoption of innovations by the subsidiary.*

Structure of Headquarters-Subsidiary Relations

In some of the companies we studied, subsidiaries enjoyed little autonomy and were highly constrained by bureaucratic controls. The national subsidiaries possessed neither the competence nor the legitimacy to initiate any new programs or even to modify any products or processes developed by the parent company. Typically, these were companies with highly centralized resources. Even if a subsidiary in such a company came to possess some local slack resources, as Matsushita's U.S. subsidiary did when the company acquired Motorola's television business and its large R&D facility in the United States, the application of the resources was controlled from the headquarters. Such subsidiaries with low levels of local autonomy neither created nor diffused innovations but tended to be effective adopters of new products and processes created by the parent companies.

In contrast, subsidiaries of companies like Unilever, ITT, and Philips enjoyed considerable strategic and operational autonomy, though the headquarters exercised varying degrees of administrative control through the budgeting and financial reporting systems. These relatively autonomous subsidiaries created and diffused more innovations. They were also more resistant to adopting innovations created elsewhere.

The effect of bureaucratic controls such as centralization and formalization on innovation has been extensively studied by organization theorists. The accepted view is that a high degree of bureaucratic control inhibits creativity and innovation (V. A. Thompson, 1967; Aiken and Hage, 1971; Amabile, 1988). As Mohr (1982) points out, even intuitively it is obvious that a certain amount of freedom to experiment and do things outside a formal role or procedure is necessary for innovation. Empirical research supports this intuitive belief (see Kanter, 1988, for a review). Moreover, research, in the context of MNCs, confirms this view. Scholars have found that greater levels of centralization and formalization have a negative impact on the innovativeness of subsidiaries (Picard, 1977; Gates and Egelhoff, 1986; Egelhoff, 1988a).

The negative association between bureaucratic controls and the creation of innovation also applies to the diffusion of innovation, since the possibility of diffusion arises only if local innovations are first created. However, the very dependence of the subsidiary on the headquarters facilitates adoption, since the subsidiary has neither the authority nor the capability to resist. These arguments are supported by the positive correlation between centralization and global product standardization observed by Picard (1977) and the negative correlation he found between centralization and the extent of local modification of products. Therefore, considering local autonomy to be the obverse of bureaucratic control, we hypothesize:

HYPOTHESIS 4.2: *High levels of local autonomy will facilitate creation and diffusion but impede adoption of innovations by the subsidiary.*

Socialization Patterns

In contrast to the effect of bureaucratic controls, there is considerable evidence of positive associations between creation, adoption, and diffusion of innovations by a subsidiary and the extent to which the subsidiary is normatively integrated with the parent company and shares its overall strategy, goals, and values. In the companies we studied, high levels of normative integration were achieved through socialization mechanisms such as the extensive travel and transfer of managers between the headquarters and the subsidiary and through joint work in teams, task forces, and committees. A typical illustration of such normative integration was the "ization" program of Unilever a systematic effort to "Unileverize" the company's operations in different countries and "internationalize" Unilever management worldwide. Supported by an elaborately planned system of executive transfers, management development programs, and regular meetings, it succeeded in convincing managers that these investments helped in developing a common context, significantly improving subsidiary contributions to the company's innovation processes. Similar experiences were also reported by companies as diverse as Ericsson, Procter & Gamble, and NEC.

Received theory suggests that two sets of conditions must be met for any organization to engage in the act of creating innovations: the act must be feasible, and it must be desirable (Mohr, 1969). For national subsidiaries of an MNC, local resources and autonomy are necessary to meet the condition of feasibility. Normative integration helps satisfy the condition of desirability (Baliga and Jaeger, 1984; Jaeger, 1983). Inclusive goals and shared values facilitate the creation of innovation not only by motivating subsidiaries to be entrepreneurial (Kanter, 1983) but also by enhancing the headquarters' responsiveness to subsidiary needs and initiatives. Similarly, by deemphasizing turf issues, shared objectives moderate the normal hierarchy of managerial loyalties whereby local interests tend to be given higher priority than global interests. The goal congruence and shared organizational context created by normative integration and extensive socialization facilitate both the adoption and the diffusion of innovation. Therefore, we hypothesize:

HYPOTHESIS 4.3: *A high level of normative integration between the headquarters and the subsidiary will facilitate creation, adoption, and diffusion of innovations by the subsidiary.*

Patterns of Communication

The effects of intrasubsidiary, headquarters-subsidiary, and inter-subsidiary communication on the creation, adoption, and diffusion of innovations vary. Each is discussed in turn.

Intrasubsidiary Communication

Consistent with our previous findings, national subsidiaries creating a relatively higher number of innovations also had relatively higher densities of internal communication among diverse managers. Most of these subsidiaries, such as Philips's in the United Kingdom and Brazil, had many formal and informal mechanisms, including cross-functional teams, committees, and task forces, to enhance internal communication across vertical and horizontal boundaries.

Our field research findings are consistent with an extensive literature in organization theory that emphasizes the importance of dense lateral relations across functional and departmental boundaries for the creation of innovation (Burns and Stalker, 1961; Lawrence and Lorsch, 1967; Aiken and Hage, 1971). These lateral linkages are a valuable source of diverse inputs that stimulate idea generation. They also prevent "segmentalism" or factional conflicts across functions, creating instead an "integrative" atmosphere that facilitates the implementation of innovative ideas (Kanter, 1983, 1988).

The importance of cross-functional cooperation has been reinforced by recent studies on the new-product development process (Hayes, Wheelwright, and Clark, 1988). These studies have found that interfunctional barriers lead to discrete handoffs—the "throwing it over the wall" syndrome—which can greatly impede innovation in organizations. Lack of communication across functional boundaries also leads to each function being trapped in its own "thought world," unable to appreciate and learn from the perspective of others who may be crucial to the success of the innovation (Dougherty, 1987). Structural arrangements such as cross-functional teams and dense interfunctional communication have been found to help break down these barriers and stimulate innovation.

Dense communication flows within a subsidiary have the greatest impact on a subsidiary's capacity to generate innovations locally. Such flows are useful but much less relevant for the diffusion of innovations to other subsidiaries or the adoption of innovations developed elsewhere in the MNC. For diffusion and adoption, flows between headquarters and subsidiaries and between the subsidiaries themselves are more important. Thus we hypothesize:

HYPOTHESIS 4.4: *A high level of interfunctional communication within a subsidiary will facilitate creation of innovations by the subsidiary. It will be less significant for the adoption and diffusion of innovations by the subsidiary.*

Headquarters-Subsidiary Communication

Most of the adoption cases pertained to innovations created in the headquarters. Subsidiaries especially effective at adopting parent-company innovations were like the U.S. subsidiary of Matsushita, with manifestly dense communication between local managers and managers at the headquarters. Most departmental managers communicated with one or more headquarters managers daily, via telex or telephone, and often through regular travel to subsidiaries by headquarters managers. These case studies suggest that a subsidiary's adoption of central innovations will be facilitated if headquarters-subsidiary communication is intense.

Extensive headquarters-subsidiary communication can also promote the diffusion of innovation, with the headquarters playing the role of a broker or clearinghouse for transferring innovations across subsidiaries. By being closely linked to its various subsidiaries, a headquarters organization can identify what we might think of as arbitrage opportunities more readily. The headquarters may learn about an innovative solution to a problem in one location and encourage its adoption in another location where it knows that local managers are struggling with a similar problem. Of course, the recognition of relevant knowledge that lies elsewhere would be even higher if the subsidiaries had direct links with one another. But transfers mediated by the headquarters are better than none at all.

Extensive headquarters-subsidiary communication, though useful for the adoption and diffusion of innovations, may, however, be less helpful for the creation of innovations by the MNC's subsidiaries. The subsidiary may come to rely too much on the headquarters for new ideas to adopt and invest less effort in generating such ideas itself. Accordingly, we hypothesize:

HYPOTHESIS 4.5: A *high level of communication between the headquarters and subsidiaries will facilitate the adoption and diffusion of innovations by the subsidiaries. It will be less helpful for the creation of innovation by subsidiaries.*

Intersubsidiary Communication

The position of an organization in various relational networks has important implications for its power, access to resources, and autonomy (Burt, 1982). In the context of innovation, an organization's position in communication networks is of particular importance. Early research on communication networks found that actors at the center of the network were better at solving problems and completing ambiguous tasks than those in more peripheral positions (Bavelas, 1950; Guetzkow and Simon, 1954). This finding has been repeatedly supported in later research on the diffusion of innovation (Rogers, 1983; Burt 1987).

Centrality in communication networks, in the sense of "betweenness" or being in the middle (directly or indirectly) of chains linking other actors (Freeman, 1979), can be a source of a diverse set of inputs as well as power (Krackhardt, 1989). By being central in intersubsidiary networks of communication flows, a subsidiary can learn about interesting developments in other national locations. Moreover, it can use the network to search more efficiently for the resources required for innovation.

Being at the center of intersubsidiary communication networks has the greatest benefit in enabling a subsidiary to diffuse innovations (Rogers, 1983). However, such a network location also has significant benefits in enabling the creation and adoption of innovations. Therefore:

HYPOTHESIS 4.6: *The diffusion of innovations by a subsidiary will be facilitated by high levels of intersubsidiary communication; adoption and creation will be facilitated as well, though to a lesser extent.*

Empirical Analysis Based on In-Depth Survey of Three Companies

The hypotheses proposed in this chapter were tested using data gathered from both the second and third phases of our research design. We first discuss the results obtained from the second phase of our study, in which data were collected through an in-depth survey completed by headquarters and subsidiary managers in three of the nine companies studied in the first phase—Philips, Matsushita

Electric, and NEC. Respondents were asked to enumerate and describe the innovations that were created, adopted, and diffused by their departments during the preceding twelve months. Subsidiary-level scores for each of these dependent variables were obtained by adding the total number of innovations created, adopted, and diffused by the different departments of the subsidiary. Responses obtained from the different departmental managers within a subsidiary were averaged to create indicators for levels of slack, local autonomy, normative integration, intrasubsidiary communication, headquarters-subsidiary communication, and inter-subsidiary communication. (See the Methodological Appendix for more details.)

For each company, the ranks of each subsidiary for all measured variables were computed. Subsidiary ranks for creation, adoption, and diffusion of innovations were then compared with the ranks for the different organizational attributes. Results of these comparisons are shown in the Spearman's rank correlations in Table 4.1. The rank correlation approach was adopted to avoid the excessive influence of outliers. The findings, however, remain unaltered even if absolute measures are considered and Pearson's correlation coefficients are employed.

The significance levels (one-tailed test) for each of the correlation coefficients is based on Olds's method (1938) for estimating the significance of rank correlations for small samples when variables are not assumed to be distributed normally. Given the small number of subsidiaries in each company, the statistical significance of these rank correlation coefficients should not be overemphasized. Keeping this caveat in mind, we can draw the following conclusions.

Several of the proposed hypotheses are supported by the data. This is particularly true with regard to the hypothesized effects of normative integration and patterns of communication on the creation, adoption, and diffusion of innovations by MNC subsidiaries. In all three companies, normative integration is positively and significantly correlated with creation and adoption of innovations. Similarly, the relationships between intra- and

Table 4.1. Spearman's Rank Correlations Between Creation, Adoption, and Diffusion of Innovations and the Different Organizational Attributes.

Organizational Attributes	Matsushita (N = 8)			Philips (N = 7)			NEC (N = 5)		
	Creation	Adoption	Diffusion	Creation	Adoption	Diffusion	Creation	Adoption	Diffusion
Slack resources	.66	.71*	.85**	.96***	.73**	.78**	.89*	.58	.66
Local autonomy	.52	.17	−.22	.89***	.83**	.65	.48	.63.	.71
Normative integration	.67*	.71*	.67*	.86**	.79**	.91***	.89*	.94*	.86
Intrasubsidiary communication	.86***	.76*	.72*	.85**	.55	.81**	.90*	.71	.77
Headquarters-subsidiary communication	.61	.83***	.69*	.68	.87**	.79**	.71	.93*	.90*
Intersubsidiary communication	.56	.80**	.91***	.61	.81**	.86**	.43	.69	1.00*

Notes: Significance for a one-tailed test (*α = .05, **α < .025, ***α < .01) based on Olds (1938). N is the number of subsidiaries in each company.

interunit communication and creation, adoption, and diffusion of innovations are all significant in the right direction. Dense intraunit communication has the greatest impact on the creation of innovations, headquarters-subsidiary communication on their adoption, and intersubsidiary communication on their diffusion.

Some of the proposed associations are, however, not strongly supported by the data. The hypothesized effects of local autonomy, in particular, have mixed support. While there is some evidence that local autonomy facilitates the creation of innovation, there is little evidence that it promotes the diffusion of innovation or that it impedes the adoption of innovations developed outside the subsidiary.

Results on the effects of local slack resources are also mixed. There is some evidence that slack facilitates creation and diffusion (correlations significant in two out of three companies), but its hypothesized effect on adoption is rejected. Contrary to our hypotheses, the association between slack and adoption is not negative in any of the three companies.

Further analysis revealed that the subsidiaries naturally clustered into three groups. Group 1 consisted of subsidiaries found to create but not adopt or diffuse innovations. Group 2 was composed of subsidiaries that created and adopted innovations but did not diffuse them. And group 3 included a few subsidiaries engaged simultaneously in all three tasks of creation, adoption, and diffusion. Interestingly, subsidiaries that engaged in all three innovation activities (group 3) were also the ones that recorded the highest scores on all three tasks.

Table 4.2 shows the numbers of innovations created, adopted, and diffused by the eight subsidiaries of Matsushita on which we had complete data and also their scores for the different organizational attributes. Group 1 subsidiaries include E and F; group 2 consists of G and H; and subsidiaries A, B, C, and D are in group 3.

The different organizational attributes of Matsushita subsidiaries belonging to the different groups are compared in Table 4.3. For each group, the table shows the mean levels of local slack

Table 4.2. Creation, Adoption, and Diffusion of Innovations by Subsidiaries of Matsushita.

Subsidiary	Number of Innovations			Slack Resource (Scale 1–5)	Local Autonomy (Scale 1–5)	Normative Integration (Scale 1–3)	Communication Density (Scale 1–3)		
	Created	Adopted	Diffused				Intra-subsidiary	Headquarters-Subsidiary	Inter-subsidiary
A	20	3	1	3.9	3.4	2.1	1.9	1.4	.0
B	16	8	4	4.3	3.2	2.6	1.6	1.4	.1
C	17	6	9	5.0	3.5	1.9	1.9	1.5	.3
D	22	12	7	4.1	4.2	1.7	2.2	1.8	.4
E	14	0	0	2.2	4.5	.7	.8	.1	.0
F	11	0	0	3.4	3.7	.6	1.1	.7	.0
G	8	2	0	3.2	3.0	1.1	1.3	1.6	.1
H	7	4	0	2.8	2.9	.8	1.4	1.5	.0

resources, local autonomy, normative integration, and the densities of intrasubsidiary, headquarters-subsidiary, and intersubsidiary communication. Results of one-way ANOVA tests revealed significant (F statistic significant at the .01 level) differences among subsidiaries across the three groups for all organizational attributes.

Further investigation of the pairwise differences among the three groups (Scheffe's test) showed the following:[2]

1. Subsidiaries in group 1—those that created innovations but did not diffuse them or adopt innovations developed elsewhere—had significantly higher levels of local autonomy but significantly lower levels of slack resources, normative integration, and intrasubsidiary, headquarters-subsidiary, and intersubsidiary communication compared to subsidiaries in the other two groups. It appears that these subsidiaries simply take advantage of the autonomy they enjoy to create local innovations. They do not, however, derive any significant advantage from being a part of a larger knowledge-creating system.

Table 4.3. Organizational Attributes of Subsidiaries Belonging to the Three Groups: Matsushita.

Organizational Attributes	Group			F Statistic	Scheffe's Test (pairs that are not significantly different)
	1	2	3		
Slack resources	2.8	3.0	4.3	8.3*	(1, 2)
Local autonomy	4.1	2.9	3.6	14.9*	None
Normative integration	.6	1.0	2.1	17.6*	None
Intrasubsidiary communication	1.0	1.3	1.9	11.6*	None
Headquarters-subsidiary communication	.4	1.5	1.5	8.4*	(2, 3)
Intersubsidiary communication	0.0	0.0	.2	1.9	All

*Significant at .01 level.

2. Subsidiaries in group 2 had significantly lower levels of local autonomy compared to subsidiaries in the other two groups. The reliance and dependence of these subsidiaries on the headquarters organizations, as also reflected in their high levels of communication with the headquarters, explain why this group is so good at adopting innovations developed at the headquarters.

3. Subsidiaries in group 3 had significantly higher levels of local resources, normative integration, and intra- and inter-subsidiary communication compared to subsidiaries in the other two groups. Not surprisingly, this is the group that is able to create, adopt, and diffuse innovations more readily than the others.

Normatively, group 3 subsidiaries have the most desirable innovation characteristics: not only do they engage in all three tasks of creating, adopting, and diffusing innovation; but they also record the highest scores on each task. In all three companies, these subsidiaries were differentiated from the others by higher scores on normative integration and higher densities of intra- and interunit communication. These results suggest that formal and informal organizational mechanisms that promote the creation of shared values and build communication links within and across organizational boundaries are especially important for enhancing the value-creating capacity of MNCs. We will explore the factors that build such social capital later in Chapters Seven and Eight of this book.

Empirical Analysis Based on Large Sample Survey of Sixty-Six MNCs

To test further the generalizability and robustness of the results obtained through our in-depth survey of three MNCs, we analyzed data obtained from sixty-six North American and European MNCs. Unfortunately, we were unable to collect data on the diffusion of innovations by the subsidiaries in each of these companies, so our analysis is restricted to hypotheses pertaining to their relative propensities to create and adopt innovations.

Table 4.4 shows the correlations between the subsidiary scores on creation and adoption of innovations and their scores on local slack resources, local autonomy, normative integration, and head-quarters-subsidiary communication.[3]

To develop a better understanding of these innovation-organizational associations, an analysis was undertaken to look for differences between high- and low-performing subsidiaries in both creation and adoption of innovations. The creation and adoption scores were first normalized for all subsidiaries of the same company, and these normalized scores (z scores) were divided into three categories: high ($z > 1$), medium ($1 > z > -1$), and low ($z < -1$).

Table 4.5 shows the mean values of the different organizational attributes for subsidiaries scoring high, medium, and low on creation of innovations. The F probabilities indicate whether the differences among the categories are statistically significant. The Scheffe's test results indicate whether the differences between the high- and low-scoring groups are statistically significant. The results support several of our hypotheses: subsidiaries with higher scores on creation of innovations have significantly higher levels of local resources, local autonomy, and normative integration, compared to other subsidiaries

Table 4.4. Zero-Order Correlation Matrix.

Subsidiary Attributes	Creation of Innovations	Adoption of Innovations	Local Resources	Local Autonomy	Normative Integration
Local resources	.63	N.S.			
Local autonomy	.54	N.S.	.51		
Normative integration	.37	.15	.45	.20	
Headquarters-Subsidiary communication	.23	.21	.39	N.S.	.32

N.S. = not significant; all other correlations are significant at the .001 level.

of the company. Interestingly, counter to our expectations (hypothesis 4.5), these subsidiaries also had higher levels of communication with the headquarters. One explanation for this anomalous finding is that such communication is helpful, provided that the subsidiary maintains autonomy. When the subsidiary is heavily dependent on the headquarters, extensive headquarters-subsidiary communication reinforces this sense of dependence and inhibits the creativity of the subsidiary. However, if it enjoys autonomy, the subsidiary may actually be stimulated by a communication channel with the headquarters because this link can serve as a valuable conduit for access to information and resources that enable local innovations.

Table 4.6 shows the results of the same analysis for subsidiaries scoring high, medium, and low on adoption of innovations. Just as we found in our in-depth analysis of the surveys from three companies, contrary to our hypotheses 4.1 and 4.2, local resources and local autonomy do not discriminate among the different categories of subsidiaries in terms of their propensity to adopt innovations developed elsewhere. Contrary to our expectations, these subsidiaries are no

Table 4.5. Distinguishing Attributes of Subsidiaries
Scoring High, Medium, and Low on Creation of Innovations.

| Subsidiary Attributes | Creation of Innovations by the Subsidiary (Scale 1–5, low to high) | | | F Statistic | Scheffe's Test (Is high-low pair distinguished at the .05 level?) |
	High	Medium	Low		
Local resources	4.3	3.2	1.9	97.5*	Yes
Local autonomy	3.0	2.2	1.2	75.0*	Yes
Normative integration	4.2	3.5	2.9	28.9*	Yes
Headquarters-Subsidiary communication	3.5	3.2	2.7	19.6*	Yes

*Significant at the .001 level.

more likely to suffer from the "not invented here" syndrome than others. Again, this result can be explained by the fact that what does indeed differentiate subsidiaries that are most likely to adopt innovations developed elsewhere is high levels of normative integration and headquarters-subsidiary communications (in keeping with our hypotheses 4.3 and 4.5). Both these latter factors are likely to reduce the problems that autonomy and local resources might create. Because they share the same goals and are tightly tied to the headquarters, these subsidiaries are unlikely to resist adopting innovations that might be helpful locally merely because they were created elsewhere. What our results suggest is that by investing in the creation of social capital that binds different organizational units together, MNCs are most likely to benefit from the resources possessed by their various autonomous subsidiaries.

Finally, to analyze the joint effects of the different organizational attributes on a subsidiary's ability to create and adopt innovations, a stepwise regression analysis was undertaken. The results of this analysis are shown in Table 4.7 with the independent variables listed in

Table 4.6. Distinguishing Attributes of Subsidiaries Scoring High, Medium, and Low on Adoption of Innovations.

Subsidiary Attributes	Adoption of Innovations by the Subsidiary (Scale 1–5, low to high)			F Statistic	Scheffe's Test (Is high-low pair distinguished at the .05 level?)
	High	Medium	Low		
Local resources	3.3	3.1	3.0	1.3*	No
Local autonomy	2.2	2.1	2.3	3.2*	Yes
Normative integration	3.7	3.5	3.2	6.5*	Yes
Headquarters-Subsidiary communication	3.5	3.2	3.0	11.6*	Yes

*Significant at the .05 level.

the order in which they entered the equation. Given the high corre-lations among the influencing variables, the beta coefficients cannot be interpreted unambiguously. The results are presented only to high-light that the four variables—local resources, local autonomy, nor-mative integration, and headquarters communication—collectively explain 52 percent of the total variance in the subsidiary scores on creation of innovation. Variance in adoption scores, by contrast, can-not be explained to any significant extent by these variables, though both normative integration and headquarters-subsidiary communi-cation appear to have a statistically significant impact.

Conclusions

Our objective in adopting a relatively complex multiphased and multimethodology research design was to achieve the benefits of triangulating multiple research approaches and comparing the results from each approach. Each approach we adopted had its lim-itations, some inherent in the methodology itself, and some imposed by the practical problems we faced in implementing this study. Our hope, however, was that some of the findings would be robust enough to be confirmed by each methodology. Table 4.8 summarizes our findings on the factors that promote the creation, adoption, and diffusion of innovations from each of the different methods we employed. The similarities and differences across our findings lead to the following conclusions.

Normative integration and intra- and interunit communica-tion have significant positive effects for the creation, adoption, and diffusion of innovations by an MNC's subsidiaries. This finding is consistent across the three methodologies. Less consistent findings are obtained with regard to the effects of local resources and auton-omy. Local resources facilitate the creation and diffusion of inno-vations, but their effect on adoption is inconclusive. For local autonomy, the inconsistencies in the findings across the different methodologies are even more severe. The inconclusive effects of local resources and autonomy can, however, be explained if it is

Table 4.7. Regression Results.

			Influencing Variables			
				Headquarters- Subsidiary Communication	F Statistic (significance)	Adjusted R^2
Dependent Variable	Local Resources	Local Autonomy	Normative Integration			
Creation of innovations by the subsidiary	.43 (11.69)	.30 (9.06)	.12 (3.70)	.10 (2.41)	187.7 (0.00)	.52
Adoption of innovations by the subsidiary	—	—	.21 (5.76)	.19 (4.62)	2.22 (0.00)	.09

Notes: The values in the table are the beta coefficients; the t statistics are shown in parentheses. Coefficients not significant at .05 level are not shown.

Table 4.8. Comparison of
Findings from the Different Methodologies.

Effects of Various Attributes	Case Research in Nine Companies (Phase 1)	Multiple-Indicator, Multilevel, Multiple-Respondent Survey in Three Companies (Phase 2)	Single-Indicator, Headquarters-Level, Single-Respondent Survey in Sixty-Six Companies (Phase 3)
Creation			
Local resources	+	+	+
Local autonomy	+	0	+
Normative integration	+	+	+
Headquarters-Subsidiary communication	0	+	+
Intrasubsidiary communication	+	+	N.M.
Intersubsidiary communication	0	0	N.M.
Adoption			
Local resources	–	+	0
Local autonomy	–	0	0
Normative integration	+	+	+
Headquarters-Subsidiary communication	+	+	+
Intrasubsidiary communication	0	+	N.M.
Intersubsidiary communication	+	+	N.M.
Diffusion			
Local resources	+	+	N.M.
Local autonomy	+	0	N.M.
Normative integration	+	+	N.M.
Headquarters-Subsidiary communication	+	+	N.M.
Intrasubsidiary communication	0	+	N.M.
Intersubsidiary communication	+	+	N.M.

Notes: Symbols indicate positive (+), negative (–), or insignificant (0) associations.
N.M. = not measured.

assumed that the effects of these organizational attributes on the various innovation tasks are mediated by the level of normative integration and the communication density in the organization. As we discuss at greater length in the next chapter, the relationship between the headquarters of a multinational and its national subsidiaries represents a situation of mixed motives wherein each party may have both convergent and conflicting interests and perspectives (Schmidt and Kochan, 1977). High levels of normative integration and information exchange can enhance the salience of the convergent interests. This convergence of interests may encourage even subsidiaries with considerable local resources and autonomy to participate in the tasks of creating, adopting, and diffusing innovations that benefit the company as a whole (Edstrom and Galbraith, 1977; Galbraith and Edstrom, 1976). In the absence of such integration, however, the conflicting interests may become relatively more salient, in which case the effects of local resources and autonomy may be negligible or even negative. Building a shared context that binds the MNC together thus emerges as the most salient factor in promoting distributed innovation in the MNC.

In Part Two, we discuss how MNCs can achieve both differentiation—to respond to the unique local circumstances of each subsidiary—and integration—to bind together these disparate organizations so that the whole is greater than the sum of the parts. Before we turn to this discussion, let us quickly review the major themes of Part One.

First, the organizational advantage of the modern MNC rests in its capacity to tap the full distributed potential for innovation that exists in all its organizational units. MNCs must move beyond their traditional focus on center-for-global innovations and recognize that local-for-local, local-for-global, and global-for-global innovations are all going to be increasingly important for them to sustain their competitive edge.

Second, the global distribution of organizational capabilities and slack resources, the structure of headquarters-subsidiary relations, socialization mechanisms that lead to normative integration, and intra- and interunit communication are the major factors that influence an MNC's capacity to foster distributed innovation.

Third, intermediate levels of organizational slack distributed throughout the various organizational units are most likely to facilitate distributed innovation in MNCs. Maintaining too little slack in the interest of efficiency risks killing innovation. But maintaining too much slack does not lead to additional innovation and hence must be avoided in the interest of efficiency.

Fourth, though slack and organizational autonomy are important considerations that influence the creation, adoption, and distribution of innovations by an MNC's subsidiaries, the real leverage lies in creating a shared context and common purpose and in enhancing the communication densities within and across the organization's internal and external boundaries.

Notes

1. There can be a fourth task, that of *participation* in global innovations that are created jointly by the headquarters and a number of national subsidiaries of the MNC. We do not consider this task here because it can vary widely in both nature and extent and therefore cannot be defined or measured precisely. However, our case research suggests that subsidiaries that are effective simultaneously in all three tasks of creation, adoption, and diffusion are also effective in the task of participation. See Bartlett and Ghoshal (1989) for illustrations of such global innovations and descriptions of the organizational attributes that facilitate such innovations in MNCs.

2. Identical patterns were observed at NEC and Philips. The results are not reported here for the sake of brevity.

3. Data on intrasubsidiary and intersubsidiary communication were not gathered in this survey; consequently, hypotheses pertaining to these variables are not discussed here.

Part Two

Differentiation and Integration

Chapter Five

Internal Differentiation Within the MNC

When James Thompson (1967, p. 70) proposed that "under norms of rationality, organizations facing heterogeneous task environments seek to identify homogeneous segments and establish structural units to deal with each," he may have had more than multinational corporations in mind. Nevertheless, it is fair to say that the MNC is the quintessential case of an organization facing heterogeneous task environments: its various national subsidiaries often operate under different environmental conditions (Robock, Simmons, and Zwick, 1977) and may have done so under very different historical circumstances (Stopford and Turner, 1985). From the perspective of contingency theory, therefore, one can expect that the internal structure of a multinational corporation will not be homogeneous but will be differentiated to match the contexts of its various national subsidiaries (Lawrence and Lorsch, 1967).

In this chapter, we begin to explore the issue of internal differentiation within MNCs. We propose a contingency framework and develop conditions of "fit" between the particular contextual conditions that characterize a subsidiary and the structure of the headquarters-subsidiary relation. We argue that the subsidiary context can be differentiated into four categories based on the joint conditions of its local resource levels and its environmental complexity relative to the other subsidiaries in the MNC. The fit structure of the headquarters-subsidiary relation in each contextual category is a correspondingly differentiated combination of the following elements: (1) centralization, the direct headquarters control of subsidiary decision making; (2) formalization, the use of systematic rules and procedures in decision making; and (3) normative integration, consensus, and shared values as a basis for decision making.

The discussion in this chapter is organized into three sections. The first develops the theoretical motivation for the proposed contingency framework. Central to the argument is the conceptualization of the headquarters-subsidiary relation as a mixed-motive dyad in which members have both interdependent and independent interests. Since each of the four contextual conditions presents a very different situation in terms of the nature of interdependence and independence in the headquarters-subsidiary exchange relation, each presents unique challenges to management. We examine centralization, formalization, and normative integration as the primary mechanisms for governing headquarters-subsidiary relations and meeting these challenges. Based on the dual considerations of the relative efficacy of each of these elements in addressing the mixed-motive situation described earlier and the administrative costs associated with each element, we develop several hypotheses that describe a fit between the contingent conditions that characterize a subsidiary and the structure of the headquarters-subsidiary relation.

The second section of the chapter presents both the methods used to test the hypotheses developed in the first section and the results of these tests. The final section discusses these results and their implications for the literature on headquarters-subsidiary relations in MNCs.

Internal Differentiation in MNCs:
A Contingency Framework

It has been well established by authors such as J. D. Thompson (1967) and Lawrence and Lorsch (1967) that the structures of organizations, in which classification they include formal structural arrangements as well as formal and informal management processes, are and should be differentiated according to the characteristics of the external environment they face. This argument is a direct corollary of the open-systems view of organizations and has demonstrated empirical and theoretical support (see Pfeffer, 1982, for an exhaustive review).

Authors such as Pfeffer and Salancik (1978) have proposed a different motivation for differentiation, namely, that organizational processes are dependent on internal power relationships, which are in turn critically contingent on the internal distribution of organizational resources. According to this view, resource dependence is the key determinant of the structure of internal exchange relationships in complex organizations (Pfeffer and Salancik, 1978; Pfeffer, 1981).

Though Lawrence and Dyer (1983) have proposed a synthesis of these two views, they have treated the entire organization as the unit of analysis, using different industrial contexts to derive different environmental complexity and resource scarcity situations. The approach we take in this chapter is to extend this synthesis to multiunit organizations, such as MNCs, in which different components, such as the various national subsidiaries, face vastly different environmental and resource contingencies. We may then compare the observed internal differentiation within MNCs vis-à-vis headquarters-subsidiary relations to the position of the subsidiaries within this contingency framework.

Adopting an exchange-theoretic perspective (Levine and White, 1961; Emerson, 1962; Aiken and Hage, 1968), we can treat the relation between the headquarters and any subsidiary of an MNC as an exchange relation involving a series of resource transactions embedded in a structured context. In turn, such a relationship may then be conceived of as a mixed-motive situation (Schmidt and Kochan, 1977). This view recognizes that headquarters-subsidiary relations involve both interdependent interest situations (for example, multipoint competition with a global competitor where each member is internally motivated to interact because each perceives that it will be better able to attain its goals by interacting than by remaining autonomous) and independent interest situations (such as a transfer-pricing decision in which the motivation to interact may be asymmetrical, including the extreme case when one member is motivated to interact but the other is not).

Conceptualizing the nature of headquarters-subsidiary relations in this way enables us to examine more clearly the contingencies posed by the different conditions of environmental complexity and local resource levels on the nature of interdependence and independence. For example, increased environmental complexity results in increased interdependence as both the headquarters and the subsidiary face a situation of mutual vulnerability. Imperfect knowledge and fluctuations in the environment induce both the headquarters and the subsidiary to engage in reciprocal exchange relationships to make the realization of even independently disparate goals more predictable over time. As the complexity of the local environment in which the subsidiary is located increases, the importance of local knowledge increases, and the subsidiary must be allowed greater influence in the decision-making process. Extensive collaboration yields benefits for both headquarters and the subsidiary; consequently, interaction in these circumstances is usually characterized by cooperation and problem solving rather than conflict and bargaining (Schmidt and Kochan, 1977).

In contrast, as the resource levels of the subsidiary increase, the independent interests of the subsidiary and the headquarters may diverge substantially. The subsidiary may desire increasing autonomy, including the right to commit resources to pursue local interests, that may not necessarily coincide with the interests of the headquarters. The risk associated with the subsidiary's acting in its own partisan interest increases as it becomes more important to the local economy and hence subject to stronger local institutional pressures to pursue certain independent goals. Furthermore, a well-endowed subsidiary may command a disproportionate share of the overall resource distribution within the MNC that cannot be altered at will by the headquarters (Zeitz, 1980; Kogut, 1983). When a subsidiary becomes critically important to the performance of the MNC because it represents a large fraction of the MNC's total asset base, a situation of headquarters dependence on the subsidiary may arise. This dependence, combined with greater subsidiary assertiveness, engenders the conditions for a situation in which bargaining and conflict are the potential forms of interaction as each party attempts to attain its own goals at the expense of the other's (Doz and Prahalad, 1981).

On the basis of the foregoing arguments, and as summarized in Figure 5.1, we may establish a fourfold classification scheme for the contextual conditions faced by the subsidiary in headquarters-subsidiary relations: C1, low environmental complexity and low local resource levels; C2, low environmental complexity and high local resource levels; C3, high environmental complexity and low local resource levels; and C4, high environmental complexity and high local resource levels. Each of these four contingent conditions presents a very different situation with regard to the nature of dependence and interdependence in the exchange relation between the headquarters and the subsidiary. It follows that each of these situations will require different structural arrangements.

The Structural Elements
of Headquarters-Subsidiary Relations

We must now establish a framework for classifying the structure of headquarters-subsidiary relations. Since the landmark studies of the Aston Group, centralization and formalization have become central constructs in the analysis of the structure of internal relations in complex organization (Pugh, Hickson, Hinings, and Turner, 1968; Pugh, Hickson, and Hinings, 1969). Following Edstrom and Galbraith (1977) and Ouchi (1980), who argued for the importance of normative integration as another primary structural element in multiunit organizations, we can plausibly assert that centralization, formalization, and normative integration, analyzed singly and together, constitute a fairly comprehensive characterization of the structure of headquarters-subsidiary relations.

Centralization has been the focus of several studies of headquarters-subsidiary relations. It refers to a governance mechanism whereby the decision-making process is hierarchically organized, with the headquarters often making most of the crucial strategic and

**Figure 5.1. Classification of Subsidiary Context and
Nature of Interdependence and Dependence in Each Context.**

		Low	High
Environmental Complexity	High	**C3** Interdependence: High Subsidiary dependence: Low	**C4** Interdependence: High Headquarters dependence: High
	Low	**C1** Interdependence: Low Subsidiary dependence: Low	**C2** Interdependence: Low Headquarters dependence: High

Local Resources

policy decisions (see Gates and Egelhoff, 1986, for a review). Because centralization shifts the focus of power asymmetrically in favor of the headquarters, it can lead to severe dissonance if the subsidiary is a powerful actor in the exchange relation. The subsidiary is likely to resent overt hierarchical control and is in a strong bargaining position due to the power that accompanies its large resource endowment. Centralization, then, does not reflect the realities of relative power in the headquarters-subsidiary relationship when the subsidiary possesses significant resources. Thus we expect the prevalence of centralization as a governing mechanism to be positively correlated primarily with situations in which the subsidiary is dependent on the headquarters. This proposition is consistent with the negative association between subsidiary size and centralization observed by Alsegg (1971) and Hedlund (1980), since size can serve as a proxy for the subsidiary's resources and power.

Centralization is also inversely related to situations of high interdependence in that it causes decisions to reflect the competencies and perspectives of the headquarters only and constrains reciprocity in exchange relations. Greater environmental complexity enhances the value of the subsidiary's local knowledge and hence requires that the subsidiary be granted greater autonomy and flexibility in making decisions. By stifling such subsidiary input in the decision-making process, centralization puts the firm at a competitive disadvantage in situations of high environmental complexity that demand well-formulated responses to rapidly changing market conditions. Local managers may resent direction from headquarters when they feel that they have the best sense of the evolving local environment, especially when these managers have a substantial level of resources at hand. Putting these arguments together, we may advance the following hypothesis:

HYPOTHESIS 5.1: *Centralization is negatively correlated with both environmental complexity and local resource levels.*

The second structural element is formalization. Formalization represents decision making through bureaucratic mechanisms such as formal systems, established rules, and prescribed procedures; it may be interpreted as the routinization of decision making and resource allocation and has been studied in this sense as an element of headquarters-subsidiary relations by Hedlund (1980, 1981). Formalization decreases the power of both the headquarters and the subsidiary as it constrains the exchange relation to an impersonal set of rules that often assume a power independent of the motivations of the actors. Thus formalization is positively correlated with situations of potential conflict between the headquarters and the subsidiary. The subsidiary is likely to be more receptive to impersonal rules and procedures that the headquarters may wish to install to keep potential agency problems in check than it would be to direct headquarters control of decision making. Formalization thus provides a mechanism for headquarters to prevent a resource-abundant subsidiary from freely pursuing an independent course of action while at the same time recognizing the realities of the internal power distribution in the company.

We also expect formalization to increase with higher interdependence to the extent that it provides the structured context for reciprocity in exchange (Burgelman, 1983). Rules could be seen as a disadvantage in highly complex environments if they promote institutional inertia and the inability to respond flexibly to changing external circumstances. When conforming to the rules becomes an end and not a means in the corporate environment, this potential shortcoming may become particularly acute. For the most part, however, the routines of formalization establish a framework within which both the headquarters and the subsidiary may react flexibly to complex environments while assuring continued pursuit of the mutually beneficial company goals that underlie the system of rules. Further, formalization facilitates through routinization the sharing of market intelligence and other valuable knowledge that is vital to informed decision making in these environments. We may therefore hypothesize:

HYPOTHESIS 5.2: *Formalization is positively correlated with both environmental complexity and local resource levels.*

Normative integration is the third structural element. It involves socializing the members of the organization to have a common set of values that minimizes divergent interests, emphasizes mutual interdependence, and leads to domain consensus (Van Maanen and Schein, 1979). Normative integration relies neither on direct headquarters involvement nor on impersonal rules but rather on the socialization of managers into a set of shared goals, values, and beliefs that then shape their perspectives and behavior. By pooling the goals of the subsidiary and the headquarters into an inclusive and shared goal, normative integration facilitates cooperation and participative decision making (Ouchi, 1980). Because the organizational mechanisms that can best address the exigencies of a complex environment operate freely under a system of normative integration, we expect normative integration to be positively correlated with interdependence. The exchange of information and market knowledge that produces strong corporate responses to environmental challenges follows from the desire among all actors to advance the interests of the company. Individual flexibility and creativity are allowed to flourish to the greatest extent possible with the expectation that decision making and eventual action will be the result of close deliberation among individuals with the same value structure.

Normative integration can mitigate potential conflict between the headquarters and the subsidiary by promoting integrative bargaining (Walton and McKersie, 1965). In addition, the establishment of a system of shared values reduces the impulse of country managers to pursue local interests at the expense of firmwide interests to the extent that the socialization process emphasizes the larger goals of the MNC as whole. Thus the problems that arise from headquarters dependence on the subsidiary due to a skewed resource distribution can be ameliorated with normative integration. Combining this observation with our earlier discussion, we can again hypothesize:

HYPOTHESIS 5.3: *Normative integration is positively correlated with both environmental complexity and local resource levels.*

The Structure-Context Fit in Headquarters-Subsidiary Relations

The theoretical argument so far for the existence of a context-structure fit in headquarters-subsidiary relations in multinationals has been based on independent and separate considerations of how each element of structure might be linked to each of the different context variables. However, as argued by Drazin and Van de Ven (1985), for a more complete contingency theory it is necessary to consider the context-structure relationships more holistically and to explore how the different elements of structure, considered jointly and simultaneously, might be linked to the different categories of subsidiary contexts shown in Figure 5.1.

In developing such a holistic model, it is necessary to recognize that while organizational adaptiveness might be enhanced by matching the heterogeneity in the context with appropriate differentiation in structure, for organizational effectiveness such differentiation must also be accompanied by suitable integrative processes (Lawrence and Lorsch, 1967). Furthermore, these processes are expensive, and it is necessary for the MNC to economize on its limited resources for achieving organizational integration. Such an economizing perspective, inherent in Thompson's norm of "administrative rationality," suggests that the most efficient structure for each context may not simply be the sum of the unidimensional context-structure patterns proposed earlier and is more likely to be a combination of the structural elements that reflects the optimal trade-offs between the costs of each element and its efficacy in the specified contexts.

Normative integration of members to share an inclusive goal is the most costly administrative mechanism, involving a significant investment of administrative resources for both initial socialization and continued cultural fidelity. Its key comparative advantage is its ability to pool the resources and competencies of both actors involved in the exchange relation, thereby allowing the organization to benefit from the complementarities in those competencies. Formalization is a less costly administrative mechanism, an assertion that is at the core of Weber's claim (1946)that the bureaucracy— the organization that governs primarily through well-developed rules and systems—is the most efficient of all organizational forms. Compared to normative integration, formalization requires less in administrative resources to institutionalize and, once established, needs little administrative energy to maintain. Though formalization provides a structured context for exchange, a comparative disadvantage is the potential inertia it creates and the constraints it may impose on rapid adaptation to changing environmental conditions. Centralization is the least expensive administrative mechanism in that it permits administration by fiat. Requiring almost no resources to institutionalize, it does, however, require administrative resources for continuous monitoring and decision making. While comparatively advantageous in terms of control over decision making, decision outcomes under centralization reflect the competencies available at the headquarters and underutilize the supplementary or complementary competencies of the subsidiary.

Having developed these premises regarding the comparative costs and benefits of the various governance mechanisms, we can now hypothesize the way in which an MNC may deploy its limited administrative resources most efficiently for the management of national subsidiaries operating within different contexts. (For a summary of the various hypotheses, see Figure 5.2.)

Clearly, the greatest returns to coordinating resources accrue if they are deployed where the MNC has abundant local resources and faces complex external environments (C4). Centralization is most unsuited to this context, as it is likely to invoke considerable dissonance in that the subsidiary is resourceful and would be unwilling to accept the dependence that centralization implies. Although formalization is desirable to constrain autonomous interests and to provide a framework for coordinated decision making, it must be limited because it creates an inertia with regard to adapting quickly to the environmental pressures. Normative integration, though most expensive, is clearly the most appropriate administrative element in this context, since its comparative advantage in greatly facilitating interdependence is most beneficial in this situation. This combination of high normative integration, moderate formalization, and low centralization resembles most closely the structure that Kanter (1983) calls integrative.

Figure 5.2. Hypothesized Fit Structure of the Headquarters-Subsidiary Relation in Each Context.

		Low ———————— Local Resources ———————— High	
Environmental Complexity	**High**	Clans (C3) Centralization: Moderate Formalization: Low Socialization: High	Integrative (C4) Centralization: Low Formalization: Moderate Socialization: High
	Low	Hierarchy (C1) Centralization: High Formalization: Low Socialization: Low	Federative (C2) Centralization: Low Formalization: High Socialization: Low

In situations in which subsidiaries with low levels of local resources are facing environments of relatively low complexity (C1), administrative resources are expected to yield the lowest benefit. Economizing on administrative costs is most important in this context. Centralization is therefore the fit structure in this situation. It is feasible because the local capabilities are often so impoverished that they almost mandate continuous monitoring and headquarters support in decision making. Although centralization does restrict the ability to respond to interdependent relationships, the use of formalization and normative integration is inappropriate in this context as there are few benefits to be gained by facilitating such interdependence. The overall structure that fits this situation may thus be said to resemble a hierarchy (Williamson, 1975).

The abundance of local resources in a subsidiary facing low environmental complexity (C2) is often the legacy of history. These are usually the older subsidiaries of a multinational that owe their resource concentration to historical processes of accumulation. Because the MNC is often dependent on this sizable pool of sticky resources, a greater investment of administrative resources than in the previous context is warranted. Centralization is inappropriate because of the potential conflict and dissonance it may create between the headquarters and the subsidiary. Normative integration wastes administrative resources, considering that the critical interdependencies in this situation are limited. Formalization is clearly the most suitable administrative mode in this situation because it facilitates exchange in a conflict-prone situation, in addition to making such exchange more predictable over time by constraining it to a set of well-developed rules and routines. This structure resembles that of federated interorganizational networks such as the United Way and may therefore be described as federative (see Provan, 1983).

Subsidiaries that have scarce local resources in complex environments (C3) either are very young or represent contexts where local organizational resources have not kept pace with rapidly changing external conditions. These are subsidiaries that face a crisis and require significant administrative resource commitments. The critical dependence of the subsidiary on the headquarters for both resources and decision making makes centralization both feasible and necessary. The critical interdependencies, however, cannot be addressed by formalization because it is too soon for standardization and routinization. Normative integration as an administrative structure is critical to this situation, as it allows pooling of the competencies of the headquarters and the subsidiary and also facilitates mutuality in decision making that eases implementation. Similar structural forms have been described by Ouchi (1980) and labeled clans.

Testing the Fit Hypothesis

In this section, we test the theoretical propositions suggested in the preceding section in a number of ways. We begin by examining the simple relationships we predicted between the structural mechanisms of administrative control in headquarters-subsidiary relations and the associated subsidiary contexts. The correlations shown in Table 5.1 provide significant support for all the univariate context-structure relationships proposed in hypotheses 5.1 and 5.3. As hypothesized, centralization is negatively associated with both environmental complexity and local resources. Formalization and normative integration, in contrast, are positively associated with both these context variables.[1]

We argued earlier that the different structural and contextual elements relating to headquarters-subsidiary relations could not merely be considered separately but also had to be analyzed together in order to build a more complete contingency theory of the MNC. Theoretically, subsidiary contexts can be meaningfully differentiated into four categories based on the joint conditions of relatively low or high local resource levels of the subsidiary and the associated low or high environmental complexity. Although a median split on these two contextual variables could be used to classify subsidiaries into these contexts based purely on theoretical grounds, a clustering

Table 5.1. Correlation Matrix for Selected Standardized Variables.

	1	1a	1b	2	3	4	5	6	μ^a	SD^a
Clustering variables										
1. Environmental complexity[b]									0.00	.96
(a) Technological dynamism	.88*								0.00	.95
(b) Competition	.86*	.55*							.02	.95
2. Local resources	.50*	.56*	.33*						.02	.95
Structural variables										
3. Centralization	−.27*	−.32*	−.15*	−.48*					0.00	.91
4. Formalization	.31*	.35*	.20*	.50*	−.18*				0.00	.88
5. Socialization	.26*	.35*	.08*	.51*	−.22*	.42*			0.00	.93
Dependent variable										
6. Performance	−.01	.10	−.12	.12	−.06	.06	.28*		0.00	.95

$N = 618$

*$p < .001$.

[a]Although all variables are normalized, the fact that normalization is within each MNC accounts for the slight departures of the overall means from zero and the standard deviations from unity.

[b]Environmental complexity is an additive scale (Cronbach's $\alpha = .7$) of the two items technological dynamism (1a) and competition (1b).

approach was used to determine if there was a natural empirical pattern that coincided with this a priori scheme. McQueen's K means clustering method was employed using resource scarcity and environmental complexity as the clustering variables.[2] The cluster algorithm indicated the existence of four different categories of subsidiaries based on these clustering variables (see Everitt, 1980).

The robustness of the membership in the various clusters was checked by comparing the K means four-cluster solution with the solution from Ward's method. Ninety-one percent of the cases were classified into the same cluster by both methods. A graphical representation of the four clusters and the cluster centroids is presented in Figure 5.3.

Given two input variables, the emergence of a four-cluster solution is not surprising. However, as is evident from Figure 5.3, the four clusters represent combinations of local resource and environmental conditions that are very consistent with the a priori theoretical scheme. Therefore, in further analysis, this natural empirical

Figure 5.3. Empirically Derived Clusters of Subsidiary Based on Contextual Conditions.

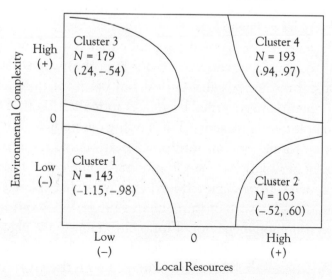

Note: (x, y) represents the standardized value of the local organizational resources.

classification is preferred to a forced theoretical classification based on median splits.

Having established empirical support for our contextual classification scheme, we may now proceed to test the multivariate hypotheses of fit summarized in Figure 5.2. First, the top-performing subsidiaries (z score > 1.0) were selected to determine the ideal combination of the three structural elements for each contextual situation. The mean scores of each structural variable for these top-performing subsidiaries in the different clusters were considered as empirically derived representations of the ideal structural combination for the four categories of subsidiary context. These ideal types were tested using one-way ANOVA and MANOVA tests to determine if the patterns actually differed across the clusters. A comparison was also made between these results and the theoretically derived structural forms shown in Figure 5.2 to determine if the derived values matched the hypothesized relationships. The results are shown in Table 5.2. The significant F-statistic ($p < .01$) for every structural variable shows that these ideal types are very different. An overall MANOVA using all three structural variables was also significant ($F = 32.9$; $p < .001$). Furthermore, the empirically derived profiles are very well matched to the theoretically proposed profiles in Figure 5.2.

However, there is one discrepancy that is worth noting. The results indicate that contrary to our hypothesis, in situations of high local resources, subsidiaries that confront more complex environments are governed by greater formalization that those in less complex environments. This finding contradicts the received view that formal systems inhibit adaptation and responsiveness, so crucial in situations of environmental complexity. Though this finding needs to be explored further, a possible explanation may be found in the work of Burgelman (1983), who contends that even autonomous behavior or innovation must take place within a structured context if it is to be effective. Perhaps this is the reason why these subsidiaries are managed with the greatest degree of formalization.

Table 5.2. Differences in the Mean Value of Top-Performing Subsidiaries Across Clusters.

	Cluster Membership				Scheffe's	F
	1 (n = 30)	2 (n = 16)	3 (n = 15)	4 (n = 49)	Test	Statistic
Structural variables						
3. Centralization	.40	−.46	.12	−.56	(1,3) (2,4)	1.8*
4. Formalization	−.52	.21	−.20	.44	(2,4)	13.2*
5 Socialization	−.17	.08	.32	.84	(2,3)	12.0*

Notes: Top-performing subsidiaries are those with z scores > 1.0. Scheffe's test is a pairwise comparison of differences in group means (Scheffe, 1953). The pairs listed in the column are for groups for which the means are not significantly different ($p < .01$).

*F values in ANOVA ($p < .001$).

Having found support for the empirically derived structural profiles, deviations from these ideal profiles for the remaining subsidiaries were calculated using an Euclidean weighted distance metric. The distance calculations represent the extent to which a particular subsidiary deviates from its ideal type, which is determined according to the subsidiary's contingency category. The distance measure is calculated as follows:

$$\text{Distance} = \sqrt{SB_s (X_{is} - X_{js})^2}$$

where X_{is} is the score of the ideal type on the sth structural dimension, X_{js} is the score of the jth particular subsidiary on the sth dimension, and SB_s is a weight given by the standardized beta or contribution of the sth dimension in a multiple regression with performance as the dependent variable and all the structural dimensions as the independent variables.

The central question that remains to be answered is this: What is the relationship between the structure-context fit of a headquarters-subsidiary relation, as described in this chapter, and subsidiary performance? To answer this question and to test the usefulness of the multivariate approach toward a more complete contingency theory of headquarters-subsidiary relations, the calculated distance measure was correlated with the performance of the subsidiary. A negative correlation would demonstrate fit because the greater the distance from the respective ideal type, the lower the hypothesized performance. The results of this analysis are shown in Table 5.3. As predicted, there is a significant negative correlation between subsidiary performance and the distance measure of the deviation of the structure of the headquarters-subsidiary relation from its ideal type ($r = -.14$; $p < .001$). Table 5.3 shows the component correlations between distance and performance within each contextual category. A significant negative correlation was observed for C4 ($r = -.17$; $p < .05$) and C3 ($r = -.18$; $p < .01$) subsidiaries. The correlations were insignificant for C1 and C2 subsidiaries. This suggests that although there is information to be gained overall by the multivariate approach, it is perhaps more relevant to situations of high environmental complexity.

Conclusions

Though it is almost a truism that there are differences both among and within organizations, much of the effort of past research on multinational organizations has been focused on developing contingency models for explaining differences of the first kind. Thus

Table 5.3. Correlations of Distance Measures with Subsidiary Performance (Excluding High-Performance Units).

Distance	Performance	n	p Value
Cluster 1	−.08	113	.201
Cluster 2	−.11	87	.160
Cluster 3	−.18	164	.012
Cluster 4	−.17	144	.022
All subsidiaries	−.14	508	.001

researchers have tried to explain differences among companies in departmentalization (Daniel, Pitts, and Tretter, 1984), centralization (see review in Gates and Egelhoff, 1986), formalization (Hedlund, 1981),and other structural attributes. In contrast, very little effort has been expended on explaining differences within an MNC. In this chapter, we have sought to correct this oversight with an exploratory analysis of the relationship between subsidiary performance and the pattern of internal differentiation in headquarters-subsidiary relations within the multinational.

Our empirical analysis provides consistent support for the logic of internal differentiation within MNCs that has been proposed in this chapter. It is clear that within an MNC, the various national subsidiaries are and should be differentiated in terms of both the complexity of their environmental contexts and their local resource levels. Furthermore, depending on the nature of these contingencies, there is a fit structure of the headquarters-subsidiary relation that leads to improved subsidiary performance. Thus as described in the theory section, an integrative structure fits subsidiaries that face complex environments and have abundant local resources, a hierarchical structure fits subsidiaries that face relatively stable environments and have limited local resources, a federative structure fits subsidiaries that face stable environments and have abundant local resources, and a clan structure fits subsidiaries that face complex environments and have limited local resources. According to the theory, managers must adjust the control mechanisms of centralization, formalization, and normative integration in the proper manner to achieve the administrative form that matches the structure appropriate for a particular subsidiary.

In this chapter, we have initiated the task of building a theory of internal differentiation by describing its underlying logic and presenting empirical evidence confirming its predictions for subsidiaries within the multinational. In the next chapter, we take the level of analysis up one level to that of the MNC as a whole and suggest broad approaches for managing the nexus of headquarters-subsidiary relations.

Notes

1. All correlations are significant at the .001 level.
2. The existence of clusters and number of clusters were determined using Calinski and Harabasz's C-ratio, as recommended by Milligan and Cooper (1985), who found this to be the best stopping rule among thirty examined. As we varied the number of clusters in the solution from two to eight, the C-ratio came to 600, 473, 656, 571, 610, 560, and 544, respectively. The maxima at the 4-cluster solution suggested that this was optional.

Chapter Six

Formal Structure and Shared Values

In Chapter Five, we proposed that in an MNC, the structure of each headquarters-subsidiary relation must be differentiated to fit its context. In this chapter, we extend our analysis from the level of the subsidiaries to that of the MNC as a whole. We suggest that there are two broad ways by which headquarters-subsidiary relations may be effectively managed. The first can be thought of as adopting a principle of differentiated fit so that the formal structure of each headquarters-subsidiary relation in the MNC matches the subsidiary context. The second requires adoption of shared values in which the headquarters and all its subsidiaries develop common and closely aligned interests and values through various socialization mechanisms. In this second approach, unlike the first, little emphasis is given to explicit and formal internal structural differentiation.

The astute reader may wonder why we make this division here, especially since we did not draw a distinction of this nature between centralization and formalization, on the one hand, and normative integration, on the other, in Chapter Five. The answer is that conceptual and practical differences between formal control mechanisms and normative control mechanisms justify such a division. Differentiated fit is a strictly contingent approach that relies on a strong link between formal structure and action. Because formal structure often serves as a tight constraint on action, adopting the right combination of centralization and formalization that fits the different circumstances of the subsidiaries responds to both control issues as well as to the differences across the various subsidiaries. The issue of internal diversity is addressed by differentiating the governance of each subsidiary to fit its context. And by using hierarchical and bureaucratic governance procedures as appropriate, agency and control issues are also taken into account.

There is a much weaker link between formal structure and action in the shared values approach. Rather, the emphasis lies in creating common and shared understandings of goals, values, and practices to influence both how subsidiaries perceive their interests and how they act. Agency and control issues are addressed by closely aligning the interests of the subsidiary and the headquarters organization. The issue of internal diversity within the MNC is addressed by creating norms that legitimize actions that respond to these differences in the interest of the overall organization. Stated another way, in the case of differentiated fit, the link between means and ends is formally specified and constrained, whereas in the case of shared values, it is not. Ends, though, in the case of shared values, are commonly agreed on, as are norms that shape the means that may be adopted to achieve them.

The distinction between the two approaches we have described is similar to the contrast between "administrative control" and "normative-cultural control" drawn by Baliga and Jaeger (1984). In the case of differentiated fit, as with administrative control, action is constrained by formal structure and administrative procedures. In contrast, in the case of shared values, as with normative-cultural control, action is constrained by linking it to common values or common objectives.

In addition to these conceptual differences, the implementation of centralization and formalization as control mechanisms differs practically from the implementation of normative integration. It is simply more difficult to differentiate the degree of normative integration among various subsidiaries within the MNC than it is to differentiate formal structures. One reason for this is that individuals typically move among different subsidiaries during the course of their careers rather than remaining at a single location. Rules governing operations may be made to differ, but individuals do not leave their shared values at the door when they enter a new

subsidiary. The rotation of personnel consequently makes it difficult to implement and sustain differing levels of shared values.

Another related practical difference concerns the costs associated with the various control mechanisms. In addition to administrative costs, centralization and formalization may exact costs in the
form of a diminished ability for a subsidiary to compete in a particular market. For example, in a highly complex national environment, centralization may be disadvantageous to the company even
if there were zero administrative costs associated with its implementation. The same is true of formalization. Conversely, though in
the extreme there may be some costs associated with "groupthink,"
normative integration within reasonable limits would be desirable
if it demanded no administrative costs to implement.

Of course, there are significant administrative costs associated
with the requisite socialization mechanisms of normative integration. Because, however, a large proportion of these costs occur up
front, the administrative costs of maintaining the shared values of
an individual are low in comparison. When personnel rotation
occurs and a company must decide whether to maintain the normative integration of an individual or not, it faces a situation in
which there is definitely a competitive upside while the administrative cost is relatively low. Further, if the individual is transferred
again in the future to a subsidiary whose environment demands a
high level of normative integration, the company may have again
to pay the fixed cost if shared values are not maintained. All of
these considerations illustrate the difficulty and inherent undesir-
ability of differentiating the level of normative integration among
subsidiaries within the firm, providing a practical reason for the distinction between differentiated fit and shared values.

The analysis in this chapter suggests not only a distinction
between these two approaches but also equifinality. While we contend that differentiated fit and shared values are equally effective
alternatives for managing headquarters-subsidiary relations, we do
not wish to suggest that the two approaches are mutually exclusive.
MNCs may be able to achieve a high degree of differentiated fit

and shared values simultaneously. Indeed, such firms, as we shall see, perform better than firms that adopt any one administrative approach exclusively.

Although both differentiation and shared values have been discussed in earlier chapters, they have not been examined specifically as potential solutions to practical management problems. In this chapter, we attempt to forge a link between theory and practice by analyzing the two approaches in this context. First, we present the theory behind these propositions; then we describe the methods of the study and present the results of the analysis. We end the chapter with our conclusions and implications for theory and practice.

Subsidiary Management in Theory

As noted in Chapter Five the attributes of headquarters-subsidiary relations make them very similar to the principal-agent relationship (Jensen and Meckling, 1976). As the principal, the headquarters cannot effectively make all the decisions in the MNC because it does not possess extensive knowledge of the subsidiaries and must consequently depend on the subsidiaries for that. At the same time, the headquarters cannot relinquish all decision rights to the subsidiaries because the local interests of subsidiaries may not always be aligned with those of the headquarters or the MNC as a whole. This poses a classic control problem that has spawned an extensive literature on how headquarters-subsidiary relations should be governed and especially on the degree of decision-making autonomy that the subsidiaries of an MNC should have (see Egelhoff, 1988a, 1988b, for an exhaustive review).

Following our analysis in Chapter Five, we recall that to address differences across subsidiaries adequately, two aspects of the subsidiary context have to be considered: the complexity of the subsidiary's local environment and the level of resources possessed by the subsidiary. One approach to managing headquarters-subsidiary relations that takes these differences in subsidiary context into account is based on contingency theory and follows directly from our prior analysis. This approach requires understanding the different contingencies (or specific control problems) that each subsidiary context presents and employing an appropriate combination of formal structural elements to manage these contingencies. Thus the structure of each headquarters-subsidiary relation is expressly differentiated to fit the distinctive environmental and resource conditions of the subsidiary.

This explicit structural differentiation is achieved through varying combinations of centralization and formalization. The differentiated fit approach adopts an economizing perspective in its specification of the appropriate combination of structural elements by which each headquarters-subsidiary relation should be managed. Conditions of fit are said to obtain when the optimal trade-offs exist between the cost of each structural element and its efficacy in the context of the subsidiary under consideration. The specific way in which the formal structure of each headquarters-subsidiary relation must be differentiated to fit various subsidiary contexts is discussed at length in Chapter Five and shown in Figure 6.1.

An alternative approach to differentiated fit is suggested by Parsons (1956), who proposed that the solution to the problem of control was the creation of "shared values" that if properly internalized by the actors in a social system guarantee that the actors want what

Figure 6.1. A Framework for a Differentiated Fit Between Subsidiary Context and Structure.

		Low	High
Environmental Complexity	High	(C3) Centralization: Moderate Formalization: Low	(C4) Centralization: Low Formalization: Moderate
	Low	(C1) Centralization: High Formalization: Low	(C2) Centralization: Low Formalization: High

Low   High
Local Subsidiary Resources

they should want and act as they should act. Shared values were also seen by Barnard (1939) as offering a solution to the problem of creating and managing complex organizations. The idea of share values as the basis of organization was also anticipated by Etzioni (1965) in his conception of a normative organization and has more recently been discussed by Deal and Kennedy (1982) under the label of "strong cultures." Minimizing the divergence of preferences and interests among the members of an organization has been explicitly portrayed by several scholars as a way to achieve control in principal-agent relations. As Ouchi (1980, p. 138) notes, "Common values and beliefs provide the harmony of interests that erase the possibility of opportunistic behavior." In the same spirit, Eisenhardt (1985, p. 135) adds, "Members cooperate in the achievement of organizational goals because the members understand and have internalized these goals."

As proposed in Chapter Five, instilling shared values and beliefs among the managers of the subsidiaries and the headquarters makes it more likely that even in the absence of formal oversight by the headquarters, the subsidiaries will use their specific local knowledge and resources to pursue the interests of the MNC as a whole and not just their own partisan interests. To build these common norms and values, as described by Edstrom and Galbraith (1977), a strong emphasis is placed on mechanisms such as the selection, training, and rotation of managers. Importance is also attached to extensive and open communication between the headquarters and subsidiaries and among the subsidiaries. By paying careful attention to the initial and ongoing socialization of all organizational members, as well as to communication among them, the MNC can encourage the adoption of a set of shared values.

Although these two approaches are equally effective alternatives for managing the nexus of headquarters-subsidiary relations, it is certainly possible for an MNC to achieve a high degree of shared values and differentiated fit simultaneously (see Bartlett and Ghoshal, 1989, for detailed case illustrations of such companies). Although it is difficult to socialize all the subsidiaries to share a common set of goals and values and to then treat them differently in terms of the degree of centralization and formalization to which they are subject, it is possible, as in a strong family that has several children with different personalities, to have a strong set of shared values and yet different rules for each child. Indeed, as Lawrence and Lorsch (1967) observed three decades ago, an approach that achieves high levels of "differentiation" and "integration" simultaneously is likely to yield the best performance. In an MNC, this simultaneous approach both ensures a congruence of interests between headquarters and subsidiaries and provides formal mechanisms that take differences in subsidiary contexts into account.

Empirical Analysis

Of the sixty-six companies in the database, fifty-four reported data on five or more subsidiaries, and only these responses were used for the statistical analysis reported here. We chose this cutoff because we wanted to capture a robust pattern of differentiated fit or shared values in each MNC. For firms on which we had data on fewer than five subsidiaries, we could not be certain that we were measuring a reliable companywide pattern.[1] Three different financial measures of performance were employed: average return on assets, average annual growth in return on assets, and average annual growth in sales, between 1982 and 1986 (see the Methodological Appendix for details).

To obtain a measure of differentiated fit for each MNC, all the subsidiaries were tested for context-structure fit described earlier and summarized in Figure 6.1. The manner in which each subsidiary was governed, in terms of the relative degree to which centralization and formalization were employed, was compared with the theoretical ideal proposed in the figure. If the pattern of governance was consistent with the proposed ideal, the subsidiary was considered to have a "fit" structure; if not, it was considered to be a "misfit." For every company, the measure of differentiated fit (DF) was then calculated as the fraction of fit subsidiaries.[2]

We chose the operationalization we describe previously because it was most consistent with our theoretical arguments and had face validity. Operationalizing fit involves making several conceptual and statistical choices. Drazin and Van de Ven (1985), for instance, distinguish between selection, interaction, and system views of fit. Theoretically, we do not presume that fit automatically results from natural selection forces. Nor do we believe that fit involves bivariate consistency between contextual and structural factors. Our notion of differentiated fit is systemic and can be understood as the degree of adherence to an ideal structure. It is thus consistent with what Drazin and Van de Ven (1985) call a systems view of fit. A systems view of fit is best operationalized by developing a theoretical or empirical ideal profile and then measuring deviations from this profile (Drazin and Van de Ven, 1985; Venkatraman, 1989). Our measure of differentiated fit is based precisely on such a procedure. Its face validity lies in the fact that if the structure of no headquarters-subsidiary relation is suited to its context, the degree of differentiated fit for the MNC as a whole equals zero. Conversely, if the structure of each and every headquarters-subsidiary relation is differentiated to fit its context, the degree of differentiated fit equals unity.

A potential criticism of this measure is that it ignores the extent to which the structure of each headquarters-subsidiary relation is fit or misfit. To address this criticism, we developed another measure of differentiated fit. For each MNC, we computed the aggregate of the Euclidean distance of the structural profile of each headquarters-subsidiary relation from its empirical ideal type based on the results reported in Chapter Five. This alternative measure was very highly correlated (.87; $p < .001$) with our measure and produced nearly identical results in our subsequent analyses. As a result, we have dropped it from the discussion in favor of our simpler, more face-valid measure (Table 6.1 shows the intercorrelations between our two measures of differentiated fit and the other variables in our study).

For each subsidiary, the extent to which it had shared values with the parent was operationalized as the average of two indicators: the level of normative integration between the headquarters

Table 6.1. Means, Standard Deviations, and Correlation Matrix Intercorrelations.

	Mean	SD	RoA	RoAGR	SLSGR	DF1	DF2
					Intercorrelations		
Average return on assets (RoA), 1982–1986	6.29	4.61					
Average annual growth in return on assets (RoAGR), 1982–1986	8.10	5.06	.46**				
Average annual sales growth (SLSGR), 1982–1986	13.62	9.42	.27**	.21			
Differentiated fit (DF1)(ratio measure)	.65	.24	.24**	.41**	.15		
Differentiated fit (DF2) (distance measure)	.43	.10	.25**	.37**	.17	.87**	
Shared values (SV)	2.90	1.08	.33**	.31**	.39**	.15	.13

*p < .10; **p < .05. N = 54.

and the subsidiary and the level of informal communication between the headquarters and the subsidiary. Based on this average, the extent of shared values for any MNC was operationalized as the minimum level of shared values across all of its subsidiaries. We chose this operationalization because our theoretical conception of shared values is based on consistency across subsidiaries. As a result, only companies that had high levels of shared values across all subsidiaries were considered to have a high degree of shared values. This is a conservative measure of shared values because if a single subsidiary was reported to have low shared values, even in a company with a high degree of shared values across most of its subsidiaries, the MNC as a whole would be rated low on shared values. Nevertheless, it is important to use this conservative measure (as opposed to a measure such as the average level of shared values across the subsidiaries) to ensure that we are capturing a uniformly consistent pattern of shared values across all the subsidiaries.

To explore the effects of differentiated fit and shared values on MNC performance, firms in the sample were categorized into those that exhibited high versus low differentiated fit, depending on whether they were above or below the median value of differentiated fit for the sample as a whole. Based on our data, only firms that had fit governance structures in at least 70 percent of their subsidiaries were classified as fit. A similar categorization procedure was employed for the shared values dimension. In this case, only firms that reported their minimum level of shared values across all their subsidiaries as being at least 3 on a scale of 1 (low) to 5 (high) were classified as having a high degree of shared values. Based on this classification scheme, a cross-tabulation of the performance measures was conducted. The results of this analysis are shown in Figure 6.2.

A statistical comparison of cell means (using t tests) across all three performance indicators provides strong support for the arguments presented. Out of eighteen pairwise comparisons (six for testing the independent effects of our two structural variables on each of three performance indicators and twelve for testing the interaction effects across four cells for the same three performance

Figure 6.2. The Effect of Differentiated Fit and Shared Values on Firm Performance.

		Low	High
Shared Values (SV)	High	RoA = 6.91 RoAGR = 7.2 SLSGR = 15.44 (Cell 3, n = 12)	RoA = 6.99 RoAGR = 13.88 SLSGR = 19.47 (Cell 4, n = 15)
	Low	RoA = 5.16 RoAGR = 4.16 SLSGR = 9.81 (Cell 1, n = 15)	RoA = 6.28 RoAGR = 8.47 SLSGR = 10.76 (Cell 2, n = 12)

Differentiated Fit (DF)

indicators), fourteen revealed results that were statistically significant as expected. There was broad support as we had hypothesized for the relative performance benefits of a greater degree of differentiated fit (except for the performance indicator average annual sales growth) and shared values.

There was also support for our equifinality hypothesis in that the performance of MNCs that exhibited a high degree of differentiated fit and a low degree of shared values (cell 2) was not statistically different (with the exception of the performance indicator average annual sales growth) from those that had a high degree of shared values and a low degree of differentiated fit (cell 3). Finally, we also found empirical support for our simultaneity hypothesis. The performance of MNCs that exhibited a high degree of both differentiated fit and shared values (cell 4) was significantly greater (except in the case of return on assets) than that of those in all the other categories. Moreover, the performance of firms that had low degrees of both shared values and differentiated fit (cell 1) was significantly lower than those in any other category.

To confirm the analysis further, two-way ANOVA tests were conducted to check the significance of the independent and joint effects of differentiated fit and shared values on each of the three measures of performance. These results are presented in the top half of Table 6.2. Differentiated fit had significant and positive main effects on both return on assets and average annual growth in return on assets but not on average annual sales growth. Shared values had significant and positive main effects on all three performance indicators. The joint effect of differentiated fit and shared values was significant and positive for average annual growth in return on assets and average annual sales growth but not for return on assets. These results are entirely consistent with our earlier exploratory analysis.

As a final step, to check that our results were not biased due to the manner in which we dichotomized firms as having high or low levels of differentiated fit and shared values, we conducted a regression analysis, with the performance measures as the dependent variables, and our continuous measures of differentiated fit, shared values, and a simple multiplicative interaction of these two variables as our independent variables. As we hypothesized, all the independent variables had positive and significant effects (at the $p < .05$ level), except for the case of average annual sales growth, for which differentiated fit was not significant, and for the case of return on assets, for which the interaction term was not significant (see Table 6.2). The consistency of the results of the ANOVA and regression analyses, though not surprising, is heartening because it shows the robustness of our findings across the various ways in which scholars have tested fit.

Conclusions

Our results provide strong empirical support for our proposition of differentiated fit: they confirm that differentiating the structure of headquarters-subsidiary relations to fit the context of each subsidiary enhances the performance not only of the subsidiary itself (Chapter Five) but also of the MNC as a whole.

At the same time, the results also provide empirical support for a previously untested assertion that instilling shared values across headquarters and subsidiaries represents an alternative solution to

Table 6.2. Independent and Interaction Effects of
Differentiated Fit and Shared Values on Firm Performance:
F Values and Standardized Regression (Beta) Coefficients.

		Indicators of Firm Performance	
Independent Variables	Average Return on Assets (RoA)	Average Annual Growth in Return on Assets (RoAGR)	Average Annual Sales Growth (SLSGR)
F Values from ANOVA			
Differentiated fit (DF)	2.91*	6.67**	1.01
Shared values (SV)	3.47**	3.01*	8.10**
Interaction effect (DF × SV)	.52	4.31**	3.26**
Overall F	1.16	4.15**	3.01*
Standardized Coefficients from OLS Regression (β)			
Differentiated fit (DF)	.25**	.37**	.12
Shared values (SV)	.30**	.25***	.38**
Interaction effect (DF × SV)	.19	.27***	.25**
Adjusted R^2	.21	.33	.19
Overall F	4.36**	7.67**	4.88**

*p < .10; **p < .05. N = 54.

the governance problem in MNCs. Not only do our results support this equifinality hypothesis, but they also support a simultaneity hypothesis—that firms that can simultaneously create both a strong set of shared values and differentiated fit will outperform those that rely on one or the other of these administrative approaches.

Of course, to be confident that these findings are both valid and usable, several additional issues need to be addressed. We must consider the relative costs and benefits of each approach. Differentiated fit, though clearly an approach to enhanced performance, can lead to a complex and difficult-to-manage organization structure. Homogeneity is certainly easier to manage than diversity. The differentiated fit approach may also lead to an inflexible structure that may be difficult to adapt dynamically. Managing by shared values, though structurally simpler, involves a significant investment of resources for both initial socialization and continued normative allegiance. In certain contexts, this approach could well entail inefficiencies resulting from redundant communication channels and undue effort spent in negotiating consensus.

In addition to these considerations, there may be overall company-level contingencies (so far, we have looked primarily at subsidiary-level contingencies) that affect the assessment of these alternatives. For example, the overall size of the MNC (in terms of revenue or the number of subsidiaries) or its degree and nature (related or unrelated) of diversification in different product markets may well affect which approach is the more efficient. One could argue that the shared values approach becomes less effective as the number of subsidiaries increases and as the company is diversified into unrelated product markets or into very different cultural contexts.

We will examine some of these company-level contingencies in Chapter Nine. However, in spite of these limits of our present findings, we believe that the results have some important implications for both theory and practice.

Our findings on the performance implications of the differentiated fit approach, both at the subsidiary and at the corporate level of analysis, provide resounding support to contingency theory and thereby strengthen Donaldson's recent defense of this theory (1995). At the same time, our findings on the efficacy of the shared values approach is also of considerable theoretical impact, particularly for organizational economists who, in extending the traditional theory of the firm to the domain of multinationals, have tended to emphasize the hierarchical organization of the firm as a solution to market imperfections (see Buckley and Casson, 1985; Hennart, 1982; and Rugman, 1981).

The conceptualization of firms as hierarchies has come to dominate the organizational economics literature in two steps. First, following the seminal article by Coase (1937), most organizational economists have explicitly or implicitly accepted the employer-employee relationship as the archetype of the firm. Second, following the work of Williamson (1975), they have tended to view this relationship as primarily concerned with the task of attenuating human opportunism. The combination of such focus on the employment relationship as the essence of the firm and on opportunism as the focal aspect of human nature has naturally led to the view that control of opportunism is the central function of organizations. This view has in turn led to the hierarchy as the taken-for-granted—indeed, necessary—mechanism for the governance of firms.

In these two steps, organizational economists have made a fundamental break from the implicit assumptions of the neoclassical framework. Instead of assuming that a firm behaves as a single coherent rational actor, always in its own best interests, modern theories of the firm acknowledge that the interests of the firm and those of its employees differ. In other words, they assume the firm to represent what Coleman (1990) described as a disjointed authority system. But in acknowledging the possibility of differences between employer and employee interests, these theories have made the assumption that is opposite to, but just as extreme as, the assumption of neoclassical economics. Instead of assuming that the interests of the firm and the employees are always in perfect alignment (at equilibrium), theories like transaction cost economics and agency theory assume that the interests of an organization and those of its members are inherently different and often in conflict and that this situation is unlikely to change. Further, the gap between the interests of the firm (or the principal headquarters) and those of the employees (or the agent subsidiaries) is treated as exogenous in these models. This leads to a conclusion that is fundamental to these theories that the firm (or the principal headquarters) knows—indeed, must know—best and is—must be—able to specify, and later to evaluate, either what is expected from the employees (or agent subsidiaries) or how they should provide it. Under these assumptions, hierarchical governance within the firm becomes a structural necessity required to ensure a level of coherent behavior that is possible only when the disjointed authority of one party over another cannot be abrogated.

As Coleman (1990) has pointed out, such a line of reasoning based on the assumption of a disjointed authority system can provide neither explanation nor guidance for organizations where more than just a few individuals must have discretionary power for the firm to succeed. "The evolution of the corporation has made the classic concept of agency no longer applicable to the employment relationship, or only after considerable revision. . . . The evolution of the corporation has so fully intertwined and combined the interests of the corporation and the interests of the persons who work in it that such a (machine-like) separation (of the functions of each of the parts—i.e., the obligations and expectations associated with positions) becomes increasingly difficult" (Coleman, 1990, p. 436).

The evidence presented in this chapter provides considerable support to Coleman's arguments about both the need for and the practical possibility of achieving a conjoint authority system as a prerequisite for effective governance of firms—particularly of large and complex firms such as the multinational corporations. Though some element of hierarchy and control is necessary in any company to ensure adequate enforcement of rules and expectations, hierarchy—as our results show—is not the only or even the most important internal governance mechanism. Beyond the enforcement of rules and expectations, the effectiveness of multinationals depends on their ability to tap into the local resources and knowledge of their dispersed units and to transfer and integrate those resources and knowledge throughout the company. To be able simultaneously to exploit these benefits of distributed and localized resources and to achieve efficiency and a reduction of transaction costs, MNCs cannot rely either wholly or even primarily on hierarchical governance; they need to create a coherent institutional context that motivates "individuals to do the desirable things without anyone having to tell them what to do" (Hayek, 1945, p. 527). In other words, shared values play a fundamental role in shaping the institutional context of a firm. This context, within which social relations are embedded and through which the preferences and behaviors of individuals are altered, allows MNCs simultaneously to achieve decentralized authority and initiative, lateral coordination and sharing, and central control and overall organizational cohesiveness.

These findings and conclusions should be heartening to managers of MNCs who want to take advantage of the insights academic research has provided into the issue of organizational fit. We have established the utility of certain categorizations of environment and structure and the empirical connections between organizational fit and firm performance. In developing an understanding of internal differentiation within MNCs, we have contributed significantly to the formulation of a complete contingency model of multinationals. However, although such a model may be helpful to business academics studying organization theory, it is less clear that the ideal types of the model offer readily applicable prescriptions for managers. It was the purpose of this chapter to examine the methods by which managers may translate theory into action—action that transforms the structure of their organizations to promote optimal efficiency in whichever business environments prevail. In Chapter Nine, we will continue our analysis at the level of the company as a whole and provide additional motivation for a complete contingency model of multinational organizations. But before we get to those issues, we turn in the next two chapters to a more detailed examination of the factors that promote integration across the MNC and serve as the glue that holds the differentiated network together.

Note

1. Of the fifty-four companies, thirty-one were headquartered in North America and the remaining twenty-three in Europe; forty-three companies had annual sales between $1 billion and $10 billion, and the other eleven had annual sales above $10 billion. Of the fifty-four, thirty had subsidiaries in eight to twelve of the nineteen countries prespecified in the questionnaire; the remaining twenty-four companies had subsidiaries in more than twelve of these locations.

Chapter Seven

Integration Through Interunit Communication

In a world characterized by transnational linkages among individuals and institutions, improved transportation and communication, and competition as well as cooperation among multinational corporations, the geographically dispersed subunits of the MNC are increasingly interdependent (Prahalad and Doz, 1987). As we saw in Chapter Six, coherent worldwide management of organizations characterized by such dispersal, differentiation, and interdependence requires extensive interunit coordination and integration. Interunit communication is a key mechanism for achieving this integration. A systematic analysis of the factors that influence communication flows within MNCs is thus of considerable importance to persons interested in designing more effective MNCs (Hedlund, 1986; Bartlett and Ghoshal, 1989).

The information processing view of organization design offers a useful foundation for such an analysis (Galbraith, 1973; Egelhoff, 1988a). According to this view, organizations can cope with increasing uncertainty in two ways. The first is to reduce information processing needs by creating slack resources or by eliminating interdependence by creating entirely self-contained organizational units. The second is to increase the information processing capacity through investments in vertical information systems or through lateral relations.

For the modern MNC, the first alternative of reducing information processing needs is available only to a limited extent. As we saw in Chapter Three, although some slack has to be maintained for innovation, too much slack is increasingly unaffordable in the face of intensifying global competition. Moreover, interdependence among the various organizational units cannot be minimized without seriously reducing the competitive strengths of the MNC. Therefore, increasing information processing capacity becomes a key strategic imperative for the MNC if it is to cope with the challenge of growing environmental and organizational complexity.

Though many mechanisms are available for increasing information processing capacity, direct communication is both one of the simplest and one of the most effective (Galbraith, 1973). As Gupta and Govindarajan (1991, p. 778) conclude after a review of the relevant literature, "More intense communication patterns create higher information processing capacity, and these patterns become especially desirable in contexts where such capacities are needed."

Although internal communication is vital to the effectiveness of the modern MNC, few systematic empirical investigations have been conducted into factors that promote such communication. Martinez and Jarillo (1989), for instance, list eighty-five publications on coordination mechanisms in MNCs. Though a number of these publications emphasize the importance of interunit communication for effective MNC management (including Edstrom and Galbraith, 1977, and Baliga and Jaeger, 1984), none directly measure interunit communication flows, nor do they investigate empirically the factors that influence these flows. Even studies that explicitly adopt an information processing perspective on the design of MNCs do not directly measure such information flows because of measurement difficulties (Egelhoff, 1982).

The larger body of research on organizational communication has similar deficiencies (see Jablin, Putnam, Roberts, and Porter, 1987, for a comprehensive review). In much of this work, communication is treated as an independent variable to explain outcomes such as innovation and overall performance, much as we did in earlier chapters of this book (see, for example, Allen, 1977; Tushman, 1978; and Snyder and Morris, 1984). In the few instances where communication is the dependent variable, the studies have usually been conducted on small groups (as in Guetzkow and Simon,

1954). As Egelhoff (1990) has correctly pointed out, these small group results cannot be easily extended to the context of interunit communication in large complex organizations like MNCs.

In this chapter, we attempt to address this gap in the literature by providing a systematic empirical evaluation of the influence of some key organizational attributes on the frequency of managerial communication between subsidiaries and headquarters as well as among the subsidiaries of two large MNCs. Though we are initiating empirical research on an important but relatively unexplored topic, we must at the outset acknowledge some of the limitations of our study. Confronted by complex theoretical and measurement problems, we limited the scope of our study of communication flows in MNCs in several ways:

Communication is a multidimensional phenomenon that can be conceptualized and measured across a number of attributes, including frequency, mode, informality, openness, density, and directionality (Jablin, 1979; Gupta and Govindarajan, 1991). Here communication is operationalized and measured only in terms of frequency. Frequency does not adequately capture either the content or the quality of information exchange. Yet as an indicator of the intensity of the communication flows between two persons, frequency has a long academic tradition and has been effectively used as a measure of communication in diverse settings (Homans, 1950; Granovetter 1973; Allen 1977; Tushman, 1978). We follow these studies in adopting frequency as our measure of communication, but both the theoretical and the normative implications of our findings remain constrained because of this restricted operationalization.

In addition, of the many factors that can potentially influence interunit communication in complex organizations, only two are examined: (1) formal organization structure as reflected in the subsidiary manager's autonomy or discretion in making key decisions and (2) informal relationships among managers formed through networking in teams, task forces, conferences, and so on. Our focus on these two factors is motivated by the distinction between formal and informal organizations first drawn by Barnard (1939). The importance of these two factors is also reflected in the empirical literature on coordination mechanisms in the MNC (Martinez and Jarillo, 1989). For many years, the primacy of the first factor—formal organization structure—went unquestioned (Stopford and Wells, 1972; Galbraith and Nathanson, 1978; Egelhoff, 1982). Recently, the primacy of formal structures has been seriously questioned, with scholars arguing that the second factor—informal relationships between managers—has become increasingly important in managing the modern multinational (Hedlund, 1986; Bartlett and Ghoshal, 1989). The salience of the underlying dimensions and the relevance of the current debate explain why we chose these two factors to study. However, we do not pretend that this is an exhaustive list of the factors that can influence communication flows within MNCs.

Factors Explaining Interunit Communication in MNCs

Our focus in this chapter is to assess the influence of formal organization structure and informal networking relationships between managers on interunit communication. The empirical analysis is guided by the relatively parsimonious theoretical model shown in Figure 7.1. In this model, formal organization structure is operationalized in terms of subsidiary autonomy, a latent variable construct. Informal relationships between managers are operationalized in terms of a second latent variable construct, networking. We measure two types of interunit communication, headquarters-subsidiary and intersubsidiary communication, and present a series of hypotheses that relate the autonomy and networking constructs to the two measures of interunit communication.

Interunit Communication

Whereas interunit communication is the dependent variable, two kinds of interunit linkages in the MNC are clearly distinguished: the vertical linkage between each of the national subsidiaries and

Figure 7.1. A Structural Model
for Interunit Communication in MNCs.

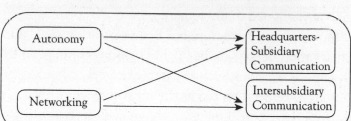

the headquarters and the horizontal linkages among the subsidiaries themselves.

The headquarters represents the strategic apex of the MNC. Ultimate responsibility for strategic direction, decision making, and overall coordination rest with the headquarters. Effective communication with each subsidiary is necessary for the headquarters to carry out these direction-setting and coordination tasks effectively.

At the same time, as highlighted by Hedlund (1993), Gupta and Govindarajan (1991), and others, MNCs increasingly face the need for leveraging the resources and capabilities of their national subsidiaries on a worldwide basis. As a result, subsidiary managers are often allocated strategic roles for the MNC as a whole (Bartlett and Ghoshal, 1986). The resulting dispersal of assets and resources, and of global roles and responsibilities, creates systemwide interdependence that requires effective intersubsidiary communication.

Formal Organization Structure

Contingency theory in general (for example, J. D. Thompson, 1967; Lawrence and Lorsch, 1967), and the information processing perspective in particular (for example, Galbraith, 1973; Galbraith and Nathanson, 1978), argue that formal organization structure powerfully influences internal communication in complex organizations. As described by Egelhoff (1990, pp. 10–11), this influence is in fact the "primary reason strategy-structure fit is important. By improving structural fit, one increases the likelihood that communication patterns, information flows and decision-making are better aligned to implement strategy."

Although formal structure has been operationalized and measured in a variety of ways (as by Pugh, Hickson, Hinings, and Turner, 1968), a few dimensions, such as complexity, centralization, and formalization, have been touted as the most important (Van de Ven, 1976). Even these core dimensions have been seen as being related to a "single bureaucratic dimension consisting of a number of Weberian characteristics" (Blackburn, 1982, p. 60). Galbraith (1973, p. 41) echoes this notion of a single structural dimension when he writes that various structural elements "fit together . . . and appear as parts of one total strategy." In the context of MNCs, the degree of centralization of the headquarters-subsidiary relation has long served as one of the fundamental dimensions of organization design and has been found to influence a whole host of organizational outcomes (Egelhoff, 1988a). Accordingly, to study the influence of formal structure on interunit communication within MNCs, we chose centralization as our primary dimension of the MNC's formal structure.

Following De Bodinat (1975), we operationalized centralization by its obverse, subsidiary autonomy, and measured it by the influence exercised by the subsidiary, relative to the headquarters, in making the following decisions: (1) major reorganizations in the subsidiary involving creation or dissolution of departments, (2) career development plans for subsidiary managers, and (3) changes in product design.

Existing research on multinational organizations suggests contradictory hypotheses on how centralization might influence interunit communication in MNCs. These contradictions are in turn reflections of two very different perspectives that are represented in this body of work.

Developed and refined over two decades through the contributions of a number of authors grounded in structural contingency theory, the first perspective adopts a hierarchical view of the MNC organization in which most organizational-level processes are

assumed to occur "within the context of a formal hierarchical organizational structure" (Egelhoff, 1990, p. 11). From this perspective,
centralization is seen as having an overall positive influence on
information processing, even though its use may be limited by
managerial and organizational constraints. With regard to vertical
information processing between the headquarters and each subsidiary, this assumption of a positive influence of centralization is
explicit, at least in Egelhoff's work (1988a): "Frequent strategic and
environmental change at the subunit level means that more information processing is required to maintain integration between the
subunit and the rest of the organization. Centralizing decision-
making for the subunit higher in the organization is one way to
provide this information-processing capacity" (pp. 131–132).

To the extent that communication is the mechanism by which
information is processed, Egelhoff's argument leads to the following hypothesis:

HYPOTHESIS 7.1(A): *A lower level of subsidiary autonomy (higher
centralization) will have a positive effect on headquarters-subsidiary
communication.*

The influence of centralization on direct intersubsidiary communication is not explicitly dealt with by authors contributing to
this first perspective except in the suggestion that "decision making for a given subunit should be more centralized when there is a
higher degree of interdependency between the subunit and the rest
of the organization . . . [because] centralization provides coordination and integration across the interdependency" (Egelhoff, 1988a,
p. 131). This assumes that all or most interunit communication is
mediated by the headquarters.

Developed through the cumulative work of another set of
authors and typically grounded in contextual case research is a second perspective that challenges this hierarchical view of the
MNC and describes it instead as a "heterarchy" (Hedlund, 1986)
or a "transnational" (Bartlett and Ghoshal, 1989). In this view,

horizontal and informal processes and shared beliefs and values replace vertical structure and authority as the prime mechanisms for organizational coordination and control. Centralization, in this view, puts limits on the initiative the subsidiary may take and reduces the subsidiary manager's propensity to initiate communication with the headquarters. Moreover, centralization impedes intersubsidiary exchange by increasing the relative centrality of the headquarters within the overall MNC network. This perspective suggests the following two hypotheses on the effects of centralization on vertical and lateral communication among the subunits of the MNC, the first of which runs directly counter to hypothesis 7.1(a):

HYPOTHESIS 7.1(B): *A higher level of subsidiary autonomy (lower centralization) will have a positive effect on headquarters-subsidiary communication.*

HYPOTHESIS 7.2: *A higher level of subsidiary autonomy (lower centralization) will have a positive effect on intersubsidiary communication.*

Informal Relationships Between Managers

Galbraith (1973) clearly highlights the importance of what he calls "lateral relations" as a key mechanism for expanding the information processing capacity of organizations. Contrasting centralization, an attribute of the formal structure, he describes lateral relations as aspects of the "informal organization" that arise spontaneously. Their efficacy, though, can be "substantially improved by designing them into the formal organization" (p. 47). More recent literature (including Martinez and Jarillo, 1989) describes these lateral processes of direct horizontal contact among managers through joint work in teams, task forces, and so on, as "networking" mechanisms that are part of organizational processes even if they are not elements of formal structure. These networking mechanisms are accordingly incorporated as the second set of influencing factors in our model explaining interunit communication.

Focused as they have been on attributes of the formal structure, researchers working within what we have called the hierarchical perspective on MNCs have paid little attention to networking mechanisms. Although their existence and relevance to interunit communication are acknowledged, it is generally assumed that such mechanisms have only a secondary role, derived from and subservient to the attributes of formal structure (Egelhoff, 1990).

For scholars who embrace a more process-oriented perspective, such lateral networking mechanisms are important ways of shaping information flows in MNCs. These scholars suggest that interunit activities such as joint work in task forces and meetings play a powerful role in building interpersonal relationships, which in turn facilitate ongoing communication among people in different parts of the company (Hedlund, 1986, 1993; Prahalad and Doz, 1987; Bartlett and Ghoshal, 1989).

Based on specific networking mechanisms described by these more process-oriented scholars, we operationalized this factor through the following three indicators: (1) time spent on interunit committees, teams, and task forces; (2) time spent in interunit meetings and conferences; and (3) time spent in the corporate headquarters; all measured in days, on the most recent annual basis.

Based on the work of the aforementioned scholars, the hypothesized relationship between networking and both headquarters-subsidiary and intersubsidiary communication is quite straightforward:

HYPOTHESIS 7.3: *A higher level of networking among managers in the various units of the company will have a positive effect on headquarters-subsidiary communication.*

HYPOTHESIS 7.4: *A higher level of networking among managers in the different units of the company will have a positive effect on intersubsidiary communication.*

Relative Influence of Structure Versus Networking

Our last set of hypotheses concerns the relative influence of subsidiary autonomy and networking on both headquarters-subsidiary and intersubsidiary communication. These hypotheses follow directly from the debate between the two strands of international management research we have just described.

The first perspective, exemplified by Egelhoff, considers formal structure to be the primary and key antecedent to headquarters-subsidiary communication. It does not explicitly deal with inter-subsidiary communication and regards lateral networking mechanisms as secondary to and influenced by formal structure. The hypothesis suggested by this perspective is consequently this:

HYPOTHESIS 7.5(A): *Subsidiary autonomy has a greater relative influence than networking on headquarters-subsidiary communication.*

The second perspective emphasizes both headquarters-subsidiary and intersubsidiary communication and argues for the primacy of networking mechanisms over structure in facilitating interunit communication. Bartlett and Ghoshal (1989) exemplify this view, as the following quote illustrates: "Companies like Procter and Gamble, Ericsson, Philips, Unilever, and NEC recognized that formal structure is a powerful but blunt weapon. . . . Administrative systems, communication channels, and interpersonal relationships often provided tools that are more subtle but also more effective than formal structure" (p. 32).

This perspective thus leads to the following two hypotheses, the first of which directly counters hypothesis 7.5(a):

HYPOTHESIS 7.5(B): *Subsidiary autonomy has a smaller relative influence than networking on headquarters-subsidiary communication.*
HYPOTHESIS 7.6: *Subsidiary autonomy has a smaller relative influence than networking on intersubsidiary communication.*

Empirical Analysis

Data for the analysis reported in this chapter were obtained from the in-depth surveys conducted in the second phase of our research. A total of 164 responses from Matsushita managers located in fourteen national subsidiaries and 84 from Philips managers located in nine national subsidiaries were used here as they had provided complete data on all the variables of interest.

Headquarters-subsidiary and intersubsidiary communication were both measured by asking the respondents to indicate the typical frequency of their communication with the head office and with each of the other national subsidiaries of the company that were included in the survey (see the Methodological Appendix for additional details). An aggregate intersubsidiary communication score for each respondent was calculated by totaling the individual's intersubsidiary communication frequency scores.

A structural model (see Figure 7.1) was posited and used to test the hypotheses relating the latent variable constructs, subsidiary autonomy and networking, to the dependent variables of interunit communication. In addition to hypothesis testing, we were also interested in ascertaining the validity of our constructs and the quality of the model.

In recent years, the LISREL structural equation modeling framework has gained increasing acceptance as the appropriate tool with which to carry out this kind of testing (Joereskog and Soerbom, 1989; Venkatraman,1989). LISREL follows a causal indicator model in which the measured variables reflect the latent theoretical constructs of interest; it allows the specification of measurement error and the assessment of measurement properties.[1]

Table 7.1 shows the means, standard deviations, and Spearman's rank correlations for the eight measured variables for Matsushita and Philips, respectively.

Table 7.2 shows results for the measurement models for Matsushita and Philips. The composite reliability scores for each of the two constructs, autonomy and networking, vary from a low of .54 to a high of .74 and are all within the acceptable range (Werts, Linn, and Joereskog, 1974; Baggozi and Yi, 1988). This suggests that the constructs have the requisite validity, at least in the specific empirical setting of the two companies studied.

Table 7.1. Means, Standard Deviations, and Spearman's Rank Correlations.

Variable	Mean	SD	1	2	3	4	5	6	7
Matsushita									
1. Intersubsidiary communication (aggregate)	89.01	9.95							
2. Headquarters-subsidiary communication	3.5	1.89	.30**						
3. Days per year in task force	7.66	11.60	.08*	.26**					
4. Days per year in cross-unit meetings	12.26	16.42	.18*	.25**	.31**				
5. Days per year at headquarters	6.99	9.72	.35**	.39**	.32**	.34**			
6. Product manager career changes	3.91	1.36	.26**	.16*	.11	.16*	.17*		
7. Major reorganizations	3.62	1.33	.09	.22**	0.00	.14	.09	.56**	
8. Changes in product design	3.52	1.34	.26**	.11	.03	.04	.18*	.50**	.32**
Philips									
1. Intersubsidiary communication (aggregate)	85.70	12.81							
2. Headquarters-subsidiary communication	3.46	1.82	−.01						
3. Days per year in task force	6.07	9.77	.23*	.07					
4. Days per year in cross-unit meetings	10.89	9.01	.13	.10	−.04				
5. Days per year at headquarters	9.62	8.29	.25*	.34**	.28**	.32**			
6. Product manager career changes	3.36	1.44	−.09	−.07	.01	−.07	.14		
7. Major reorganizations	3.37	1.16	.11	.09	−.05	.08	.18	.33**	
8. Changes in product design	3.08	1.36	.00	.07	−.30**	.06	−.08	.06	.21

$*p < .05; **p < .01.$

Table 7.2. Results of the LISREL Measurement Model.

Latent Variables (Indicators)	Factor Loading	Standard Error	t Value	Squared Multiple Correlation
Matsushita (n = 164)				
Autonomy (composite reliability = .74)				
Product manager career changes	1.00	—	—	.85
Major reorganizations	.65	.12	5.64	.36
Changes in product design	.59	.11	5.36	.30
Networking (composite reliability = .58)				
Days per year in task force	.92	.24	3.89	.21
Days per year in cross-unit meetings	1.00	—	—	.25
Days per year at headquarters	1.44	.32	4.47	.52
Philips (n = 84)				
Autonomy (composite reliability = .54)				
Product manager career changes	1.00	—	—	.85
Major reorganizations	5.24	9.07	.58	1.70*
Changes in product design	.67	.40	4.68	.03
Networking (composite reliability = .58)				
Days per year in task force	.85	.42	2.01	.08
Days per year in cross-unit meetings	1.00	—	—	.10
Days per year at headquarters	3.16	1.81	1.75	1.03*

*Not significantly different from zero.

We also posited that the constructs are unique, that is, different from each other. A correlation between a construct pair significantly different from unity implies discriminant validity. Based on this criterion, the construct pairs in both companies pass the discriminant validity test (z value = 1.96, $p < .05$).

The overall fit of the structural model for communication is assessed by the chi-square test, the adjusted goodness-of-fit index (AGFI), and the Bentler and Bonett normed-fit index. There is no clear theoretical basis to demarcate cutoff points, based on any of these tests, between acceptable and unacceptable fit. However, in practice, a p value above .10 for the chi-square test and a score in the vicinity of .90 for both AGFI and Bentler-Bonett are considered minimum thresholds for acceptable goodness of fit (Baggozi and Yi, 1988). As can be seen from Figure 7.2, in the case of Matsushita, all indices are higher than these minimum acceptable levels. For Philips, as shown in Figure 7.3, except for the Bender-Bonett index, which falls below the threshold, the other test statistics are satisfactory.

Table 7.3 shows the parameter estimates for the structural model for Matsushita and for Philips, respectively. Hypothesis 7.1(a)—that subsidiary autonomy is inversely related to the frequency of headquarters-subsidiary communication—is clearly rejected in the cases of both Philips and Matsushita. The rival hypothesis 7.1(b)—that subsidiary autonomy is directly related to the frequency of headquarters-subsidiary communication—is also rejected. There is no evidence in our data regarding either a negative or a positive effect of subsidiary autonomy on headquarters-subsidiary communication.

Hypothesis 7.2 fares better. In the case of Matsushita, subsidiary autonomy has a significant positive influence on intersubsidiary communication. However, in the case of Philips, though its influence is positive, it is not significant.

Hypotheses 7.3 and 7.4 are both strongly supported by the data. In both companies, networking appears to have significant positive effects on both headquarters-subsidiary and intersubsidiary communication.

The total variance explained for each dependent variable can be decomposed into a linear combination of the variance contributed by each of the explanatory constructs and by their covariance. LISREL does not provide a direct estimate for the

Figure 7.2. Results of the LISREL Model
for Interunit Communication at Matsushita.

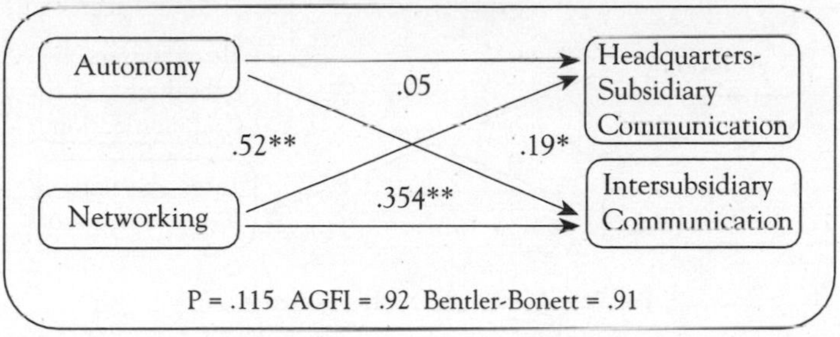

*p < .05; **p < .01.

extent of variance explained by each of the explanatory constructs. However, it does provide as output a regression matrix of the standardized dependent variables on the standardized independent variables. The weights of the linear combination can be computed using the standardized coefficients. These estimates are presented in Table 7.3.

For headquarters-subsidiary communication, subsidiary autonomy accounts for about 1 percent of the total variance explained by the model in the cases of both Philips and Matsushita, while networking explains more than 90 percent. For intersubsidiary communication, the networking factor explains between three (for Matsushita) and ten (for Philips) times the variance that is explained by subsidiary autonomy.

These results clearly indicate the greater influence of networking and thereby provide support for hypotheses 7.5(b) and 7.6. This broadly reinforces the contention that networking has a greater relative influence on interunit communication than formal structural elements such as subsidiary autonomy.

To examine the robustness of these conclusions further, the tests were run again with a more limited definition of interunit communication that included only daily or weekly interaction. Table 7.4 shows the results of these additional tests. In both companies, autonomy has no significant effect on high-frequency

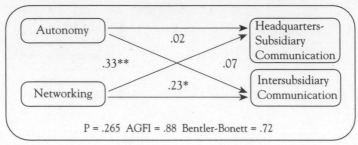

Figure 7.3. Results of the LISREL Model
for Interunit Communication at Philips.

*p < .10; **p < .05.

communication. The effect of networking is positive and significant (at least at the p = .10 level) for both headquarters-subsidiary and intersubsidiary communication. These results confirm
those of the original operationalization of communication and
indicate that networking and communication are indeed independent measures.

Conclusions

In this chapter, we investigated some of the organizational factors
that influence interunit communication in MNCs. The analysis
focused on the relative influence of one important dimension of formal structure, subsidiary autonomy, and characteristics of the informal organization, as represented by interpersonal networking
mechanisms, on both headquarters-subsidiary and intersubsidiary
communication. Our findings suggest that while subsidiary autonomy
has almost no effect on either headquarters-subsidiary or intersubsidiary communications, interpersonal networking has significant
positive effects on the ongoing communication of subsidiary managers, both with their counterparts in the headquarters and with
managers in other subsidiaries.

The implications of our findings are clear. A number of authors
have emphasized the importance of lateral networking mechanisms

Table 7.3. Estimates of the Structural Parameters from the LISREL Model.

Independent Variables	Dependent Variables	Headquarters-Subsidiary Communication	Intersubsidiary Communication
Matsushita			
Autonomy	Standardized path coefficient	.05	.19
	t value	.528	2.164
	Share of variance explained[a]	1%	18%
Networking	Standardized path coefficient	.52	.35
	t value	3.98	3.078
	share of variance explained[a]	94%	62%
Overall share of variance explained		29%	20%
Philips			
Autonomy	Standardized path coefficient	.02	.07
	t value	.217	.816
	Share of variance explained[a]	< 1%	9%
Networking	Standardized path coefficient	.33	.23
	t value	2.237	1.801
	Share of variance explained[a]	> 99%	91%
Overall share of variance explained		20%	17%

[a]The share of variance explained may not add up vertically to 100 percent. The residual percentage is explained by the interaction term of the two independent latent variables.

to facilitate information exchange within MNCs (Bartlett and Ghoshal, 1989; Martinez and Jarillo, 1991). Others have argued that the costs incurred in supporting such mechanisms may be too high and the benefits too uncertain (Egelhoff, 1990). The strong influence of the networking variables on promoting both headquarters-subsidiary and intersubsidiary communication in MNCs, coupled with the manifest importance of communication as a key source of the MNC's ability to develop, share, and leverage knowledge, reinforces the prescription that managers should invest in interunit networking.

While investing in networking, it is important to remember that the organizational task of information processing involves not

Table 7.4. Estimates of the Structural Parameters from the LISREL Model (daily and weekly communications only).

Independent Variables	Dependent Variables	Headquarters-Subsidiary Communication	Intersubsidiary Communication
Matsushita			
Autonomy	Standardized path coefficient	.001	.06
	t value	.009	.654
Networking	Standardized path coefficient	.43	.19
	t value	3.182	1.681
Philips			
Autonomy	Standardized path coefficient	.135	.19
	t value	.833	1.273
Networking	Standardized path coefficient	1.399	.879
	t value	2.20	1.822

only managing its flow but also facilitating its interpretation (Huber and Daft, 1987). Information is transformed whenever it is transferred, and information interpretation requires the development and use of a mutually validated grammar for creating meaning out of ambiguous and equivocal information (Weick, 1980). It is in creating this shared meaning system that the networking mechanisms and organizational processes may play a vital role. It is plausible that the information flows that formal structure attempts to induce can actually function properly only when the lateral processes needed for interpretation are also in place. Thus in addition to structural considerations, managers must be cognizant of informal processes that facilitate communication in organizations and enable coordinated action among dispersed yet interdependent organizational units. Such networking mechanisms are especially important for MNCs that aspire to tap all the distributed capabilities that reside in their various national subsidiaries.

Note

1. In using LISREL, we made the standard assumptions of multivariate normality and diagonal error structure. Concerning sample size adequacy, we followed Baggozi and Yi (1988), who suggest a minimum of five sample points per parameter estimate. Because we were working with ordinal variables, we faced the problem of nonnormality in the computation of the covariance matrix (Joereskog and Soerbom, 1989). We addressed this problem by using Spearman's rank correlations.

Chapter Eight

Integration Through Interpersonal Networks

In Chapter Seven, we examined the factors that promote interunit communication in MNCs. Here we focus on the formation of interpersonal networks. In MNCs, interpersonal networks are vital because they serve as the glue that holds these vast geographically dispersed and internally differentiated organizations together. Interpersonal links act as integrative mechanisms because they are conduits for information exchange. The exchange of information that takes place through these ties enables the various interconnected parts of the multinational enterprise to coordinate their activities with one another. In the absence of such informal ties, coordination would break down because organizational members would have to rely solely on formal structural mechanisms, which would quickly get overloaded. As we all know from experience, much of organizational life depends on knowing whom to call to get relevant information. Indeed, such informal contacts are often the only way to get things done (Ibarra, 1992).

Interpersonal contacts are vital for achieving the multinational's goals of efficiency and innovation. For instance, efficiency is enhanced because the exchange of information allows the various subunits of the multinational to take advantage of opportunities for arbitrage. Knowing, for example, that a plant in France has excess inventory that can be shipped to meet an unexpected need of a customer in the United States is the kind of exchange that an interpersonal network facilitates that can greatly enhance the efficiency of the multinational organization. Similarly, to the extent that innovation is stimulated by chance discoveries and by putting together combinations of ideas in novel ways, information obtained through interpersonal contacts can greatly enhance innovation.

Interpersonal ties are also mechanisms for building trust and shared values within the MNC. Trust is typically built on repeated interaction and contact among individuals who over time develop mutual expectations and obligations (Coleman, 1990). The creation of shared values or norms also requires interpersonal communication between an organization's members. Interpersonal ties are often the primary means for individuals to learn the appropriate codes of conduct within an organization. They also serve to monitor conduct and to ensure compliance with norms (Van Maanen and Schein, 1979). Both trust and shared values reduce coordination costs within organizations (Arrow, 1974; Ring and Van de Ven, 1992).

Given the importance of interpersonal contacts, one would ideally want everyone in the multinational to be directly connected with everyone else. But that is, of course, not humanly possible. No individual could possibly maintain the thousands of contacts that a fully connected network would require. Individuals simply do not have enough time or cognitive capacity to maintain such an extensive number of ties, especially since many of these ties have to span the globe, extending across countries separated by time zones, language, and culture.

Given the impossibility of building a fully connected network across all the individuals in the organization, what is the alternative? The alternative is a network that relies on having at least a few individuals in each subsidiary who have a wide range of ties within and across the subsidiary's boundaries. These individuals can serve as gatekeepers or brokers of information across the disparate parts of the network (Allen, 1977; Tushman, 1977). They can be the linking pins or bridging ties that connect the otherwise disconnected parts of the network and help plug the structural holes in it (Granovetter, 1973; Burt, 1992b).

Thus from the standpoint of enhancing the value-creating potential of an MNC, it is vital to understand the factors that enable key individuals in each subsidiary to develop interpersonal ties that reach across the various departments within the subsidiary and the various subsidiaries of the multinational. In this chapter, we explore some key factors that affect the social capital or range of ties developed by department-level managers in MNCs. We provide empirical evidence to support our arguments using data from the three multinationals surveyed in depth during phase 2 of our study.

Social Capital

The performance of individuals in an organization depends on various forms of capital that they possess. Burt (1992a) argues that physical capital, human capital, and social capital are three such forms of capital that are particularly salient. Physical capital refers to the resources, such as money, equipment, and land, that an individual has access to. Human capital is the personal knowledge, ability, and skills, as well as charisma and flair, that an individual brings to the performance of the job. Social capital is the individual's network of contacts, the people he or she knows and who they in turn know.

Although all these forms of capital are valuable, Burt (1992a) argues that social capital is perhaps the final arbiter of success because it provides individuals with the benefits of access, timing, and referrals that allow them to make the most of their stock of physical and human capital. The benefits of access refer to the valuable information we receive from our contacts. No one in an organization of any significant size, let alone of the complexity and dispersion of an MNC, has access to all the relevant information necessary to put the company's resources to their best use. Our social capital often shapes the quality of the information we receive and thus the degree to which our resources are employed. Contacts, in a sense, serve to compensate for our limited information processing capacity, serving, as Burt nicely puts it, "as an army of people processing information who can call your attention to key bits—keeping you up to date on developing opportunities, warning you of impending disaster" (p. 62).

Related to access is the benefit of timing. The quality of our contacts shapes not only what we learn but also how quickly we learn so that we can take advantage of the information. Reading in a newspaper that a competitor in another country is suffering from production problems that create an opportunity for you to unload excess inventory is of less use than learning about this in advance from a contact in that country. Personal contacts often get information to us before it reaches the general public.

The third critical benefit that results from social capital, Burt (1992a) suggests, is referrals. Not only do our contacts provide us with information, but they also provide information about us to others. These referrals shape our reputations. To the extent that having a good reputation is a valuable resource, we benefit from our social capital.

Individuals with greater social capital are likely to do better in the organizational arena. They are more likely to succeed at their jobs and to get ahead in their careers. There are also organizational benefits because the social capital of its members aggregates to the social capital of the entire organization. An organization that has more individuals with extensive contacts inside and outside the organization is likely to be at a competitive advantage relative to another that has fewer such individuals.

Given the importance of social capital for individual and organizational performance, the key question is what defines an individual's social capital. The simplest definition and measure of social capital is, of course, the size of the individual's network. The larger the number of contacts, the greater the individual's social capital. The problem with this measure, however, is that it assumes that all contacts are equally valuable. Given the limits of time and energy, there are only so many contacts that we can possibly maintain. To procure the greatest benefit from the limited number of contacts we can maintain, we should seek to minimize what Burt (1992a, 1992b) calls redundant contacts. Contacts are redundant when they tap into the same information or resource pool. We are better off having one key contact in two different information pools than two contacts in one pool. The range of nonredundant contacts we have is thus a more powerful indicator of our social capital than the total size of our network.

In the context of complex multiunit organizations like MNCs, we believe that an individual's range of contacts across departmental or functional boundaries within a subsidiary and the range across different subsidiaries are two important indicators of social capital. Within a subsidiary, each department or function represents a different pool of information and resources. Across subsidiaries, we can similarly view each subsidiary as representing a nonredundant and unique pool of resources and information. Accordingly, the two measures of social capital we focus on in this chapter are the number of different departments in which an individual has at least one contact and the number of national subsidiaries in which an individual has at least one contact.

As we have seen in Part One, aggregate measures of such individual social capital—namely, the density of intra-and intersubsidiary communication—have a significant impact on the creation, adoption, and diffusion of distributed innovation in MNCs. Understanding the factors that enhance individual social capital is therefore critical to organizing efforts that aim to enhance the value creation potential of the MNC.

Factors Influencing the Formation of Social Capital

In principle, a large number of factors, including organizational factors such as formal and informal structure and individual factors such as personality and motivation, can influence an individual's social capital. Here we focus on just a few key career-related factors: tenure, mobility, expatriate status, initial socialization, and mentoring relationships. We focus on these factors because they have been regarded in both organization theory and the MNC literature as having a significant influence on an individual's ability to form social ties.

Tenure

The effects of tenure on social capital are intuitively obvious. The longer an individual has worked in any organization, the more opportunities he or she has had to meet and form contacts throughout the organization. Even the everyday performance of a job brings us, over the course of time, into contact with people from other parts of the organization, if only for some special occasion or assignment.

Experience also creates knowledge of the network we need to get things done. Thus more experienced individuals may maintain key contacts in other areas whom they have found over time to be helpful to their own performance.

Another benefit of experience is that it is itself a resource that an individual possesses that others seek to tap into. An experienced individual is often seen as a credible and valuable source of information and may thus be sought out by other individuals trying to build their own contact network. Inasmuch as ties tend to be reciprocal, this can lead to an expansion of the experienced individual's network. We thus make the following hypothesis:

HYPOTHESIS 8.1: *Individuals with longer tenure will have a greater range of both interdepartmental and intersubsidiary contacts.*

Mobility

Although tenure is important, an individual's mobility during a career may have a more significant effect on his or her social capital. Horizontal mobility, or the number of different functions and subsidiaries in which an individual has worked during his or her tenure, may be particularly important. There is no better way to develop contacts outside one's own department or subsidiary than to work there for some period of time. Such rotational assignments have several benefits, as highlighted by Edstrom and Galbraith (1977) in their study of human resource flows in MNCs. Horizontal mobility increases the knowledge individuals have of the scope of the total organizational network. It makes them aware of the different activities and perspectives within the organization and allows them to develop a broader, more cosmopolitan, firmwide perspective. It helps them develop and learn skills and form new contacts. Indeed, horizontal mobility may be one of the best ways for organizations to achieve control through normative integration or shared values because such transfers reduce parochial attachments that individuals may have and bind them more tightly to the organization as a whole.

Another key benefit of horizontal mobility is that it can disseminate skills and knowledge that reside in different parts of the organization. Because these capabilities are often tacit, they cannot be easily codified and transferred through formal mechanisms (Kogut and Zander, 1992). One of the best ways to transfer knowledge within an MNC is thus through the transfer and rotation of organizational members through different parts of the organization. Such transfers not only allow individuals to learn these capabilities themselves but also, through the contacts they form, permit them to continue to tap these capabilities as needed.

Horizontal intraorganizational mobility is thus viewed as a key mechanism for building social capital. Accordingly, we hypothesize:

HYPOTHESIS 8.2: *Horizontal mobility will increase an individual's social capital. The greater the number of departments an individual has worked in, the larger the range of interdepartmental contacts; and the greater the number of subsidiaries an individual has worked in, the larger the range of intersubsidiary contacts.*

Expatriate Status

Expatriates can be defined in many ways, the broadest definition being individuals working outside their home country (Edstrom and Galbraith, 1977). Here we focus on a more limited class of expatriates, namely, individuals whose home country is the MNC's corporate headquarters who have been deputed to work abroad in one of the MNC's national subsidiaries. Our field research indicated that in many of the companies we studied, there was a cadre of such parent-country expatriates who were assigned, over the course of their careers, to multiple subsidiaries. We expect such individuals to be especially likely to have a large range of inter-subsidiary contacts, even relative to a local country executive who may have worked in an equal number of foreign subsidiaries. This is because parent-country expatriates are able to play a unique brokerage or mediating role in MNCs that derives from their association with the corporate headquarters, the central node in the network. Indeed, MNCs often maintain such a cadre of expatriates precisely because they can play such a mediating role, owing to the credibility they typically enjoy with both the headquarters and the subsidiary. Such individuals are trusted by subsidiary managers because they have worked there. And being parent-country nationals, they naturally enjoy the trust of the corporate headquarters. Thus we hypothesize:

HYPOTHESIS 8.3: *Expatriates will have a larger range of intersubsidiary contacts, though not necessarily a larger range of interdepartmental contacts.*

Initial Socialization

To this point, we have discussed factors that shape movement and exposure over several years of an individual's career. We now discuss a factor that can influence an individual's social capital at the very outset of his or her career: the initial training and socialization that the individual receives.

As Van Maanen and Schein (1979) point out, initial socialization is especially important because it "provides the individual with an ordered view of the work life that runs ahead and guides experience, orders and shapes personal relationships in the work setting, and provides the ground rules under which everyday conduct is to be managed" (p. 212). Initial socialization plays a key role in educating new organizational members to the range of solutions to the problems they can expect to encounter on the job, the rules for choosing particular solutions, and the goals and values of the organization that serve to justify, legitimize, and define the ends toward which their activities are guided.

Initial socialization builds social capital by introducing the newcomer to key individuals in different parts of the organization. In many of the organizations we studied, new managers were formally assigned for short training periods to the various departments and functions in the subsidiary they had joined. Occasionally, they were also assigned, for a brief period, to work at the corporate headquarters. On such assignments, these individuals had the opportunity to form contacts with peers from other national subsidiaries who had also been sent to the corporate headquarters as part of their initial training. Several managers we interviewed indicated that contacts they made with other members of their cohort from different countries during this initial training period had developed into durable relationships and a network of contacts across the organization's boundaries. This leads us to hypothesize:

HYPOTHESIS 8.4: *Individuals that received formal initial training are more likely to have a broad range of interdepartmental and intersubsidiary contacts.*

Mentoring Relationships

Much organizational socialization takes place through informal rather than through formal mechanisms like training. The mentoring relationship, defined as an informal advisory relationship with a more senior member of the organization, plays a central role in informal socialization. Mentors transfer knowledge, norms, customs, and understandings. They help individuals learn and master the skills necessary to succeed in their jobs and advise them on how to assess and navigate the organization's political landscape (Kram, 1985; Caruso, 1992). They also help an individual develop social capital, primarily through the mechanism of referrals mentioned earlier. Beyond making direct introductions, mentors also lay the groundwork for their mentees to form contacts of their own by spreading a positive reputation for them. The literature on the formation of networks highlights the cascading role such ties play in the formation of a more extensive set of contacts (Granovetter, 1982).

Although mentoring has generally been thought to have positive consequences, scholars have also pointed out some of its potential pitfalls. For example, we have been cautioned that mentoring can lead to overdependence and smothering (Kram, 1985). In such circumstances, contrary to helping, mentoring relationships may hinder the individual's personal development and development of social capital.

The potentially negative effects are likely to be most salient early in an individual's career. Indeed, Higgins and Nohria (1994) suggest that early on, an individual runs the risk of being seen merely as the mentor's "sidekick." Therefore, though the mentor's introductions may indeed provide the protégé with visibility, they may not translate into durable relationships for the protégé because they are inextricably linked to the accomplishments and reputation of the mentor, not the protégé. Riding on the mentor's coattails may create the illusion of building contacts, but these are unlikely to be long-lasting for the mentee.

Later in a manager's career, once he or she has established a reputation independent of the mentor, a mentor's introductions and advocacy can be of benefit. At this stage, exposure and visibility provided by a sponsor can open doors to new opportunities and to new people that the protégé can pursue more readily. The mentor is now more likely to abet, rather than overshadow, the protégé. Accordingly, we advance this hypothesis:

HYPOTHESIS 8.5: *Having a mentor early in one's career will negatively affect an individual's formation of social capital, whereas*

having a mentor later in one's career will positively affect one's for-
mation of social capital.

Empirical Analysis

We test the hypotheses in this chapter using the questionnaire data
we collected during phase 2 of our research project from managers
in the subsidiaries of three major multinational corporations. After
eliminating incomplete responses, the final number of managers in
our analysis was 177. The composition of our final sample was not
significantly different from the population surveyed.

The dependent variable in our analysis was social capital. We
operationalized social capital as the range or number of national
subsidiaries of the firm in which the respondent had at least one
contact and the range or number of different departments in this
subsidiary in which the respondent had a contact. A contact was
someone with whom the respondent communicated at least once
a year. Following Burt's recommendation (1992a), we did not focus
as much on the strength of these ties as on the number of nonredundant bridging contacts—ties that tap into separate social clusters. Accordingly, more than one contact in any particular
department and subsidiary counted as only one tie in our calcula-
tion of range because each was considered a separate social cluster.

We included as independent variables measures of our respondents' tenure in the firm, the number of other functions within the
firm in which they had worked, the number of other subsidiaries in
which they had worked, and whether they were of expatriate status. We also asked individuals if they had received initial training
when they joined the company.

To determine the mentoring relationships of our respondents, we
asked them if they had developed a "close personal relationship with
any senior manager in the company in their first two years of employment" or if they had such an "informal adviser or sponsor" now. The
first of our two independent variables indicates whether the respondents had a mentor early in their tenure, when they first joined the

company. The second variable indicates whether the individuals had a mentor late in their tenure, at the time of the survey.

We included several control variables in our analysis to account for factors other than those identified here that may influence an individual's range of intersubsidiary contacts. A brief description and rationale for including these controls follows. See Table 8.1 for a full listing of these variables.

To control for the fact that our respondents were from three different multinationals, we included two dummy variables to identify if the respondent was an employee of Matsushita or of Philips. The base case is thus employees of NEC. These dummy variables were intended to control for any firm-specific variations.

Within any multinational system, some subsidiaries may be more important and central than others in the internal resource flow network. In such subsidiaries, managers may have more opportunities to form intersubsidiary contacts. To control for this source of internal variation within any MNC, we included a variable that measured the relative importance of the respondent's subsidiary in the multinational system. This measure was based on ratings of each subsidiary's relative strategic importance provided by several headquarters-level respondents in each multinational.

Because our respondents were either functional departmental heads or general managers in their respective subsidiaries, we controlled for their job responsibilities. Several dummies were included to control for the possibility that being a general manager, as opposed to a functional head of marketing, manufacturing, research and development, finance, purchasing, or legal affairs and administration, could have an influence on an individual's social capital. We expected general managers to have a broader range of contacts than the heads of functions by virtue of their more integrative organizational role.

Although we attempted to control for several factors that might influence the range of contacts possessed by our managers, we recognize that there are other factors that we cannot control for. For instance, recent research suggests that an individual's personality, on

Table 8.1. Means, Standard Deviations, and Correlation Matrix.

Description	Mean	SD	1	2	3	4	5	6	7	8	9	10	11	12	13	14	15	16	17	18	19	20
1. Dummy for company (Matsushita)	.60	.49	1.00																			
2. Dummy for company (Philips)	.17	.38	-.55*	1.00																		
3. Importance of subsidiary	3.71	.76	-.09	.10	1.00																	
4. General manager	.14	.34	-.21*	.22*	.05	1.00																
5. Marketing	.22	.42	-.04	.01	.06	-.21*	1.00															
6. Manufacturing	.19	.39	.16*	-.10	-.19	-.19*	-.25*	1.00														
7. Purchasing	.07	.25	-.01	0.00	-.03	-.11	-.14	-.13	1.00													
8. Research and development	.06	.23	.10	-.11	-.07	-.10	-.13	-.12	-.07	1.00												
9. Finance	.15	.36	.01	.03	.05	-.16*	-.2?*	-.20*	-.11	-.10	1.00											
10. Legal/administrative	.10	.30	.03	-.10	.09	-.1?	-.?*	-.16*	-.09	-.08	-.14	1.00										

Table 8.1. (Continued)

Description	Mean	SD	1	2	3	4	5	6	7	8	9	10	11	12	13	14	15	16	17	18	19	20
11. Tenure at current firm	13.58	7.69	.18*	.21*	-.04	-.03	-.07	.18*	-.04	-.02	.07	-.14	1.00									
12. Tenure at other firms	7.10	8.58	-.17*	-.02	.12	.08	.03	-.12	-.01	-.11	-.09	.12	-.55*	1.00								
13. Number of other functions worked in	2.20	1.98	-.06	.05	.02	.22*	-.05	.08	-.04	-.05	-.24*	.08	.18*	0.00	1.00							
14. Number of other subsidiaries worked in	.98	1.56	-.03	.13	.05	.03	.03	.13	-.05	-.06	-.03	-.06	.18*	-.08	.49*	1.00						
15. Expatriate	.41	.49	.12	.05	.06	-.10	-.03	.13	.05	-.06	.11	-.20*	.46*	-.46*	-.07	.17*	1.00					
16. Initial training	.47	.50	.41*	-.22*	.01	-.11	-.12	.16*	.06	.01	-.04	-.08	.33*	-.36*	.02	.13	.51*	1.00				
17. Early mentor	.46	.50	-.04	-.02	-.13	.17*	-.13	0.00	.02	-.03	-.03	.09	-.09	.06	.18*	.02	-.24*	-.12	1.00			
18. Late mentor	.65	.50	.20*	-.14	.06	-.12	-.01	.05	.01	-.03	.07	0.00	.09	-.17*	.02	0.00	.23*	.32*	.18*	1.00		
19. Range of intersubsidiary ties	9.95	6.91	-.12	.06	.17*	-.05	.14	-.17*	.05	.01	.12	-.05	-.05	.03	-.16*	-.02	.18*	-.01	-.23*	.12	1.00	
20. Range of intrasubsidiary ties	9.92	1.59	-.12	.12	.28*	.05	-.11	-.03	-.11	.04	.14	.04	-.02	-.04	.06	.13	.12	.19*	-.04	.13	.21*	1.00

*p < .05. N = 177.

which we collected no data, influences the extent to which the person seeks out and uses network contacts (Turban and Dougherty, 1994). It has also been shown that gender and race play a significant role in the pattern of relationships that individuals develop (Ibarra, 1993; Thomas, 1993). We do not have data on gender or race, so we cannot control for such effects.

Multiple linear regression was used initially to explore the effects of the various independent variables on the two range variables. The output of these analyses suggested that for the case of intersubsidiary contacts, respondents fall into two clear groups: those with many ties, or high range, and those with some ties, or low range. This conclusion was drawn after reviewing the plot of residuals versus predicted values, which showed two parallel lines of scattered points, and after examining the frequencies table of the dependent variable. To avoid violating the random distribution of errors assumption for efficient estimation in ordinary least squares (OLS) regressions, we used a logistic regression analysis.

Managers with "many ties" were found to have eleven to seventeen ties with other subsidiaries, while those with "some ties" had from one to ten ties with other subsidiaries. No individual reported having no ties at all with other subsidiaries. Given these results, it seemed most appropriate to recode the subjects into the two groups—$y = 0$ (some ties) or 1 (many ties)—and to perform a logistic regression analysis based on this new dichotomous dependent variable.

The results of the logistic regression are shown in Table 8.2. The logistic model fits the data nicely. Overall, 72.32 percent of the respondents were correctly classified by our model. The goodness-of-fit statistic further confirms that the model fits the observed data (chi-square of 171 with 151 degrees of freedom). The large observed significance level ($p = .13$) indicates that our model does not differ significantly from a "perfect" model in which the observed probabilities exactly match those predicted by the model. Finally, similar to the overall F test for multiple linear regression, the logistic model chi-square allows us to reject the null hypothesis that all of the coefficients in our model are 0, except the constant (chi-square = 50.7; df = 25; p = .0017). In sum, our model fits the observed data quite well.

Our results show that having a mentor late or early is the only variable that has a significant effect at the $p < .05$ level on the respondent's range of intersubsidiary contacts. Specifically, having a mentor early decreases the odds of an individual's being in the group with high range, whereas having a mentor late increases the odds of an individual's being in the high-range group. The only other variable that had any significant influence was expatriate status, which had a positive impact on range if we relax the confidence level to $p < .10$.

The values shown in Table 8.2 allow us to gauge the magnitude of these effects. They indicate the amount by which the odds are increased that a respondent would fall in the category of those with a broad range of contacts, given a unit increase in the independent variable. Our results indicate that if a respondent had a mentor early in his or her career, the odds of the respondent's being in the high-range group fall significantly. In fact, an individual with an early mentor is only 40 percent as likely as someone who does not have an early mentor to fall into the high-range group. In contrast, we find that if the respondent has a mentor later in his or her career, the odds of the respondent's being in the high-range group increase dramatically. These odds ratios confirm hypothesis 8.5.

Expatriate status also had a sizable effect on an individual's range of intersubsidiary contacts. A respondent who was an expatriate was much more likely to be in the high-range group, consistent with hypothesis 8.3.

The results of the OLS regression for the range of interdepartmental or intrasubsidiary contacts also showed little support for most of our hypotheses (see Table 8.3). The only factor that had a significant effect was initial training, which had the expected positive effect on the range of interdepartmental ties (hypothesis 8.4).

Table 8.2. Results of Logistic Regression Analysis for Intersubsidiary Communication.

Classification Table

Observed	Predicted		Percentage Correct
	1.0	*2.0*	
1.0	58	29	66.67
2.0	20	70	77.78
			Overall: 72.32

Goodness-of-Fit Statistics	*Chi-Square*	*df*	*Significance*
Model chi-square	50.706	25	.0017
Goodness of fit	170.998	151	.1268

Regression Coefficients

Description	Beta	Standard Error	Significance
1. Dummy for company (Matsushita)	−.611	.532	.251
2. Dummy for company (Philips)	.058	.728	.937
3. Importance of subsidiary	.303	.264	.251
4. General manager	.516	.955	.589
5. Marketing	1.130	.926	.223
6. Manufacturing	.100	.934	.915
7. Purchasing	1.156	1.114	.300
8. Research and development	1.191	1.158	.304
9. Finance	1.018	.973	.295
10. Legal/administrative	.740	.986	.453
11. Tenure at current firm	−.005	.049	.919
12. Tenure at other firms	.033	.046	.478
13. Number of other functions worked in	−.091	.118	.444
14. Number of other subsidiaries worked in	.042	.158	.789
15. Expatriate	.983	.520	.059
16. Initial training	−.477	.508	.348
17. Early mentor	−.896	.410	.029
18. Late mentor	1.337	.461	.004

Table 8.3. Results of OLS Regression Analysis for Intrasubsidiary Communication.

Description	Beta	Standard Error	Significance
1. Dummy for company (Matsushita)	−.176	.342	.097
2. Dummy for company (Philips)	.103	.464	.349
3. Importance of subsidiary	.213	.167	.009
4. General manager	−.021	.580	.864
5. Marketing	−.097	.555	.504
6. Manufacturing	.002	.559	.991
7. Purchasing	−.116	.651	.264
8. Research and development	.093	.714	.364
9. Finance	.138	.583	.290
10. Legal/administrative	.046	.607	.683
11. Tenure at current firm	.010	.025	.887
12. Tenure at other firms	.052	.020	.628
13. Number of other functions worked in	.019	.076	.839
14. Number of other subsidiaries worked in	.074	.090	.406
15. Expatriate	−.036	.337	.735
16. Initial training	.313	.317	.002
17. Early mentor	−.014	.263	.865
18. Late mentor	.072	.268	.375

Adjusted R^2 = .127.

Conclusions

Our objective in this chapter was to identify the potential determinants of an individual's social capital in the MNC. We examined the role of several factors that could potentially exert an influence.

Our results suggested that most of these factors were insignificant. A single factor had a significant effect on social capital within a particular subsidiary (ties across departmental boundaries): it was increased if an individual had received initial training. The results underscore the importance of investing in initial socialization. They suggest that ties formed early in our careers are the most important and durable contacts we form, at least within our organization. Other contacts formed later during our tenure or through horizontal mobility are less durable.

A speculative explanation for these results is that the most intensive interactions individuals have during their initial training is with their peers who may have been recruited into the same subsidiary. Ties formed within this cohort by virtue of their common initial training experience are lasting bonds. The strength of cohort effects has been highlighted by studies of socialization in institutions like the military and the police. These organizations have intense initial socialization programs (Van Maanen and Schein, 1979). Perhaps a similar cohort effect is at work in the multinationals we studied.

The reason why this initial training effect does not extend to ties formed across subsidiary boundaries is that in most of the companies we studied, the period of contact that newcomers from different countries had was very brief, if they had any contact at all. As we mentioned, such contact was typically at the corporate headquarters, where the newcomers were assigned for a short training period. The weak effect of this minimal interaction on the formation of durable social contacts suggests that MNCs that wish to use their initial training for the purpose of building intersubsidiary links may need to invest more heavily in keeping new managers from different countries together for a longer period. If possible, they should rotate new managers through assignments in the various countries rather than through the headquarters alone.

In the absence of such formal training, what does influence the formation of a broader range of intersubsidiary ties is having a senior mentor who provides exposure later in a manager's career. Usually, mentors for such senior subsidiary managers are located at the corporate headquarters and can thus serve as brokers, introducing their mentees to important individuals in other subsidiaries of the MNC. Early mentors, by contrast, are typically local subsidiary managers

A strong relationship with such a mentor may in fact potentially create a parochial perspective that has a negative effect on the range of intersubsidiary contacts an individual develops.

It might also be that having a mentor early in one's career can produce a "sidekick effect" whereby mentees are so overshadowed by their sponsors that development of their own social capital as individuals is difficult. However, this sidekick effect disappears once the person has developed a reputation as an individual contributor in the firm. At this later point in time, a senior sponsor or mentor may be quite helpful in facilitating the formation of new ties since the manager is no longer walking in anyone's shadow.

Finally, our results indicate that expatriates play a central role in facilitating intersubsidiary ties in MNCs. This result is entirely consistent with the work of Edstrom and Galbraith (1977), who highlighted the linking and mediating roles played by expatriates in the MNCs they studied. MNCs must thus invest in creating a pool of expatriates who can serve this vital function. Given the enormous personal and organizational expense that is involved in supporting this difficult role, MNCs may have to work extra hard to ensure that there is a critical mass of such expatriates. As Edstrom and Galbraith's research showed, the payoffs from such an investment can be great in terms of both reducing coordination costs and making the best use of the dispersed knowledge that resides in the MNCs.

In sum, individual social capital is the glue that binds the dispersed nodes of the multinational network together. Individual networks form the microfoundations of the macrostructure we have called the differentiated network. As the need to tap the full potential of an MNC's dispersed assets increases, MNCs will have to devote ever-greater resources to enhancing the social capital of their members because only then will they be able to realize their objective of maximizing their potential for value creation.

Part Three

Limits and Extensions
of the Differentiated Network

Chapter Nine

Requisite Complexity

One of the most enduring ideas of organization theory is that an organization's structure and management processes must fit its environment. In this book, we have argued that the modern MNC is increasingly confronting an environment that demands a more complex organization structure than the traditional hierarchy or other unitary structures such as the area, global product, or matrix proposed by scholars such as Stopford and Wells (1972). To be effective in an environment that requires simultaneous emphasis on local responsiveness and global integration, the MNC must adopt a differentiated network structure. Its structure must be internally differentiated to respond to the unique contingencies presented by the various environments in which it operates. At the same time, if the MNC is to be more than simply a chain of units strung across the world, these units must be integrated into a network, bound by a common purpose and values and by ongoing resource and communication flows.

Though the differentiated network is the new ideal toward which we see MNCs evolving, it is important to recognize that this new structure is more complex than traditional structures. The additional administrative complexity should be embraced only if it is warranted by the environment in which the MNC operates. It is most worthwhile if the environment requires both local responsiveness and global integration. If one, or both, of these demands is less stringent, it may not be worthwhile for the MNC to assume the added complexity. Put simply, in organizing the MNC, we should be guided by Ashby's principle of requisite complexity (1956): the complexity of a firm's structure must match the complexity of its environment.

This chapter offers a framework for classifying the environments and structural forms of MNCs and hypothesizes fit relationships based on these classifications. We demonstrate that organizational fit is positively correlated with multinational performance. Data on forty-one companies from the third phase of our study—the large sample survey of U.S. and European MNCs—are used to develop and test these ideas (see Table 9.1 for a listing of these companies and their principal businesses).

Classifying the Environments of MNCs

Each MNC subsidiary operates in a different national environment. In each country, the local subsidiary must be responsive to local customers, institutions, governments, and regulatory agencies for its ongoing institutional legitimacy and economic success. To some extent, then, the MNC must respond to the different contingencies presented by each of the multiple environments in which it operates. These local contingencies are categorized in the multinational management literature as "forces for national responsiveness" (Prahalad and Doz, 1987).

The different local environments in which the MNC operates may also be linked for a number of reasons: common customer preferences across countries; economies of scale, scope, and national comparative advantage that create incentives for global specialization and interdependence; knowledge developed in one environment that is transferable or adaptable in another; and transnational customers, suppliers, competitors, and even regulatory agencies (such as the European Union). These linkages across national boundaries pressure the subsidiaries to coordinate their activities; they are described as "forces for global integration" (Prahalad and Doz, 1987).[1]

These two forces—for national responsiveness and for global integration—are not opposite ends of a spectrum. Rather, they

Table 9.1. The MNCs Surveyed and Their Principal Businesses.

Company	Home Country	Principal Industry
Air Products and Chemicals	United States	Industrial chemicals
Alcan	Canada	Nonferrous metals
Baker International	United States	Machinery
Bertelsmann	Germany	Printing and publishing
Blue Bell	United States	Textiles
British-American Tobacco (BAT)	United Kingdom	Tobacco
BSN Groupe	France	Food
Caterpillar	United States	Construction and mining machinery
Colgate-Palmolive	United States	Packaged Goods
Continental Group	United States	Metals
Cummins	United States	Engines
Deere	United States	Construction and mining machinery
Digital Equipment	United States	Computers
Du Pont	United States	Chemicals
Electrolux	Sweden	Household appliances
Emhart	United States	Machinery
Firestone	United States	Rubber
Freuhauf	United States	Automobiles
Friedrich Krupp	Germany	Metals
General Foods	United States	Food
General Motors	United States	Automobiles
Glaxo	United Kingdom	Drugs and pharmaceuticals
Hoechst	Germany	Chemicals
Honeywell	United States	Scientific measuring instruments
ICI	United Kingdom	Chemicals
Jacobs Suchard	Switzerland	Food
Kodak	United States	Photographic equipment
Mannesmann	Germany	Metals
Norsk Hydro	Norway	Chemicals
Norton	United States	Machinery
R.J. Reynolds	United States	Tobacco
Reckitt & Colman	United Kingdom	Drugs and pharmaceuticals
Rio Tinto-Zinc	United Kingdom	Metals
Schneider	France	Machinery
Seagram	Canada	Beverages
Siemens	Germany	Machinery
Solvay	Belgium	Chemicals
Swedish Match	Sweden	Paper and forestry
Timken	United States	Machinery
United Biscuits	United Kingdom	Food
Volvo	Sweden	Automobiles

represent separate and somewhat orthogonal dimensions: a company with a weak force for national responsiveness does not automatically have a strong force for global integration, or vice versa. Consequently, the environmental contingencies faced by the MNC as a whole can be conceived as the extent to which it must respond to strong and unique national environments and the linkages across these national environments (Prahalad and Doz, 1987). On the basis of these two contingencies, we distinguish broadly among four environmental conditions that MNCs face: (1) a *global environment* in which the forces for global integration are strong and for local responsiveness weak, (2) a *multinational environment* in which the forces for national responsiveness are strong and for global integration weak, (3) a *transnational environment* in which both contingencies are strong, and (4) an *international environment* in which both contingencies are weak.[2]

Proceeding with this classification scheme requires a way to measure the forces for global integration and national responsiveness for a particular industry. To measure global integration, we use Kobrin's "index of integration" (1991): the ratio of the total intrafirm trade (the sum of affiliate-to-affiliate, affiliate-to-parent, and parent-to-affiliate sales) to the total international sales (sum of total sales of parent and of all affiliates) of the MNCs in an industry.

Kobrin (1991) argues that global integration cannot be measured simply on the basis of bilateral flows. One must also consider the overall system of interdependent relationships: "Transnational integration implies more than interdependence in the sense that events in one business environment significantly influence those in another; it implies dependence of subsidiaries on the multinational system" (p. 21). According to Kobrin, the cross-flow of products within the total MNC system, aggregated to all MNCs in the industry, provides one of the most effective ways to measure the forces of global integration. It allows for a systematic and data-driven specification of global industries and avoids the pitfalls of anecdotal and descriptive evidence. Also, the actual measures based on this approach correlate highly with industry research and development intensity (a widely used proxy for the forces of global integration) and are, as Kobrin argues, "certainly in accord with an intuitive, case-study based concept of global integration" (p. 21).

Kobrin's index is a continuous variable, and as he notes, any particular cutoff point to delineate "high" and "low" categories is bound to be somewhat arbitrary. The cutoff point we choose here is 20 percent (intrafirm trade as a percentage of total sales). Based on this threshold, businesses such as automobiles (44 percent), computers (38 percent), photographic equipment (32 percent), engines (30 percent), scientific measuring instruments (29 percent), industrial chemicals (26 percent), nonferrous metals (23 percent), pharmaceuticals (21 percent), and construction and mining machinery (21 percent) are seen as confronting strong forces of global integration. The remaining businesses confront weak forces for global integration.

To measure national responsiveness, two indicators are used. The first is the advertising-to-sales ratio of the industry, as published in *Advertising Age*. The second is an average of the values received on the questionnaire for the extent of local regulation, by industry (for example, the ratings given by computer companies surveyed on the extent of local regulations were averaged to determine the computer industry average). The two measures are only weakly correlated (rank correlation .32, p = 0.11). Given that both regulations and customer preferences can act as powerful forces for local responsiveness, any business falling above the sample mean on either of these indicators is categorized as facing strong forces of national responsiveness, and one that falls below on both indicators is assumed to face relatively weak forces of national responsiveness.

Figure 9.1 shows how juxtaposition of these two indicators leads to the assignment of the various business environments to the international, multinational, global, and transnational categories. Businesses such as pharmaceuticals, telecommunications, automobiles, and computers simultaneously face strong demands for both global integration and local responsiveness, corresponding to a transnational environment. In computers, for instance, the growing commoditization of hardware, high capital intensity, and scale economics constitute powerful forces for global integration. At the same time, the increasing market demands for integration of hardware with software and services providing "solutions" to customer problems create equally strong needs for local responsiveness. Similarly, while pharmaceutical companies require a strong global network through which they may quickly and efficiently diffuse innovations to all national subsidiaries, dramatic differences in governmental drug-testing regulations and in health care delivery systems across countries demand simultaneously a high degree of national responsiveness.

The weak-weak combination of national responsiveness and integration forces means that MNCs dealing in metals, machinery, paper, textiles, and printing and publishing confront international environments. The business of producing and marketing cement

**Figure 9.1. The Environment of MNCs:
Classification of Businesses.**

		Global Environment	Transnational Environment
Forces for Global Integration	Strong	Construction and mining machinery Nonferrous metals Industrial chemicals Scientific measuring instruments Engines	Drugs and pharmaceuticals Photographic equipment Computers Automobiles
	Weak	International Environment Metals (other than nonferrous) Machinery Paper Textiles Printing and publishing	Multinational Environment Beverages Food Rubber Household appliances Tobacco
		Weak	Strong

Forces for Local Responsiveness

provides a tangible demonstration of this environment's attributes. Cement products are highly standardized, and marketing and distribution systems are similar across countries. As a result, demands for local responsiveness are weak. However, the trade-offs between the economics of cement production and transportation costs are such that global integration of cement production is not attractive.

Global environments contain strong forces for global integration alongside weak forces for local responsiveness. MNCs in the businesses of construction and mining machinery, nonferrous metals, industrial chemicals, scientific measuring instruments, and engines operate in global environments. For instance, with their high capital intensities and significant scale economies, semiconductors and airplane engines confront strong forces for global integration but relatively weak forces for national responsiveness because product standardization is relatively high and customer demands are relatively uniform in different geographic markets. The presence of scale economies and uniform product standards also combine to make construction machinery and industrial chemical businesses global environments.

Finally, strong forces for national responsiveness and weak forces for integration in the beverages, food, rubber, household appliances, and tobacco industries classify them as multinational environments. To illustrate, nonbranded foods and household appliances are likely to face weak forces for global integration due to an absence of scale economies and lack of dependence on an innovation infrastructure. Both of these businesses, however, face strong demands for national responsiveness because of differences in consumer preferences and variations in the nature and extent of government regulation across countries.

Classifying the Structure of MNCs

The main criticism of models that define MNC structure in terms of function, geography, product division, or a matrix has been that the formal organizational chart is a poor representation of how an organization actually functions. Organizations represent a set of relationships among individuals, groups, and units; and very different relationship patterns can flourish within the same formal structure. Consequently, to understand, describe, or categorize organizations, one must focus on the pattern of these relationships. One of the ways in which an MNC's structure may be better conceived is in terms of the nexus of the relationships between the various national subsidiaries and the headquarters.

The nature of each headquarters-subsidiary relationship is the basic unit in this conceptualization. As explained earlier, these relationships can be described in terms of the three basic governance mechanisms that underlie them: centralization, formalization, and normative integration. Whereas analyses of MNC organizations have often assumed that headquarters-subsidiary relationships are identical for all subsidiaries throughout the company, as we showed in Chapter Five, each headquarters-subsidiary relation can be governed by a different combination of various structural mechanisms.[3] In this chapter, the understanding of internal differentiation within the multinational is advanced by conceptualizing the MNC's overall structure in terms of the pattern of variation in its different headquarters-subsidiary relationships.

Using Lawrence and Lorsch's dimensions of differentiation and integration (1967), MNC structures are seen as exhibiting four patterns. In the first structure—*structural uniformity*—there is little variance in how the different subsidiaries are managed, and a common "company way" is adopted for the governance of all headquarters-subsidiary relationships. The emphasis may be on one of the three governance mechanisms or a combination. Of central importance is a strong and uniform governance mechanism for the whole company; overall integration is high, and there is little attention to differentiation.

A second structure—*differentiated fit*—represents companies that adopt different governance modes to fit each subsidiary's local context. In Chapter Five, a scheme was developed that matches structures to subsidiary contexts.[4] When a company recognizes differences in these local contexts, it can explicitly differentiate its headquarters-subsidiary relationships to ensure that the management processes fit each local context. A company that applies this strategy to every headquarters-subsidiary relation in the firm adopts the differentiated fit structure. Stated another way, a manager who strictly applies the prescriptions of Chapter Five will create a set of headquarters-subsidiary relations that correspond exactly to differentiated fit for the MNC as a whole as defined here. Note that differentiation is the dominant characteristic of this structure and that it lacks a strong firmwide integrative mechanism.

A third pattern is one in which there is neither a dominant integrative mechanism nor an explicit pattern of differentiation to match local contexts. We believe that the structure of these MNCs betrays a lack of a coherent organizing logic and accordingly label this pattern *ad hoc variation*.

The final structural pattern is evident when a firm adopts the logic of differentiated fit but overlays the distinctly structured relationships with a dominant overall integrative mechanism—whether through strong centralization, formalization, or normative integration. Such structures are *differentiated networks* the model of MNCs we have advocated in this book.

The following procedure was adopted to place each of the forty-one companies in one of these four structural categories. First, the measures of centralization, formalization, and normative integration were aggregated for all of a company's subsidiaries to arrive at a firmwide average of these measures. These averages were used as indicators of the strength of the firm's integrative mechanisms. When a firm's average measure for any of these three structural variables exceeded the median value across all the firms in the sample, the company was considered to have a strong integrative mechanism along that dimension; otherwise, it was considered to have a weak integrative mechanism along that dimension (see Figure 9.2).

Some of the companies appear to have strong integrative mechanisms along a single dimension.[5] For example, Seagram, Jacobs Suchard, Reckitt & Colman, and Colgate-Palmolive appear

Figure 9.2. Mapping Integration and Differentiation.

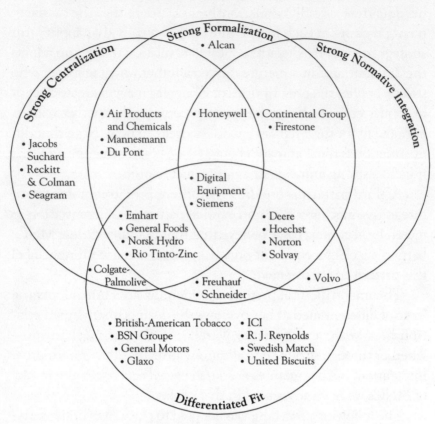

Weak Differentiation and Weak Integration

Baker International

Bertelsmann

Blue Bell

Caterpillar

Cummins

Electrolux

Friedrich Krupp

Kodak

Timken

to have a high level of centralization; Alcan, Freuhauf, and Schneider demonstrate a high level of formalization; and Volvo exhibits strong normative integration throughout the company. Detailed case studies on all of the companies do not exist to cross-check these survey findings, but the results are consistent with some widely known management systems in these firms. Seagram, for example, is known for its extremely strong and highly centralized financial control system: all sales proceeds deposited in its subsidiaries' bank accounts are transferred daily to a central account managed by corporate headquarters while the central account remits to each local bank account the amounts required to cover specific operating expenses. Alcan's worldwide planning systems are well known, and Volvo's long-term efforts to pioneer a new work style and corporate culture have often been hailed as unique among Western automobile companies.

Other firms appear to have strong integrative mechanisms along multiple dimensions. Du Pont, Air Products and Chemicals, Mannesmann, General Foods, Emhart, Norsk Hydro, and Rio Tinto-Zinc appear to have strong levels of both centralization and formalization; Deere, Firestone, Continental Group, Hoechst, Norton, and Solvay combine formalization with strong firmwide normative integration. Others, like Digital Equipment, Siemens, and Honeywell, exhibit high levels of all three mechanisms. Again, the findings are consistent with what little we know about some of these companies. Digital, for example, has long had highly centralized engineering, product development, and base product marketing functions; has built elaborate formal rules and systems for revenue and profit planning, pricing and discounts, and manufacturing; and enjoys a strong set of shared values concerning management of people, commitment to individual initiatives, and working through consensus.

The remaining companies in the sample show a lack of strong firmwide integration along any of the three dimensions. They do not have uniform, centralized control over their worldwide activities to any significant extent. They lack institutionalized rules and procedures as well as the glue of any strongly shared norms, values, and culture.

The extent of structural differentiation was measured by comparing the fit between each subsidiary's local context and the type of relationship it had with headquarters in the manner employed in Chapter Five. For each company, the extent of differentiation was measured as the ratio of the number of its "fit" to its "misfit" subsidiaries. When this ratio for a company exceeded the median value for the sample, it was classified as strongly differentiated in its structure; otherwise, the company was classified as weakly differentiated.

Figure 9.3 shows the results of this analysis, superimposed on the preceding analysis of integrative mechanisms. It shows how the forty-one companies in our survey are distributed among the four structural categories we have proposed.

Some of the companies in the sample, such as Caterpillar, Cummins, Baker International, Bertelsmann, Blue Bell, Friedrich Krupp, Kodak, Timken, and Electrolux, appear to lack systematic differentiation and have no strong integrative mechanism either. These correspond to the overall category of ad hoc variation.

Others, such as General Motors, Glaxo, BSN Groupe, British-American Tobacco, ICI, R.J. Reynolds, Swedish Match, and United Biscuits, appear to have strong and systematic internal differentiation but lack strong firmwide integration; these correspond to our differentiated fit category.

Firms such as Digital, Siemens, General Foods, Emhart, Norsk Hydro, Rio Tinto-Zinc, Colgate-Palmolive, Freuhauf, Schneider, Deere, Hoechst, Norton, and Solvay have strong differentiation as well as strong integration (through one or more of the three integration mechanisms); these are placed in the differentiated network category.

Finally, the remaining companies demonstrate high integration through one mechanism or a combination of the three mechanisms but are not systematically differentiated internally. These firms belong to the category we have described as structural uniformity.

**Figure 9.3. The Structure of MNCs:
Classification of Companies.**

	Structural Uniformity	Differentiated Network
High	Air Products and Chemicals Alcan Continental Group Du Pont Firestone Honeywell Jacobs Suchard Mannesmann Reckitt & Colman Seagram	Colgate-Palmolive Deere Digital Equipment Emhart Freuhauf General Foods Hoechst Norsk Hydro Norton Rio Tinto-Zinc Schneider Solvay Volvo
	Ad Hoc Variation	Differentiated Fit
Low	Baker International Bertelsmann Blue Bell Caterpillar Cummins Electrolux Friedrich Krupp Kodak Timken	British-American Tobacco BSN Groupe General Motors Glaxo ICI R. J. Reynolds Swedish Match United Biscuits
	Low	High

Structural Integration (vertical axis)

Structural Differentiation (horizontal axis)

Organization-Environment Fit

Our basic argument is that for effective performance, the MNC's organization structure should fit its overall environmental contingencies. We hypothesize that structural uniformity is best suited to global environmental conditions, differentiated fit to multinational environments, differentiated networks to transnational environments, and the ad hoc variety to international environments.

The logic underlying these hypotheses is straightforward. In global environments, cross-national linkages create forces for firmwide coordination that predominate over the local environmental forces. A common integrative structure in these situations not only enables the MNC to respond to these linkages across these environments but also economizes on the administrative burden that managing a highly differentiated system imposes.

In multinational environments, in contrast, the MNC must respond to the local environments to be competitive. The most effective structures are likely to be those that are differentiated to respond to the local environments' needs. Here the administrative burden of a complex differentiated system is almost a cost of doing business, but the MNC must avoid the additional administrative complexity of a strong overlying integrative mechanism.

Placid international environments have neither strong forces of differentiation nor strong forces of integration, and a company in such a situation derives little benefit from systematic organization design. Such a firm can probably avoid the costs of both differentiation and integration.

In transnational environments, it is important for the MNC to be responsive not only to local contingencies but also to cross-national linkages. It needs a structure of requisite differentiation overlaid with a strong companywide integrative mechanism. Here the administrative costs of a complex organizing structure like the differentiated network are both necessary and justified.

It is the competing costs and benefits of differentiation and integration that underlie these issues of fit. In principle, if there were no administrative cost associated with organizational complexity, one might always recommend the differentiated network structure because such a structure would be best able to respond to minor variations in environments as well as to a great variety of linkages. But the costs associated with administrative complexity are significant and thus lead us to the idea of requisite complexity.

To test these hypotheses, the environmental (Figure 9.1) and structural (Figure 9.3) classifications of the forty-one companies were juxtaposed, as shown in Figure 9.4; each cell in this figure represents a particular environment-structure combination. Cell 1, for example, identifies those companies that, during the study period, confronted an environment of relatively weak forces of both global integration and local responsiveness and whose organizations were neither strongly differentiated internally nor strongly integrated through firmwide mechanisms. Such a combination—an international environment and an ad hoc variation organization—represents a good fit and, according to our theory, should on average outperform firms in cells 2, 3, and 4, which operate with the same relatively simple organizational approach but face the more complex multinational, global, or transnational environments. Similarly, the firms in cell 1 should also outperform, on average, firms in cells 5, 9, and 13 because these companies adopt the more complex organizational approaches, thereby expending effort and resources on organizational integration and differentiation that are not necessary for responding to the demands of their relatively simple international environment.

Following this logic, it becomes clear that the seventeen companies in the four diagonal cells (1, 6, 11, and 16)—all of which represent good environment-structure fits—should, on average, outperform the twenty-four companies in the other twelve cells, all of which represent misfits. As shown in Table 9.2, the actual performance of these forty-one companies conforms to our prediction. On all three dimensions of performance—average return on net assets, growth in these returns, and revenue growth—the seventeen companies representing good environment-structure fit outperform the twenty-four companies that lack such fit by statistically significant margins.

Conclusions

In the recent past, MNC managers have been on the receiving end of a diverse and often conflicting set of organizational prescriptions. On the one hand, influential academics and consultants have urged them to abandon simplistic structures and processes and to build multidimensional network organizations

Figure 9.4. Mapping Environment and Structure.

Structure	International	Multinational	Global	Transnational
Differentiated Network	Emhart Norton Rio Tinto-Zinc Schneider Siemens (Cell 13)	General Foods (Cell 14)	Deere Hoechst Norsk Hydro Solvay (Cell 15)	Colgate-Palmolive Digital Equipment Freuhauf Volvo (Cell 16)
Structural Uniformity	Continental Group Mannesmann (Cell 9)	Firestone Jacobs Suchard Seagram (Cell 10)	Air Products and Chemical Alcan Du Pont Honeywell (Cell 11)	Reckitt & Colman (Cell 12)
Differentiated Fit	Swedish Match (Cell 5)	British-American Tobacco BSN Groupe R. J. Reynolds United Biscuits (Cell 6)	ICI (Cell 7)	General Motors Glaxo (Cell 8)
Ad Hoc Variation	Baker International Bertelsmann Blue Bell Friedrich Krupp Timken (Cell 1)	Electrolux (Cell 2)	Caterpillar Cummins (Cell 3)	Kodak (Cell 4)

Environment

with distributed management roles and tasks, overlapping responsibilities and relationships, and built-in ambiguity and redundancy (see Hedlund, 1986). On the other hand, equally strong voices have argued that the performance problems faced by many large MNCs are attributable to the complexities of their organizations and that managers must reestablish organizational simplicity by reverting to direct decision making and unambiguous accountability (Tichy and Charan, 1989; Eccles and Nohria, 1992). The intense advocacy accompanying these arguments has made it difficult for managers to get a perspective on such diverse prescriptions.

The issues raised in this chapter can be useful to these managers. What managers must remember is that it is the *appropriate*

Table 9.2. Performance of Companies with Environment-Structure Fit and Misfit.

Performance Measures	Companies in Cells 1, 6, 11, and 16 (Diagonal = Fit)	Companies in Cells 2, 3, 4, 5, 7, 8, 9, 10, 12, 13, 14, and 15 (Others = Misfit)	p Value Difference
Average RONA (1982–1986)	5.72	3.69	< .001
RONA growth (1982–1986)	6.41	2.32	< .001
Revenue growth (1982–1986)	7.19	4.98	< .001

level of organizational complexity that leads to effective performance in multiunit organizations like MNCs. Managers thus require a detailed understanding of their companies' environmental demands to evaluate the kind of organizational capabilities they need to build. Unnecessary organizational complexity in a relatively simple business environment can be just as unproductive as unresponsive simplicity in a complex business environment. What we have offered in this chapter is a simple framework for analyzing these environmental demands and for selecting the appropriate organization structure.

As a brief aside, though our focus is on the MNC, the argument we have advanced here can easily be extended to any multidivisional firm. Consider the case of a firm in which each division operates in a different market or business segment. The overall environmental contingencies this firm faces can be characterized by the extent to which each of its business segments has unique and strong forces for local responsiveness and by the extent to which these businesses are linked. This is similar to identifying the nature of the firm's diversification, whether it is in related or unrelated business segments. Similarly, the firm's overall structure can be conceived in terms of the pattern of variation in the governance of the different corporate-division relationships. Again, the same four structural patterns may be identified, and we would expect the environment-structure fit to follow the logic of requisite complexity. In this situation, then, all we have done is change the source of environmental variation from geography, in the case of MNCs, to different business segments, in the case of the multiproduct firm. Of course, in some situations, the source of environmental variation in the firm's units may well be driven by both geography and product markets. Though operationally more complex, this situation can just as easily be accommodated under the same general theoretical rubric.

None of the foregoing analysis should be interpreted to imply that determining and adopting the optimal organizational form for a company is a simple or seamless process. As pointed out, managers must possess a profound understanding of the business environment in which they are operating to decide which organizational form is most appropriate for addressing the challenges of the particular environment. Even if a manager successfully identifies the ideal type of structure the firm needs, achieving the institutional change necessary to implement it presents an additional obstacle. Selecting the appropriate structure is not an easy task; learning to manage it may be just as difficult.

Moreover, environmental demands evolve over time, and managers need to adopt a dynamic view of their organizational capabilities. In the food and beverage business, for example, the forces of global integration appear to be getting stronger by the day, driven by, among other factors, the growing importance of international brands. In scientific measuring instruments, by contrast, the need for local responsiveness is increasing as stand-alone products are giving way to integrated systems consisting of packages of hardware, software, and related services. These and many other businesses are thus evolving toward the transnational category, and companies operating in them may need to embrace a differentiated network structure. Managers have to be sensitive to such changes in environmental demands; ideally, they should anticipate and drive such changes. Nevertheless, the first step in successful management of an MNC is an understanding of the relationship between the structure of the multinational and its operating environment. The framework proposed in this chapter is designed to advance this understanding.

Notes

1. For one of the earliest descriptions of MNC environments in these terms, see Fayerweather (1978); for one of the most comprehensive elaborations, see Prahalad and Doz (1987). For a discussion of the factors that drive the needs for global integration and national responsiveness, see Yip (1989).

2. Our characterization and terminology need some clarification. Bartlett and Ghoshal (1989) considered three sets of environmental forces: global integration, national responsiveness, and worldwide learning. Strong demands along each of these dimensions were characterized as "global," "multinational," and "international" industries, respectively, whereas "transnational" industries were defined as those facing strong demands simultaneously along all three dimensions. In this chapter, we use the relatively simpler two-dimensional conceptualization proposed by Prahalad and Doz (1987). In our framework, global and multinational industries are defined the same way as in Bartlett and Ghoshal (1989), but international and transnational industries are defined as those facing weak-weak and strong-strong combinations of the forces of global integration and national responsiveness. This characterization is consistent with the use of the terminology in Bartlett (1986), except that he did not define the "international" industry environment explicitly in that paper.

3. For a review of the evidence and arguments for internal differentiation in headquarters-subsidiary relationships, see Gupta and Govindarajan (1991).

4. See Chapter Five. For alternative conceptualizations of subsidiary context, see Poynter and Rugman (1982) and Gupta and Govindarajan (1991).

5. It is interesting to observe that there is one null set in this analysis: none of the companies combines high levels of centralization and socialization while lacking formalized systems. Perhaps this is merely an artifact of the sample or a reflection of measurement error. Or this combination may be administratively infeasible. This may be a starting point for future study, although it is only speculative at this stage.

Chapter Ten

Beyond the Differentiated Network

In this book, we proposed a new model of the multinational corporation—the differentiated network. This model has several virtues over traditional models of the MNC. First, it is descriptively a more accurate conceptualization of the structure of most contemporary MNCs. As we saw in Chapter One, the structure of MNCs such as Philips can no longer be easily understood in terms of broad structural archetypes such as an area, product, or matrix form. A network perspective is almost mandatory for capturing the inherent complexity of the modern MNC.

The second virtue of the differentiated network is that in addition to being a descriptive model, it is also an ideal type, on the same order as Weber's hierarchy (1946). The differentiated network provides a normative ideal for the design of the modern MNC. It recommends that the internal organization of the MNC be differentiated to meet the contingencies of its various national subsidiaries. At the same time, these differentiated parts must be integrated by means of mechanisms such as shared values and formal and informal communication flows.

Finally, viewing the MNC as a differentiated network also has significant analytical advantages. As we have demonstrated through the various empirical analyses in this book, this model offers a powerful framework that can be used to examine structural effects in MNCs. The model offers new ways for us to extend our understanding of organization-environment relations in MNCs and their effect on firm performance.

In Chapter Nine, we argued that although MNCs increasingly need to be organized as differentiated networks, this model should not be regarded as universally applicable. Indeed, it should be embraced only if the MNC is facing a transnational environment. In a sense, we placed some bounds on the scope of the differentiated network as defined by the principle of requisite complexity.

In this chapter, we explore two directions in which the differentiated network model may be extended. The first is to recognize that the environment of the MNC is itself a network of other organizations such as customers, suppliers, regulators, and competitors with which the different units of the MNC interact (Nohria and Eccles, 1992). Hence the MNC can in fact be viewed as a differentiated network embedded in a larger network. Although we do not explore this idea empirically in this chapter, we outline some ways in which this broader network perspective can be pursued.

The second direction in which we extend our thinking is to explore more fully the theme of value creation as the source of the MNC's organizational advantage. We argue that traditional theories of the firm—which have also been used to explain the existence of MNCs—are essentially negative theories. They explain the existence of firms as the outcome of market failures. Markets serve as the optimal way to organize economic activity in these theories. We suggest that a positive theory of the MNC can be constructed on the premise that the shared social context that a firm provides allows it to combine and exchange resources, including knowledge, far better than markets ever can. Thus if value creation rather than value appropriation is the engine of economic progress, firms may have a positive role in society that market failure–based theories of the firm are unable to identify or illuminate.

The Multinational Within an External Network

Consider a multinational corporation with operating units in a number of countries and a headquarters unit. For the purpose of analytical simplicity, assume that all units of this multinational are engaged in a single and common business. All the relationships and linkages existing among the different units of this multinational constitute the multinational network studied in the preceding chapters.

Each of the national operating units of the multinational is in turn embedded in a unique context in which each has connections to various units outside the multinational (Aldrich and Whetten, 1981). For example, a national subsidiary can have existing or potential exchange relationships with a specific set of suppliers, buyers, and regulatory agencies; it competes for resources with an identifiable set of competitors. These different entities in each national environment are also connected to each other in various ways. The density of a particular national environment is one measure of the extensiveness of exchange ties within it (Aldrich and Whetten, 1981). For example, density may be thought of as the percentage of actual to potential ties among the different units in a single national context.

Of course, the density of such connections in different national contexts may vary. For example, it has been noted by many authors that the level of connectedness among different members of an industry group is significantly higher in Japan than in some Western countries. Similarly, it has been shown in the management literature that in the same national environment, the level of cohesiveness among customers, suppliers, and competitors may be higher in certain businesses (such as construction, publishing, textiles, and investment banking) than others (see Granovetter, 1985).

The national environments in which the multinational has subsidiaries may themselves be interconnected through exchange ties. For example, one of the supplying organizations in the local environment of one country may be an affiliated unit of another multinational company, and it may have exchange linkages with its counterpart in the local environment of another country. Similarly, the actions of regulatory agencies in one nation may influence the actions of their counterparts in other nations, as demonstrated by recent events surrounding the outbreak of mad cow disease in the United Kingdom. Such influence may be manifested in actions such as retaliation by one nation to another's perceived protectionist action or deregulation by a regulatory agency in response to similar actions taken elsewhere (Mahini and Wells, 1986). These linkages may also exist among suppliers and competitors. In fact, much of the current literature on global strategy considers such cross-border linkages among customers, competitors, and other relevant participants as a key factor that influences the behaviors of MNCs (see Eccles, 1981; Powell, 1985; Sabel, Herrigel, Kazis, and Deeg, 1987; and Eccles and Crane, 1987).

Because of such linkages among the national environments, all entities in all national environments in which the multinational has subsidiaries collectively constitute the external network within which the multinational network is embedded (Tichy, Tushman, and Fombrun, 1979). In the same manner as the construct of density was defined for each of the different national contexts, one can also describe the density of this external network as the ratio of actual to potential ties among all the MNC's external constituents. For purposes of analysis, it is important to differentiate between these two densities—density within a single national environment versus density across the various national environments.

The basic argument we wish to advance is that different attributes of the MNC can be explained in terms of selected attributes of the external network within which it is embedded. Indeed, each of the four major structural characteristics of the MNC's internal network—the configuration of resources, the formal structure of headquarters-subsidiary relations, the extent of normative integration, and lateral and vertical communication—will be influenced by the external network in which the MNC is embedded. Discussing all these influences is beyond the scope of this chapter—that would require a whole new book. Here we simply illustrate the utility of this extended network perspective by briefly sketching how the two types of densities in the external network identified earlier can potentially influence one of the key features of the internal network—the configuration of resources.[1]

Resource Configuration in MNCs

Resources such as production equipment, finance, technology, marketing skills, and management capabilities may be located in one or more of the various subsidiaries of the multinational. The term *resource configuration* refers to the way in which the resources of a multinational are distributed among the national subsidiaries (see Porter, 1986). In companies Bartlett (1986) described as "centralized hubs," most of these resources are concentrated in one location, typically the parent company. For example, 90 percent of the manufacturing investments of Matsushita, the Japanese consumer electronics company, and 100 percent of its research facilities are located in Japan. In contrast, for Philips, Matsushita's European competitor, which Bartlett categorized as a "decentralized federation," over 77 percent of total assets are located outside the company's home in the Netherlands, and no single national subsidiary has more than 15 percent of the company's worldwide assets. This difference illustrates dispersal, a dimension of the resource configuration indicating the extent to which a company's resources are concentrated in one unit or dispersed among different units.

However, although both Philips and Electrolux, the Swedish home appliance company, have a relatively high level of dispersal, with both companies having significant parts of their total assets distributed in a number of countries, the pattern of asset distribution is very different in the two cases. Consider their resources within Europe. Even though Electrolux's resources are dispersed, they also are very specialized; that is, the resources and associated activities located in any one country are of sufficient scale to meet the company's worldwide or regional requirements for that activity, avoiding the need to carry out that activity or task in multiple locations. For example, Electrolux's washing machine factory in France produces top-loading washing machines only, and it meets the company's requirements in that product category for all of Europe. Similarly, the washing machine factory in Italy produces only front-loading models to meet Europe-wide demand. Its research centers, product development laboratories, and component-producing units are all similarly differentiated and specialized. By contrast, despite considerable recent efforts to increase specialization, Philips owns five factories in Europe that produce identical or near-identical models of television sets, each basically for a local market. In other words, the resources of Philips are dispersed on a local-for-local basis. They are dispersed but undifferentiated, with identical resources being used by each unit to carry out essentially similar tasks in and for its own local environment. This dimension of resource configuration is referred to as *specialization;* it represents the extent to which the resources located in each unit are differentiated from those in others.

Resource configuration in MNCs is traditionally analyzed from an economic perspective, typically under the assumption that resource location decisions are based on rational, self-interested considerations such as increasing profitability, gaining access to new markets or desired factors of production, protecting competitive position, and minimizing costs and risks.[2] Explanations of both dispersal and specialization have therefore focused on factors such as differences in costs of inputs, potential scale economies in different activities, impacts of transportation and other "friction costs," imperfections in information and other intermediate product markets, defense against opportunism, and potential benefits of risk diversification (see Buckley and Casson, 1985; Caves, 1982; Dunning, 1981; and Hennart, 1982).

Much of this analysis can be criticized as undersocialized or oversocialized conceptualizations ignoring the important and ongoing effects that surrounding social structures have on economic behaviors of organizations (Granovetter, 1985). An alternative framework is presented here relating dispersal and specialization to the densities of interactions both within and across the different national environments of the multinational. This conceptualization is strongly influenced by the work of institutional theorists who argue that the structure and behavior of organizations are influenced by both technical and institutional factors and that "organizations compete not just for resources and customers, but for political power and institutional legitimacy, for social as well as economic fitness" (Di Maggio and Powell, 1983, p. 150). As suggested by Westney (1989), for MNCs, strong needs for legitimacy and local isomorphism in each host-country environment coexist with a strong demand for efficiency within the worldwide system. Therefore, the institutional structure of the environment—the attributes of the local contexts and the external network—plays an important role in moderating the influence of technical and economic considerations. Even though different from traditional economic analysis, these arguments are much more consistent with recent work of economists such as Kogut (1988), who has shown the importance of institutional structures in determining the competitiveness of different countries and companies in different businesses.

Effects of Dense Interlinkages in the Subsidiary's National Environment

As Bower (1987) showed in his in-depth study of American, European, and Japanese companies in the petrochemical industry, the density of linkages among key players in a national industrial context greatly influences industry performance and company strategy. For a variety of economic, legal, sociological, cultural, and historical reasons, some countries, such as Japan, are characterized by dense linkages among the suppliers, producers, regulators, customers, and others involved in a particular field of industrial activity (Westney and Sakakibara, 1985). Such linkages among the various participants may involve different kinds of exchanges (funds, people, information), and they may be established and maintained through many different mechanisms such as integration of governmental agencies, interlocking boards of directors, cross-holding of equity, institutionalization of systems of personnel flows, reliance on long-term contracts and trust-based relationships, and organizations that play mediating roles such as trade associations, banks, and consultants (see Stevens, 1974; Porter, 1986; Hirsch, 1976; Magee, 1977; Rugman, 1981; Teece, 1986; and Lessard and Lightstone, 1986). Bower's study (1987) shows how Japanese petrochemical companies capitalized on such linkages, not only to build entry barriers in the local market but also as a means of restructuring and rationalizing the industry.

In locations where units in the local environment are densely connected, the implications for local units of MNCs are clear. Strong and multiplexed ties among the existing members within the national environment leads to exclusion of those who cannot establish equally strong and multiplexed ties with each member (Granovetter, 1985). Westney and Sakakibara's study (1985) on the R&D activities of Japanese and American computer companies illustrates this effect of density within a national environment. According to these authors, the Japanese R&D centers of some of the American computer companies could not tap into local skills and technologies because the absence of associated manufacturing and marketing activities prevented them from building linkages with the local "knowledge networks" embedded in the dense interactions among the various players in the Japanese computer industry.

Where the links in the national environment are sparse, no such barriers are created. This is clear in the U.S. Department of Commerce account of the American television industry in the early 1970s (Paul, 1984). The absence of ties among producers because of rivalry and antitrust laws, as well as their arm's-length relationships with suppliers, labor, and government, created an environment that made it easy for Japanese producers to enter the U.S. market and set up local sales offices to import finished products from the parent companies. However, when the American companies responded in a unified manner through the Electronics Industry Association and, with the support of labor unions and suppliers, were able to obtain government support on antidumping suits, the resulting politically negotiated import quotas forced the Japanese companies to establish local manufacturing facilities.

Therefore, the following propositions can be made about the effects of dense interlinkages within a national environment on the dispersal and specialization of resources in a multinational. When interaction densities within each national context are low, the social context is of limited influence, and intended economic rationality becomes dominant in resource configuration decisions. In this situation, the MNC will concentrate research, production, assembly, and other similar activities by considering potential scale and scope economies; it will locate them by the resource niches that exist in different countries as a result of their comparative advantages—for example, R&D in the United States or Japan, manufacturing in Singapore or Brazil (Aldrich, 1979). As a result, as shown in Figure 10.1, its overall resource configuration will show relatively low dispersal and high specialization. When such densities are high, however, the company will be forced to fragment its activities and locate more of the different kinds of resources in each market to provide the variety necessary to match the structures of the local environments. Consequently, in this case, dispersal will increase and specialization will decrease.

Effects of Dense Interlinkages Across the External Network

When the linkages across the national environments are sparse, the MNC's resource configuration follows the pattern described previously, based on consideration of the interlinkages within each national context alone. However, the existence of dense interactions among members of the various national contexts changes the situation significantly.

Consider the case of sparse interlinkages in each national context and dense interlinkages among different national environments. Low density within a local environment will lead to low dispersal and high specialization, and the company will locate its resources according to the resource niches in different countries. But with high cross-densities, many of these national resource niches are eliminated because of freer flows. If technologies developing in one

Figure 10.1. Effects of the External Network on Resource Configuration Within the MNC.

Density Within National Environment		Low (Density Across National Environment)	High (Density Across National Environment)
	High	Disperal: High Specialization: Low	Disperal: Moderate Specialization: High
	Low	Disperal: Low Specialization: High	Disperal: Low Specialization: Moderate

Density Across National Environment

location can be accessed instantaneously from another, or if excess capital available in one environment can be borrowed in markets located elsewhere, there is no longer a need to locate specific activities in specific places to benefit from access to local resources. Therefore, with high cross-densities, resource-seeking concentration will decline (though it will not necessarily be eliminated because regulatory and other barriers may selectively prohibit flows of certain people and products).

Chandler (1986), among others, has documented that improvements in communication and transportation infrastructures around the world have increased the density of interlinkages among different national environments and affected a wide range of industries in the recent past. The observed consequences of this trend are entirely consistent with the arguments advanced here. For example, until the late 1970s, the telecommunications switching industry was characterized by high density within each local context and low density across these contexts. Interactions among members of the industry were high within each country because of its status as a strategic industry and the resulting coordinating role of the national governments. However, until the advent of digital technology, the industry was highly regulated in most countries, and the need to synchronize the switching equipment with the idiosyncrasies of local terminal equipment constrained opportunities for cross-border linkages. As a result, the resources of most multinational companies were highly dispersed, with low levels of specialization. ITT provides a good illustration: each of its national subsidiaries in Europe had its own local facilities for product development, manufacturing, and marketing, and the corporate staff, including the top management, consisted of fewer than one hundred employees.

The context of this industry changed significantly in the 1980s. Although interlinkages within each national environment have remained dense, the density of interlinkages among these environments has increased substantially due to the emergence of digital technology and the growing trends of standardization and deregulation, all of which facilitated cross-border integration among suppliers, customers, and other industry participants. As a result, resource configurations of the producers also changed. Even though the overall level of dispersal was reduced to a limited extent, the level of specialization increased dramatically. Ericsson, for example, closed a few of its factories around the world, but many others were converted into focused manufacturing centers producing a narrow range of components. Similarly, each of the laboratories of Alcatel, the company created by the merger of ITT and CIT-Alcatel, has been given the mandate and resources to pursue a specific and well-defined technology or development task. This is in contrast to an earlier situation when most of them operated independently, developing the entire range of products for their local markets.

The Forces of Convergence

In the foregoing discussions of resource configuration in MNCs under different conditions of local and global interlinkages, several simplifying assumptions were made. The enormous complexity of several disparate country-level contexts and the diversity of the heterogeneous international business environment were dichotomized into high-low categories of densities of each type. In reality, the levels of connectedness within and across the national environments can be expected to vary across countries and groups of countries. Density of interactions across the national contexts may be high for the developed countries or among regional groupings but low in developing countries, particularly the more regulated and autarkical. Similarly, interactions among members within each local context may be high in homogeneous societies that have a tradition of strong interinstitutional linkages but low in countries where such linkages are discouraged through legislation, impeded because of societal heterogeneity, or rendered ineffective because of poor communication infrastructures or the absence of linking institutions.

Therefore, the configuration of resources in multinationals engaged in such businesses will be influenced by multiple criteria. In some locations, internal interactions within the national environment may be high, but external linkages with other environments may be low. In such locations, the MNC may provide all the required resources in appropriate measures so that its local unit can build and maintain linkages with key members of its own community. The environments in some other countries may be sparsely connected internally, but different elements of the local environment may be strongly connected with their counterparts in other countries. For these locations, the MNC may create a resource structure that is concentrated and specialized, and in some cases, the location of the specialized resources may reflect the desire to access special resource niches, whereas in other cases, the location choice may be motivated by the modalities in the external network. Finally, the environments in a third group of countries may be characterized by dense interlinkages both within and across national environments. In these locations, the MNC may establish all the complementary resources for integrated operations but may link these locations with others so as to leverage the resources and achieve economies of concentration and specialization.

The overall resource configuration for a company like Philips, then, will reflect a mix of some resources that are dispersed among some units on a purely local-for-local basis (for example, product development, manufacturing, marketing, and other resources for the lighting business in India), some that are concentrated in different countries to access specialized local resource pools (the global-scale audio factory in Singapore), and others that are concentrated in lead markets (development and manufacturing facilities for teletext television sets in the United Kingdom). In sum, its resource configuration will resemble that of the ideal differentiated network model of the MNC described in this book. Studies have shown that a number of large multinational companies, including Procter & Gamble, Unilever, Ericsson, NEC, and Matsushita, are increasingly converging to this structural form despite differences in business focus and parent-company nationality (Bartlett and Ghoshal, 1989).

Such a convergence is consistent with the theoretical arguments presented here because in most businesses, the interlinkages among actors, both within and across national boundaries, are increasing. When such linkages are low, the influence of structural embeddedness is low. MNCs have a greater degree of freedom to locate their activities and resources to benefit from local resource niches in line with the economic and technological characteristics of their businesses. In such situations, the resource configurations of different MNCs can be expected to differ as a reflection of differences in their businesses and as a result of their freedom to exercise strategic choices. However, in the context of dense interlinkages within and across different national environments, such freedom is reduced because of the network's influence. Both dispersal and specialization now become essential, at least for the very large MNCs that have been the focus of attention in this book. If density within a national market is a country trait and density among national environments is a world system trait, the pattern of linkages in the overall structure of the external network is going to be increasingly similar for large multinational companies, irrespective of their field of endeavor. In other words, mimetic and normative forces of isomorphism may be getting stronger as the world jolts along to Levitt's "global village" (1983), and the observed trend of convergence to the differentiated network structure may be an outcome of these broader societal changes (Di Maggio and Powell, 1983).

As indicated at the beginning of this chapter, extending the differentiated network model of the MNC developed in this book beyond the internal boundaries of the firm to include external networks requires further theoretical and empirical research. The necessary improvement and extension of these preliminary ideas will require both deductive theory building and more sophisticated use of network theory than has been presented here. In addition, empirical studies are also needed to test finer-grained propositions and hypotheses. This does not mean that the theory as presented is unsupported. On the contrary, where it has been tested, the theory has been strongly substantiated. Overall, the foregoing discussion should provide a hint of the potential of a broader network view of the multinational corporation.

Toward a Positive Theory of the Firm

The differentiated network model of relations within the MNC suggests a cogent reason for its extension to relations outside of the organization. At the same time, the idea of extending the network perspective in this way raises additional fundamental questions: If the components of the multinational are simply entities embedded within a larger external network, what determines what is inside and outside the firm? Are ownership and control relations simply historical and legal contingencies, or do they serve a more meaningful economic purpose? In other words, it raises questions that lie at the heart of the theory of the firm in general and the theory of the MNC (or foreign direct investment) in particular.

Historically, the literature on the strategy and organization of the multinational—the literature to which this book aims to contribute—has evolved largely independently of the literature that aims to explain why such companies exist. This separation between these two literatures has reflected a similar separation that has existed between theories of the firm, on the one hand, and theories of strategy and organization of firms, on the other.

However, as Conner and Prahalad (forthcoming) have so convincingly argued, this separation has become increasingly untenable. The question of how to structure and coordinate the various parts of a firm requires, as an essential component, a theory of when and what kind of advantages might be gained by organizing economic activity within a company instead of through arm's-length market relationships. Conceptualizing the firm as a differentiated network has only made the inherent link between these two issues even more obvious.

Our empirical studies were not aimed at answering the question of why a firm exists. Yet the different aspects of our analysis and findings do collectively suggest a coherent answer to this question that is considerably at variance from the currently dominant answers. We do not, at present, offer this answer as anything other than a plausible theoretical speculation. But it is an interesting speculation that has the potential for opening up a fruitful new line of academic inquiry.

The Multinational as an Agent for Value Creation

As we described in the very first paragraph of this book, currently dominant theories of the multinational firm emphasize the advantages of internalization for appropriation of the returns that are generated by a firm's internal resources and capabilities, more specifically by its internal stock of knowledge. Reflecting the more general formulation of the theory of the firm as it has evolved within the discipline of economics (Coase, 1937; Williamson, 1975, 1985; Milgrom and Roberts, 1992), theories of the MNC are grounded in the premise that under certain contingencies, markets do not provide adequate safeguards against opportunistic actions by human agents, and under such conditions of market failure, foreign direct investment provides the control necessary for the firm to enjoy the due benefits from its internalized knowledge, resources, and capabilities (Buckley and Casson, 1985; Hennart, 1982; Rugman, 1981).

In contrast to this view, focused as it is on value appropriation as the primary benefit of internalization, we have argued in this book that a key advantage of the multinational arises from its ability to create new value through the accumulation, transfer, and integration of different kinds of knowledge, resources, and capabilities across its dispersed organizational units. In the first part of the book, we provided evidence of such value creation in the form of a variety of innovation processes that utilize the dispersed resources of the multinational to create new products, processes, and administrative practices that are exploited both locally and globally. In other words, we have posited value creation instead of value appropriation as the *raison d'être* of the multinational.

Why might internalization offer some advantages over markets for such value creation? Kogut and Zander (1992) have already offered an initial answer to this question, grounded in their concept of "combinative capacity," that focuses on the factors that might allow a firm to generate, transfer, and integrate knowledge in a way that is not easily accessible to markets. One of the reasons for this advantage of firms over markets in creating new knowledge may lie in their ability to develop a shared code (Monteverde, 1995; Moldoveanu, Nohria, and Stevenson, 1996) that facilitates the transfer and integration of tacit knowledge (Polanyi, 1969) and enhances absorptive capacity (Cohen and Levinthal, 1990). Building on their arguments but generalizing beyond just knowledge creation, we believe that the value-creating role of firms may well lie in their broader ability to stimulate the combination and exchange of resources (of all types, including knowledge) in a way that markets cannot.

The creation of economic value, be it by individuals or by organizations (such as firms) in an economy, is a process that involves the use of economic resources. However, to produce something of value, these economic resources must somehow be combined. In other words, combining resources provides the basis for the creation of new and better products or new and better ways of making products (that is, obtaining greater productivity from given resources). To do this, either new resources have to be combined, or given resources have to be combined in new ways. In either case, as Schumpeter (1934, p. 66) argued, "to produce things, or the same things by a different method" or to "combine these materials and forces differently" constitutes "economic development." Such combinations represent "simply the different employment of the economic system's existing supplies of productive means" (p. 68).

However, although such combinations create and add to the economic system a new source of "potential" value, this potential value does not contribute directly to the creation of wealth. It shows up as wealth-enhancing economic value only when it becomes a part of the fabric of the economic system itself, as reflected in enhanced social productivity. Exchange is the primary mechanism through which this potential value is realized. Exchange validates the value of the resources exchanged and thereby promotes and sends a signal of the realization of the potential value that was previously created by new resource combinations. But exchange does more than just promote the realization of value and validate the process. It also assigns a value to and reorders the resources that are available for new combinations. Hence exchange also influences the way in which resources are deployed and the path taken in creating value. One can identify three conditions that must exist for any kind of resource to be exploited intentionally and voluntarily. First, the opportunity to deploy the resource in question must exist. Second, it must also be perceived to exist by the parties in question. Finally, the parties must be motivated to engage in the process of deploying the resource; in other words, the parties must expect to appropriate some value from the deployment.

It is important to note that although many resource deployments occur by accident (that is, without meeting any of these conditions) and many more are exploited on the faulty perception of an opportunity for value realization (that is, they fail to meet the first or second condition), all three conditions must be met before any purposive action can lead to the realization of potential value. Consequently, the significance of these three conditions for the deployment of resources arises from certain characteristics of resource accessibility and deployability in the real world. If we imagine a hypothetical world where people are completely rational, possess perfect foresight of future events and the ability to evaluate them, and otherwise experience no constraints on the accessibility and deployability of resources, there would be no reason why all possible resource combinations that would create value for the whole system would not be expected to occur. However, this hardly seems to be the case in the real world, where people are only boundedly rational (Simon, 1945) and where uncertainty and the costs associated with the deployment of resources will result in a different (and substantially smaller) set of executed combinations than what could be expected theoretically.

For example, if we assume satisfaction of the first condition (the existence of a resource and an opportunity to deploy it productively) as given, the satisfaction of the remaining two criteria is likely to be impeded, if not distorted, by uncertainty. Uncertainty surrounds many beneficial deployment opportunities and their associated effects, including the returns from such deployment. Information costs are incurred in defining, maintaining, and exercising the right to the resources, as well as in perceiving the opportunity. Note that these costs affect the deployment of resources and are incurred independent of any transaction taking place. Thus they have the potential to influence the exchange of the resources in ways that transaction costs alone may not. As a result, only a small fraction of the set of all potentially value-adding combinations will actually be executed because most combination opportunities will not be fully motivated or even perceived by the parties involved. Furthermore, the set of executed combinations will also include many combinations that are value-destroying, largely because of distorted perceptions of what constitutes a value-creating combination.

Like resource combination, exchange requires that all three necessary conditions for intentional and purposeful deployment must be satisfied. That is, some potential opportunity for exchange must exist, and that opportunity must also be perceived and be motivated. In addition, because exchange, by definition, requires more than one party, an additional and potentially demanding condition is that the three conditions must be satisfied by all parties whose resources are to be exchanged. This additional condition is commonly referred to as "double coincidence." In a hypothetical world of no transaction costs, each opportunity or need for exchange would independently provide all the motivation that is necessary for any exchange to take place. However, in the real world, transaction costs are likely to distort an exchange opportunity's appropriability or the perception of its appropriability or of the opportunity itself. Thus the added constraint imposed by the double coincidence is likely to accrue potentially large additional transaction costs in locating suitable exchange partners and in assessing the availability and usefulness of the resources in question.

Under these circumstances, the institutional logic of markets as arenas of exchange imposes severe limits on the scope of value-adding resource deployments that are supported by exchange. There are two reasons for this. First, markets may be "missing" (incomplete) because of their failure to meet the need for double coincidence. Even though the opportunity or need for deployment is recognized, the market conditions or conventions necessary for exchange may be incomplete or absent. Such situations can include exchanges for which pricing is difficult, money is inappropriate, or rights are unclear, inadequately specified, or insufficiently protected or enforced. The nature of these "market failures" stems in part from the conservative standards that must be applied by most markets in establishing exchange viability and not from the distribution of resources and rights per se. In the markets of the most developed economies, conventions have evolved that support and reinforce an institutional logic that enables actors to enter into and exit from a variety of exchange relations at relatively little cost and thereby preserve their independence from all other actors. The very advantage of this independence of individual actors, which makes it easier (and therefore more efficient) for these market participants to adapt autonomously to changing conditions without the need to consult others, necessarily restricts the form of viability that must exist around each exchange transaction. Consequently, market exchanges must satisfy the condition of what Coleman (1990) has described as "reciprocal viability": each exchange must be viable, by itself, for each of the parties to that exchange.

Second, many resource deployments are systematically discouraged by markets to the extent that in the presence of transaction costs, some resource deployments are always discouraged by any single institution, whether one market or one firm. In the presence of transaction costs, any institution that induces behavior through a system of incentives (say, by allocating resources, assigning rights, or restricting access) encourages the pursuit of some opportunities and necessarily discourages the pursuit of others. That is, each institution favors the conduct of a unique set of economic activities over all other activities—and the set of favored activities comprises those that are more efficient, as defined by that institution. Therefore, some resource deployments critical for future economic development may be unlikely to come about from market exchange, given the current distribution of resources, rights, and individual perceptions (North, 1990). In other words, markets (as single institutions) fail to adapt institutional incentives to new opportunities, which results in some degree of lock-in to the current set of opportunities that are motivated.

Consequently, for economic progress of societies, some other institution besides markets alone is required. It is this role that organizations generally, and firms in particular, play, and it is through playing such a role that these institutions help create value for society beyond what markets alone can create. Firms broaden the scope of exchange in ways that systematically address both of these limitations of markets by creating their own unique institutional logic for overcoming the market's stringent demands for viability and for circumventing (at least for a while) the severely constraining forces of static efficiency that exist in the market. Firms possess the ability to pursue resource deployment strategies that are difficult (costly) or impossible to pursue in markets. Such strategies include those that require resources that are difficult to acquire or accumulate through market exchange (perhaps because prices or markets are "missing") or the use of which is difficult to coordinate among independent actors, subject to the stringent demands of "reciprocal viability," as well as those that cannot be created, accumulated, or deployed in ways that viably satisfy the market's stringent demands for static efficiency yet appear promising to parties with the requisite local knowledge.

First, the organization's advantage in overcoming the market's reciprocal viability constraint dramatically broadens the scope of resources that are exchanged and considered for deployment within firms relative to markets. As our empirical analysis throughout this book has highlighted and as we specifically emphasized in Chapter Six, an organization's internal institutional context shaped by a set of shared values permits it to ensure the viability of exchange under less restrictive conditions. Two such less restrictive conditions of viability have been referred to by Coleman (1990) as "independent viability" and "global viability." Whereas independent viability requires only that each actor have a positive account balance with the organization as a whole and not with each of the other exchange parties, global viability is even less restrictive, in that individual actors themselves do not all require a positive balance for the exchange to be globally viable. Because the organization itself is an implicit third party to every exchange relation, members are able to enter into and maintain relations that may be beneficial to the organization itself even if such relations are not directly beneficial to the members themselves (Coleman, 1990). Thus by permitting individuals and groups to enter voluntary exchanges that benefit the organization directly but benefit themselves only indirectly, organizations open up and make accessible to members a much broader range of resource deployments (including exchanges) than would be possible were exchange required to satisfy the stringent condition of the double coincidence.

The second advantage of organizations as additions to the market system lies in their ability to overcome the constraint that is present in any single institution (this is known as "institution-specific efficiency"). In structuring incentives, all institutions, whether market or organizational, and the conventions and norms that have evolved to support them, largely determine what economic activity is efficient and what is inefficient, given the institutional structure these institutions have helped put in place. The conventions and norms of markets in most developed societies tend to be biased toward the achievement of what North (1990) has described as "allocative efficiency." Instrumental in making a set of available options as efficient as possible by directing resources away from the less efficient and toward the more efficient uses, market adaptation tends to be guided by current relative efficiency and is independent of the efficiencies of future states. In other words, a highly efficient future state that must be preceded by the occurrence of relatively inefficient states is unlikely to be reached through market exchange, regardless of how efficient the future state may be (Arthur, 1989).

Firms relax this constraint of market exchange by creating a unique context within their boundaries—not an instrumental one that mirrors the market or responds to market failures (though, undeniably, some firms may do this) but a coherent institutional context consisting of a combination of its own unique mix of incentives and muted market incentives that encourages the assimilation, sharing, and combination of local knowledge in ways that are difficult to carry out under the alternative institutional context of the market. This unique context of each firm enables its members to defy for a time the relentless gale of market forces and thereby set in motion the countervailing forces necessary for a society to achieve adaptive efficiency (North, 1990).

As North (1990, p. 26) has said, "Institutions alter the price paid for one's convictions." The institutional context of a firm, supported by a coherent set of values, rules, incentives, and expectations, can make it easier for its members to follow a particular path that reduces their cost of accessing certain kinds of knowledge and allows them to combine that knowledge in ways that would otherwise be impossible. By creating an internal environment that is so different from the market (and other firms) in incentive structure, internal vocabulary, and shared codes, a firm can create a context from which its members can collectively challenge, overcome, and alter the forces of the market in which they must interact. In this way, firms may accomplish more than damage control in the process of market adaptation; they may alter the course of adaptive efficiency that the overall institutional matrix (including markets and other firms) ultimately pursues (see North, 1990).

The theory and evidence presented in this book suggest a potential starting point for the formulation of such a positive theory of the firm. In several chapters, a shared social context or a high degree of normative integration has been empirically shown to enhance efficiency, promote innovation, and encourage communication within the MNC. By establishing the organizational context within which subsidiaries and individuals may employ their unique knowledge, skills, and creativity for the purpose of working toward a common goal, normative integration actively encourages greater efficiency and innovation. A shared context also alters the preference structures of members so that they apply their personal talents and expertise to advance the company's goals. In other words, the firm, by providing a context of shared values over and above the benefits of hierarchical and bureaucratic control, has some unique advantages that explain why economic activity is dominated by large organizations like MNCs.

Of course, the argument presented here is intended to be suggestive. The positive theory of the firm is only sketched in, and any systematic development of such a theory would require substantially more theoretical and empirical work.[3] Nevertheless, the study of MNCs presented in this book implies that a positive theory of the firm that emphasizes the role of shared values in creating a unique organizational context is not out of reach. Further study of the differentiated network model will advance our understanding of the myriad relations within and outside MNCs and reveal how they can be organized to enhance firm performance. It will also inform attempts to construct a positive theory of the firm in which the primary role of managers will be value creation.

Notes

1. See Ghoshal and Bartlett (1990) for a discussion on how such a perspective can help illuminate other aspects of MNC organizations, such as the internal distribution of power that over time influences the pattern of internal resource configuration.
2. We use the word *resource* in the sense of Cook (1977, p. 64), to refer to "any valuable activity, service, or commodity."
3. These ideas on how firms can create value are developed further in Moran and Ghoshal (1996).

Methodological Appendix

The empirical analyses conducted in this book are based on data gathered from a research project that consisted of three phases, with a different methodological approach used in each phase (see Figure A.1; this figure has also appeared earlier as Figure 1.4).

Research Design

The purpose of this three-phase research design was to seek triangulation by covering the spectrum from relatively fine-grained to relatively coarse-grained methodologies within the same project to address the same set of issues. The motivations for and methods of each of the three phases are described here.

Phase 1: In-Depth Studies of Nine Companies

The first phase of the project involved case studies of the organization structures, systems, and management processes in nine large multinational companies and led to a normative scheme proposing four generic organizational roles that could be assumed by MNC subsidiaries (Bartlett and Ghoshal, 1986). We interviewed a large number of managers in the corporate headquarters and in a number of national subsidiaries of the nine subject MNCs.[1] Given the concept development and hypothesis-generating objectives, our selection of companies for conducting the case studies was based on the logic of sampling for maximum variety (Cook and Campbell, 1979). We chose three industries, consumer electronics, branded

Figure A.1. The Research Process.

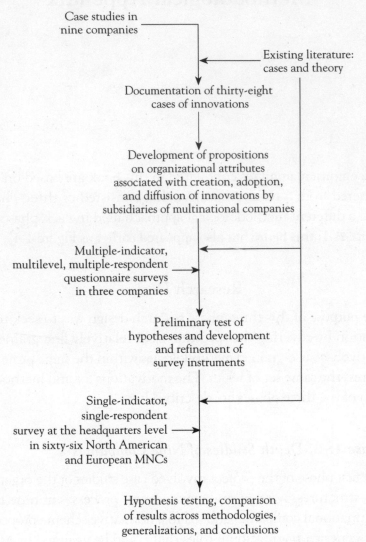

Case studies in
nine companies

Existing literature:
cases and theory

Documentation of thirty-eight
cases of innovations

Development of propositions
on organizational attributes
associated with creation, adoption,
and diffusion of innovations by
subsidiaries of multinational companies

Multiple-indicator,
multilevel, multiple-respondent
questionnaire surveys
in three companies

Preliminary test of
hypotheses and development
and refinement of
survey instruments

Single-indicator,
single-respondent
survey at the headquarters level
in sixty-six North American
and European MNCs

Hypothesis testing, comparison
of results across methodologies,
generalizations, and conclusions

packaged products, and telecommunications switching. Each of these businesses was highly international but represented a very different set of environmental conditions in terms of the strategic needs for global integration and national responsiveness (Prahalad and Doz, 1987). The first offered the greatest benefits of global integration, the forces of national responsiveness were especially strong in the second, and the third represented a situation where both global and local forces were prevalent. Within each industry, we selected a group of companies that represented the greatest variety of administrative heritage, including differences in nationality, internationalization history, and corporate culture (Bartlett, 1986). Philips, Matsushita Electric, and General Electric in consumer electronics; Unilever, Kao, and Procter & Gamble in branded packaged products; and L.M. Ericsson, NEC, and ITT in telecommunications switching offered such variety and were chosen as our sample of nine companies.

Figure A.2 provides a schematic representation of this sample in terms of the strategic characteristics of the industries and the administrative heritages and competitive postures of the firms. For each box in the figure, the vertical axis represents the strength of globalizing forces in the industry or the extent of global integration in the company's strategic posture, and the horizontal axis represents the need for national responsiveness in the business or the extent of country-by-country differentiation in the company's overall competitive strategy (for further details, see Bartlett and Ghoshal, 1989).

The knowledge we acquired in this first phase of the project shaped our study of various issues in the subsequent phases. For example, in the case of innovation, our objective was to identify and document the histories of as many specific cases of innovation as possible. This process yielded reasonably rich and complete descriptions of thirty-eight innovation cases in these companies. Analysis of the organizational attributes that were associated with these innovation cases led to our identification of four different generic processes through which innovations come about in MNCs (see Bartlett and Ghoshal, 1989) and also to a set of propositions regarding the associations among a set of organizational characteristics of an MNC and the ability of its subsidiaries to create, adopt, and diffuse innovations. These propositions in turn served as the hypotheses for the second phase of the study.

Figure A.2. Phase 1: The Sample of Nine Companies.

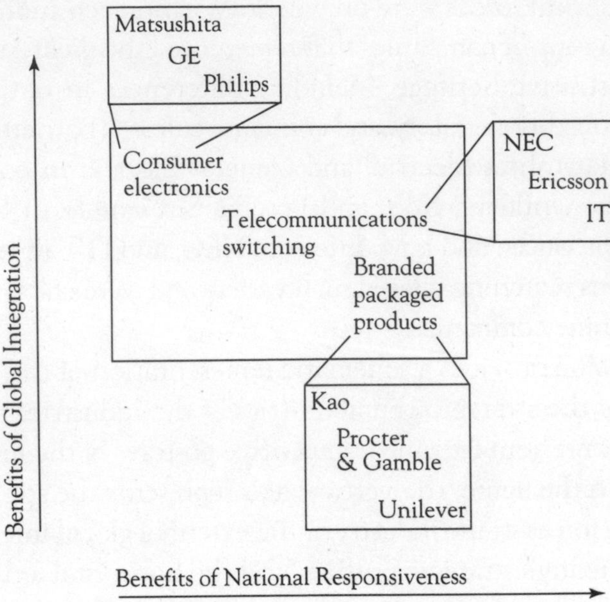

Phase 2: Questionnaire Surveys in Three Companies

In the second phase of the project, we mailed questionnaires to a fairly large number of managers in three of the nine companies surveyed in the first phase. The objectives of the surveys were to formalize the hypotheses that were generated in the first phase, to carry out preliminary tests of some of those hypotheses, and to develop suitable instruments for conducting a large sample survey to test the generalizability of our findings in the third phase of the study.

Data for the second phase of the study were collected through a multiple-indicator, multirespondent, mailed questionnaire survey completed by headquarters and subsidiary managers of Philips, Matsushita, and NEC. This was purely a convenience sample, these being the three of the nine companies that agreed to host the survey. Ideally, we would have liked to include RCA, then the largest U.S. multinational competitor in this business. However, the ownership of RCA was in flux at the time of our study, and we were unable to obtain its agreement to participate. The subsidiaries were selected in consultation with corporate managers of the companies and represented a wide variety in terms of size, activities undertaken locally, and characteristics of host country environments (for further details, see Ghoshal, 1986).

In each of these selected subsidiaries, questionnaires were mailed to all departmental managers appearing on lists and organizational charts furnished by the companies. A total of 323 managers completed the survey, representing an overall response rate of 83 percent. In no subsidiary did we get a response rate of less than 60 percent. We were fortunate to receive such a high response rate because of the close cooperation we received from the managers at the three firms.

Two different instruments were developed for the survey. One was designed for response by headquarters managers, in which all constructs were operationalized by single variables measured on centrally anchored 5-point scales, as described in detail in the following descriptions of each variable. The other questionnaire was designed for response by subsidiary managers and sought subsidiary responses for the same constructs used in the instrument described earlier. In this instrument, though, the structural constructs were operationalized through multiple indicators, again as summarized in the following variable descriptions.

Both questionnaires were implemented in the three large MNCs. In each company, two senior headquarters managers responded to the first questionnaire, providing single indicators for the various constructs for the various national subsidiaries of the company. At the same time, between six and eight managers from each of those subsidiaries responded to the second questionnaire and provided multiple indicators for each of the constructs as applicable to their own subsidiary. Analysis of the data so obtained revealed the following:

1. In each MNC, interrater convergence was high for the two headquarters-level respondents. For each variable measured, the ranks of the different subsidiaries were assessed similarly

by both respondents, as is clear from the rank correlations shown in Table A.1.

2. In each MNC, interrater convergence was also consistently high among headquarters and subsidiary-level respondents. The rank correlation between the ranks for the different structural elements for the subsidiaries obtained by aggregating the responses of the subsidiary managers and the corresponding ranks obtained by aggregating the responses of the two headquarters managers are reported in Table A.1.

Phase 3: Large Sample Survey of U.S. and European MNCs

In the third phase of the study, a single-respondent questionnaire survey was carried out at the headquarters level in some of the

Table A.1. Spearman's Rank Correlation for Assessing Interrater Convergence on Selected Variables.

MNC to Which Raters Belong	Headquarters-Headquarters Raters			Headquarters-Subsidiary Raters[a]		
	A	B	C	A	B	C
Clustering variables						
1. Environmental complexity[b]						
a. Technological dynamism	.63	.79	.76			
b. Competition	.88	.63	.71			
2. Local resources	.79	.84	.76			
Structural variables						
3. Centralization	.71	.69	.86	.95	.70	.75
4. Formalization	.92	.88	.83	.65	.50	.70
5. Socialization	.62	.59	.43	.60	.75	.70
Dependent variable						
6. Performance	.84	.76	.73			

[a]Only structural variables were assessed for convergence of headquarters and subsidiary rater assessments.

[b]No correlations are available for environmental complexity directly because this is merely an additive scale of technological dynamism and competition.

largest North American and European multinationals. Needless to say, the framework used in the survey was not developed purely on prior theoretical principles but drew heavily on the earlier stages of the overall research project.

A review of the options available suggested that the only feasible way to collect data was via a mail questionnaire that would require a single knowledgeable respondent at the headquarters of each MNC to furnish, for each of a number of national subsidiaries of the MNC, single measures for each of the constructs we wished to measure. Such a procedure, however, involved a number of possible shortcomings, including dependence on a single respondent, dependence on single indicators for complex constructs, and the questionable reliability of subsidiary-level information provided by corporate-level respondents. To adopt this procedure, it was necessary to assess the implications of each of these shortcomings on the reliability and validity of the data. Based on the findings of high interrater convergence among headquarters-level respondents as well as the congruence of data obtained through multiple indicators and multiple respondents at the subsidiary level and single indicators and single respondents at the headquarters level, it was decided that a single corporate-level respondent could provide reliable data for the study.

This survey instrument was mailed to the chairman or CEO of all the 438 North American and European MNCs listed in Stopford's *World Directory of Multinational Enterprises* (1983). We did not receive any response from 281 (64 percent) companies, and another fifty wrote to us declining participation on different grounds; 31 questionnaires were returned due to wrong mailing addresses, and completed questionnaires were received from the remaining seventy-six (17 percent) companies. Of these, sixty-six (15 percent) were complete in all respects. Although the response rate was modest, the respondents were distributed across geographical boundaries and industries in a manner quite similar to that of the relevant population, and no discernible response bias could be observed (for further details, see Ghoshal and Nohria, 1987).

In fifty of these sixty-six companies, the respondent was the corporate vice president responsible for all international operations or someone with greater responsibility, such as the CEO or the chairman. Thirty-six of the sixty-six companies were headquartered in North America and the remaining 30 in Europe. Four had annual sales below $1 billion, and eleven had annual sales above $10 billion; the rest were within the $1 billion to $10 billion range. A wide variety of industries were represented, including aerospace (two companies), building products (three), health care (three), industrial equipment (nine), metals (eleven), motor vehicles (three), office equipment (two), paper and wood products (two), petroleum products (seven), rubber (two), and textiles (two).

Collectively, the sixty-six companies reported data on 618 national subsidiaries—only wholly owned operations were considered so as to maintain uniformity within the sample. Five of the companies had fewer than five subsidiaries, forty-four had between five and fifteen subsidiaries, and twelve had more than fifteen subsidiaries in the nineteen countries that were specified in the questionnaire.

Variables and Measures

Our focus on differences within MNCs was addressed by measuring the properties of each case (for example, headquarters-subsidiary relations) as standardized deviations (z scores) from the mean conditions of the company of which it was a part.

Structural Variables

Distribution of Slack Resources. Operationalizing and measuring organizational slack is a difficult task, especially for an organizational subunit. In Chapter Three, where our unit of analysis is each department, we measured the degree of slack within each department by asking the departmental managers the following two questions:

1. Assume that due to some sudden development, 10 percent of the time of all people working in your department has to be spent on work totally unconnected with the tasks and responsibilities of your department. How seriously will your work be affected?

2. Assume that due to a similar development, your department's annual operating budget is reduced by 10 percent. How significantly will your work be affected?

In both cases, managers were given five choices, ranging from 1 (output will not be affected) to 5 (output will be affected by 20 percent or more). The midpoint of 3 could be chosen to indicate that output will fall by about 10 percent. Due to the high correlation between these measures, the mean of these two responses (reverse-scored) was used to construct our measure of slack. These responses were aggregated for all respondents from a subsidiary to compute a subsidiary-level measure for slack. In the third phase of the study, where data were obtained from a corporate respondent, slack was measured by asking the corporate respondent the extent to which the subsidiary could expand oper ations without significant additional resources. A scale of 1 (with great difficulty) to 5 (with great ease) was used to anchor these responses.

Centralization. For corporate-level respondents, this was operationalized simply as the opposite of autonomy measured by this question:

> Different national organizations in your company may enjoy different levels of autonomy for deciding their own strategies and policies. On a scale of 1 (very low) to 5 (very high), rate the extent of local autonomy enjoyed by each of the following national organizations.

For subsidiary-level respondents, centralization was operationalized as the opposite of autonomy and measured by estimates of subsidiary managers on the extent of headquarters or subsidiary influence on the following six decision situations (De Bodinat, 1975): introduction of a new product, minor but significant modification of an existing product, modification of a production process, restructuring of the subsidiary organization involving creation or abolition of departments, recruitment and promotion to positions just below that of the subsidiary general manager, and career development plans for departmental managers. The empirical studies in each chapter specify which of these decision situations are captured by the measure of centralization used in that chapter.

For each of these situations, the relative influences could be scored on a 5-point scale: (1) the headquarters decides alone; (2) the headquarters decides, but the subsidiary can and does provide suggestions; (3) both the headquarters and the subsidiary have roughly equal influence on the decision; (4) the subsidiary decides but the headquarters can and does provide suggestions; (5) the subsidiary decides alone. Average scores for these decisions for all the respondents from the subsidiary were aggregated to yield a subsidiary-level measure for local autonomy.

Formalization. For corporate-level respondents, this was measured by the following question:

> The extent to which policies and systems are formalized may vary within the company, being different for different national organizations. On a scale of 1 (low formalization) to 5 (high formalization), rate the extent of formalization of policies and systems (through instruments such as manuals, standing orders, standard operating procedures, etc.) in each of the following national organizations.

For subsidiary-level respondents, formalization was measured by the assessment of subsidiary managers of the extent of truth or falsehood of the following three statements:

1. For most tasks, the headquarters has provided a fairly well-defined set of rules and policies.

2. To the extent possible, there are manuals that define the courses of action to be taken under different situations.

3. The headquarters continuously monitors to ensure that rules and policies are not violated.

Responses could be scored on a 4-point scale, indicating (1) definitely true, (2) more true than false, (3) more false than true, or (4) definitely false. Average scores for these statements for all the respondents from the subsidiary were aggregated to yield a subsidiary-level measure for the degree of formalization in the headquarters-subsidiary relation.

Socialization, Shared Values, and Normative Integration. For corporate-level respondents, these factors were measured by this question:

> Some of your national organizations, compared to others, may be relatively more in tune with the overall goals and management values of the parent company. Let us call this the extent of shared values. On a scale of 1 (low shared values) to 5 (high shared values), rate each of the following national subsidiaries.

For subsidiary-level respondents, normative integration was measured by aggregating the responses of subsidiary managers on the following four indicators: extent of time the respondent actually worked in the headquarters, scored as 1 if the duration was one year or more and 0 otherwise; number of headquarters visits per year over the last three years, scored as 1 if the count was one or more and 0 otherwise; having a mentor at the headquarters, positive responses being scored as 1 and negative responses as 0; and whether the person had undergone a period of formal training at the parent company, positive responses being scored as 1 and negative as 0. These four scores were aggregated to yield a single composite measure of the level of normative integration for each respondent; the scores of all respondents from the subsidiary were then aggregated to provide a subsidiary-level measure for the variable.

Interfunctional or Interdepartmental Communication. This was operationalized as the extent to which the managers in the subsidiary communicated on task- or work-related matters across functional and departmental boundaries. Respondents in the survey were asked to report the frequency with which they communicated with managers in all other prespecified departments within their subsidiary (on a scale of 1, less than yearly, to 5, daily). Unless stated otherwise in a specific chapter, the extent of each manager's cross-functional communication was then calculated as the fraction of the total number of other departmental managers with whom the manager communicated on a monthly basis (scored 3) or more often. Finally, the scores of the respondents were averaged to measure the density of interfunctional and interdepartmental linkages within each subsidiary.

Measures of such intrasubsidiary communication could not be reliably obtained from a headquarters-level respondent, and hence such data were not collected in the third phase.

Headquarters-Subsidiary Communication. For corporate-level respondents, headquarters-subsidiary communication was measured by asking this question:

> Communication between headquarters and subsidiary managers can take place for a variety of reasons. Consider the kind of communication aimed more at coordination and sharing of information than at control. On a scale of 1 (low) to 5 (high), rate the average level of such communication with the headquarters of each of the following national subsidiaries of your company.

For subsidiary-level respondents, headquarters-subsidiary communication was measured by the responses of subsidiary managers to the typical frequency with which they communicated with the corporate headquarters, scored as 5 if daily, 4 if weekly, 3 if monthly, 2 if yearly, and 1 if less than yearly.

Intersubsidiary Communication. This was measured by asking the respondents to indicate, on a scale of 1 to 5 similar to that for the other communication measures, the typical frequency of their communication with each of the other national subsidiaries of the company that were included in the survey. Based on these responses, various measures of intersubsidiary communication, including total frequency, density, centrality, and range, were constructed as indicated in the various chapters in which these variables are employed. A measure of intersubsidiary communication could also not be reliably obtained from headquarters respondents and hence was not collected in the large-sample survey.

Environmental Variables

Environmental Complexity. This measure used an additive 5 point scale consisting of two equally weighted variables, local competition and technological dynamism (Cronbach's α – .7). These variables were proposed by Lawrence and Dyer (1983) as important constituents of environmental information complexity. Competition was measured by asking corporate-level respondents the following:

> On a scale of 1 (not much competition) to 5 (extremely intense competition), rate the intensity of competition your company faces in each of the following markets.

This was followed by a list of nineteen countries, with a centrally anchored 5-point scale associated with each and the option of specifying the nonexistence of a subsidiary in each case. The same pattern was adopted for all the other questions.

Technological dynamism was measured by this question:

On a scale of 1 (very slow) to 5 (very rapid), indicate the relative rate of product and process innovations (for the industry as a whole) that characterizes each of the national markets of the following subsidiaries.

Local Subsidiary Resources. This was measured by corporate-level respondents' answers to this question:

Some national organizations in your company may have relatively advanced physical resources (such as technology or capital) and managerial capabilities. Some others, in contrast, may not have such resources to the same extent. On a scale of 1 (low) to 5 (high), rate the overall level of resource availability in your national organizations in each of the following countries.

Global Integration. This measure is a variation on Kobrin's "index of integration" (1991). Kobrin's index is the ratio of total intrafirm trade (the sum of affiliate-to-affiliate, affiliate-to-parent, and parent-to-affiliate sales) to total international sales (the sum of total sales of the parent and all affiliates) of all the MNCs in an industry. We classify industries with Kobrin's index of greater than 20 percent as facing strong forces for global integration and those less than 20 percent as facing weak forces for global integration.

Local Responsiveness. To measure national responsiveness, we used two indicators. The first is the advertising-to-sales ratio of the industry, as published in *Advertising Age*. The second is an average of the values received on the questionnaire for the extent of local regulation, by industry (for example, we averaged the ratings given by computer companies on the extent of local regulations to come up with the computer industry average). The two measures are only weakly correlated (rank correlation .32, $p = 0.11$). Given that both regulations and customer preferences can act as powerful forces for local responsiveness, we categorize any business that falls above the sample mean on either of these two indicators as facing strong forces of national responsiveness and one that falls below on both indicators as facing relatively weak forces of national responsiveness.

Performance Outcomes

Subsidiary Performance. This subjective measure was based on the following question asked of corporate-level respondents:

> Please evaluate the average overall performance over the last three years (based on financial, strategic, and other considerations that you feel are relevant) of each of the following national organizations. Rate each organization on a scale of 1 (much lower than expected) to 5 (much better than expected).

Subsidiary Innovation. Each of the departmental managers in each subsidiary was asked how many innovative accomplishments they were responsible for over the preceding year and the estimated dollar benefit of their three most valuable innovative accomplishments. Using these data, we computed two measures of innovation creation that captured different dimensions of the innovativeness of each subsidiary. The *scale* of innovations was computed as the average of the self estimated dollar benefit (revenues or savings) of the top three innovations reported by the respondents. The *number* of innovations refers to the average total number of innovations reported by the respondents in each subsidiary.

The final value for each of the three other innovation performance measures—*creation*, *adoption*, and *diffusion*—were based on our own evaluation of the descriptions of the innovations provided by the subsidiary-level respondents. In some instances, additional information was sought from the respondents and also from the subsidiary general managers to decide if the cases should be included in the final count. As indicated, subsidiary-level scores for each of these variables were arrived at by simply adding the total number of innovations created, adopted, and diffused by the different departments of the subsidiary. Corporate-level respondents assessed each subsidiary's ability to create and adopt innovations on a scale of 1 to 5. Data on the subsidiary's ability to diffuse innovations could not be reliably obtained from the corporate respondents.

Corporate Performance.   Corporate performance was measured by three financial indicators over a five-year period: the average return on assets from 1982 to 1986, the average annual growth in return on assets over the same period, and the average annual growth in sales over the same period. These performance data were all obtained from the annual financial reports of the firms studied.

Note

1. Nitin Nohria was not involved in this phase of the research, which was conducted by Chris Bartlett and Sumantra Ghoshal.

References

Aiken, M., and Hage, J. (1968). Organizational interdependence and intraorganizational structure. *American Sociological Review, 33*, 912–930.

Aiken, M., and Hage, J. (1971). The organic organization and innovation. *Sociology, 5*, 63–82.

Aldrich, H. E. (1979). *Organizations and environments*. Englewood Cliffs, NJ: Prentice Hall.

Aldrich, H. E., and Whetten, D. A. (1981). Organization-sets, action-sets, and networks: Making the most of simplicity. In P. C. Nystrom and W. H. Starbuck (Eds.), *Handbook of organizational design*. London: Oxford University Press.

Allen, T. J. (1977). *Managing the flow of technology*. Cambridge, MA: MIT Press.

Alsegg, R. A. (1971). *Control relationships between American corporations and their European subsidiaries*. AMA Research Study 107. New York: American Management Association.

Amabile, T. M. (1988). A model of creativity and innovation in organizations. In B. M. Staw and L. L. Cummings (Eds.), *Research in organizational behavior*, Vol. 10. Greenwich, CT: JAI Press.

Antle, R., and Fellingham, J. (1990). Resource rationing and organizational slack in a two-period model. *Journal of Accounting Research, 28*(1), 1–24.

Arrow, K. J. (1974). *The limits of organization*. New York: Norton.

Arthur, W. B. (1989). Competing technologies, increasing returns, and lock-in by historical events. *Economic Journal, 99*, 116–131.

Ashby, W. R. (1956). *An introduction to cybernetics*. New York: Wiley.

Baggozi, R. P., and Yi, Y. (1988). On the evaluation of structural models. *Journal of the Academy of Marketing Sciences, 16*(1), 74–94.

Baldridge, J. V., and Burnham, R. A. (1975). Organizational innovation: Individual, organizational, and environmental impacts. *Administrative Science Quarterly, 20*, 165–176.

Baliga, B. R., and Jaeger, A. M. (1984). Multinational corporations: Control systems and delegation issues. *Journal of International Business Studies, 15*, 25–40.

Bandura, A. (1986). *Social foundations of thought and action: A social cognitive theory.* Englewood Cliffs, NJ: Prentice Hall.

Barnard, C. (1939). *The functions of the executive.* Cambridge, MA: Harvard University Press.

Bartlett, C. A. (1986). Building and managing the transnational: The new organizational challenge. In M. E. Porter (Ed.), *Competition in global industries.* Boston: Harvard Business School Press.

Bartlett, C. A., and Ghoshal, S. (1986). Tap your subsidiaries for global reach. *Harvard Business Review, 4*(6), 87–94.

Bartlett, C. A., and Ghoshal, S. (1987a). Managing across borders: New organizational responses. *Sloan Management Review, 27,* 43–53.

Bartlett, C. A., and Ghoshal, S. (1987b). Managing across borders: New strategic requirements. *Sloan Management Review, 27,* 7–17.

Bartlett, C. A., and Ghoshal, S. (1989). *Managing across borders: The transnational solution.* Boston: Harvard Business School Press.

Bavelas, A. (1950). Communication patterns in task-oriented groups. *Journal of the Acoustical Society of America, 22,* 725–730.

Benson, J. K. (1975). The interorganizational network as a political economy. *Administrative Science Quarterly, 20,* 229–249.

Blackburn, R. S. (1982). Dimensions of structure: A review and reappraisal. *Academy of Management Review, 7,* 59–66.

Bourgeois, L. J. (1981). On the measurement of organizational slack. *Academy of Management Review, 6,* 29–39.

Bourgeois, L. J., and Singh, J. V. (1983). Organizational slack and political behavior within top management teams. *Academy of Management Proceedings,* pp. 43–47.

Bower, J. L. (1987). *When markets quake.* Boston: Harvard Business School Press.

Bromiley, P. (1991). Testing a causal model of corporate risk-taking and performance. *Academy of Management Journal, 34,* 37–59.

Buckley, P. J., and Casson, M. C. (1976). *The future of the multinational enterprise.* London: Holmes & Meier.

Buckley, P. J., and Casson, M. C. (1985). *The economic theory of the multinational enterprise.* London: Macmillan.

Burgelman, R. A. (1983). A model of the interaction of strategic behavior, corporate context, and the concept of strategy. *Academy of Management Review, 8,* 61–70.

Burns, T., and Stalker, G. M. (1961). *The management of innovation.* London: Tavistock.

Burt, R. S. (1982). *Toward a structural theory of action.* Orlando, FL: Academic Press.

Burt, R. S. (1987). Social contagion and innovation: Cohesion versus structural equivalence. *American Journal of Sociology, 92,* 1287–1335.

Burt, R. S. (1992a). The social structure of competition. In N. Nohria and R. G. Eccles (Eds.), *Networks and organizations: Structure, form, and action.* Boston: Harvard Business School Press.

Burt, R. S. (1992b). *Structural holes*. Cambridge, MA: Harvard University Press.

Calvet, A. L. (1981). A synthesis of foreign direct investment theories and theories of the multinational firm. *Journal of International Business Studies, 12*, 43–59.

Caruso, R. E. (1992). *Mentoring and the business environment: Asset or liability?* Hanover, NH: Dartmouth University Press.

Caves, R. E. (1982). *Multinational enterprise and economic analysis*. Cambridge, UK: Cambridge University Press.

Chandler, A. D. (1986). The evolution of modern global competition. In M. E. Porter (Ed.), *Competition in global industries*. Boston: Harvard Business School Press.

Child, J. (1972). Organization structure, environment, and performance: The role of strategic choice. *Sociology, 6*, 1–22.

Coase, R. H. (1937) The nature of the firm. *Economica, 4*, 386–405.

Cohen, W. M., and Levinthal, D. A. (1990). Absorptive capacity: A new perspective on learning and innovation. *Administrative Science Quarterly, 35*(1), 128–152.

Coleman, J. S. (1990). *Foundations of social theory*. Cambridge, MA: Harvard University Press, Belknap Press.

Conner, K. R., and Prahalad, C. K. (forthcoming). A resource-based theory of the firm: Knowledge versus opportunism. *Organization Science*.

Cook, K. S. (1977). Exchange and power in networks of interorganizational relations. *Sociological Quarterly, 18*, 62–82.

Cook, T. D., and Campbell, D. T. (1979). *Quasi-experimentation* Boston: Houghton Mifflin.

Cyert, R. M., and March, J. G. (1992). A *behavioral theory of the firm*. Englewood Cliffs, NJ: Prentice Hall. (Originally published 1963.)

Damonpour, F. (1987). The adoption of technological, administrative, and ancillary innovations: Impact of organizational factors. *Journal of Management, 13*, 675–688.

Daniel, J. D., Pitts, R. A., and Tretter, M. J. (1984). Strategy and structure of U.S. multinationals: An exploratory study. *Academy of Management Journal, 27*, 292–307.

Davenport, T. H. (1993). *Process innovation*. Boston: Harvard Business School Press.

Davis, S. M. (1979). *Managing and organizing multinational corporations*. New York: Pergamon Press.

De Bodinat, H. (1975). Influence in the multinational corporation: The case of manufacturing. Unpublished doctoral dissertation. Boston: Graduate School of Business Administration, Harvard University.

De Meyer, A., and Mizushima, A. (1989). Global R&D management. *R&D Management, 19*, 135–146.

Deal, T. E., and Kennedy, A. A. (1982). *Corporate cultures: The rites and rituals of corporate life*. Reading, MA: Addison-Wesley.

Delbecq, A. L., and Mills, P. K. (1985). Managerial practices that enhance innovation. *Organizational Dynamics, 14*, 24–34.

Di Maggio, P. J., and Powell, W. W. (1983). The iron cage revisited: Institutional isomorphism and collective rationality in organizational fields. *American Sociological Review, 48*, 147–160.

Donaldson, L. (1995). *American anti-management theories of organization: A critique of paradigm proliferation.* Cambridge, UK: Cambridge University Press.

Dougherty, D. J. (1987). New products in old organizations. Unpublished Ph.D. dissertation, Sloan School of Management, Cambridge, MA.

Downs, G. W., and Mohr, L. B. (1976). Conceptual issues in the study of innovation. *Administrative Science Quarterly, 21*, 700–714.

Doz, Y. L., and Prahalad, C. K. (1981). Headquarters influence and strategic control in MNCs. *Sloan Management Review, 22*, 55–72.

Drazin, R., and Van de Ven, A. H. (1985). Alternate forms of fit in contingency theory. *Administrative Science Quarterly, 30*, 514–539.

Drucker, P. F. (1985). *Innovation and entrepreneurship.* New York: HarperCollins.

Dunning, J. H. (1981). *International production and the multinational enterprise.* London: Allen & Unwin.

Eccles, R. G. (1981). The quasi firm in the construction industry. *Journal of Economic Behavior and Organization, 2*, 335–357.

Eccles, R. G., and Crane, D. B. (1987). Managing through networks in investment banking. *California Management Review, 30*, 176–195.

Eccles, R. G., and Nohria, N. (1992). *Beyond the hype: Rediscovering the essence of management.* Boston: Harvard Business School Press.

Edstrom, A., and Galbraith, J. R. (1977). Transfer of managers as a coordination and control strategy in multinational organizations. *Administrative Science Quarterly, 22*, 248–263.

Egelhoff, W. G. (1982). Strategy and structure in multinational corporations: An information-processing approach. *Administrative Science Quarterly, 27*, 435–458.

Egelhoff, W. G. (1988a). *Organizing the multinational enterprise: An information-processing perspective.* New York: Ballinger.

Egelhoff, W. G. (1988b). Strategy and structure in multinational corporations: A revision of the Stopford and Wells model. *Strategic Management Journal, 8*(1), 1–14.

Egelhoff, W. G. (1990). Exploring the limits of transnationalism. Paper presented at the annual meeting of the Academy of International Business, Toronto.

Eisenhardt, K. M. (1985). Control: Organizational and economic approaches. *Management Science, 31*, 134–149.

Emerson, R. M. (1962). Power-dependence relations. *American Sociological Review, 27*, 31–41.

Etzioni, A. (1965). Organizational control structures. In J. G. March (Ed.), *Handbook of organizations.* Skokie, IL: Rand McNally.

Everitt, B. (1980). *Cluster analysis* (2nd ed.). New York: Wiley.

Fayerweather, J. (1978). *International business strategy and administration*. New York: Ballinger.

Fisher, D. H . (1970). *Historian's fallacies*. New York: HarperCollins.

Freeman, L. C. (1979). Centrality in social networks: Conceptual clarification. *Social Networks, 1*, 215–239.

Galbraith, J. R. (1973). *Designing complex organizations*. Reading, MA: Addison-Wesley.

Galbraith, J. R., and Edstrom, A. (1976). International transfer of managers: Some important policy considerations. *Columbia Journal of World Business, 11*(2), 100–112.

Galbraith, J. R., and Nathanson, D. A. (1978). *Strategy implementation: The role of structure and process*. St. Paul, MN: West.

Garvin, D. A. (1994). The processes of organization and management. Harvard Business School Working Paper No. 94–084.

Gates, S. R., and Egelhoff, W. G. (1986). Centralization in parent headquarters-subsidiary relationships. *Journal of International Business Studies, 17*(2), 71–92.

Gecas, V. (1989). The social psychology of self-efficacy. *Annual Review of Sociology, 15*, 291–316.

Ghoshal, S. (1986). The innovative multinational: A differentiated network of organizational roles and management processes. Unpublished doctoral dissertation, Graduate School of Business Administration, Harvard University.

Ghoshal, S. (1987). Global strategy: An organizing framework. *Strategic Management Journal, 8*(5), 425–440.

Ghoshal, S., and Bartlett, C. A. (1988). Creation, adoption, and diffusion of innovations by subsidiaries of multinational corporations. *Journal of International Business Studies, 19*(3), 365–388.

Ghoshal, S., and Bartlett, C. A. (1990). The multinational corporation as a differentiated interorganizational network. *Academy of Management Review, 15,* 603–625.

Ghoshal, S., and Nohria, N. (1987). Multinational corporations as differentiated networks. INSEAD Working Paper No. 87/13, European Institute of Business Administration (INSEAD), Fontainebleau, France.

Ginzberg, E., and Reilly, E. (1957). *Effective change in large organizations*. New York: Columbia University Press.

Granovetter, M. (1973). The strength of weak ties. *American Journal of Sociology, 78*, 1360–1380.

Granovetter, M. (1982). The strength of weak ties: A network theory revisited. In P. V. Marsden and N. Lin (Eds.), *Social structure and network analysis*. Thousand Oaks, CA: Sage.

Granovetter, M. (1985). Economic action and social structure. The problem of embeddedness. *American Journal of Sociology, 91*, 481–510.

Gross, N., Giacquinta, J. B., and Bernstein, M. (1971). *Implementing organizational innovations: A sociological analysis of planned educational change*. New York: Basic Books.

Grossman, G., and Shapiro, C. (1987). Dynamic R&D competition. *Economic Journal, 97,* 372–387.

Guetzkow, H., and Simon, H. A. (1954). The impact of certain communication nets upon organization and performance in task-oriented groups. *Management Science, 1,* 233–250.

Gupta, A. K., and Govindarajan, V. (1991). Knowledge flows and the structure of control within multinational corporations. *Academy of Management Review, 16,* 768–792.

Hambrick, D., and Snow, C. (1977). A contextual model of strategic decision making in organizations. In R. L. Taylor, J. J. O'Connell, R. A. Zawacki, and D. D. Warrick (Eds.), *Academy of Management Proceedings*.

Hamel, G., and Prahalad, C. K. (1994). Competing for the future. *Harvard Business Review, 72*(4), 122–128.

Hammer, M., and Champy, J. (1993). *Reengineering the corporation*. New York: HarperBusiness.

Hayek, F. (1945). The use of knowledge in society. *American Economic Review, 35,* 519–530.

Hayes, R. H., Wheelwright, S. C., and Clark, K. B. (1988). *Dynamic manufacturing: Creating the learning organization*. New York: Free Press.

Hedlund, G. (1980). The role of foreign subsidiaries in strategic decision making in Swedish multinational corporations. *Strategic Management Journal, 1,* 23–36.

Hedlund, G. (1981). Autonomy of subsidiaries and formalization of headquarters-subsidiary relations in Swedish MNCs. In L. Otterbeck (Ed.), *The management of headquarters-subsidiary relations in multinational corporations*. Hampshire, UK: Gower.

Hedlund, G. (1986). The hypermodern MNC: A heterarchy? *Human Resource Management, 25*(1), 9–35.

Hedlund, G. (1993). Assumptions of hierarchy and heterarchy—with applications to the management of the multinational corporation. In S. Ghoshal and D. E. Westney (Eds.), *Organization theory and the multinational corporation*. London: Macmillan.

Hedlund. G. (1994). A model of knowledge management and the N-form corporation. *Strategic Management Journal, 15,* 73–90.

Hennart, J. F. (1982). *A theory of multinational enterprise*. Ann Arbor: University of Michigan Press.

Higgins, M., and Nohria, N. (1994). The sidekick effect: Mentoring relationships and the development of social capital. Working Paper No. 94–088, Harvard Business School.

Hirsch, S. (1976). An international trade and investment theory of the firm. *Oxford Economic Papers, 28,* 258–270.

Homans, G. C. (1950). *The human group*. Orlando, FL: Harcourt Brace.

Huber, G. P., and Daft, R. L. (1987). The information environments of organizations. In F. M. Jablin, L. L. Putnam, K. H. Roberts, and L. W. Porter (Eds.), *Handbook of organizational communication*. Thousand Oaks, CA: Sage.

Ibarra, H. (1992). Homophily and differential returns: Sex differences in network structure and access in an advertising firm. *Administrative Science Quarterly, 37*, 422–447.

Ibarra, H. (1993). Network centrality, power, and innovation involvement: Determinants of technical and administrative roles. *Academy of Management Journal, 36*, 471–501.

Jablin, F. M. (1979). Superior-subordinate communication: The state of the art. *Psychological Bulletin, 6*, 1201–1222.

Jablin, F. M., Putnam, L. L, Roberts, K. H., and Porter L. W. (Eds.). (1987). *Handbook of organizational communication*. Thousand Oaks, CA: Sage.

Jaeger, A. M. (1983). The transfer of organizational culture overseas: An approach to control in the multinational corporation. *Journal of International Business Studies, 14*, 91–114.

Jensen, M. C. (1986). Agency costs of free cash flow, corporate finance, and takeovers. *American Economic Review, 76*, 323–239.

Jensen, M. C. (1993). The modern industrial revolution, exit, and the failure of internal control systems. *Journal of Finance, 48*, 831—880.

Jensen, M. C., and Meckling, W. H. (1976). Theory of the firm: Managerial behavior, agency cost, and ownership structure. *Journal of Financial Economics, 3*, 305–360.

Joereskog, K. G., and Soorbom, D. (1989). *LISREL: A guide to the program and applications* Chicago. 3PSS.

Kamin, J. Y., and Ronen, J. (1978). The effects of corporate control on apparent profit performance. *Southern Economic Journal, 45*, 181–191.

Kanter, R. M. (1983). *The Changemasters*. New York: Simon & Schuster.

Kanter, R. M. (1988). When a thousand flowers bloom: Structural, collective, and social conditions for innovation in organizations. In B. M. Staw and L. L. Cummings (Eds.), *Research in organizational behavior*. Vol. 10. Greenwich, CT: JAI Press.

Katz, R., and Allen, T. J. (1982). Investigating the not invented here (NIH) syndrome: A look at the performance, tenure, and communication patterns of 50 R&D project groups. *R&D Management, 12*, 7–19.

Kidder, T. (1981). *The soul of a new machine*. New York: Little, Brown.

Knight, K. (1967). A descriptive model of the intra-firm innovative process. *Journal of Business, 40*, 478–496.

Kobrin, S. J. (1991). An empirical analysis of the determinants of global integration. *Strategic Management Journal, 12*, 17–31.

Kogut, B. (1983). Foreign direct investment as a sequential process. In C. P. Kindelberger and D. B. Audretsch (Eds.), *The multinational corporation in the 1980s*. Cambridge, MA: MIT Press.

Kogut, B. (1985a). Designing global strategies: Comparative and competitive value-added chains. *Sloan Management Review, 26*, 15–28.

Kogut, B. (1985b). Designing global strategies: Profiting from operational flexibility. *Sloan Management Review, 26*, 27–38.

Kogut, B. (1988). Country patterns in international competition: Appropriability and oligopolistic agreement. In N. Hood and J. E. Vahlne (Eds.), *Strategies in global competition*. London: Croom Helm.

Kogut, B., and Zander, U. (1992). Knowledge of the firm and the replication of technology. *Organization Science, 3*, 383–397.

Krackhardt, D. (1989). Graphing theoretical dimensions of the informal organization. Presentation at the European Institute of Business Administration (INSEAD), Fontainebleau, France.

Kram, K. E. (1985). *Mentoring at work: Developmental relationships in organizational life*. Glenview, IL: Scott, Foresman.

Lant, T. (1985). Modeling organizational slack: An empirical investigation. Stanford University Research Paper No. 856.

Lawrence, P. R., and Dyer, D. (1983). *Renewing American industry*. New York: Free Press.

Lawrence, P. R., and Lorsch, J. W. (1967). *Organization and environment: Managing differentiation and integration*. Boston: Graduate School of Business Administration, Harvard University.

Leibenstein, H. (1969). Organizational or frictional equilibria, X-efficiency, and the rate of innovation. *Quarterly Journal of Economics, 83*, 600–623.

Lessard, D., and Lightstone, J. B. (1986). Volatile exchange rates can put operations at risk. *Harvard Business Review, 64*(4), 107–114.

Levine, S., and White, P. E. (1961). Exchange as a conceptual framework for the study of interorganizational relations. *Administrative Science Quarterly, 5*, 583–601.

Levinthal, D., and March, J. G. (1981). A model of adaptive organizational search. *Journal of Economic Behavior and Organization, 2*, 307–333.

Levitt, T. (1983). The globalization of markets. *Harvard Business Review, 61*(3), 92–102.

Lewin, K. (1951). *Field theory in social science*. New York: HarperCollins,

Lorange, P., Scott-Morton, M., and Ghoshal, S. (1986). *Strategic control*. St. Paul, MN: West.

Magee, S. P. (1977). Information and the multinational corporation: An appropriability theory of direct foreign investment. In J. N. Bhagwati (Ed.), *The new international economic order*. Cambridge, MA: MIT Press.

Mahini, A., and Wells, L. T. (1986). Government relations in the global firm. In M. E. Porter (Ed.), *Competition in global industries*. Boston: Harvard Business School Press.

Majumdar, S. K., and Venkataraman, S. (1993). New technology adoption in U.S. telecommunications: The role of competitive pressures and firm-level inducements. *Research Policy, 22*, 521–536.

Mansfield, E. (1963). Size of firm, market structure, and innovation. *Journal of Political Economy, 41*, 556–576.

March, J. G. (1976). The technology of foolishness. In J. G. March and J. P. Olsen (Eds.), *Ambiguity and choice in organizations*. Bergen, Norway: Universitetsforlaget.

March, J. G. (1981). Footnotes to organizational change. *Administrative Science Quarterly, 26*, 563–577.

March, J. G., and Simon, H. A. (1958). *Organizations*. New York: Wiley.

Marquis, D. G. (1969, Nov.). The anatomy of successful innovations. *Innovation*, pp. 35–48.

Martinez, J. I., and Jarillo, J. C. (1989). The evolution of research on coordination mechanisms in multinational corporations. *Journal of International Business Studies, 20*, 489–514.

Martinez, J. I., and Jarillo, J. C. (1991). Coordination demands of international strategies. *Journal of International Business Studies, 22*, 429–444.

Meurling, J. A. (1985). *Switch in time*. Chicago: Telephony.

Meyer, A. D. (1982). Adapting to environmental jolts. *Administrative Science Quarterly, 27*, 515–537.

Milgrom, P. R., and Roberts, J. (1992). *Economics, organizations, and management*. Englewood Cliffs, NJ: Prentice Hall.

Milligan, G. W., and Cooper, M. C. (1985). An examination of procedures for determining the number of clusters in a data set. *Psychometrika, 50*, 159–179.

Mohr, L. B. (1969). Determinants of innovation in organizations. *American Political Science Review, 63*, 111–136.

Mohr, L. B. (1982). *Explaining organizational behavior*. San Francisco: Jossey-Bass.

Mokyr, J. (1990). *The lever of riches: Technological creativity and economic progress*. New York: Oxford University Press.

Moldoveanu, M., Nohria, N., and Stevenson, H. (1996). The path-dependent evolution of organizations. Working Paper No. 96–005, Graduate School of Business Administration, Harvard University.

Monteverde, K. (1995). Applying resource-based strategic analysis: Making the model more accessible to practitioners. Working Paper No. 95–1, St. Josephs University.

Moran, P., and Ghoshal, S. (1996). Value creation by firms. In J. B. Keys and L. N. Dosier (Eds.), *Academy of Management Proceedings*, 41–45.

Moses, D. O. (1992). Organizational slack and risk-taking behavior: Tests of product pricing strategy. *Journal of Organizational Change Management, 5*(3), 38–54.

Nelson, R., and Winter, S. G. (1982). *An evolutionary theory of economic change*. Cambridge, MA: Harvard University Press.

Nohria, N. (1992). Is a network perspective a useful way of studying organizations? In N. Nohria and R. G. Eccles (Eds.), *Networks and organizations: Structure, form, and action*. Boston: Harvard Business School Press.

Nohria, N., and Eccles, R. G. (Eds.). (1992). *Networks and organizations: Structure, form, and action*. Boston: Harvard Business School Press.

Normann, R. (1971). Organizational innovativeness: Product variation and reorientation. *Administrative Science Quarterly, 16*, 203–215.

North, D. C. (1990). *Institutions, institutional change and economic performance*. Cambridge, UK: Cambridge University Press.

Olds, E. G. (1938). Distribution of sums of squares of rank differences for small samples. *Annals of Mathematical Statistics, 9*, 1–13.

Otterbeck, L. (Ed.). (1981). *The management of headquarters-subsidiary relations in multinational corporations*. Aldershot, U.K.: Gower.

Ouchi, W. G. (1980). Markets, bureaucracies, and clans. *Administrative Science Quarterly, 25*, 129–141.

Parsons, T. (1956). A sociological approach to the theory of organizations. *Administrative Science Quarterly, 1*, 63–85, 225–239.

Paul, J. K. (Ed.). (1984). *High-technology international trade and competition*. Park Ridge, NJ: Noyes.

Peters, T. (1990). Get innovative or get dead (pt. 1). *California Management Review, 32*(1), 9–26.

Pfeffer, J. (1981). *Power in organizations*. Boston: Pitman.

Pfeffer, J. (1982). *Organizations and organization theory*. Boston: Pitman.

Pfeffer, J., and Salancik, G. R. (1978). *The external control of organizations: A resource dependency perspective*. New York: HarperCollins.

Picard, J. (1977). Factors of variance in multinational marketing control. In L. G. Matsson and P. F. Widersheim (Eds.), *Recent research on the internationalization of business*. Uppsala: Stockholm School of Economics.

Polanyi, M. (1969). *Knowing and being*. Chicago: University of Chicago Press.

Porter, M. E. (1986). Competition in global industries: A conceptual framework. In M. E. Porter (Ed.), *Competition in global industries*. Boston: Harvard Business School Press.

Powell, W. W. (1985). *Getting into print: The decision-making process in scholarly publishing*. Chicago: University of Chicago Press.

Poynter, T. A., and Rugman, A. M. (1982). World product mandates: How will multinationals respond? *Business Quarterly, 47*(3), 54–61.

Poynter, T. A., and White, R. A. (1984). The strategies of foreign subsidiaries: Responses to organizational slack. *International Journal of Management and Organization, 1*, 91–106.

Prahalad, C. K., and Doz, Y. L. (1987). *The multinational mission: Balancing local demands and global vision*. New York: Free Press.

Provan, K. G. (1983). The federation as an interorganizational linkage network. *Academy of Management Review, 8*, 78–109,

Pugh, D. S., Hickson, D. J., and Hinings, C. R. (1969). The context of organizational structure. *Administrative Science Quarterly, 14*, 91–114.

Pugh, D. S., Hickson, D. J., Hinings, C. R., and Turner, C. (1968). The dimensions of organization structure. *Administrative Science Quarterly, 13*, 65–105.

Quinn, J. B. (1985). Managing innovation: Controlled chaos. *Harvard Business Review, 63*, 73–84.

Ring, P. S., and Van de Ven, A. H. (1992). Structuring cooperative relationships between organizations. *Strategic Management Journal, 13*, 483–498.

Roberts, E. B. (1980). New ventures for corporate growth. *Harvard Business Review, 68*(4), 130–144.

Robock, S. H., Simmons, K., and Zwick, J. (1977). *International business and multinational enterprises*. Homewood, IL: Irwin.

Roethlisberger, F. J. (1977). *The elusive phenomenon*. Boston: Division of Research, Graduate School of Business Administration, Harvard University.

Rogers, E. (1983). *Diffusion of innovations* (3rd ed.). New York: Free Press.

Ronstadt, R. C. (1977). *Research and development abroad by U.S. multinationals*. New York: Praeger.

Rugman, A. M. (1981). *Inside the multinationals: The economics of internal markets*. New York: Columbia University Press.

Sabel, C., Herrigel, G., Kazis, R., and Deeg, R. (1987). How to keep mature industries innovative. *Technology Review, 90*(3), 26–35.

Scheffe, H. A. (1953). A method of finding all contrasts in the analysis of variance. *Biometrika, 40*, 87–104.

Schmidt, S. M., and Kochan, T. A. (1977). Interorganizational relationships: Patterns and motivations. *Administrative Science Quarterly, 22*, 220–234.

Schumpeter, J. A. (1934). *The theory of capitalist development*. Cambridge, MA: Harvard University Press.

Scott, R. W. (1987). *Organizations: Rational, natural, and open systems* (2nd ed.). Englewood Cliffs, NJ: Prentice Hall.

Sharfman, M. P. (1988). Antecedents of organizational slack. *Academy of Management Review, 13*, 601–614.

Simon, H. A. (1945). *Administrative behavior*. New York: Macmillan.

Singh, J. V. (1986). Performance, slack, and risk-taking in organizational decision making. *Academy of Management Journal, 29*, 562–585.

Snyder, R. A., and Morris, J. H. (1984). Organizational communication and performance. *Journal of Applied Psychology, 69*, 461–465.

Staw, B. M., Sandelands, L. E., and Dutton, J. E. (1981). Threat-rigidity effects in organizational behavior: A multi-level analysis. *Administrative Science Quarterly, 26*, 501–524.

Stevens, G.V.G. (1974). The determinants of investment. In J. H. Dunning (Ed.), *Economic analysis and the multinational enterprise*. London: Allen & Unwin.

Stopford, J. M. (Ed.). (1983). *World directory of multinational enterprises*. Detroit: Gale Research.

Stopford, J. M., and Turner, L. (1985). *Britain and the multinationals*. Chichester, UK: Wiley.

Stopford, J. M., and Wells, L. T., Jr. (1972). *Managing the multinational enterprise*. New York: Basic Books.

Teece, D. J. (1986). Transaction cost economies and the multinational enterprise. *Journal of Economic Behavior and Organization, 7*, 21–45.

Thomas, D. A. (1993). Racial dynamics in cross-race developmental relationships. *Administrative Science Quarterly, 38*, 169–194.

Thompson, J. D. (1967). *Organizations in action*. New York: McGraw-Hill.

Thompson, V. A. (1967). *Bureaucracy and innovation*. Huntsville: University of Alabama Press.

Tichy, N. M., and Charan, R. (1989). Speed, simplicity, and self-confidence: An interview with Jack Welch. *Harvard Business Review, 67*(5), 112–120.

Tichy, N. M., Tushman, M. L., and Fombrun, C. (1979). Social network analysis for organizations. *Academy of Management Review, 4*, 507–519.

Turban, D. B., and Dougherty, T. W. (1994). Role of protégé personality in receipt of mentoring and career success. *Academy of Management Journal, 37*, 688–702.

Tushman, M. L. (1977). Communication across organizational boundaries: Special boundary roles in the innovation process. *Administrative Science Quarterly, 22*, 581–606.

Tushman, M. L. (1978). Technical communication in R&D laboratories: The impact of project work characteristics. *Academy of Management Journal, 4*, 624–645.

Urban, G. L., and Hauser, J. R. (1980). *Design and marketing of new products*. Englewood Cliffs, NJ: Prentice Hall.

Van de Ven, A. H. (1976). A framework for organization assessment. *Academy of Management Review, 1*, 64–78.

Van Maanen, J., and Schein, E. H. (1979). Toward a theory of organizational socialization. In B. M. Staw (Ed.), *Research in organizational behavior*. Greenwich, CT: JAI Press.

Venkatraman, N. (1989). A concept of fit in strategy research: Toward verbal and statistical correspondence. *Academy of Management Review, 14*, 423–444.

Vernon, R. E. (1966). International investment and international trade in the product cycle. *Quarterly Journal of Economics, 80*, 190–207.

Vernon, R. E. (1979). The product cycle hypothesis in a new international environment. *Oxford Journal of Economics and Statistics, 41*, 255–267.

Walton, R. E., and McKersie, R. B. (1965). *A behavioral theory of labor negotiations*. New York: McGraw-Hill.

Warren, R. L. (1967). The interorganizational field as a focus for investigation. *Administrative Science Quarterly, 12*, 396–419.

Weber, M. (1946). *From Max Weber: Essays in sociology*, H. H. Gerth and C. Wright Mills (Trans. and Eds.). New York: Oxford University Press.

Weber, M. (1978). *Economy and society*. Berkeley, CA: University of California Press.

Weick, K. E. (1980). *The social psychology of organizing* (2nd ed.). Reading, MA: Addison-Wesley.

Werts, C. E., Linn, R. L., and Joereskog, K. G. (1974). Interclass reliability estimates: Testing structural assumptions. *Educational and Psychological Measurement, 34*, 25–33.

Westney, D. E. (1989). Institutionalization theory: The study of the multinational enterprise. Paper presented at the conference on organization theory and the multinational enterprise, European Institute of Business Administration (INSEAD), Fontainebleau, France.

Westney, D. E. (1993). Institutionalization theory and the multinational corporation. In S. Ghoshal and D. E. Westney (Eds.), *Organization theory and the multinational corporation*. London: Macmillan.

Westney, D. E., and Sakakibara, D. (1985). Comparative study of the training, careers, and organization of engineers on the computer industry in Japan and the United States. Mimeograph, MIT–Japan Science and Technology Program.

Williamson, O. E. (1964). *The economics of discretionary behavior: Managerial objectives in a theory of the firm*. Englewood Cliffs, NJ: Prentice Hall.

Williamson, O. E. (1975). *Markets and hierarchies*. New York: Free Press.

Williamson, O. E. (1985). *The new institutional economics*. New York: Free Press.

Yip, G. S. (1989). Global strategy . . . in a world of nations? *Sloan Management Review, 30*, 29–41.

Zajac, E. J., Golden, B. R., and Shortell, S. M. (1991). New organizational forms for enhancing innovation: The case of internal corporate joint ventures. *Management Science, 37*, 170–184.

Zaltman, G., Duncan, R., and Holbeck, J. (1973). *Innovations and organizations*. New York: Wiley.

Zeitz, G. (1980). Interorganizational dialectics. *Administrative Science Quarterly, 25*, 72–88.

The Authors

Nitin Nohria is a professor at the Harvard Business School and is also a visiting professor at the London Business School. His recent books include *Fast Forward: The Best Ideas on Managing Business Change* (coedited with Jim Champy), *Beyond the Hype: Rediscovering the Essence of Management* (coauthored with Bob Eccles), *Networks and Organizations* (coedited with Bob Eccles), and *Building the Information Age Organization* (coauthored with Jim Cash, Richard Nolan, and Bob Eccles). Professor Nohria's teaching, research, and consulting focus on designing and transforming organizations to achieve superior performance. He is currently investigating the dynamics of change in large industrial corporations (the Fortune 100) by studying changes in their strategy, structure, governance, and culture over the last two decades.

Holder of the Robert P. Bauman Chair in Strategic Leadership, *Sumantra Ghoshal* joined the faculty of the London Business School in 1994. Prior to this he was professor of business policy at INSEAD and taught international business at the Sloan School, MIT. Professor Goshal's research, writing, and consulting focus on the management of large, worldwide firms. He has published a number of books, articles, and award-winning case studies including *Managing Across Borders: The Transnational Solution* (coauthored with Christopher A. Bartlett) and *Organisation Theory and the Multinational Corporation* (with Eleanor Westney). His latest book, *The Strategy Process: European Perspective*, written with Henry Mintzberg and J. B. Quinn, was published in 1995.

Index

SCORPION SHARDS

ALSO BY NEAL SHUSTERMAN

NOVELS
Antsy Does Time
Bruiser
The Dark Side of Nowhere
Dissidents
Downsiders
The Eyes of Kid Midas
Full Tilt
The Schwa Was Here
The Shadow Club
The Shadow Club Rising
Speeding Bullet
Unwind
UnWholly
What Daddy Did

THE SKINJACKER TRILOGY
Everlost
Everwild
Everfound

THE STAR SHARDS CHRONICLES
Scorpion Shards
Thief of Souls
Shattered Sky

THE DARK FUSION SERIES
Dreadlocks
Red Rider's Hood
Duckling Ugly

STORY COLLECTIONS
Darkness Creeping
Kid Heroes
MindQuakes
MindStorms

Visit the author at storyman.com

THE STAR SHARDS CHRONICLES
BOOK 1

SCORPION SHARDS

Neal Shusterman

SIMON & SCHUSTER BFYR

NEW YORK   LONDON   TORONTO   SYDNEY   NEW DELHI

SIMON & SCHUSTER BFYR

An imprint of Simon & Schuster Children's Publishing Division

1230 Avenue of the Americas, New York, New York 10020

For information about special discounts for bulk purchases,
please contact Simon & Schuster Special Sales at 1-866-506-1949
or business@simonandschuster.com.

The Simon & Schuster Speakers Bureau can bring authors to your live event.
For more information or to book an event,
contact the Simon & Schuster Speakers Bureau at 1-866-248-3049
or visit our website at www.simonspeakers.com.

Book design by Hilary Zarycky

The text for this book is set in Granjon.

Manufactured in the United States of America

2 4 6 8 10 9 7 5 3 1

Library of Congress Cataloging-in-Publication Data

Shusterman, Neal.

Scorpion shards / Neal Shusterman.

(The star shards chronicles ; book 1)

Originally published by Tor, 1995.

Summary: Six teenagers, each tormented by what seems to be an exaggerated
adolescent affliction, come together to try to stop the "beasts" that threaten
to destroy them and the world.

ISBN 978-1-4424-5836-9 (hardcover)

ISBN 978-1-4424-5116-2 (eBook)

[1. Supernatural—Fiction. 2. Horror stories.] I. Title.

PZ7.S55987

[Fic]—dc20

2012049166

For Anne McD., a star-shard of the highest order,
and for Mike and Christine,
who now shine like a double sun

ACKNOWLEDGMENTS

SCORPION SHARDS BEGAN AS A SMALL IDEA, BUT RAPIDLY EVOLVED INTO a trilogy, this being the first of three books. Along the way there were a great many people whose support and expertise made this book possible.

First, I'd like to thank the regional and scientific experts I met online through Prodigy, who lent an air of authenticity to the story. In Alabama, Matt Dakin, David Camp, Louis Davis, and R. D. McCollum. In the Midwest, Vicki Erwin and Tammy Hallberg. In Boise, Marilyn Friedrichsmeyer and Bradford Hill. In the Northwest, Rick Reynolds, Kim Guymon, Carol Hunter, and Jerry Morelan. And the astronomy and scientific experts John Winegar, Laura L. Metlak, Frank Sheldon, Charles Mielke, Stephen Kelly, and Paul Erikson.

Thanks also to Kathy Wareham, Diane Adams, and Scott Sorrentino, whose comments on early drafts helped to shape the story.

My deepest gratitude and admiration to Kathleen Doherty, who believed this book into existence in its initial Tor Books publication; and to my sons, Brendan and Jarrod, who, when they were young, made me a whole boxful of Creepy-Crawler scorpions, to paste on copies of the book; and thanks to their mother, Elaine, who was of great support and encouragement while this book was being written.

The new and improved incarnation of the Star Shards Chronicles could not have been possible without the support of my agent, Andrea Brown, as well as David Gale and Justin Chanda at Simon & Schuster, who are great luminous souls themselves, and saw fit to breathe new life into these books. They have always been among my favorite books. I'm thrilled that Simon & Schuster are getting them to a new audience!

My only disclaimer is that the star Mentarsus-H does not really exist. But if it did, then this might be what happens . . .

CONTENTS

Part I
American Dregs

1. THE DESTROYER

A SHATTERING OF GLASS.

A monstrous crash echoing through the glass-domed restaurant—and then a second sound so horrid and final it could have meant the very end of the world. The way thunder must sound to a man struck by lightning. The ear-piercing rattle of breaking glass, combined with the deep wooden crunch that followed, pinned the high and low ends of human hearing, and what remained between were dying dissonant chords like that of a shattered—

—piano?

The restaurant's maitre d' could not yet believe his eyes. He stood dumbfounded, trying to figure out what on earth had happened.

The final tinkling of ruined crystal fell from the ornate glass roof of the Garden Court Restaurant—the pride and joy of the Palace Hotel—the most beautiful restaurant in all of San Francisco. Until today. Today shards of the crystal ceiling were stabbing the plush Victorian furniture to death.

And it *was* a piano—or what was left of it, lying like a shipwreck in the center aisle.

Is God dropping pianos on us today? thought the maitre d'. *I should have called in sick.*

The restaurant was closed, thank goodness—Sunday brunch did not begin until eight—but workers and early-rising guests had already gathered to gawk.

Of course it must have been the piano from the new Cityview lounge, up on the top floor, but how could it have come crashing down seventeen floors, through the glass roof?

"Should I notify security?" asked one of the waiters, but somehow the maitre d' was sure security had already figured out there was a problem.

IN LIKE A FLASH and out in the blink of an eye.

The boy called Dillon Cole was in the street in an instant and vanished into the foggy morning. The streets were not crowded, but there were enough people for Dillon to lose himself among unknown faces. He wove through them, brushing past their shoulders, leaving a wake of chaos behind him. The souls he bumped into lost their concentration and sense of direction—a woman stopped short, forgetting where she was going; a man lost his train of thought in the middle of a conversation; a girl, just for a moment, forgot who she was, and why she was even here . . . but then Dillon passed, and their thoughts returned to normal. They would never know that their confusion was caused by Dillon's mere touch. But Dillon knew. He wondered if believing such a thing was enough to send him to the nuthouse. If that wasn't enough to have him locked away, certainly the other things would do the job.

Things like that business with the piano. For all the commotion it had caused, it had been an easy enough stunt. It was a simple thing to get into the deserted top-floor lounge on a Sunday morning. Since the grand piano was on wheels, it hadn't been that hard to ease it across the floor, out onto the patio. As he moved the piano, his fury had grown along with

the burning, screaming need to finish this act of destruction—
a need that ate at his gut like an uncontrollable hunger.

A wrecking-hunger.

Adrenaline coursed through his veins, giving him incredible strength as he heaved the piano onto the ledge—but all he could feel was that wrecking-hunger, forcing him on like a hot iron drilling down to his very soul. He hoisted the heavy beast of a piano onto the ledge, where it balanced for a moment, floating between possible futures, and then it disappeared, taking the railing with it.

One second. Two seconds. Three seconds.

The impact came as a deafening scream of dying crystal as the great glass roof seventeen floors below was shattered . . . and the wrecking-hunger was instantly quelled. That pressure deep inside was released by some invisible escape valve. Dillon took a deep breath of relief and didn't spare the time to look at his handiwork. He got out.

Wearing a bellhop uniform he had taken from a storage closet, Dillon took the elevator to the lobby and left without anyone giving him a second glance—and why should anyone suspect him? He was fifteen, but could pass for seventeen; he was an attractive, clean-cut, redheaded kid who simply looked like one of the kids the bell captain was training. So no one noticed him as he slipped out into the street, where he quickly took off his bellhop jacket and vanished into the morning.

Now, the hotel was far behind him and, in front of him, the stairwell of a BART station descended into darkness. Fog swirled around it as if it were the mouth of a black cave, but to Dillon it was a wonderfully welcome sight.

Once he was down the stairs and heard the approaching train that would carry him away, he knew he was home free. He dropped the bellhop jacket in the trash as he hurried to catch the train. He was not caught. He was never caught.

The train stopped, Dillon found a seat, and it rolled on. Only now, as the hotel fell farther and farther behind, did he relax enough for the worries to fill his head.

Please, he begged. *Let no one be hurt. Please let no one be hurt.* The restaurant was closed—but what if a waiter had been setting tables? What if a housekeeper had been vacuuming the rug? Dillon was always careful—he was always good at predicting exactly how his little disasters would unfold, and so far there had been no major injuries . . . but he was starting to slip—the wrecking-hunger was making him careless. When the hunger to destroy came, it was all-consuming and didn't allow him second thoughts. But now in the aftermath of his horrible deed, when his spirit seemed to hang like that piano on the edge of its drop, he could clearly see the ramifications of these awful, awful acts.

People could have died! And I won't know until I see the news. The weight that now burdened his soul was truly unbearable . . . yet it was more bearable than the hunger, which always came back, making him forget everything else. He would fall slave to it again, and the only way to escape was to destroy something. Anything. Everything. The bigger the better. The louder the better. And when it was done the pressure would be gone. The hunger would be fed, and the relief would be rich and sweet like a fat piece of chocolate melting in his mouth.

But the wrecking-hunger had been getting worse lately. It didn't come once a week anymore. Now it came almost every day, pushing him, pressing him, demanding to be fed. Even now as he sat on the train, he felt the hunger again. How could it be? So soon! Wasn't the piano enough? It was the biggest, it was the loudest, it was the worst he'd done yet.

What more did he have to do to be free of this terrible hunger?

The woman sitting next to him on the train eyed him with a look of motherly concern—a look Dillon hadn't seen for the entire year he had been out on his own. She glanced at his shaking hands.

"Are you all right?" asked the woman.

"Sure, fine."

And then she touched his hand to stop it from shaking.

"No!" said Dillon, but it was too late. She had touched him. Her face became pale and she shrank away.

"Ex . . . excuse me," she said in a daze, and she wandered off to find a seat far away from Dillon. Then she sat down to begin the task of unscrambling her mind.

"WHAT ARE YOU AFRAID of, Deanna?"

"Everything. Everything, that's all."

Deanna Chang's pale hands gripped the arms of her chair as if the chair were the only thing keeping her from being flung into space. The room around her was painted a hideous yellow, peeling everywhere like flesh, to reveal deep red underneath. The place smelled musty and old. Faces on fading portraits seemed to lean closer to listen. The walls themselves seemed to be listening. And breathing.

"I can't help you, Deanna, if you won't be specific."

The man who sat across the old desk shifted uncomfortably in his chair. *I make him nervous,* thought Deanna. *Why do I even make psychiatrists nervous?*

"You *can't* help me, okay?" said Deanna. "That's the point." He tapped his pencil on the desk. The eraser fell off the end and rolled onto the stained floor.

I hate this place, thought Deanna. *I hate this room, I hate this man, and I hate my parents for making me come here to hear the same questions the other shrinks have asked, then give the same answers, and have nothing change. Nothing. Ever.*

A woman's voice wailed outside, and Deanna jumped. She couldn't tell whether the sound was a shriek, or a laugh.

"I'm afraid," said Deanna. "I'm afraid of dying."

"Good. That's a start."

Deanna began to rub her pale, slender arms. Behind her and beneath her, the springs within the padding of the chair poked and threatened her through the fabric of the worn upholstery. "At first I was just afraid of walking outside alone. I thought it would end up being a good thing, because it made my parents move us to a better neighborhood—but it didn't stop when we moved. I started to imagine all the terrible things that could happen to me." She leaned forward. "That was two years ago. Now I see myself dying every day. I see my body smashed if our house were to collapse. I see a man with a knife hiding in the closet, or the basement, or the attic in the middle of the night. I see a car with no driver leaping the curb to pull me beneath its wheels . . ."

"You think people are out to get you?"

"Not just people. Things. Everything."

The shrink scribbled with his eraserless pencil. Somewhere deep within the building a heater came on, moaning a faint, sorrowful moan.

"And you imagine these awful things might happen to you?"

"No!" said Deanna. "I *see* these things happening to me. They happen, I feel them—I see them—It's REAL!" Deanna reached up and brushed cool sweat from her forehead. "And then I blink, and it—"

"And it all goes away?"

"Sometimes. Other times the vision doesn't go away until I scream."

The shrink in the cheap suit loosened his tie and put his finger beneath his collar. He coughed a bit.

"Stuffy," he said.

"I'm not safe going out," said Deanna. "I'm not safe staying in. I'm not safe here—because what if the stupid light fixture above my head right now is slowly coming unscrewed and waiting for the perfect moment to fall and crack my skull?"

The shrink looked up at the fixture, which did, indeed, seem loose. He leaned back, unfastened his collar button and took a deep breath, as if the air were thinning. He was becoming frightened, Deanna noted—just like everyone else did when they were near her. She could feel his fear as strongly as her own.

"I think I might drown," Deanna said. "Or suffocate. I always feel like I'm suffocating. Have you ever felt like that?"

"On occasion." His voice sounded empty and distant. He seemed to shrivel slightly in his chair.

Deanna smiled. Feeling his fear somehow made *her* fear begin to diminish. "I give you the creeps, don't I?"

"Your mother is very concerned about you."

"My mother can take a flying leap, if she thinks *you* can help me."

"That's not a healthy attitude."

"You know what? *I* think you're gonna screw me up worse than I was before. Can you guarantee that you won't? And are you sure this stuff is *all* inside my head? Are you *certain*? Are you?" Deanna waited for an answer.

If he said he was sure, she would believe him. If he swore up and down that he could take away the darkness that shrouded her life, she would believe—because she wanted to believe that it was a simple matter of her being crazy. But he didn't answer her. He couldn't even look at her. Instead, he glanced down at his watch and breathed a sigh of relief.

"Is my time up?"

"I'm afraid so."

"FORGIVE ME, FATHER, FOR I have sinned."

"Tell me what your sins are, my son." The priest on the other side of the confessional sighed as he spoke. He must have recognized Dillon's shaky voice from the many times Dillon had come to confess.

"I've done terrible things," said Dillon, cramped within the claustrophobic booth.

"Such as?"

"Yesterday I broke a gear in the cable house—that's why the cable cars weren't running. This morning I shattered the glass roof of the Garden Court Restaurant."

"Dear Lord." The priest's voice was an icy whisper. "I can't give you absolution for this, Dillon."

Dillon stiffened, suddenly feeling as if the booth had grown smaller, tighter, pressing against him. "Please," he begged, "no one was hurt—the news said so—*please!*"

"Dillon, you have to turn yourself in."

"You don't understand, Father. I can't. I can't because it wouldn't stop me. I would find a way to escape and wreck something else—something even bigger. It's not like I want to do this stuff—I *have* to. I don't have a choice!"

"Listen to me," said the priest. "You're . . . not *well*. You're a very sick boy and you have to get help."

"Don't you think my parents tried that?" fumed Dillon. "That kind of help doesn't work on me. It only makes me worse!"

"I . . . I'm sorry, I can't absolve you."

Dillon was speechless in his terror. To go without forgiveness for the things he was forced to do—that was the worst nightmare of all. He gripped the small cross around his neck, holding it tightly, feeling the silver press into his palm.

"But I'm not guilty!" Dillon insisted. "I have no choice—I'm *poisoned*! I'm *cursed*!"

"Then your penance is taking this confession to the police."

"It's not their job to absolve me!" screamed Dillon. "It's *your* job. You're supposed to take away my sins, and you can't judge me! You can't!"

No answer from the priest.

"Fine. If you won't absolve me, I'll find a priest who will."

Dillon flung the cherrywood door out so hard, it splintered when it hit the wall. A woman gasped, but Dillon was past her, and out the door as quickly as his anger could carry him. The wrecking-hunger was already building again, and he didn't know how much longer he could resist it. He had half a mind to throw bricks through the stained glass window of the church, but it wasn't God he had a gripe with. Or was it? He didn't know.

He had told the priest his name a week before in a moment of weakness, and now it could very well be his ruin. Would this priest betray the secrecy of the confessional and point a finger at Dillon?

Dillon didn't want to find out. He would have to leave tonight and find a new place to wreak his havoc. He had worked his way up from Arizona without getting caught, and there were still lots of places to go. There was a freedom in feeling completely abandoned by life, Dillon tried to convince himself. It was easy to keep moving when every city was just as lonely. When every face in every crowd was just as uncaring.

But there had to be one more feeding—just one more before he left. It would need to be something grand and devastating—something that would put the wrecking-hunger to sleep for a while.

Are you proud of me, Mom and Dad? he thought bitterly. *Are you proud of your little boy now?* He thanked God that they were dead, and hoped they were far enough away from this world not to know the things he had done.

NOT FAR AWAY, DEANNA Chang climbed a steep sidewalk, trying to forget her appointment with the psychiatrist. She didn't dare to look at the people she passed—they all eyed her suspiciously, or at least it seemed that they did—she could never tell for sure. It made her want to look down to see if her socks were different colors, or if her blouse was bloody from a nose-bleed she didn't even know about. Now that she was outside, her claustrophobia switched gears into agoraphobia—the fear of the outside world. It wasn't just that her fears were abnormal—they were unnatural, and it made her furious. She had had a warm, loving childhood—she had no trauma in her history—and yet when she had turned twelve, the fears began to build, becoming obsessions that grew into visions, and now, at fifteen, the world around her was laced with razor blades and poison in every look, in every sound, in every moment of every single day. The fear seemed to steal the breath from her lungs. So strong was the fear that it reached out and coiled around anyone close to her; her parents, the kids who had once been her friends— even strangers who got too near. Her fear was as contagious as a laughing fit and as overwhelming as cyanide fumes.

As she reached the corner, her fear gripped her so tightly that she couldn't move, and she knew that she was about to have another waking-vision of her own death. That it was only in her mind didn't make it any less real, because she felt every measure of pain and terror.

Then it happened: Confusion around her, loud noises. She blinked, blinked again, and a third time, as she tried to make the horrific vision go away. But the vision remained. The driverless car leapt from the curb, and it swallowed her.

DILLON WATCHED FROM THE top of the hill, his horror almost overwhelming the wrecking-hunger in his gut. His eyes took it in as if it were slow motion.

The truck was hauling six brand-new Cadillacs to a dealership somewhere. A few minutes ago, Dillon had jaywalked across the street. He had searched for the chains that fastened the last car onto the lower deck of the truck and picked the locks with the broken prong of a fork. Another human being could have spent all day trying to figure out how to pick those locks—but chains, ropes, and locks were easy for Dillon. He was better than Houdini.

He had clearly anticipated the entire pattern of how the event would go, like a genius calculating a mathematical equation. The car would spill out of the transport truck; the bus driver behind it would turn the wheel to the right; the bus would jump a curb; cars would start swerving in a mad frenzy to get out of the way of the runaway car; many fenders would be ruined—some cars would be totaled . . . but not many people would get hurt.

Maximum damage; minimal injury. This was the pattern Dillon had envisioned in his unnaturally keen mind. What Dillon did not anticipate was that the driver of the bus was left-handed.

Dillon walked up hill and watched as the truck lurched forward, got halfway up the steep hill, and then the last car on its lower ramp slid out and down the hill. Horns instantly began blaring, tires screeched, the escaping Cadillac headed straight for the bus . . .

. . . And the bus driver instinctively turned his wheel to the left, instead of the right—*right into oncoming traffic.*

That simple change in the pattern of events altered everything. Dillon now saw a new pattern emerging, and this time there would be blood.

Horrified, he watched as car after car careened off the road into light posts and storefronts. People scattered. Others didn't have the chance.

Dillon watched the driverless car roll through the intersection and toward a corner. A man ran out of the way, leaving a solitary girl directly in the path of the car—an Asian girl no older than Dillon, who stood frozen in shock. Dillon tried to shout to her, but it was too late. The driverless Caddy leapt the curb, and the girl disappeared, as if swallowed by the mouth of a whale.

For Dillon Benjamin Cole, it was a moment of hell . . . and yet in that moment something inside him released the chokehold it had on his gut. The hunger was gone—its dark need satisfied by the nightmare before him. Satisfied by the bus that crashed deep down the throat of a bookstore; and by the ruptured fire hydrant that had turned a convertible Mercedes into a fountain; and by the sight of the girl disappearing into the grillwork of the Cadillac. Dillon felt every muscle in his body relax. Relief filled every sense—he could smell it, taste it like a fine meal. A powerful feeling of well-being washed over him, leaving him unable to deny how good it made him feel.

And Dillon hated himself for it. Hated himself more than God could possibly hate him.

A HOSPITAL WAS AN indifferent place, filled with promises it didn't keep, and prayers that were refused. At least that's how Dillon saw it ever since he watched his parents waste away in a hospital over a year ago. The doctors never did figure out what had killed them, but Dillon knew. They had held their son one too many times . . . and they died of broken minds. Insanity, Dillon knew, could kill like any other disease. Dillon had watched his parents' minds slowly fall apart, until the things they said became gibberish, and the things they did became dangerous. In the end, Dillon imagined their minds had become like snow on a television screen. With thoughts as pointless as that, sometimes a body knows to turn itself off and die.

Now, as he stepped into the private hospital room with a bouquet of flowers, Dillon barely recognized the girl in the bed. He had only seen her from a distance—before the Cadillac had taken her down, and then in the aftermath of his awful accident, when she was whisked into an ambulance and taken away. How could he expect to recognize a face he had seen so briefly? And yet he had seen that face long enough for it to haunt him for the rest of his life unless he paid this visit.

Her name was Deanna; he had found that much out. She was half-Asian; an only child. The nurse at reception had asked if he was family, he told her he was a cousin. Once inside the room, he told her mother that he was a classmate. He sat beside the mother, chattering lies about a school and teachers he had never heard of, and then the mother got up to make some calls, leaving Dillon alone to keep a vigil for the girl. For Deanna.

DEANNA FLOATED DEEP IN the void, hearing nothing but her own heartbeat. She opened her mouth to scream, but no sound came out. She felt far away, beneath an ocean, for she could not breathe at all. She forced herself up and up, toward the light at the surface, her head pounding, her chest cramping, until finally she broke surface, into the light of—

—a room. A hospital room. Yes. Yes, of course. The driver-less car of doom. How terrified she had been of it. She had seen it before. Only this time it had been real. It was not just there to terrify her—it was there to kill her—and it could have, too—but she wasn't dead. She wiggled her toes—she wasn't even paralyzed. She moved her right arm and felt a searing pain shoot through her wrist that made her groan.

"You're all right," said someone next to her. The voice of a man. No—a boy. She lazily turned her head to face him, and her eyes began to focus. He was her age—fifteenish, with red hair but eyes that were dark and so frighteningly deep that she couldn't look away. *Soulful,* her mother would call those eyes.

"Your wrist is sprained," he said. "You've probably got a concussion too, but still you're pretty lucky, considering what happened."

"Who are you?" she asked.

"No one important," he replied. "My name's Dillon." She still could not look away from his eyes, and what she saw there told her all she needed to know. His eyes poured forth his guilt, and she knew that somehow he had done this to her. He had sent the terrible driverless car.

"You bastard," she groaned, and yet she felt strangely relieved. This time it *had* been real, not just another vision—and yet she wasn't dead. In its own way, it was a relief.

Dillon leaned away, unnerved. "I didn't want to hurt you." He said anxiously. "I didn't want to hurt anybody. . . . It's just that . . ." He stopped. How could he hope she could ever understand?

"No, tell me," she said and grabbed his hand. Dillon gasped and tried to pull his hand back; but even in her weakened state, she held him firmly . . . and he was amazed to discover that his touch didn't scramble her mind. She did not shrink away from him.

How was this possible? Everyone he touched was affected—*everyone*.

"Your hand is warm," she said, then looked at him curiously. "You're not afraid! I don't make you afraid!"

"No," he said. She smiled, keeping her eyes fixed on his, and in that moment a brilliant light shone through the half-opened blinds—a sudden green flash that resolved into a red glow in the dark sky.

Whatever that light was, it seemed to make the rest of the world go away, leaving the two of them floating in a hospital room that was floating in space.

This, thought Deanna, *is the most important moment of my life* . . . and she immediately knew why.

"You're like me!" she whispered. "You're just like me!"

Dillon nodded, his eyes filling with tears, because he too knew it was true. In this instant, he felt closer to Deanna than he had ever felt to anyone. *I almost killed her,* he thought. *How horrible it would have been if she died, and we had never met.* He marveled at how the strange light painted a soft glow around her charcoal hair, and he felt a sudden reverence for her that was beyond words. The only words that he could speak now that would make any sense would be his confession.

"I destroy everything I touch," said Dillon.

"You don't destroy me," answered Deanna.

"I'm a monster," said Dillon.

"That's not what I see," she answered. It was the closest thing to forgiveness Dillon had ever felt. Then Deanna began to cry and began a confession of her own.

"I'm afraid," she said.

"Of what?"

"Of this place. Of my life. Of everything inside and out. I'm terrified."

Dillon gripped her hand tightly. "Then I'll protect you," he said. "I'll make sure nothing out there can hurt you."

Deanna smiled through her tears, because she knew that this boy who had almost destroyed her now meant to protect her with all his heart. He held her hand with a delicate intensity, as if having her hand in his was a miracle of the highest order. In this instant, she trusted him more than she had ever trusted anyone.

"No," she answered. "We'll protect each other."

2. 'STONE GETS COOTIES

On that same night, the dark sky over Alabama was punctuated by a million stars. Still, those stars were not bright enough to shed light on the ground, and since the moon had not yet risen, the ground was left darker than the space between the stars.

Winston Marcus Pell lay in his lightless room, wiggling his fingers, trying to see them. His dark skin could have been painted fluorescent yellow, and still he'd have seen little more than a vague shadow.

A night this black was either a good omen or a bad one—depending on which set of superstitions you chose to believe—and Winston had to keep reminding himself that he didn't believe in that silly stuff. Educated people like him didn't have superstitions—that was left to the poor folk still trapped deep in the Black Belt, tilling its cruel dark soil. People who didn't know any better.

So why, then, was Winston so afraid on nights like tonight?

The wind came and went in great and sudden gusts that rattled the windows and tore off leaves before their time. Those yellow October leaves, orphaned by the wind, would shatter against the side of their big old house, sounding like scampering mice. When the gusts had passed, there was silence as empty as the night was dark. This was wrong, Winston knew. It was terribly wrong.

There are no evil creatures out there, he told himself. Those were stories told by old folks to keep kids from wandering out into the dark—but the silence—it was all wrong!

There are no crickets.

That was it!

The realization made Winston's neck hairs stand on end and made him want to shrink even smaller beneath his blanket. There were *always* crickets, chirping all night long out here in the country—even in October. When they'd moved out from Birmingham, it was weeks before Winston could sleep because of the crickets.

What had shut the crickets up tonight?

Winston cursed himself for being so stupid about it. Damn it all, he was fifteen—no matter how he looked on the outside, he was fifteen *inside*, and shouldn't be worried about what crickets choose to do on this night. On this dark night. On this dark creepy night.

Winston knew why he was afraid, although he didn't want to think about it. He was afraid because, apart from the local superstitions, he knew there were stranger things in heaven and earth than he could shake a stick at.

Like the strange and awful thing that had been happening to him for almost three years now. Of course no one talked about that to his face anymore. No one but little Thaddy, who was just too dumb to know any better.

Winston clenched his hands into fists, wishing he had someone to fight. Well, maybe he was afraid of a night without crickets, but if something were out there, he was mad enough to beat the thing silly. He'd paralyze it and leave it helpless on the muddy ground, no matter how big it was.

A gust of wind ripped across the silence, then a thin ghostly wail flew in from the next room followed by the sound of running feet.

Thaddy was in Winston's room in a terrible fright. He

smashed his shin against Winston's wooden bed frame, and his wail turned into a howl.

"Hush up!" ordered Winston. "I don't want you waking Mama."

"There's a monster outside, 'Stone," cried Thaddy. "I seen him! He was at my window gonna rip my guts out, I know it." Thaddy wiped his eyes. "I think it was Tailybone."

Thaddy made a move to jump into bed with Winston, but thought better of it. Instead he just grabbed Winston's blanket off of him and curled up with it on the floor.

"You had best give that back, or you'll be sleepin' with no front teeth." But Thaddy didn't move.

"It's out there, 'Stone, I saw it. It was drooling on my window. I swear it was. We gotta get the rifle."

"We ain't got a rifle, you idiot!"

Winston slipped out of bed and touched his feet to the floor. In the silence, the floorboards creaked.

"Where are the crickets?" asked Thaddy.

"Hush yo' aoo, or I'm gonna paralyze your lips till morning."

"No! I'll be good. I promise. No more talking," which was like a wind-chime promising to be quiet through a hurricane.

Winston glanced out of his window. In normal moonlight, he could see the yard and beyond, all the way through the neighbor's field. Tonight, he could barely see the fence—and just beyond the fence, the cotton seemed to roll like beasts in the shadows. Tigers and big fat alligators.

"I can smell it out there," mumbled Thaddy. "It's got a dead smell, like somethin' back from the grave."

"Quit trying to scare yourself," said Winston. He didn't smell it the way Thaddy did, but Winston knew that Thaddy was right—something *was* out there—he could sense it.

Winston grabbed his baseball bat from beneath the bed and headed toward Thaddy's room with Thaddy close behind. No reason to wake their mother up until they knew for sure.

"It's Tailybone, I know it!" whined Thaddy.

"There's no such thing, that's just a dumb old story," Winston said, for himself as much as he did for Thaddy.

Then Thaddy made an observation. It probably wasn't true, but it bothered Winston just the same. "You're shorter today, 'Stone," he said. "Reckon now you've got so short you can't whoop a grave-monster."

Winston threw Thaddy an evil look and put his forefinger up, just an inch away from Thaddy's mouth as a warning. Even in the dark, Thaddy could see the silhouette of the finger about to touch his lips.

"No! No! 'Stone, I'll shut up. I promise."

Little Thaddy was ten years old—a full five years younger than Winston—but Winston was two inches shorter. Winston was, in every way, the size and shape of an eight-year-old.

It hadn't always been that way. He had grown like a weed until the time he was twelve or so. Then, when his friends started sprouting legs and knobby knees, Winston stopped growing up . . .

. . . and started growing down.

The way he figured, he'd have the body of kindergartner again when he was eighteen.

"I wish *I* could grow backward," Thaddy had once said, when he outgrew his favorite bike. But as he watched his big brother become his little brother, Thaddy's thoughts on the subject changed. Thaddy made no such wishes anymore.

The door to Thad's room was ajar, and Winston pushed it all the way open. Its hinges complained with a high-pitched creak as the door swung open to reveal . . . an open window. If there was a thing out there—it could be in the house now! It could be anywhere!

"Thaddy, was your window open before?"

Thaddy stuttered a bit.

"Think! Was your window open or closed?"

Thaddy couldn't remember.

A gnarled branch hung just outside the window, coiled as if fixing to reach in and grab something. In the tree, a rag fluttered in the breeze.

"It's my shirt," said Thaddy. "I threw it at the thing. Maybe I scared it away, maybe."

Winston stood at the threshold of the room for the longest time, not daring to go in. He squinted his eyes and looked at the tree. The light was so very dim that he could barely see the tree at all, and the more he looked the more he thought he saw a face in it. A big old twisted face. A goblin with a head the size of a pumpkin leering into the window.

"It's just the tree," explained Winston, breathing a silent sigh of intense relief. "Your fool head is playing tricks on you again."

"But what about the smell, 'Stone?"

"Dead possum, maybe—under the window, like last year," said Winston, but the smell didn't catch him the way it caught Thaddy.

Thaddy clung to this explanation, and climbed into bed. Winston tucked his brother in, making sure to touch only the blanket.

"Thank you, 'Stone," said Thaddy. "And I'm sorry about what I said before about you being too small and all. I think it's great that you're small."

"Quit talking about that!"

Winston didn't want anyone talking about it ever. The very

first sign of trouble came about three years ago. Not only had it become apparent that he had stopped growing, but something else just as alarming began to happen. It was the way Winston's touch could make a person tingle. Carpet shocks, his parents called it. Didn't think much of it. Then they had taken Winston to the doctor for a simple flu shot. The doctor noticed his height was half an inch shorter than a year before. Didn't think much of it. Must have been a mistake. A few months later, they knew it was no mistake. He was a whole inch shorter. Four doctors later, and they still didn't know what to make of it—and none of the doctors would acknowledge the strange effect Winston's touch was beginning to have on people. Vitamin deficiency, they said. Genetic fluke. One doctor named Guthry wanted to called it Guthry's Syndrome and tried to send him up to the Mayo Clinic where they'd study him like a rat.

So they stopped seeing doctors.

It was the crazy old sisters down the road who called it "Growing Down." They called Winston a witch child, and it made his dad furious. Mr. Pell had been a man of science—a pharmacist—but more than that—a scholar. He was an educated man with educated friends; he had moved back from the city to set an example and help the small town he grew up in. Those two old sisters were everything he hated about growing up black, poor, and ignorant in the Deep South.

When Winston's dad died of a heart attack, the sisters spread word that it was Winston who did it, by putting "a stunt" on his daddy's heart, the way he had put a stunt on their little vegetable garden, where nothing grew larger than the size of a finger. For all Winston knew those toothless old crones were right.

Of course, people didn't really believe he had killed his

father, but the thought was always there—and by then, Winston's touch could numb people's arms, making them tingly, like when your foot fell asleep. The family had stopped going to church soon after, because Baptists saw God or the Devil in everything. It wasn't exactly comfortable being the center of attention on Sunday. Still, Winston often wondered . . . if he could stunt vegetables, numb flesh, and grow backward, was that science or magic? God or the Devil?

Winston finished tucking Thaddy in nice and tight, just the way he liked it.

"The window, 'Stone. Gotta shut out the rotten possum smell."

Winston went to the window, and remembered Thaddy's shirt hanging in the branch, just out of his limited reach. Before closing the window, Winston leaned out into the night to get the shirt . . .

. . . and the monster, sitting in the tree limbs beside the window, hissed like a python.

Winston screamed!

The hideous thing was less than a foot from Winston's face. It was going to kill him. It was going to rip his guts out like Thaddy said. Why, of all times, did Thaddy have to be right about something *now*!

It leapt deeper into the tree, and the tree limbs clattered like bones as the thing hurried to the ground.

"It's Tailybone!" screamed Thaddy, half out of his little fool mind. "It's Tailybone!" And he screamed for their mother.

Winston pushed himself back into the room and fell to the floor. A light came on downstairs.

"Thaddy, are you all right? What's going on up there?" Winston headed downstairs with the baseball bat, and Thaddy fell in line close behind, still whimpering about Tailybone.

"Shut up!" Winston commanded his brother. "There ain't no such thing, there never was and there never will be!"

"Then what was that?"

"I don't know, but it wasn't no Tailybone. It was a some*one*, not a some*thing*," Winston was sure of that now, because the face of the beast had something very human about it. Maybe it was something that escaped from someplace. A carnival. An asylum.

"Maybe it's an alien, maybe," said Thad. "It was so UGLY!"

"What was so ugly?" shouted Mama. They passed her room downstairs, on the way out the back door. She was already scrambling out of her bed and into her wheelchair.

"Don't worry, Mama, I'll check it out."

"Don't you go out there, Winston, if it's a prowler, we'll call the sheriff!"

But nothing she could say would stop him now. At first he had been terrified, but the terror was quickly boiling itself into full-blown fury. He had his fighting fury up, and no one messed with 'Stone Pell when he was in a fighting frenzy.

The kids around town knew that you didn't fight that little freak 'Stone, unless you wanted to be laid out by the count of five—because now Winston's touch was more than just numbing. Every punch Winston threw was guaranteed to paralyze whatever it hit. First your right arm would go senseless, then your left, then your chin, then your gut, and before long you were lying on the ground, your body limp and useless for hours—maybe even till morning. Maybe longer.

It left Winston with no one to fight, and that was a horrible thing, because lately all Winston wanted to do was fight.

Winston and Thad raced through Mama's stunted garden, hopped the fence, and followed the thing out into the pasture at the edge of a field ripe with cotton.

The moon was on the rise now, making the cotton shine

like snow. There was enough light to see the shape of the thing as it lumbered behind the octopus tree, an ancient live oak with a dozen limbs perfect for climbing. The thing tried to get up into the tree, but Winston swung the bat. He missed, but the creature slipped on some Spanish moss, and fell to the ground. Thaddy pushed at it once, and then ran to hide behind the octopus tree.

"Paralyze it, 'Stone," yelled Thad. "Paralyze it good!"

Winston threw the bat down and cornered it against a hedge thick with sharp thorns. He moved in for hand-to-hand combat.

The beast wasn't as big as he had thought—but it was certainly bigger than he was. Winston dove on the thing, fists flying. It struggled, and Winston grabbed onto its arms—but the thing pulled away, and they both fell over the fence into the cotton. He couldn't paralyze it, no matter how hard he tried. All he could do was fight it, and so Winston and the beast rolled in the cotton, fighting one another, until the beast spoke.

"Stop it," it screamed in a voice that was wet and raspy, but still not evil enough for a nightmare beast. "Or I'm really gonna have to beat you silly!"

The thing threw Winston off, and he landed hard against a fence post with a thud.

By now Thaddy was scratching his arm—the one that had touched the thing.

"Why aren't you paralyzed yet?" Winston demanded. "What the hell are you?"

"I'm a freak," it said. "I'm a freak like you."

Winston took a good look at its face. It was pocked and cratered, like the face of the moon—full of peeling sores and swelling boils, as if it had been bathing in nuclear waste. It was what Winston imagined leprosy might be like—only worse.

That's when Thaddy made an amazing observation.

"I think it might be a girl," he said.

A girl? Winston regarded the grotesque face. It was hard enough for Winston to figure what color its skin was, much less its sex. The straight blond hair gave away that it was white, but the fact that the hair was short and matted didn't reveal what sex it was, if any.

"Are you a boy or a girl?" demanded Winston.

"A girl," it said, disgusted.

By now, Thaddy was scratching his arm like crazy.

"What did you do to him?"

The she-thing smiled. "He shouldn't have touched me. Guess I gave him cooties."

Thaddy looked at Winston and the pizza-faced girl in horror, as if to say *You mean there really is such a thing as cooties?* He turned and ran back to the house, screaming for Mama.

"He'll get a rash on his arm," said the girl. "Probably come down with a bad fever for a week or so, but then it'll go away . . . he shouldn't have touched me."

"Winston?" called his mother from the porch. "What's going on out there?"

"Just some girl, Mama," said Winston. "Thaddy fell in some poison ivy—better tend to him." This was far easier than trying to explain to her the truth.

When his mother had rolled back into the house, the girl-thing told Winston her name was Tory, short for Victoria.

"What's wrong with you?" Winston asked Tory.

"Acne," she said. "Ain't you ever seen acne before?"

Winston looked closely. If this was acne, it was acne gone

mad. There was a human being down there, but it was hidden far beneath an oily layer of zits built on zits. If you spread all those blemishes across ten faces, each face would still be painful to look at.

"You're damn ugly," observed Winston.

"Gee, thanks for noticing, Mighty Mouse. It just so happens that I know who you are. I've been watching you ever since my aunt and me moved here last month. Are you really a witch midget? A devil-dwarf?"

"Go to hell!" shouted Winston, and he leapt at her. So what if she was a girl? No one called him things like that.

They rolled and fought, and even though Winston wasn't really winning, it felt good. It felt wonderful to actually have someone to fight who didn't fall to the ground the second he touched them.

"You possum-rot pus-head," shouted Winston.

"You pin-headed voodoo troll!" shouted Tory.

"Slime-drippin' cesspool explosion!"

"Baby-brained diaper butt!"

"Fusion-face!"

"Shrunken head!'

"Elephant girl!"

Tory delivered a punch to the nose that was right on the mark. It hurt pretty bad, and Winston had to stagger off, collapsing by the fence.

"Why can't I paralyze you?" he asked weakly.

"I don't know," she said. "Why don't you get sick when I touch you?"

They looked at each other like boxers in separate corners.

"Sorry I hit you so hard," said Tory. "It's just that the elephant girl thing is a sore spot. It's what they used to call me when I lived in Florida."

"Where'd you live, the Everglades?" jabbed Winston. "Are you a swamp thing?"

Tory didn't answer. Even in the dim light Winston could see her puffy eyes filling with tears.

"Okay," said Winston. "Truce?"

"Truce," echoed Tory, rubbing the tears from her eyes before they had a chance to fall. *Tears would probably make her face sting*, thought Winston.

"You always go looking in people's windows at night, scarin' 'em half to death?" he asked, wiping his bloody nose.

"Sun's bad for my delicate complexion," said Tory, "so I do all my exploring at night. People don't see me that way. Suits me just fine."

"Does your face . . . hurt?"

"All the time." She leaned a bit closer to him, whispering. "Is it true you're growing backward?"

"What do you care?" snapped Winston.

"I came looking for you because I heard what people said about you. I wanted you to touch my face . . . paralyze it so I couldn't feel it at all, and maybe it would stop hurting."

Winston shook his head. "But you don't paralyze like the others. . . . Why?"

Just then their faces were lit by a light in the sky, shining brighter than the crescent moon. The cotton around them glowed green for a moment and then pink. At first Winston took it to be the sheriff's spotlight, but the color was wrong— and it was too high up.

They stood up to get a better look. It was an uneven ball of light, maybe a fourth the size of the moon. It hurt their eyes to look at it.

Winston backed up to a fence post, leaning on it for balance. The light had triggered something inside of him, and he thought he might pass out. All at once, his brain was firing like crazy, and he was filled with an overpowering sense of wonder and confusion, as if all his life he had been sleeping and was just waking up. But of all the confused feelings and thoughts that rocketed through his head, the most overwhelming feeling of all was the sense that this light in the sky, whatever it was, was meant for him.

"It's incredible," said Tory. "I've never . . . *felt* anything like it."

Winston looked over at Tory and could see in her rapid breathing and wonder-filled eyes that she was hit by the same devastating wave of emotion that he felt. She had the same revelation that this odd light in the sky did not just hit their eyes, it ignited their souls.

It made Winston furious!

Whatever that light was, it was for him and him alone. He didn't want to have to share such a special thing with this hideous girl beside him. It would mean that they didn't meet tonight by accident—they were drawn together—somehow bound like soul mates. Winston found the thought unbearable.

"I . . . know you, don't I? asked Tory. "We're the same age, you and me!" She said it with such excitement, it made Winston cringe.

"We might both be freaks," growled Winston, "but I ain't nothin' like you! We got nothin' in common, do you hear me?!"

It was then that Winston noticed the noise. It had been growing all around both of them since the light had appeared in the sky, and now its volume grew and multiplied until it buzzed in the brush like an air-raid siren. Winston knew right then that the sound was aimed at the two of them, and no one else in all of Alabama—and he knew that it was a sign he could not deny. The sound was nature itself, screaming out to tell him that this torturously ugly girl was more his sister than anyone born to his family. More like him than anyone he had known.

"What is it?" asked Tory, holding her ears. Winston tried to squeeze out the sound as well, but couldn't.

"Crickets," answered Winston. "Millions of 'em."

3. A PLANETOID, THE FULL MOON, AND THE SCORPION STAR

EARLIER THAT SAME DAY, AND A THOUSAND MILES NORTHEAST, the south fork of eastern Long Island was set upon by an unseasonably warm fog. It brooded dense and round on the weather maps like a gray cataract—an unseeing eye surrounded by cold, clear skies. Shrouded in the center of the fog stood Hampton Bays High School, where things had been normal until third period. That's when the chase began for Lourdes Hidalgo.

It started in the science lab, and the chase spread through the school as Lourdes tried to escape from the teachers who chased her. She had lost them by ducking into a broom closet, and now she descended the south stairwell, hoping that everyone would be thrown off track just long enough for her to burst out into the foggy October and freedom.

As Lourdes lumbered down the worn metal stairs of the old school, the stairs rang out in dull, heavy tolls, like an ancient mission bell. The bolts creaked, and the steel steps themselves seemed like cardboard, ready to give way under her immense weight.

Lourdes, however, had grown used to that. She was used to chairs buckling beneath her when she sat. She was used to the way her hips would brush past both sides of a door frame when she entered a room, as if the entire room was a tight pair of pants she was trying to squeeze her way into. But she would never get used to the cruel teasing.

Now Lourdes was bounding down the metal stairs, two steps at a time, running from teachers, the guidance counselor, and the principal. Ralphy Sherman had deserved what Lourdes had done to him, and so she fought back her tears, and fought the remorse that was trying to take hold of her.

Ralphy had been whispering lies about Lourdes in science lab, as if he himself believed they were true. *Did you hear that Lourdes was offered ten grand to join the circus? Did you hear that Lourdes donates fat to the Southampton Candle Factory? Did you hear they found some loose change and a TV remote in Lourdes's belly button?* Lourdes tried to control herself. She bit her tongue and gritted her teeth, but there's only so much abuse a person can take. She wanted to hurt him as much as he hurt her—as much as they all hurt her, and so she pushed Ralphy up against the wall, held her hand firmly on his chest, and felt his chest begin to crush inward. Ralphy tried to scream, but couldn't. His face turned red, purple, then blue. By then the teacher had taken notice and come running, so Lourdes stepped away from the limp blue kid, and he fell to the floor. Lourdes ran.

Now, as she lumbered down the stairs, she cursed the steps and the way they rang out every time her bursting orthopedic shoes hit them.

It was at the first floor landing that Lourdes encountered Mrs. Conroy, the principal of Hampton Bays High.

"Hold it right there, Lourdes." She stood ten steps beneath Lourdes, and her voice was well trained to wield power— power enough to stop the grossly obese girl in her tracks. Lourdes swayed just a bit, and the steps creaked like the hinges of a rusty door. There wasn't any sympathy from anyone in school this year—not even the principal. It was as if sympathy and understanding were limited to a certain waist size, and if a person grew beyond that limit, they were fair game for all forms of cruelty.

"You are coming to the office," said Mrs. Conroy, "and we're calling your parents. What you've done is very serious, do you understand?"

"Of course I understand," said Lourdes. "I'm fat, not stupid." Her voice was thick and seemed to be wrapped within heavy, wet layers of cotton. When Lourdes spoke, it sounded as if she was shouting from inside the belly of a whale.

"I didn't kill him, did I?" asked Lourdes.

"No," said Mrs. Conroy, "but you could have."

Lourdes was relieved and disappointed at the same time.

"This school has had about enough of you," growled Conroy.

"Does that mean I'm expelled?"

"We'll talk about it in my office."

"Fat chance," said Lourdes. She took one step at a time as she descended slowly toward her principal.

Boom! The steps rang out as Lourdes planted her swollen feet on them.

Boom!

In a moment she eclipsed the stairway lights, and Conroy's face was lost in shadow.

"I'm warning you, Lourdes . . ."

Boom!

As Lourdes approached, Mrs. Conroy seemed smaller and less powerful. Why, she was just a wisp of a woman after all, thought Lourdes.

Boom!

"Lourdes, I won't let you past me."

"So try and stop me."

Boom!

As Lourdes continued her descent toward the frail principal, Conroy unconsciously gripped the rail, already feeling

Lourdes's pull—her *gravity*, for Lourdes did have a gravity about her. When she was in a room, it was difficult not to find oneself leaning in her direction. If a breeze blew in through the window and scattered papers, they would all stick to Lourdes until she peeled them off. If you threw a paper airplane at her, it would curve around her and come back to you like a boomerang—and if you threw it just right, that airplane would continue to circle in orbit around her until it fell to the ground. Her classmates called her the Planetoid, and she hated them all.

"If you so much as touch me, Lourdes—"

Boom!

The final step. Lourdes stood right before Conroy, and the principal's shoulder-length hair was falling forward across her face, reaching toward Lourdes. Her immense belly pinned the principal against the wall, and they looked into each other's eyes. Fear was in the principal's eyes now. Fear and disgust.

"It's not my fault I'm like this," said Lourdes. With that the principal's body began to crush inward, from Lourdes's mere touch, collapsing in upon itself. Barely able to breathe, Conroy snarled out her words.

"You don't belong here," she said, and Lourdes knew she wasn't just talking about school. "Here," for Lourdes, meant this world. She brushed Conroy away as if swatting a fly, and the woman gasped for breath, as if she had just escaped the crushing force of a black hole.

Principal Conroy clutched the railing to keep from collapsing and shouted at Lourdes, but Lourdes didn't listen. She just continued out of the stairwell and onto the first floor.

THE FIRST FLOOR HALLWAY housed mostly English and history classrooms. The nearest exit was to the left, but the school security guard and guidance counselor were standing there, blocking Lourdes's escape route. At the other end of the hall stood the vice principal and a whole legion of teachers. They all began to close in.

Either she could run at them, hoping her momentum would take them out like bowling pins, or she could duck into an empty classroom. Since there were too many of them to bowl over, she chose the classroom. Once inside, she would be cornered, but at least she'd have an arsenal of things to throw at them as they tried to come at her. If it had to be her against the whole world, then the whole world would be made to suffer for what it was doing to Lourdes Hidalgo.

She pushed into the classroom, and instantly caught sight of Miss Benson—the new English teacher—and Michael Lipranski in the front of the classroom.

Lourdes was not prepared for what she saw. Her eyes went wide and her jaw dropped open.

Because Michael Lipranski was kissing his English teacher.

The very sight of it distracted Lourdes a moment too long, and she was caught off guard when everyone burst into the room. With so many people trying to wrestle her under control, not even her crushing gravity could save her. In the end, she had to give up. Her only consolation was that Michael Lipranski was also caught, and he would be in as much trouble as she was. Maybe more.

MICHAEL LIPRANSKI WAS AN unlikely make-out king. Sure, he was attractive, but there was something about him that was unnerving, unclean, and a bit slimy. He was a bit too thin, his dark hair was a bit too long—and always damp. When he would look at you, you could swear that he was reading your most secret thoughts and thinking great mischief.

He wasn't your typical stud—had no great muscles to speak of, and there was always a constellation of bruises over much of his body. Some of these came courtesy of his father, who was known to use his fists, but most were from fights around school. Michael wasn't much of a fighter, but he had learned to defend himself in a world that turned out to be far more cruel and vicious than he ever thought it could be.

Physically, the only thing truly special about Michael Lipranski was his eyes. He had these impossibly intense turquoise-hazel eyes, layered with rich coronas of color that made them seem as deep, warm, and inviting as a Caribbean sea. The girls in school could lose themselves in Michael's eyes, and often did. It happened last year in Baltimore, and it happened here in the Hamptons. Maybe that's why all the guys hated him.

And maybe that's why no teacher wanted him in their classroom. For several years Michael could never figure out why this was so. He was friendly, funny, and personable. He made an effort to do the work. Still, he seemed to be an epicenter for all sorts of disturbances. Since seventh grade, Michael's classrooms had always been remarkably unruly. He always assumed that this was normal. Kids hit puberty and turned into monsters, right? That's what everyone said . . . but the way his classmates acted wasn't exactly normal.

When Michael was in a room, a clamminess filled the air that pulled at the edge of everyone's senses like a smell so faint it was impossible to identify. Whatever it was, it usually attacked girls and guys differently. It made girls' hearts race and made them suddenly feel like there was something that they desperately wanted. They would begin to sweat, and their eyes would constantly seek out Michael's—for if they could look into Michael's eyes, they would begin to feel just a bit better. And if they could move closer to him, they could feel relief. Close enough to smell his breath. Closer still, to taste it.

Of course, guys didn't generally feel that way. Instead they felt like beating Michael up.

So when the posse chasing Lourdes Hidalgo burst into Miss Benson's classroom, word got around at the speed of light squared that Michael "Lips" Lipranski had taken his smooth moves to new heights. Everyone acted surprised, but no one really was.

WHILE LOURDES SAT IN the principal's office under tight guard, Michael had a pressing appointment with Mr. Fleiderman, the guidance counselor, who was everyone's friend—or at least tried to be.

The appointment wasn't held in Fleiderman's office, because when it wasn't too cold, Fleiderman liked to hold his sessions out in the quad—the courtyard in the center of the large school. More relaxed, less threatening, Fleiderman thought. It had never occurred to him that most kids didn't want to talk to the guidance counselor in view of the entire school.

When Michael crossed through the wall of steamy fog, it seemed that the rest of the world slipped off the edge of the earth into gray nothingness. It's how Michael felt inside too—lost, alone, and confused—generally fogged in, but he didn't plan on letting Fleiderman see that. *Let him think I'm calm and in control,* thought Michael as he approached the over-eager counselor.

Fleiderman shook Michael's hand and invited him to sit with him in the moist grass. Michael refused to sit.

"Why not?" asked Fleiderman, pleasantly. "I won't bite."

Michael smiled his winning smile. "Standing is better, strategically speaking," he said. "If you attack me and try to strangle me, I can run. And yes, you might bite, too."

Fleiderman laughed at the suggestion and decided to stand. "All right, we'll do it your way."

They both waited, Michael leaned against a yellowing sycamore tree with his arms folded.

"So talk to me," Fleiderman finally said.

"So talk to you about what?"

"You know what. Miss Benson."

"What about her?"

"You tell me."

Michael shrugged and looked away. "She kissed me. So?"

"Don't you mean *you* kissed *her*?"

Michael smiled slyly. "What makes you so sure?"

Fleiderman grunted slightly. Michael could see irritation building in the mild-mannered man.

"I want to understand where you're coming from, Michael."

"Baltimore."

"No, inside. I want to understand you."

That made Michael laugh out loud. "Good luck."

"I know you keep yourself pretty busy with girls in school. I know you're . . . shall we say . . . 'active.'"

"Active?" said Michael. "Like a volcano?"

"Sexually active."

"Oh," said Michael. "That." He looked away again and paced around to the other side of the sycamore. Fleiderman followed, and Michael noted how the guidance counselor's irritation had already built into frustration.

"I make out a lot," explained Michael. "I don't go much past that. Second base, maybe. You know."

"Am I supposed to believe that?"

"Believe what you want," said Michael. And then Michael smiled again. "But to tell you the truth, sex scares me."

"Why?" asked Fleiderman. "Afraid you might explode?"

Michael shrugged. "Yeah. Or that the girl might."

Fleiderman laughed uncomfortably, but Michael didn't. He became dead serious and noticed that Fleiderman's hands had involuntarily tightened into fists.

"Let's get back to Miss Benson," said Fleiderman. He reached up to wipe steam from his glasses.

"What happened wasn't all my fault, okay?" said Michael, beginning to say more than he had really wanted to. "She didn't *have* to keep me after class to talk about my book report. She didn't *have* to come up to me and touch my shoulder like that—and she didn't *have* to kiss me back when I kissed her."

Fleiderman gritted his teeth. Michael could see his anger heading toward meltdown. There was no logical reason for it; Michael wasn't antagonizing him—Michael was, in fact, being honest and spilling his guts, just like Fleiderman wanted. Still the guidance counselor seethed with anger. "Miss Benson will be dealt with," Fleiderman said. "But now we're talking about you and your problem of self-control."

"How the hell am I supposed to control myself when all the girls in school are after me, and all the guys want to beat the crap out of me?"

Fleiderman's whole face seemed clenched as he spat his words out. "Oh, I see. Everyone either loves you or hates you. You're the center of the universe and everyone's actions revolve around you."

"Yeah," said Michael. "That's it!"

"Delusions!" shouted Fleiderman. He was furious, and Fleiderman *never* got furious at anything. Staying calm was his job. "It's all in your head!" he shouted.

"Oh yeah?" Michael took a step closer to Fleiderman. Michael was five-seven, Fleiderman closer to six feet. "What do you feel now, Mr. Fleiderman? Do you feel really pissed off? Do you want to grab me and rip my head off? It's like you're turning into a werewolf inside, isn't it? An animal. Everyone who hangs around me long enough starts acting like an animal out of control. They either want to kill me or kiss me. Actually I'm glad that you'd rather kill me."

Meltdown! Fleiderman lost it, and he lunged at Michael, grabbing him by the throat. Michael pushed him away, but Fleiderman lunged again, growling—baring his teeth like a mad dog. Fleiderman smashed the boy with the back of his hand, then threw Michael to the ground; Michael tried to scramble away, but Fleiderman was too fast. He was on Michael, pinning him to the ground; he raised his heavy fist, ready to bring it across Michael's jaw with a blow that would surely break it.

"Stop!" said Michael. "They're watching!"

Fleiderman's wild uneven breath gave way to a whine as he looked up to see that the fog had lifted just enough for the school windows to be seen all around them. Faces peered out from classrooms on all sides, as if this was a Roman circus and Michael was fodder for the lion.

"Kill him, Fleiderman," shouted some kid from the third floor. "Kill the creep!"

Fleiderman could have—it was in his power, and it was certainly in his eyes; instead, the guidance counselor bit his own lip and continued biting it until it bled. Then he fell off of Michael and crouched in a humiliated heap, trying to find himself once more.

"My God!" muttered Fleiderman. "What am I doing? What's wrong with me?"

"It's not you," said Michael, refusing to let his own tears out. "It's me. I turn people crazy. I'm like . . . a full moon, only worse."

Fleiderman wiped blood from his lips as he crouched low, still unable to look up at Michael.

"You won't be going to this school anymore," he told Michael, finally getting to the bottom line.

"I'm being expelled?"

"Transferred." Which to Michael was the same thing.

Fleiderman began to breathe hard, fighting back words of anger. Michael could tell because his face was turning red, and although Michael felt like kicking Fleiderman in the gut, he didn't. Instead he dug deep within himself, to find a feeling that was decent, and when he found it, Michael took his hand and gently rested it on Fleiderman's hunched shoulder.

"It's all right," said Michael. "You can say it if it makes you feel better—it doesn't bother me."

"*I hate you!*" said Fleiderman.

"Say it again."

"*I hate you . . .*" Just saying the words seemed to release some of Fleiderman's steam. He quivered the tiniest bit.

Although those words hurt, they also gave Michael a sense of control. He could bring people down to their knees in love or hate, altering their very nature. He could turn a bright, sunny disposition into a storming fury. He could turn the heart of an ice-queen into hot steam. Such awesome power must be worth something.

Michael patted Fleiderman's shoulder and turned to leave. As Michael crossed the quad, his thoughts became a bit clearer and what fog was left in his own mind began to lift, along with the fog in the quad. Now that the worst was over, he felt relieved as he went back into school to clear out his locker.

As Michael left the quad, Fleiderman began to feel his fury fading. In a moment, Fleiderman's humanity came crawling back to him, and he began to condemn himself and obsess over this awful thing he had just done—for no reason he could figure out. He felt ashamed and terrified.

Love and hate being two sides of the same coin, Fleiderman began to wonder if the unfortunate Miss Benson also felt this way once Michael Lipranski had been removed from her company.

THAT NIGHT, WHILE THE rest of the Eastern seaboard was densely padded with storm systems, a patch of clear sky stalled over eastern Long Island, making it a perfect night for the annual star-watch. After sunset, four dozen kids gathered to spend an evening on Montauk Point with their science teacher, peering through his telescope, drawing star maps by flashlight, and calculating the speed of the earth's rotation.

Both Michael and Lourdes were advised not to come, which was more certain to assure their attendance than giving them a printed invitation. Michael, who had been sporting a fake license for almost a year now, drove up in his father's van, and no one was quite sure how or when Lourdes got there; at times she was amazingly stealthy for a girl of her size.

Montauk Point was a state park surrounded by cold, rough ocean on three sides, and the bluff beyond the lighthouse was the farthest east one could get in the state of New York. It was the tip of Long Island and simply as far as you could go. Unless, of course, you chose to take one step further east—off the cliff and into the sea.

It was around eleven that night that Michael Lipranski stood at the tip of the lighthouse bluff, contemplating that final step east that would send him plunging to his death in the cold breakers.

For Michael, the evening hadn't begun with such thoughts, but it had begun desperately. The star-watch was a great make-out opportunity—and on his last day at this school, Michael felt compelled to take advantage of that.

Upon arrival, Michael had set his charms on Melissa Brickle, who was, by nature, the school's wallflower. One smile from Michael changed her nature considerably. He took her to the high bluff behind the lighthouse—the most easterly place—and there, to the sound of waves and the pulse of the spinning light arcing over their heads, Michael got down to business.

Michael's kisses were more frantic than passionate, more compulsive than romantic, but Melissa did not notice, for, as Michael knew, no one had ever kissed Melissa Brickle this way before, and her own new and overwhelming feelings blocked out everything else. Michael could feel himself trespassing in the dark places of her mind, releasing those feelings like wild beasts from a cage. A thin ground fog carpeted the grass around them, slipping off the cliff in a slow vapor fall. The mist seemed to be flowing from the two of them.

Through it all, Michael's mind and body were exploding with emotions. Frustration, anger, confusion all fought for control—but what he felt more than anything tonight was futility. No matter what he did, no matter how many girls he lured into secret corners—even if he took them all the way and absolutely gave in to all of his urges—he still would not be satisfied. Instead his urges would only increase—they would grow and drive him insane. Michael's grip on Melissa grew stronger as they kissed—so strong that it must have been hurting her, but she didn't notice. She wouldn't notice even if Michael really did hurt her.

"Tighter," she said. "Hold me tighter."

And as he tightened his grip, Michael came to understand that this frenzied necking was a violation of the girl. He had, in some way, entered this girl's mind—he *made* her want all the things that he could do to her, and this was a violation as real as any other. Michael was terrified of what he was turning into, and what awful things he might be capable of.

Before it went too far, Michael pushed Melissa away.

"What's the matter?" she asked. "Did I do something wrong?"

She moved toward him again, then this shy, sweet girl slipped her hand into his jacket, and shirt, shamelessly rubbing his chest.

Michael gently grabbed her hand and placed it back down in her lap. "Better stop," he said.

"Better not," she whispered. She tried to snuggle up to him, but Michael stood up.

"Just go!" screamed Michael. "Get out of here!" But she did not move—so he reached down, picked up a clump of dirt and hurled it at her shoes.

Confused and humiliated, Melissa ran off in tears.

Good, thought Michael. Because there were worse things she could feel than humiliation.

Soon the sound of her footfalls faded, and Michael was left alone with his bloated, malignant urges. But those urges could be killed, couldn't they? The sound of the crashing ocean made him think of that. Those soul-searing urges that ate him alive could be destroyed by one single step east. Right now anything seemed better than having to feel That Way anymore.

And so, before he knew what he was doing, Michael found himself leaning into the wind at the edge of the cliff, daring his balance to fail him, and gravity to pull him down to his end.

"Do you really think anyone cares if you jump?"

The voice came as such a shock, Michael almost did lose his balance. He stumbled backward, away from the cliff, into the grass. His life did not so much flash before his eyes, as slap him in the face.

"If you jump, people might freak, but they'll forget soon enough," said a voice that was dense and wet, like liquid rubber. Lourdes Hidalgo lumbered out from behind a bush like a buffalo, and Michael wondered how long she had been watching.

In truth, Lourdes had been watching from the moment Michael had brought Melissa to the bluff. Lourdes enjoyed watching the other kids make out—and wasn't ashamed of it either. She had enough things to feel ashamed of—peeping was low on her shame list.

"I don't care if everyone forgets me," said Michael. "I'm just sick of feeling This Way, okay?"

"What way?"

"You wouldn't understand."

"How do you know?"

Michael looked down at the bulge in his pants. They were too tight down there, as always, and in this warped little moment, he didn't care who he told or how dumb it sounded.

"Do you know what it's like to feel totally crazed all of the time? To wake up That Way, and go to class That Way, and not be able to sleep at night because of Those Thoughts going through your head, and then when you do sleep, to be invaded by Those Kind of dreams? They say we got hormones, right? Well, I don't have hormones, I *am* a hormone—one big mutated hormone with a thousand hands and a million eyes. It's like that hormone has eaten me alive, and there's nothing left of *me*. Do you know how that feels?"

Lourdes, to her credit, took the question very seriously. "No," she said. "But I do know what it's like to be fat. So fat that I can't sit down in a movie theater. So fat that I have to ride in elevators alone. So fat that when I take a bath, there's no room for any water in the tub. If anyone should jump into the sea, it should be me."

Michael shrugged, feeling embarrassed. "Naah. You'd probably bounce."

Lourdes considered this. "Or splat like a water balloon."

"Gross!" Michael looked at Lourdes. She was truly hideous to behold, even in this dim light.

Lourdes smiled at him and Michael backed off. Was this a trick? Was she just after him like all the other girls? After all, she could not be immune to his full-moon effect, could she?

"Nice try," said Michael. "I'm not going to kiss you, so get lost." He turned toward the edge of the cliff again, contemplating it.

"Kiss you? I don't want to kiss you, your breath smells like onions."

This got Michael's interest. "What do you mean you don't want to? Don't you find me irresistible?"

"I can resist you just fine," said Lourdes. "I mean, you don't use enough deodorant, your clothes are ugly, your hair is stringy—"

Michael grinned, unable to believe his ears. "Go on! Tell me more!"

"Let's see. You've got a crooked lower tooth, your eyebrows are like caterpillars, you got no butt at all . . ."

Michael practically jumped for joy. "That's great," he said. "Do you know how long it's been since I've been able to talk to someone without them either wanting to beat the crap out of me, or make out with me? Do you know how long it's been since *I* could talk to a girl without feeling you-know-how? This is great!" Michael could have gone on for hours contemplating the deep ramifications of their mutual lack of attraction, but hearing about how unattractive Michael found her didn't seem to make Lourdes too happy. He looked at her swollen form and wondered how a girl could get this way.

"You know, you'd probably lose weight if you ate less," offered Michael.

"I'll tell you a secret," said Lourdes. Her head rolled forward on her neckless body, and she whispered in her cotton-padded voice: "I haven't eaten in months."

"No way!"

"It's true—not a bite, and still I get fatter. Almost a pound every day."

"That's wild!"

Lourdes smiled. "As wild as your man-eating hormone, maybe?"

They looked at each other, both beginning to realize that their similarities ran far deeper that they could have imagined—and then, without warning, the sky exploded.

A burst of green, and then a strange pink light lit up the heavens; it shook Michael and Lourdes to the core of their very souls.

"A supernova!" exclaimed Mr. Knapp, the science teacher. "My God! I think it's a supernova!" He frantically cranked his telescope toward the constellation of Scorpius, then flipped through his astronomy book to identify the star.

In a matter of minutes, a star in the tail of the scorpion flared to a fourth the size of the moon. Michael and Lourdes stepped out from behind the lighthouse to see everyone crowding around Knapp, who compared his star chart to the heavens above him.

"Mentarsus-H!" he announced. "It says here that it's sixteen light-years away—that means it blew up before most of you were born!"

Knapp immediately started to explain, "It took all those years for the light of the explosion to reach the earth. Like when you're in the bleachers at the ball park, you see the player swing, but don't hear the crack of the bat until a second later. Space is so vast that light takes years to get from star to star. That star blew up over sixteen years ago, but we're just finding out about it now."

While everyone else marveled at this grand cosmic display, Michael and Lourdes lingered beyond the fringe of the crowd—touched by the nova with an intensity none of the others felt. It was as if the light illuminated some part of themselves that had always been hidden in shadows.

"I have to go!" Michael suddenly exclaimed. "I have to go now!" He was already fumbling in his pockets for the keys to his van.

"I have to go with you," said Lourdes, her eyes filling with tears she could not explain.

Yes! thought Michael. *It had to be the two of them.* They were both being drawn away—drawn west. They had to travel west because . . .

. . . *Because there were others! Others who were like them.*

The truth came to him as if he had known it all along.

Michael could imagine them now—all of them looking up at the supernova at this same instant, in places far away.

"I have room in the van for you," said Michael.

"I have a credit card," said Lourdes, "if we need money."

They hurried toward Michael's van, as if they could afford no lost time.

Now those people standing around the telescope and all the other people in their lives seemed meaningless and unimportant.

Michael turned the key in the ignition with such force the starter screamed as the engine came to life.

"Where do we go?" asked Lourdes. "How will we know when we get there?"

But both of them knew there were no answers to such questions. In a moment they were gone, driving west, while their former classmates looked heavenward through a round patch of clear sky that was fixed over Montauk like an eye, staring unblinking into infinity.

Part II
Free Fall

4. THE SHADOW OF DESTRUCTION

THE SPLINTERING OF STONE.

A deafening rumble as a mountainside pounced upon an unsuspecting neighborhood below. Five homes were destroyed by the massive boulders, and Dillon Cole, his wrecking-hunger now fed, gripped Deanna Chang and collapsed in her arms.

In the dim light they sat on the mountainside, hearing the shouts from below as neighbors came out to help one another. Through it all, Deanna held Dillon tightly.

"Please let no one be hurt," Dillon whispered desperately.

Deanna had watched in horror as the row of homes on this hill above Lake Tahoe was obliterated. She watched in horror . . . but not in fear. Even now, as she held Dillon, she wasn't frightened. Her fears, which had been building for hours, vanished the moment Dillon satisfied his wrecking-hunger—and it had been that way every time.

In the four days since they had run from the hospital in San Francisco, Deanna had stood by as Dillon sent a driverless semi down a ravine; sunk an empty barge on the Sacramento River; and shorted out a switching station, plunging the entire community of Placerville into darkness. She knew she should have felt terror and revulsion at each of these catastrophes, yet, against all reason, a sudden peace always filled her in the aftermath.

All that destruction didn't feel real to her in those moments after—it seemed little more than a painted canvas before her.

But Dillon was real, and she always turned her newfound calm to him, comforting him and his conscience, which had a strong case for feeling guilty. She thought she was beginning to understand that strange calm: she was in the shadow of Dillon's destruction now—and that was far less terrifying than being in its path—for if those horrible things were happening to someone else, it meant that they weren't happening to her.

What remained in that swollen calm was a single question in Deanna's mind.

How?

How does he accomplish these things?

She looked to the night sky—to the supernova that still shone in the heavens, as if it could answer her.

"Is it winking at you?" asked Dillon, turning to look at it as well. "Is it telling you all the secrets of the universe?"

Deanna shook her head. "It's just telling me to go east."

Dillon nodded. "I know."

It was true. From the moment its light appeared in the sky, she and Dillon were falling east; carried by an irresistible current, like driftwood pulled toward a raging waterfall. Suddenly Deanna's aching wrist and aching body didn't matter. Her family didn't matter—they seemed like people from a different lifetime and, aside from a single postcard to tell them she was all right, they had been shuffled far back in Deanna's mind. All that mattered was moving east with Dillon—and all because of that star.

Maybe the others know more, thought Deanna. Oh, yes, she knew about The Others—they both did. Although they spoke of them only once, they knew that it was The Others who were drawing them east. It was Dillon who didn't want to discuss them—as if this knowledge of The Others was too important a thing to say out loud.

Deanna could swear she could sometimes hear their voices in the rustling of leaves—see their faces in dreams she couldn't quite remember. She thought to tell Dillon, but thought better of it.

Far below, at the bottom of the hillside, an ambulance could be heard arriving at the scene of the rock slide.

"No one was supposed to get hurt . . . ," said Dillon, squeezing his eyes tightly shut.

Deanna pushed the sound of the ambulance out of her mind. Instead she focused on Dillon—how he needed her and how she needed him to keep her fears away. How strong they were together.

A trickle of pebbles fell past them on the dark hillside, settling in the aftermath of Dillon's rock slide.

"I don't understand how you did it," she asked him. "All you did was throw a stone . . ."

"It wasn't just a stone," he told her. "It was the *right* stone."

But it was still beyond Deanna to understand just what he meant by that. He had thrown a stone, and that stone had begun an inconceivable chain of events—his stone hit another, which then rolled against a large boulder, and in a few moments the whole mountainside beneath them was falling away before their eyes. It would have been wonderful, if it wasn't so horrible.

"Do you hate me, Deanna?" Dillon asked. "Do you hate me for the things that I do?"

Did she hate him? She probably ought to hate him, but how could she when he was the only one who didn't run from her? How could she hate him when he treasured every ounce of comfort she gave him? The more he needed her, the more she loved him—she couldn't help it. *Whatever you do, I'll forgive you, Dillon,* she said to herself, *because I know the goodness inside you—even if no one else can see.*

But to him, she only said, "No, I don't hate you."

When Dillon heard her words, he relaxed—as if her feelings for him were all that mattered—as if Deanna was his only lifeline to the world.

Now that the wrecking-hunger had been fed, he looked stronger in the dim nova light. He looked *noble,* and when he stood from her arms he somehow seemed larger than life. Now it was her turn to take comfort in him.

"Let's go," Dillon said. "I know a way to get money."

She glanced toward the immense lake, where Tahoe's casinos glittered just over the Nevada border.

"Casino gambling?" she asked.

"We don't need a casino," he answered. "All we need is a bar." He reached out his hand and smiled. He was his old, tender self again. "Come on. I'll show you something incredible . . . I'll show you something magical!"

She reached out and gently took his hand, and he escorted her off the ruined mountainside.

A GUST OF WIND blew through the door of the roadside bar as they stepped in, sending a flurry of cocktail napkins to the sawdust-covered floor.

With the wrecking-hunger deeply satisfied, Dillon felt himself in control of his thoughts and actions. Deanna had seen him at his worst tonight, and now she would see him at his best. He would show her something special.

Dillon was tall, but his boyish features and the style of his conspicuous red hair made it clear he was underage. Still, no one seemed to care, and he had no intention of ordering drinks.

Most of the talk around the bar was about the rock slide.

"Did you hear?" the regulars were saying to one another. "Five homes got flattened. Summer homes mostly, so no one was in 'em . . . except of course for the Barnes' place, where a boulder the size of a Buick tried to come down the chimney like friggin' Santy Claus."

"Sadie Barnes got a concussion," told one old-timer, with wide eyes as if he were telling a ghost story. "Jack Barnes, well, he might lose a leg. Still too early to tell."

Dillon grimaced and tried not to think about it. He caught himself glancing at Deanna's bruised wrist, silently tallying all the injuries he had caused and cursing himself for it.

In the many quiet hours alone with Deanna, he had told her every last thing he had done since the wrecking-hunger had come two years ago. He had told her how it started—not so much a hunger, but an itch; a tiny little urge to break things, which grew with each thing he broke. He had told her how his parents eventually died of "broken minds," before Dillon understood what his touch did to people, and how he had wandered for a whole year alone. Deanna took great pains to listen and not judge. Dillon had no words to tell her how special she was.

He led Deanna to the back of the bar, where an old, worn pool table sat in an alcove. Two guys were finishing a game of eight-ball. They were cowboy types—early twenties, talking about fortunes won and lost in the Tahoe casinos that day. One of them was bursting with energy, because his wallet was bursting with cash. He would be Dillon's target.

"Watch this," Dillon whispered to Deanna. Dillon had only played pool once, years ago. Even then he had found it about as challenging as sorting mail into six different slots. He approached the cowboy with the stuffed wallet.

"I'll play you a game," offered Dillon, sounding naive and inexperienced. "I'll play you for five dollars." Dillon slapped five dollars down on the edge of the table. Cowboy and his friend laughed.

"Sure, buddy," Cowboy said, treating Dillon like a child who had just asked for a quarter for a video game. "You break."

Cowboy racked up the balls, and Dillon broke, while Deanna watched from a peeling red vinyl chair.

The game took five minutes. It was less than magical; Dillon lost miserably. He glanced at Deanna, who was beginning to look nervous.

"One more game!" insisted Dillon. "Double or nothing."

Cowboy agreed, and easily beat Dillon a second time. The smile slipped from Dillon's face now. Deanna came up to him and whispered, "Don't be dumb—we're almost out of money."

"Don't worry about it," he said loudly enough for the others to hear. "I feel lucky, okay?"

Deanna rolled her eyes and stepped away, leaning against the wall.

Cowboy won the third match and was all full of himself. Dillon, on the other hand, looked pathetic and desperate. He took out his wallet and angrily slapped it down in front of the cowboy.

"All of it," said Dillon. "I'll play you for all that's in my wallet for all that's in yours."

Cowboy grinned out of the corner of his mouth.

"Dillon, let's get out of here," said Deanna. "It's not worth it."

"I don't leave a loser," said Dillon.

Cowboy smiled even wider. The picture here was clear; a young kid trying to impress his girlfriend—willing to go to ridiculous extremes to avoid being completely humiliated.

And that was exactly how Cowboy intended on leaving him; completely humiliated, not to mention broke.

Cowboy put his wallet next to Dillon's and racked up the balls. "You break," he said.

Dillon took a deep breath and made sure Deanna was watching. Then he took his cue ball, and stared intently at the wedge of colored balls before him. Dillon stared until he stopped seeing balls, and instead saw angles, vectors, and forces of impact. He examined the lines of motion and rebounds— each one bearing a complex mathematical equation that his mind solved instantaneously. And then, once he saw every pattern of possibility on that pool table, Dillon struck the cue ball . . . sending two solid-colored balls into two different pockets.

His second shot sunk two more balls, his third shot sent his remaining three balls home, and his fourth shot sent the eight ball rebounding off three sides before disappearing into a corner pocket.

Four shots. Like sorting mail.

Cowboy just stared at the table, which was still full of his own seven striped balls. "Beginner's luck," said Dillon. He took his and Cowboy's wallets from the edge of the table, leaving Cowboy completely humiliated, not to mention broke. From behind the bar, the bartender laughed.

Cowboy was furious. He threw his cue down and grabbed Dillon. "Just who do you think you—"

But he never finished. The moment he grabbed Dillon, his pupils dilated, his jaw dropped, and his face paled. In an instant Cowboy's thoughts had become so scrambled, he couldn't even speak. Dillon slipped free from his grip.

"Good game," said Dillon.

"Duh . . . ," said Cowboy.

Dillon and Deanna left him there, his senses just beginning to come back. They breezed out the door, dragging a flurry of cocktail napkins in their wake.

"I DON'T SEE THINGS the way other people see things," Dillon told Deanna that night as they dined like kings in their hotel room above Lake Tahoe. "You want to know how I started the rock slide, and how I won that pool game. I don't know how—all I can tell you is how I see the world—and it's different than other people do."

Deanna just looked at him quizzically, so Dillon tried to explain. "Other people, they just see 'things'—but I see *patterns*—cause and effect. I can see whole chains of events that other people can't see. It's like the way a good chess player can plan ten moves in advance? Well, when I play chess, I can see the entire game the moment the first move is made, not just all my moves—*but every possible move*—all at the same time. It's the same thing with pool; all I had to do was look at the positioning of the balls, and I knew exactly how to hit them to make the balls go into the pockets."

Deanna nodded. "Sort of the way a computer can solve a really hard math equation in half a second."

"Yeah, sort of like that. It was harder for me to make myself lose than it was to win."

Deanna was amazed. "You must be a genius."

Dillon shrugged modestly. "Naah, it's just something I can do. Some people can sing or dance; I can see patterns. A while back, before things got bad, I did this trick with a Rubik's Cube. My friends would get it all completely mixed up, then hand it to me. They would give me five seconds to look at it and then blindfold me. I would remember where the colors had been and solve the cube blindfolded." Dillon began to smile as he thought about it. "There was this one time they took the cube apart and put it back together so it was impossible to solve, but I managed to solve it anyway!"

Deanna looked down and nervously began to scratch at her healing wrist, as something occurred to her. "So then . . . if you can see how things are going to happen—then you *meant* to hurt those people in the avalanche. You meant to hurt *me*."

Dillon cringed and stood up. "Boulders aren't billiard balls. A mountain's not a chessboard," he said. "And it's not like I can predict the future—I just see patterns of the way things *ought* to happen—but things don't always happen the way they're supposed to . . ."

Dillon began to pace. "There was a tree further down the mountain," he said. "The way I saw it, the tree was going to get smashed, and in the end four homes would get hit—the four that were empty. No one would get hurt, and the wrecking-hunger would be fed, right? So I threw the stone that I knew would start the whole avalanche. The pebbles started moving, the rocks started slipping, the boulders began to go, but when that tree got hit—it didn't fall! It deflected the boulder toward that fifth house."

The more Dillon thought about it, the angrier he got. "I don't want to hurt people, but people get hurt, okay? That's just the way it is, and I can't do anything about it!"

Suddenly he took his fist and punched it as hard as he could against the window. It vibrated with a loud thud.

"I don't want to talk about it anymore," he mumbled.

DEANNA WATCHED HIM CLOSELY as he sat there stewing in his own conflicted emotions. Deanna could hear that frightened voice in her head that sounded so much like her mother, telling her to run away from his crazy boy. But if he were crazy, he was no crazier than Deanna.

She sat next to him and gently touched his hand. It was hot from his anger. Hers was cold, as it always was.

"With all that money you won playing pool," suggested Deanna, "we could fly east."

"Fly where?" asked Dillon. "When you get on a plane, you need a destination, you can't just buy a ticket 'east.'"

Deanna sighed. It was true: the eastbound gravity that gripped them could deposit them anywhere between Reno and New York.

"Anyway," said Dillon with a smirk, "you're afraid of flying . . . because if you're in a plane, the plane'll do everything it can to crash."

"Are you making fun of me?"

"No," said Dillon very seriously. "I believe you. All the things you're afraid of—all those awful things you imagine happening to you—your fear is so strong that it makes them come true. It's like your fear is a virus or something running through your veins . . . only it's mutated. Now it's this thing wrapped around your neck, strangling you."

Deanna shivered. "Gee, thanks, Dillon," she said. "You know just what to say to make me feel better."

"But you *should* feel better," insisted Dillon, "because, I can *see* the pattern—and as long as you're with me, none of those bad things can happen to you. I'll push you out of the way of a speeding car, even before it comes around the bend. I'll get you off a train before it derails. I won't let you get on a plane that will crash. I'll be like a good luck charm you wear around your neck! I promise."

Deanna knew there was truth in what Dillon said.

"We're meant to do great things, Deanna—don't you feel it?" he said, gripping her hand tightly. "And every day, we're closer to knowing what those things are!"

"All of us, you mean?" asked Deanna. "Us and the others?" Deanna watched to see how Dillon would react to her bringing up The Others.

Dillon shrugged uncomfortably. "Yeah, sure," he said. "But you and me especially."

Deanna felt her eyelids getting heavy, and so she leaned back, letting Dillon put his arm around her. He did nothing more—just held her with a wonderful innocence as if they were two small children. He asked no more from her than her presence, and it made her feel safe.

In the silence she listened as Dillon's breathing slowed, and he fell asleep. She took comfort in the sound of his breathing, and soon matched the pace of her own breath to his. She imagined their hearts beating in time with each other as well, and wished that they could somehow be part of each other . . .

Then she realized that in some strange and immeasurable way, they already were.

5. GHOST OF THE RAINBOW

AT A CAMPSITE IN THE WOODS WHERE THE MISSISSIPPI AND Ohio Rivers meet, Tory Smythe tended to her aching face. She gently cleaned her cheeks, chin, and forehead with astringent alcohol, and three types of soaps—a ritual performed four times a day. It stung as if she had just wiped her face with battery acid, and although all these cleansers promised results, none of them helped. She put on some perfume, which didn't do much either, then dabbed her scaling face with Clearasil, hoping beyond hope that someday it would work.

"I want to head toward Nebraska," she shouted to Winston, who was standing by the edge of the water. "Last year I read about this astronomer . . . in Omaha, I think. Anyway, he predicted a star was about to go supernova—and since that star seems to have something to do with us, maybe he knows something we don't."

She turned to see that Winston wasn't even listening. He was just looking out over the river.

"What are you doing, praying again?"

"I'm not praying," said Winston. "I'm taking a whiz."

But Tory knew he was just using that as an excuse. Even this far away, she could tell that he was looking at that weird blue cloth again.

WINSTON PELL STOOD BY the water's edge so Tory couldn't see, fiddling with the torn piece of turquoise-blue satin that he had pulled from a trash can three days before. He felt troubled, unsure of his next move, and for some reason fiddling with that torn piece of cloth made him feel better, as if it were a tiny security blanket. He had one of those when he was little. It was just a quilt, but when he wrapped it around himself, he felt safe and secure. Now, as he stood by the edge of the water, he did say a little prayer; he wished for things to be like they once were, before his ma got paralyzed . . . before his dad died. . . . He wished for the days when an old blanket was the only protection he needed. *Please, God, make it like it was,* he prayed, as he often did. *Make everything go back.* . . .

Maybe his old life hadn't been the best in the world, but it was better than it had become in these past few years and much better than what he had to face these past few days. On that first night, suddenly roaring with crickets, he knew his legs were moving him away from home, but it was like sleepwalking. Only after dawn broke did he begin to comprehend that he was running away with this hideous, crater-faced girl.

At first they traveled west: on foot and in the beds of pickup trucks, "borrowing" clothes from clotheslines along the way, and food from unharvested fields. Once they hit the Mississippi River, they followed it north. Winston could feel himself being drawn upriver, the way salmon were drawn against a powerful current.

Winston knew they were moving toward Others like themselves—it was something he had sensed from the beginning—but where would they find them and how long would it take?

And where to go now?

As he stood at the edge of western Kentucky's woods, he looked out across the swirling waters where the Ohio and the Mississippi met—a delta that divided three different states. Where to go from here? Kentucky, Illinois, or Missouri. Decisions were getting harder and harder for Winston these days. The very thought of having to make one made him want to put his thumb deep in his mouth and suck on it to make all his problems go away. He'd been getting that thumb-sucking urge a lot lately—like he used to the first time he was little. But he reminded himself that he was fifteen and forced the urge away. Instead he focused his attention on that piece of turquoise cloth in his other hand, studying the soothing richness of its color. There was something *important* about that color—he was certain of it.

In a few minutes he returned to their campsite and slipped into his sleeping bag, which was just an old comforter he had found in a Memphis Dumpster.

"Did you hear what I said about Omaha?" Tory asked. "About that astronomer? He's supposed to be a kook, but then maybe only a kook will talk to us."

Winston rolled over, away from her. "Sure," he said. "Whatever."

Tory sighed. "It would help," she said, "if you did *some* of the thinking around here."

Winston slid deeper into his sleeping bag. "Thinkin' just makes me angry. I got no use for it anymore."

"You know," said Tory, "you're not an easy person to run away with."

Winston rolled over to face her. "Just because we ran away at the same time, in the same direction, doesn't mean I ran away *with* you." But even as he said it, Winston knew he was wrong. They were stuck with each other—and even if they were to go their separate ways, he knew they'd end up bumping right back into each other—pulled together like two magnets.

Winston began to think of his family. The faces of his mother and brother were getting harder to remember.

"My mama's probably turnin' the country upside down lookin' for me."

"I thought you called her and told her you were all right."

"I did," said Winston. "But she had more questions than I could answer, so I hung right up."

Tory sighed and slipped deeper into her makeshift sleeping bag. "You're lucky you got a mama who cares enough to ask questions. My mama's gone."

"She's dead?"

"No, just gone," said Tory. "Up and left last year. I got stuck with my aunt."

"I'm sorry."

"Just as well. My mama and I never got along anyway. She used to say 'Tory, your bulb is so dim, you'll never amount to anything.' Truth is, I get straight A's in school. But that didn't matter. I coulda been a national scholar, she still would have figured me dumber than a doorpost. Anyway, when I started getting this skin problem, my mother just gave up. She said it was my fault all her boyfriends ran away—and I hoped she was right; I would have been ugly just to spite her. When she got drunk, she would tell me things like how because of my face, I'd spend my whole life alone and unhappy."

"Like her?"

"Like her."

"Sounds like she got on the inside what you got on the outside," said Winston. "I'd rather be you than her."

"I'd rather be neither of us," said Tory. "I'd rather be a prom queen from the right family instead of a . . . a gargoyle."

"You ain't no gargoyle," said Winston. "Gargoyles got big red eyes and ugly teeth, and skin like snakes."

"I am so a gargoyle. I smell like one— my skin peels like one. One of these days my face'll probably start turning green too." Winston looked at her battle-scarred face, and she looked away, not wanting him to look at it anymore.

"You Baptists got a prayer for ugly people?" she asked.

"We got a prayer for everything," said Winston. But try as he might, he couldn't think of a prayer for the ugly.

Two HUNDRED MILES WAY, Indianapolis was pelted by heavy rain—but the rain that was falling inside Michael "Lips" Lipranski's soul seemed even worse than the rain outside. The storm raging inside him was full of acid rain, and it burned, filling him with the familiar feeling he could never make go away. He couldn't talk about that, could he? *There are some things you don't talk about,* he thought, as he lay uncomfortably in the van, which was parked in a back alley. *There are some things that are just too secret, too personal, so you just never talk about them. Ever.*

The trip from Montauk had been torture. The drenched roads all seemed the same—back roads mostly, because they knew they'd be harder to find if they traveled the back roads. Right now, Michael couldn't bear the thought of another road.

Beside him, Lourdes babbled on about a dream she had the night before, about a gray rainbow—whatever that meant. She was cramped and uncomfortable—none of the van's seats were wide enough for her. When she finally realized that Michael wasn't listening, she turned to him and asked, "How do you feel?"

"You know how I feel," said Michael, adjusting his uncomfortably tight pants. "I feel like I always feel."

"You know, you're not the only guy to feel horny all the time," Lourdes said.

Michael shifted uneasily. "Yes I am," he answered. "I'm the

only one who feels it this bad. The only one in the world."

"Maybe not."

"Yeah, sure. And maybe you're not really fat—you just wear the wrong clothes."

Michael regarded the ceiling of the van above him, listening to the clattering of the rain.

"I got a brother," said Lourdes, "who always had girls on the brain, too."

Michael let out a bitter laugh. If girls on the brain were his problem, then there were thousands of them in there, all with jackhammers.

"Whenever he got the girl crazies," continued Lourdes, "he'd go off into the bathroom. When he came out a few minutes later, he didn't feel that way no more. He thought we didn't know what he was up to, but we did. We just didn't say."

Michael cleared his throat. He just kept looking up at the spots in the roof lining.

"I do that, too," said Michael. "I do it a lot." Hearing the words come out of his mouth made tears come to his eyes—but Lourdes didn't laugh at him. She just listened.

"My brother—I'll bet he thought he was the only person in the world to do that. I'll bet he hated himself for it."

Michael felt his whole body react to his tears. His throat closed up, his feet felt even colder, his fingers felt weak. Above him, the clattering sound of the rain grew stronger.

"Sometimes . . . ," said Michael. "Sometimes I think . . . what if all my dead relatives are watching me? What if their ghosts can see the things I do?"

"Dead people don't care," said Lourdes. "Because if they really do hang around after they die, I'll bet they've seen so many secret things, nothing bothers them anymore."

"You think so?"

"At the very worst, they think it's funny."

"I don't think it's funny!"

"That's because you're not dead."

Above, the rain began to ease up. *Some things you can't talk about,* thought Michael. He never thought it would be so easy to talk about those things with Lourdes.

"We should go soon," said Lourdes, who, for obvious reasons, preferred to travel by night rather than by day. "Maybe when the rain stops we'll see the rainbow."

Michael rolled his eyes. She always brought up the thing about the rainbow.

"It's night," reminded Michael. "Whoever heard of a rainbow at night?"

"Maybe night's the only time you can find a gray rainbow."

"Maybe there's no such thing as a gray rainbow, and that dream you're having doesn't mean a thing."

Lourdes shook her head. "Dreams always mean something," she said. "Especially dreams you have more than once."

Michael cracked the window and took a deep breath. He could smell the end of the storm, the same way he could smell when it began. He could always smell the weather. An autumn storm always began with the smell of damp concrete and ended with the aroma of yellow leaves trampled along the sidewalk. A winter blizzard began clean, like the air itself had been polished to perfection, and ended with a faint aroma of ash.

As Michael sat there, breathing in the end of the storm, he had to admit that talking to Lourdes had made him feel a little bit better.

"Lourdes," said Michael, "tell me something about you

now. Tell me something about yourself you swore you'd never tell a living soul. It's only fair."

Lourdes shifted and the seat creaked, threatening to give way. Michael waited.

"I don't have secrets," she said in her deepest, most thickly padded voice.

Michael waited.

Lourdes sighed, and Michael leaned closer to listen.

"My parents . . . they love me very much," said Lourdes. "I know this because I heard them talking one night. They said that they loved me so much, they wished that I would die, so I would be put out of my misery." Lourdes spoke matter-of-factly, refusing to shed a single tear. "The truth is, I never felt misery until I heard them say that."

Outside the air began to take on a new flavor—a rich, earthy smell that Michael recognized as fog rolling in, matching the cloudy, numb feeling in his brain.

"Lourdes," said Michael, "I don't care what anyone says, I think you're beautiful."

MICHAEL AND LOURDES ARRIVED in St. Louis the next morning, their van riding the crest of the storm. The black rain clouds followed behind them like a wave rolling in from the distant Atlantic Ocean, baffling the weatherman, who always looked west for weather.

Michael, starved, stopped at the first cheap-looking fast-food place he found, but all they sold were fried brain sandwiches, a local specialty. When Michael returned to the car with his questionable sandwich and a drink for Lourdes, he looked behind him to see a sheet of rain moving across the surface of the Mississippi River, until it finally reached them, letting loose over St. Louis. Michael hopped into the van and managed not to get drenched.

He handed Lourdes her Diet Coke. "What do you know about St. Louis?" she asked.

"I know I'd rather be just about anywhere else in the world," he said, looking miserably down at the brain-burger in his hand.

"Besides that, what do you know?"

Michael shrugged. "The Cardinals," he said. "That's about it. . . ." And then he stopped dead—and started to breathe rapidly. Michael turned to Lourdes and grabbed her heavy arm, trying to speak but unable to catch his breath.

"What's wrong?" she asked.

"Lourdes . . . there's one more thing I know about St. Louis . . . something that never occurred to me until now!"

"So, tell me."

"I think maybe you should look for yourself."

Lourdes followed Michael's gaze to the south. Lourdes wiped the fog from the windshield, and her eyes traced the path of the riverbank, until she saw it, too. It was about a mile away, curving hundreds of feet into the sky—thousands of tons of gray steel, shaped and curved into the magnificent arch that graced the city of St. Louis. The sleek steel wonder stretched deep into the clouds, and back down to earth again, and the very sight of it gave Michael and Lourdes the eerie shivers—because more than anything else, the arch looked like a ghostly gray rainbow.

TORY AND WINSTON HAD already been at the arch for twenty minutes. They had stood with die-hard tourists in a line that wound through the underground museum, waiting to board the tiny car that would take them to the peak of the arch.

The logic made perfect sense. If you were supposed to meet someone in St. Louis, but didn't know where, there were cer-

tain places one ought to try: airports, bus stations, train stations, landmarks— and they knew St. Louis had to be the
place. They could sense something here they felt nowhere
else they had been—the westward current suddenly seemed
caught in a swirling eddy.

They had been to all the other places, and now they searched
the city's best-known landmark—their last hope—before con-
tinuing west. To Omaha, if Tory got her way.

Once at the top of the arch, the view was spectacular, for
the very tip of the arch pierced the dense, low-hanging storm
clouds. It was like a view from heaven.

Tory wore her scarf over most of her face like an Arabian
veil. "I've never been this high," she said. "I guess this is what
it must look like from a plane." The clouds beneath the observation window were slow-moving billows; huge cotton snails
sliding over one another.

The car brought them back down to the underground
museum, and still there was no sign of anyone on the lookout
for them. It was worse than the old needle in a haystack. At
least then you knew it was a needle you were looking for.

"There's nothing here," Tory finally had to admit. Then
Tory and Winston heard a voice deep in the crowd.

"This is a waste of time," the voice said. Tory and Winston
quickly turned and saw a boy through the crowds. He had a
thin, scraggly body and thin, scraggly hair. He seemed flushed
and sweaty. Next to him stood a girl so immense there was no
way she'd fit in the tiny car that rode to the top of the arch.

But it was the scraggly boy that caught Winston's attention—
not his face, but his eyes. Even from a distance, Winston could
see the color of his eyes.

"I know him!" said Winston. "Don't I know him?"

Winston and Tory pushed through the crowd, and as they

did, the sounds around them seemed to become distant. The people milling about and waiting in line seemed like mere shadows of people. The guard mouthed the words "Move along," but his voice sounded as if it were coming from miles away. The only sights clear and in focus were the fat girl and scraggly boy, who were now staring at them with the same troubled wonder.

Winston approached the scraggly boy, pulling his torn satin cloth out of his pocket. One glance at the cloth, and then at the boy's eyes proved to Winston what he already knew. The cloth was the exact same color as the scraggly boy's eyes. Impossibly deep—impossibly blue! This was the connection!

Michael grabbed the cloth and looked at Winston, suddenly overwhelmed with emotion. Michael felt the urge to say *It's good to see you again,* even though he knew he had never met this small black kid before.

Tory approached, staring at Lourdes, and rather than being repulsed, she felt somehow comforted by her large presence. It made Tory want to peel back her scarf, to reveal her own awful face, suddenly not ashamed of it in front of the present company.

"My God!" said Lourdes, as Tory revealed her face, and Lourdes smiled with a look of wonder instead of disgust. Still holding onto Michael, Lourdes reached out to touch Tory, who still had a hand on Winston's shoulder; Winston had put his small palm up against Michael's large one, closing a circuit of the four of them . . . and the instant the circuit was closed, something happened.

Their skin felt on fire, their bones felt like ice. They could not move.

Then an image exploded through their minds with such power and intensity, it seemed to burn the world around them away. It was a vision before sight, a tale before words. It was a memory—for it was so terrifyingly familiar to all of them it could only be a memory—not of something seen or heard but of something felt:

Bright Light! Sharp Pain! One screaming voice becoming six screaming voices. Six! There are six of us!

As the vision filled them, the clouds above began to boil and separate, as a powerful wind blew through the ghostly steel rainbow and the wet earth was finally drenched by blinding rays of sun.

6. THE UNRAVELING

At that same moment, about four hundred miles away, Dillon Cole doubled over in a pain even more intense than the wrecking-hunger. He burst into a men's room in the small bus depot in Big Springs, Nebraska, stumbled into a stall, and collapsed to the tile floor. At first he thought this must have been God striking him down for the sheer magnitude of his sins—but then as the world around him seemed to burn away, he knew it was something else. The vision—the *memory* then burst upon his mind. It was both glorious and awful at once, and so intense that he thought it would kill him.

> *Awful Awful Awful*
> *Blinding fire*
> *Tearing*
> *Shattering*
> *Unbearable pain*
> *Shard of light*
> *Piercing*
> *Screaming through the void*
> *Then silence . . .*
> *And a beat.*
> *And silence . . .*
> *A heartbeat.*
> *And warmth*
> *And comfort*
> *And the soft safety*
> *Of flesh and blood.*

It was the vision of a cataclysmic death . . . followed by life. His own life. Something died . . . and he was born . . . but not just him. Others. *The* Others.

The convulsions that racked his body subsided as the vision faded, and he felt the grip of reality once more. He picked himself up and staggered back into the waiting area.

"Deanna?" He found her still doubled over on a bench. Her head was in her hands and she was quietly crying. She had shared this earth-shattering vision as well.

"You okay?" asked Dillon, still shaking from the experience.

"What was it?" Deanna got her tears under control. "I was so scared . . . what's happening to us?"

"The Others are together," said Dillon, just realizing it himself. The fact struck him in the face, leaving him stunned—and unsure of how to feel about it.

It was all beginning to make sense to him now. There were six of them in the vision, all screaming discordant notes.

They were all here, together, for fifteen years. Maybe thousands of miles apart by human standards, but from the perspective of an immense universe, they were right beside one another . . . and moving closer. The thought of it began to make Dillon get angry, and he didn't know why . . . and then he realized why. It was the wrecking-hunger, suddenly brought to a full boil, as if the vision triggered it to attack.

"I think we somehow know each other—even though we've never met," said Deanna. "There *are* six of us, aren't there?"

"Four of *them*," said Dillon. "And two of *us*."

Dillon could see Deanna struggling to understand—but she couldn't grasp the entire truth yet. She couldn't see the pattern the way he did.

"We need to find them," insisted Deanna. "We have to join them . . ."

"We don't *have* to do anything."

"Yes we do! We have to meet The Others and find out who we really are!"

"I know who I am! I'm Dillon Cole, and that's all I need to know!"

"What's wrong with you?" she shouted. "Isn't that why we've been moving east? To find them?"

Dillon knew she was right. The thought of finding The Others had been like a carrot dangling before them. But now that carrot was quickly growing rotten in Dillon's mind. What would joining the others prove? What would it do beyond making Dillon just one of six? Yes, the wrecking-hunger was awful—but it was something familiar. Joining The Others, however, was a great dark unknown.

They're going to hurt you, the wrecking-hunger whispered to him. *They'll ruin everything. They'll take Deanna away.* He didn't know what to believe anymore.

The hunger was clawing at him now, tearing up his gut as it had done so many times before . . . and from outside came the drone of a bus and black smoke pouring through the open door.

"Oh no!" cried Deanna in a panic. They both raced to the door in time to see their bus—which had only stopped in Big Springs for a few minutes—drive off. Along with that bus went what few things they had: a bag with maps, a change of clothes, and most importantly, Dillon's wallet.

Fine, thought Dillon. *Let the bus go. Who cares, anyway?* Dillon stormed out the door and headed in the other direction. The hunger kept swelling inside of him, and he knew he would have to feed it soon.

"Where are you going?" shouted Deanna.

"Looks like I'm going to Hell," he said, then turned from her and stormed away.

Dillon Cole's pilgrimage to Hell began moments later, in a schoolyard across the street, where a tall kid, maybe a year older than he, was playing basketball alone.

Dillon was consumed by the wrecking-hunger now—and his mind was set on seek and destroy. He didn't know how or what he would destroy—but this guy on the basketball court was directly in his path and was therefore a target.

The target bounced his ball without much skill, trying to weave it through his legs. When he saw Dillon coming, he stopped his dribbling antics, and the two of them began to shoot around.

The guy introduced himself as Dwight Astor, and, as they took shots, Dillon tried to hide the wrecking-hunger like a vampire hiding his fangs.

"How about a game of one-on-one?" asked Dillon.

"Okay, winners out," said Dwight. And the game began.

Dwight played fairly well, and although Dillon knew he could beat him—for Dillon never lost any game he played—Dillon didn't try. He let Dwight drive around him for lay ups. He guarded poorly, making sure there were never any fouls—no body contact.

. . . And while they played, Dillon did something he had never done before: he studied the patterns of his human subject.

Until now, Dillon had kept away from people, never making eye contact, thinking only of ways to avoid them. He was always much more comfortable with the simple, predictable patterns of crashing cars, shattering glass, stones, and billiard balls. But today Dillon dared to peer into the workings of a human being, and he discovered something remarkable:

Human beings have patterns too. Patterns of action and behavior that can trace their histories and futures.

Dillon bristled with excitement as he watched Dwight move around the court—and in about ten seconds of basketball, Dillon was able to predict every move Dwight could make on the court—but Dillon could do better than that! He could look beyond the court, right into every aspect of Dwight's life.

It amazed Dillon just how much he was able to figure out; facts impossible for the most observant of people to uncover came to Dillon with the slightest effort.

The hesitation that made Dwight miss his shots told Dillon how long and how often his parents had punished him as a child. The way Dwight's eyes darted back and forth told Dillon of friendships lost and trusts broken. The thrill in Dwight's eyes each time he drove toward the basket told Dillon exactly how high his ambitions were and how successful he was going to be in life. Every move, every word, every breath betrayed a secret about Dwight's days and nights, hopes and dreams, fears and failures.

Dillon had heard it said that every second we live bears the pattern of our entire life, the way a single cell bears the DNA pattern of our whole body. Now Dillon knew it to be true, because what might have taken years for a psychiatrist to uncover, Dillon instinctively knew in just a few minutes on a basketball court.

The blueprint of Dwight Astor's life!

And to think that all along Dillon had this talent—this *power* to peer into the human clockwork. It was the single most thrilling moment of Dillon's life.

Dwight missed a shot, and the ball went bouncing out of bounds.

"Your ball," said Dwight. Dillon took the ball and began dribbling it around the court, thinking about the many things he discovered by watching his opponent:

Dwight Astor. He was a B-plus student. His parents fought. He had at least two brothers and at least one sister. His father was a recovering alcoholic. This was Dwight's past and present, but Dillon could also see the pattern of his future, as if the basketball were a crystal ball. If nothing changed, Dwight would go to college, would major in business, or maybe economics, and would go on to run a small company. It was all there—Dillon saw the complex tapestry of Dwight's past, present and future as if he were simply reading a road map— and in that future, Dillon could see shades of wealth, success, and some level of happiness.

Dillon now had control of the ball. At last he worked his way around Dwight as if he were standing still. Then Dillon went for the lay up and released the ball onto the rim, where it hung, perfectly balanced— not on the back of the rim, but on the front of the rim. The ball just sat there, not going into the basket, and not falling out.

"Wow!" said Dwight. "How'd you do that? That's impossible."

As Dwight innocently stared at the balanced ball, Dillon Cole moved in for the kill.

"Listen to me, Dwight." Dwight turned and was caught in Dillon's gaze. "Your father says he doesn't drink anymore, but he does. He keeps his bottles of booze hidden somewhere in the house. If you look hard enough, you can find them."

Then Dillon whispered into Dwight's ear, clearly and slowly.

"Your father would never notice," said Dillon, *"if you drank some of it."*

The words Dillon spoke were like bullets that pierced deep into Dwight's brain. There was no blood, but the damage was the same—and the only one who could see the damage was Dillon. After all, he had done something anyone could have done . . . he had tossed Dwight a simple suggestion . . . but like the stone Dillon had tossed down the mountain in Tahoe, this was exactly the *right* suggestion to begin an avalanche in Dwight Astor's life. Dillon could already see the road map of Dwight's future changing. Dillon's simple suggestion had paved Dwight a brand-new future filled with addiction. Alcohol first, and then other things. Dwight would drop out of high school. He would run far away from home. He would make the wrong friends, make the wrong choices. He would die young and alone.

Dillon had destroyed him.

There were no crashes, no carnage, no evidence. And yet the wrecking-hunger was gone—it had been more satisfied than ever before; it dawned on Dillon that destroying a hillside, or crashing cars and breaking glass were nothing compared to destroying a human mind. . . . And it had been so easy to do. Finding the weakness in Dwight's pattern was like finding the loose thread of a sweater. All Dillon had to do was to pull on the thread to make the entire fabric unravel.

Now, with the wrecking-hunger quieted, he could only beam with satisfaction, his wonder overcoming any self-loathing he might have felt.

That vague sense of destiny that had begun with the supernova was focused by what happened today. For too long, Dillon had fled from his catastrophes, racked with guilt— begging for forgiveness. But he was stronger than that now. Much stronger.

"I . . . I have to go now," said Dwight. "Good game." Bewildered, Dwight turned and left, forgetting his ball.

Dillon could sense a pattern now unfolding in his own life. A destiny. A purpose—and although he wasn't quite certain what that purpose was, he knew it would soon make itself clear. He could hardly contain the excitement that came with this new reason to be. Its very power filled him with something he thought might be joy.

I could choose this destiny, thought Dillon. . . . *Or I could fight it; I could let the wrecking-hunger make me strong . . . or I could let it kill me.*

The way Dillon felt right now, the decision was as easy as it had been to whisper in Dwight Astor's ear.

As he watched Dwight shuffle off, Dillon made a pact with himself. No more fighting the hunger. He would feed it, he would live it, he would *be* the hunger . . . and if his destination was Hell, then he would learn to accept that. But he would not be alone. There would be others he'd be taking with him. Many, many others.

INSIDE THE DEPOT, DEANNA tried to find out when the next bus came through town, but the fear of being alone overcame her, and she had to get out.

Dillon had never acted this way toward her before. He had always been thoughtful and treated her kindly. She didn't know what this change meant, but they had promised to protect each other, and she would protect him, no matter what he said or did. She drew some comfort from the strength of her own resolve.

She found Dillon playing basketball across the street, alone.

"We need to get going," said Deanna, watching him cautiously, waiting to see how he would react.

"Yes, we do," he answered. "But we're not going east anymore. . . . We're going west."

Deanna studied him, thinking that it might be a joke—but then she realized that Dillon did not joke that way. "But . . . but The Others—"

"We don't need The Others." His voice was calm, his body relaxed. Deanne could tell that he had fed the wrecking-hunger, but she saw no evidence of it . . . and something was different this time. He wasn't racked by guilt. He wasn't cursing himself. She wanted to question him, to take a step away and think about all this, before his infectious peace-of-mind drowned her panic completely.

That's when Dillon grabbed her and did something he had never done before. He kissed her. The kiss felt so perfect, so natural, that she would have agreed with anything he said. She didn't know whether to feel angry because of it, or to feel relieved.

"Listen to me, Deanna," he told her. "Forget The Others; they're nothing compared to us—you and I are the strongest, the most powerful!"

It was true—Deanna had sensed that much in the vision. How loud they were—how *bright* they were compared to The Others as they screamed in the darkness. Her fears and Dillon's hunger for destruction were certainly far more powerful than anything the other four had to deal with.

Until now she had thought the strange gravity that had been drawing all of them together was impossible to resist. But if Dillon could resist it, then she could, too. They were the strong ones. This time she leaned forward to kiss him.

"Where will we go now?" she whispered.

Dillon struggled with his answer. "Deanna, I think I was meant to do some really big things. . . . I have to find out what those things are, and I can't be afraid to do them . . . but I'm afraid to do them alone."

Her mind told her that this was wrong, but her heart was too close to Dillon's now. Traveling to The Others might solve her troubles, but she was terrified of making that journey alone. And the thought of losing Dillon was unbearable.

"These things that you have to do," asked Deanna, "are they terrible things?"

Dillon bit his lip. She knew he wouldn't lie to her. "They might be," he said.

Deanna nodded, knowing she would have given him the same answer, no matter what he said. "Then I'll go with you . . . so you don't have to face those things alone."

As she said the words, she felt something changing around her like a great river suddenly shifting course. Perhaps this was what Dillon felt when he saw a pattern change, and she wondered how large this shift must have been if she could feel it too.

It was too huge a thing to think about, so she decided not to. She ignored it, pretending it didn't matter, and after a moment, it all felt okay. In a few minutes they were hitchhiking west on the interstate.

Meanwhile, in a house not too far away, Dwight Astor poured himself a glass of scotch, downed it, and then poured himself another.

Part III
Scorpion Shards

7. THE SUM OF THE PARTS

I want to forget who I am.
I never want to leave here.
I want to stay in this tight circle of four forever.

SOMEWHERE BETWEEN DUSK AND DAWN, BETWEEN HERE AND there, Tory, Winston, Lourdes, and Michael lay close, touching each other in some way—hand to hand, toe to toe, head to chest, huddling like a litter of mice. This closed circuit of four felt more joyous, more peaceful than anything any of them had ever felt before. Their hearts beat in unison, their breath came and went in a single tide. It felt wonderful to finally be whole.

Almost whole.

The place was as solitary and secluded as a place could be; a corn silo on the edge of town, part of an abandoned farm. The dome of the silo had long since turned to rubble, the victim of storms and neglect, leaving a round hole high above them filled with stars, like a portal to another universe. The storm had been washed away when the four of them had come together, and now the air was so tranquil and calm it didn't even feel cold.

They were silent for a long time as they rested, and when they finally began to talk, the words that came out were things they never dared to speak out loud.

"I shared a room with my sisters until my parents fixed up the attic for me," said Lourdes, her voice so heavy and thick that her very words seemed to sink to the ground. "They said it was to give me more room, but I knew it was to hide me away. That first night in the attic, I dreamed I was floating down Broadway in the Thanksgiving Day parade, so bloated with helium I could burst. A hundred people held me with strings, and all I could do was hang there bouncing back and forth between the skyscrapers, while thousands of people stared and laughed. When I woke up, I could feel myself growing . . . I could feel my body drawing energy right out of the air—maybe even pulling it from other people's bodies. I had stopped eating, but I still grew. That's when I knew the problem wasn't just food."

Then Lourdes gently squeezed Michael's hand, which rested so calmly in hers; Michael focused his eyes on the distant stars. "When I was thirteen," he said, "my friends dared me to talk to this high school girl who I had a crush on. She was three years older, and a head taller than me, but the crush I had on her was out of control, so I just had to talk to her. I went up to her, but before I could open my mouth to say anything, she looked at me and WHAM! I felt there was some sort of weird connection, like I was draining something out of her, right through her eyes—and I knew right then I should have stopped and walked away, but I didn't, because I liked the way it felt. It was cold out, but suddenly the whole street began to feel hot like it was summer. I asked her out, and she said 'yes.' Ever since then no girl has ever said 'no' to me, and no guy has wanted to be my friend."

Winston moved his Nike against Tory's shoe and shifted his head against the comfortable pillow of Lourdes's sleeve, making sure not to break the circle.

"My mother used to get these swollen feet 'cause she stood all day long working at the bank," Winston began. "It was always my job to massage her feet when she got home. We already knew I had stopped growing, but that's all we knew. Then one day, I'm massaging her feet, and she tells me how good it feels, 'cause she can't feel the pain no more, so I keep on massaging. And then, when she tries to get up, she can't. She tries to feel her legs, but she can't feel nothin'. Doctors said it was some kind of freak virus, but we all know the truth, even if Mama won't say it. I paralyzed her legs. A few weeks later, we knew for sure that I was growing backward, too."

Winston wiped a tear from his eye, and Tory began to speak. "There was this blind boy in my neighborhood, with allergy problems so bad a skunk could have walked into the room, and he wouldn't have smelled it. Once I started breaking out, he was the only boy who liked me. Then one day he brushed his fingertips across my face. He pulled his hand away and turned white as a ghost, then he ran off to wash his hands over and over again, trying to wash the feel of my face off his fingers. He came down with pneumonia a few days later and was in the hospital for weeks. He was the first one to get sick from touching me. And that's how I knew it wasn't just zits."

No one spoke for a while. They rested their voices and minds, listening to the singular *whoosh* of their breaths, feeling each other's parallel heartbeats, and it seemed to make everything okay. They needed no more words to express how they felt.

I want to forget who I am.

I never want to leave here.

I want to stay in this tight circle of four forever.

But they couldn't stay like this, could they? They would freeze to death. They would starve to death. And they would never solve the mystery of who they were, and why they were dying these miserable deaths.

Yes, they were dying. Although they never dared to say it out loud, they all knew the truth. Tory's disease would eat away at her until there was nothing left. Michael's passion would consume him like a fire, Lourdes would become so heavy her bones would no longer be able to hold her, and Winston would wither until he became an infant in search of a womb to return to, but there would be none.

Better not to think about that.

I want to forget who I am . . .

While the others seemed content to shut their minds down, Tory could not. Mysteries did not sit well with her and she despised riddles of any sort. From the moment they had come together, she, more than the others, had struggled to understand the truth behind their shared vision, and their shared journey, but all she had were half-truths.

She knew they belonged together, but why?

The vision told them that two were missing, but who?

They must have known each other from somewhere, but how?

The vision had been so contorted, confusing, and overwhelming that it only left more questions in its wake. Questions—and this collective state of blissful shock.

"The truth is bigger than any of us want to know," Lourdes had proclaimed.

"The truth is something we're not supposed to know," Winston had declared.

"What we don't know can't hurt us," Michael had decreed.

But those were all just excuses. Cop-outs. Tory could not accept that.

Up above, a crescent moon was coming into view within

the circle of stars . . . but something was missing, thought Tory. What was it? Of course! It was the nova on the edge of the horizon. She could not see it, but she knew it was there. The dying star.

The dying star?

It began as a single thought, that suddenly grew until it became the key to the vision . . . but not just the vision . . . the key to everything! It was so simple, yet so staggering, she didn't know whether to believe it or just crawl up into a ball and disappear.

She broke the circle of four, and the moment the connection was broken, the world around them became cold and hostile once more. The ruined silo was no longer a haven, it was just a lonely, forgotten place where they could all die and no one would ever find them.

As they all sat up, they began to shiver. It was like coming out of a dream. "What's wrong?" Winston asked Tory. Now that they were apart, they moved away from one another, withdrawing to the walls of the silo, as if, now that their senses had returned, they were ashamed of the words they had spoken and the heartbeat they had shared.

"You sick or something?" he asked.

Tory just shook her head, still reeling from the thoughts playing in her mind.

"You figured something out, didn't you?" asked Lourdes. "Tell us."

Tory began to shake and tried to control it. "I'm afraid to tell you," she said, "'cause what I'm thinking is crazy."

"We won't think you're crazy," said Lourdes.

"I'm not afraid of that. . . . I'm afraid you'll think I'm right."

Winston looked at Lourdes, and Michael just looked down. A wind now breathed across the open silo above them, and the heavy stone ruin began to resonate with a deep moan, like someone blowing across the lip of a bottle.

"Tell us," said Lourdes.

Tory took a deep breath and clenched her fists until her knuckles were white. She forced her thoughts into words. "We know that all of this started when that Scorpion Star blew up last week, right?"

The others nodded in agreement.

"But . . . that star didn't *just* blow up, did it?" continued Tory. "We're just seeing it now, because of the speed of light, and stuff, but it really blew up sixteen years ago."

Winston shifted uncomfortably. "What are you getting at?"

"Winston, you believe we have a soul, don't you?" asked Tory.

"Yeah, so?"

"So does every living thing have a soul?"

He took a moment to weigh the question. "I don't know— maybe."

"How about a star?"

"What the hell are you talking about?" said Michael. "A star's not a living thing!"

Tory looked him right in the eye. "How do you know?"

"Because it's just a ball of gas."

"So? When it comes right down to it, we're all just piles of dirt, aren't we? Dirt and a whole lot of water."

Michael zipped his jacket as high as it would go, but it wasn't just the cold he was trying to keep out. "Speak for yourself," he said.

"Let her talk!" demanded Lourdes.

"I know this sounds wild," said Tory, "but the more I think about that vision we had, the more it makes sense . . . because it wasn't a vision at all. It was a memory."

Tory took a deep breath and finally spat out what she was thinking. "What if the Scorpion Star was alive? What if it had a soul, or a spirit, or whatever you want to call it . . . and when it blew up all those years ago, its soul blew up, too . . . into six pieces that flew through space a zillion times faster than light, and ended up right here on earth. What if it became *our* souls? What if it became us?"

Lourdes heaved herself closer to Tory. "And sixteen years later," added Lourdes, "when we saw the light of the explosion, it reminded us . . . and we started to move toward one another like it was an instinct."

"No!" Winston shook his head furiously. "No, you're crazy." He put his hands over his ears and pulled his knees up. "And anyway," he said, "if it's true, we'd all have been born on the same day, wouldn't we? The same day the star exploded."

Tory hesitated for a moment. She hadn't thought it through that far yet.

"When's your birthday?" Winston asked her.

"May twenty-third?" she offered.

"Ha!" shouted Winston. "My birthday's June fifteenth! You're wrong!"

"Maybe not," said Michael, and all eyes turned to him. "I was born on April twentieth, *but* I was six weeks premature. I was *supposed* to be born at the beginning of June." He turned to Tory. "Were you early or late?"

Tory shrugged. "Don't know. My mother and me . . . we didn't talk much."

"I was right on time," chimed in Lourdes. "June second."

Everyone turned to Winston.

"June fifteenth, huh?" said Michael. "I'll bet you were two weeks late, weren't you?"

Winston wouldn't look him in the eye. He pulled his knees up to his chest again.

"Well, Winston?" said Tory.

Winston picked the ground with a twig and finally said, "My mom always said I was too stubborn to come into this world when I was expected. I came in my own time . . . two weeks late."

Tory gasped. "Then we were all *supposed* to be born on the same day!"

Michael nodded. "Not just the same day . . . but the same second, I'll bet." He looked down, and found in the debris of the silo the shattered remains of an ancient Coke bottle— he picked it up and pieced the shards of the bottle together. "Check this out—sixteen years ago, our parents conceived each of us at the same instant in time . . . and at that same moment . . . BOOM!" He dropped the bottle, and the shards scattered as they hit the hard earth. ". . . The star died . . . and we got ready to be born."

Winston stared at the broken glass, looking a little bit sick. He didn't say anything—just closed his eyes and held his knees tightly to his chest. Tory could tell that he was trying desperately to make this information go away. The way he looked at things—it's like he wanted all of creation to fit nice and neatly in a little box, and whatever didn't fit he just ignored. Well, this time Tory knew he couldn't ignore it—he'd have to stretch that little box.

"C'mon, Winston, you can deal with it," said Tory. "Make the stretch."

"I ain't no bungee cord, okay? I don't stretch that way." Winston shut his eyes even tighter, and Tory could hear him grinding the last nubs of his teeth in frustration.

The soul of a star, thought Tory. *How big—how powerful was the soul of a star?* Even one sixth of it must have been brighter than any other on Earth. "We must be the most powerful human beings in the world!" she told her friends.

"Then why are we dying?" Winston looked at her coldly and left the silo. Since no one had an answer, they silently followed him out.

Why were they dying? thought Tory. *Not just dying—but suffering hideous afflictions. Why would the brightest lights on earth be so consumed by darkness?* This answer she had found was only half an answer, and it made her furious.

Outside the silo, the ground was covered by a thick fog that swirled around their ankles, and the air smelled rich with the decaying remains of an early harvest. A hint of blue on the eastern horizon told of the coming dawn, and although they had not slept, they were too tightly wound to sleep now.

"Yesterday when I closed my eyes," said Michael, "I could almost see the faces of the others . . . but now they feel further away." And then he dared to voice something they were all too afraid to admit might be true. "I don't think they're coming," he said. "Something's gone wrong."

"We have to go to Nebraska," said Tory. "To Omaha. I'm telling you some astronomer at some school there predicted the explosion of the star; he has to know something that can help us."

They *did* have a sense that they had to move northwest, and although Omaha didn't leap out at them as a must-see town, it wasn't out of their way, either—and it was the closest thing to a lead that they had, so Tory got her way. Omaha it was.

By now Lourdes had squeezed her way out of the stone entrance to the silo and joined them. Winston, however, was standing by himself, pondering the glow of the nova, which was quickly being overcome by the light of dawn. Tory reached out to touch Winston gently on the shoulder, but Winston quickly pulled away.

"Don't!" His sleeves fell over his hands, and he had to fight to stick his arms through them again. The jacket seemed much larger on him than it had yesterday, and his boyish voice seemed a little bit higher. "Just don't touch me, okay?"

"Winston . . ."

"I like being one person, okay? I don't want to be one sixth of something, or even one fourth of something."

"But, Winston, if what I've said is right, it could mean so many things—look at the possibilities!"

Winston's face hardened into the expression of a stubborn old man or a very small boy. "I don't care to," he said. Winston's hand began to twitch at his side, and he turned away from Tory, but Tory still watched. He brought his hand up a little, then forced it back down, as if fighting some inner battle—but it was a battle he lost. Tory could only stare in growing dread as Winston Pell, the incredible shrinking boy, brought up his hand, slipped his thumb into his mouth, and kept it there for a long, long time.

THAT AFTERNOON, AT ANOTHER farm hundreds of miles away in Torrington, Wyoming, Dillon Cole tore through a wheat field, putting distance between himself and the farmhouse behind him. He would not look back; he would not *think* back, and what he left behind in that house would be put completely out of his mind.

He felt the wrecking-hunger curl up and go to sleep well fed, and when the hunger was fed, Dillon felt strong—stronger than anyone alive. *What would I be without the wrecking-hunger?* he thought. The hunger answered like a rumbling from his stomach: he would be nothing. Sometimes he felt as if the hunger were a living thing; a weed that had coiled around his soul and he couldn't tell where it ended and where he began. He didn't know whether that was a good thing or a bad thing.

But whatever it was, those four Others wanted to take it away, didn't they? Even now they were drawn toward him, across the miles, and if they found him, they would weaken him; maybe even destroy him. They would drive a wedge between him and Deanna, and Dillon could not allow that. So they had to keep moving until . . .

Until what?

Until the hunger no longer needed to be fed.

He raced across the wheat field to the place where he had left Deanna, but when he got there, she was gone.

Dillon had left Deanna in the wheat field with little warning. They had just left a farmhouse where a family had been kind enough to give them lunch—they were crossing a field, when suddenly Dillon had told her to wait, and then doubled back over the hill toward the house again.

He had gone to feed the hunger—Deanna knew that—she could see in his face how he had been suffering—strangling—but why did he have to leave her alone? He knew what happened to her when she was alone.

A wind swept across the rolling hills of wheat. The ground beneath her seemed to move, and fear gripped her. She felt one of her waking nightmares coming on again, and although she knew it could not be real, it terrified her all the same. Was there something there under the ground? Something coming for her? Yes! She could see it burrowing beneath the wheat. Why had Dillon left her here?

She began to run, but the fear ran with her. Finally she

stumbled into a field that had already been harvested, where thick black mud swallowed her to her ankles. Something was reaching for her. She could feel it. She screamed in terror.

She fell to the mud, and the ground seemed to swallow her. Was the ground alive? Was it climbing up around her, dragging her down into darkness? She couldn't see now—the mud was in her eyes, in her mouth. She swore she could feel a beast coming out of the mud wrapping around her like a snake, and she screamed again to chase the terror-mare away, but her screaming didn't help.

Then something grabbed her by the wrists. At first she thought it was the ground itself reaching up to pull her even deeper, but then there was a voice. A familiar voice.

"Deanna, it's all right!" She could barely hear Dillon through her own screams. "Look at me," he said. "*See* me. Make it go away."

Deanna, her sight still blurry, fixed on his dark eyes, pushing the foul vision of fear away.

When the terror-mare had ended, it was like coming out of a seizure, which is exactly how Dillon treated it. He held her tightly, as if she had been in the throes of convulsions. Deanna was exhausted and let all her muscles go slack, feeling the steady pressure of Dillon as he held her.

"You left me," she said weakly.

"I'm sorry. I was wrong to—I won't do it again." Dillon picked her up and carried her to a place where the wheat was tall and the ground was dry, then he lay her down, and tenderly wiped away the mud that had caked on her arms. Dillon was calm and relaxed. Deanna knew what that meant.

"What happened at the farmhouse?" she asked. "How bad was it?"

"I didn't touch a thing," said Dillon. "I just sort of planted a seed. That's all."

"What did you do?"

Dillon stared at her, considering her question. "I'll tell you, if you want to know."

But the truth was, she *didn't* want to know, so she didn't press the issue. Instead she just lay there staring up at the sky, feeling her fear curl up inside her and go to sleep as she listened to far-off birds crying somewhere over the hill. Their voices sounded like screams in the distance.

"We need to keep moving," said Dillon, helping Deanna up.

"Do we know where we're going yet?" she asked.

"We're not 'going' anywhere," Dillon answered. "We're getting away from The Others."

Dillon had been saying that since they left Nebraska—but it wasn't entirely true, was it? *Dillon knows where he's going,* thought Deanna. *He just doesn't know he knows.* It was clear to Deanna that he was doing what he did best—tracing a pattern—but this pattern was so complex and intricate not even he could see its end.

Deanna kept her faith in Dillon, knowing that wherever this journey was leading, she and Dillon would be together. She held onto that thought as they headed west out of Torrington, leaving behind the farmhouse and the screaming birds.

8. DR. BRAINLESS AND THE SIX OF SWORDS

It was a small observatory in a small university, where a man of small recognition worked feverishly to get his telescope up and running.

Winston was doubtful about the entire thing—but then he was doubtful of everything since Tory came up with that crazy stuff about the Scorpion Star. Winston feared he'd never be able to stretch himself around that one—but the others had, and now Tory was in the lead wherever they went.

In the two days the quartet had been together, Winston had felt his disease, or whatever it was, start to accelerate. A day ago he had chewed a sandwich on his seven-year molars. But when he ran his tongue through his mouth today, those molars were gone, receding back into his head. His front teeth were starting to get smaller and smaller. Soon all his adult teeth would be gone, and he would have no teeth at all, because his baby teeth had long since been exchanged for quarters beneath his pillow.

The others were no better off: Lourdes's blouse looked like a patch quilt because they kept having to sew scraps of material into it to make it larger. Tory had begun complaining that her joints ached something fierce, which meant that whatever was devouring her skin was beginning to move deeper into her body, and Michael . . . well, sometimes he looked like a madman on the verge of turning into a werewolf. He complained his girl-crazies were getting worse and that his heart beat so fast, he was afraid it might blow up in his chest.

They had all hoped that coming together would slow down their deterioration, but it hadn't—in fact, things were progressing faster, and they all could be dead in a matter of days. Winston didn't know how an astronomer could help, but he was desperate enough to try anything now.

Finding the man was not very difficult. A simple Web search uncovered several articles on the eccentric astronomer. Dr. Bayless was his name, but his crueler colleagues were more fond of calling him Dr. Brainless.

Winston fought to stay ahead of Michael and Lourdes and right behind Tory as they crossed the small college campus toward the physics building. Tory still shuffled through printouts of the articles they had found, trying to read in the late twilight.

"Listen to this—it says here that Bayless's mother was a carnival psychic, and she gyped rich people out of thousands of dollars!"

"So?" scoffed Winston.

"So, the scientific community thinks Bayless is a quack as well and gives him the cold shoulder."

"But he predicted the explosion of Mentarsus-H," chimed in Lourdes, in her deep whale-belly voice. "So who's quacking now?"

Winston turned to Michael, who seemed distracted and bothered as if the air itself was pricking his whole body with needles as he walked.

"What do *you* think?" asked Winston.

"He probably won't help us unless we bring him the broomstick of the Wicked Witch," said Michael.

BEHIND THE PHYSICS BUILDING stood the observatory—a small domed structure painted a peeling institutional green. It was no more an emerald city than their path had been a yellow-brick road.

As they pushed their way through the squeaky doors of the observatory, they were met by the smell of old floor varnish and a twelve-foot telescope with pieces missing. It was an unimpressive observatory, consisting of little more than the crippled telescope, a desk in a far corner, and an arrow on the floor pointing north—in case anyone couldn't figure that out by themselves.

Across the room, a thin man, with thinner hair, fought with workers—trying to keep them working on the telescope, even though it was way past five o'clock. He was tall, with a slight roundness to his back from too many years making calculations at a desk. The four kids approached the ranting astronomer solemnly like a small minion of misery, and when he saw them, he waved them off.

"No classes today. Go home." His voice had a hostile, unfriendly tone that could only come from many years of bitter disappointment.

Tory cleared her throat and stepped forward. "Dr. Bayless, we've come a long way—we have to talk to you."

Bayless turned to take a better look at them, then, with a disgust he didn't even try to hide, said, "My God! What happened to you?"

"That's what we're trying to find out," said Winston.

Around them the workers were starting and moving toward the doors, whispering to each other about the freaks that had just walked in.

"Go on," Bayless shouted to the workers. "Get out—see if I care." They were more than happy to oblige. "The cosmic event of a lifetime, and the telescope had to break down this month."

He took a moment to look at the four of them again, shook his head—shuddering with revulsion—and let loose a bitter laugh. "Life's misfortunes just fall at my doorstep, don't they?

If it's not a ruined telescope, it's the wretched of the earth. Well, how can I help you?"

"What can you tell us about supernovas?" asked Tory.

"What *can't* I tell you?" he replied, slipping into professor-speak. "Supernovas are the reason we're all here. Oxygen, carbon, silicon—all the heavier elements are created in the explosions. Without novas, the whole universe would be little more than hydrogen gas . . ." He paused and looked at them again, shuddering, but this time not laughing. "But you didn't come here for an astronomy lecture, did you?"

"You predicted the explosion of Mentarsus-H," said Tory. "We think our condition's got something to do with that."

Now Bayless's look turned from revulsion to suspicious interest. He studied them intensely and began to pick at his ragged yellow fingernails.

"My prediction was luck," he said. "At least that's what my colleagues say."

"Don't go playing games with us, all right?" said Winston, pulling his thumb from his mouth. "If you know something, tell us."

"You got a big mouth for a little kid," said Bayless.

"I'm fifteen," growled Winston.

Bayless sighed and nodded reluctantly. "All right, come on and sit down."

Bayless led them to a corner of the observatory that had been set up as his office. Winston noticed that Michael kept his distance, breathing in gasps, like someone suffering from asthma, and shifting his weight from one foot to another like a caged animal. *He's got it bad today,* thought Winston.

"The Scorpion Star," said Lourdes to Bayless. "Tell us how you knew."

Bayless leaned back in his desk chair, took a sip of cold

coffee, and focused on his uneven fingernails, picking at them with an unpleasant click-click-click. Finally he spoke.

"It's a curious talent," said Bayless, "to look at the universe and know what it's thinking. To sense that countless galaxies would be discovered in dark space. To feel that the universe is even older than most scientists think it is. To glance at a star chart and see one star missing in the tail of the Scorpion, only to see it reappear when you blink."

"Intuition?" suggested Tory.

"My mother had it," said Bayless. "She chose to use it to separate fools from their money and turned herself into a sideshow freak. I chose to use it for more noble purposes. Biology . . . astrophysics." Then he angrily flicked a fingernail in an arc over their heads. It landed on the dark floor, where it lay like a crescent moon. "Unfortunately science has no room for intuition. Scientists find a million ways to spell 'coincidence,' and so I've become a sideshow freak after all." Then he smiled grimly, and added, ". . . like the four of you."

His smile made them all squirm. Everyone but Tory.

"The star blew up sixteen years ago," said Tory. "We've figured out the exact date."

"Students of astrophysics, are you?" said Bayless, beginning on a new fingernail.

"No," said Tory. "That was the day each of us was conceived."

Bayless raised his attention from his marred fingertips to the four of them. "Remarkable," he said, studying their faces, and movements. "Remarkable. Perhaps these exploding stars have more to do with us than I've dared to imagine." He pulled out a digital recorder from his desk and hit the record button. "Do you mind if I record all this?"

"We'd rather you didn't," said Lourdes.

He put his recorder in his desk, but Winston couldn't tell if he turned it off.

"Tell me everything," he said. "Everything to the last detail . . ."

THEY TOOK A GOOD hour to go through their stories, and Bayless listened, attentive to every word. When they were done, the astronomer was practically drooling with excitement.

"Shards!" he exclaimed, laughing with glee. "Shards of a shattered star!" He peered at them as if they were subjects he planned to study. The slight hunch of his back made him resemble a vulture.

"I've written about this sort of thing," he said, pacing a short, sharp path, "but never dared to publish it—but now I can present you as proof!" He looked at them with such awe, it made Winston roll his eyes. "Do you have any idea how special—how *luminous* you are? Why, the rest of us are mere smithereens compared to you!"

"Yeah?" said Michael. "So if we got these fantastic kick-ass souls, how come we're so screwed up?"

His words stopped Bayless in mid-pace. "I don't know," he said. "By my estimation you should be living lives like no others— glorious lives with—"

"Shut up," shouted Winston. Hearing what his life *should* have been made it all seem even worse. He started to stomp around like a small child, and Tory put her hand on his head to calm him down. It only made him angrier.

"We don't need ought-a-be's," said Tory. "We need some why-not's."

Bayless looked at them and sighed. The answers they needed were clearly not easy to come by. Bayless pondered his inoperable telescope for a moment, then turned back to them decisively.

"Science can't help you," said Bayless. "Not unless you want to wait and see what they find in your autopsies."

The thought made Winston shiver, and he swore he could feel himself shrink a fraction of an inch.

"Then what do you suggest?" said Michael, his breathing heavier, his voice even more impatient than it had been an hour ago.

Bayless thought about it, sighed in resignation, and reached into his bottom drawer, pulling out an old deck of cards that looked like they hadn't been used in ages.

"When I was young, my mother made me read cards for rich old women. I once told a woman she was going to die before the sun went down. She stormed out of the tent in a huff and was promptly trampled by the fair's elephant."

Michael stood engulfed in his own growing frustration. "We need *real* help and *real* answers, can't you see that? We didn't come all this way to read dumb old tarot cards!"

"And I didn't get degrees in biology and astrophysics to read dumb old tarot cards, but here we are, aren't we?"

Michael, his breathing helplessly heavy, his body uncontrollably tense, his pants unrelentingly tight, looked to the others. "Are you going to sit here for this garbage?" Clearly his frustration had little to do with tarot cards—so Lourdes gently took his hand.

"Just relax," she told him. "Take deep breaths. What you're feeling will go away."

"No it won't," he said. "You know it won't."

He shook off Lourdes's hand and stormed along the arrow on the floor, until he crashed out of the observatory, into the night.

"Don't mind him," Winston told Bayless. "He's just pointing north."

Tory was about to go after him, but Lourdes stopped her. "He just needs some air," she said. "He'll be all right."

When the echo of Michael's exit had faded, Bayless returned to shuffling the cards.

"Does it have to be tarot cards?" asked Winston. "Where I come from only ignorant folk use 'em. They're hard to believe in."

Bayless continued to shuffle. "It's not the cards you need to believe in, it's the skill of the dealer," he said. He pulled out a card and handed it to Winston. "It's like playing poker. Any idiot can deal cards—but how many people can deal a straight-flush every time?"

Winston looked at his card. A small boy on a golden ram, racing out of control through the sky. In one hand the boy held a torch that fought to survive a brutal wind. To Winston the boy seemed terrified.

"The Page of Wands," noted Bayless. "Unless I've lost my touch, that card is you."

Winston studied the card. He didn't quite know what it meant, but he did have a sense of identification—as if he truly could be this boy clinging helplessly to the back of the wild wooly ram.

"If I wanted to," said Bayless, "I could tell your fortune with baseball cards and the result would be exactly the same."

Winston cast his eyes down.

"All right, then," said Tory. "Deal us a fortune."

Bayless smiled. "Yes—let's desecrate the halls of science, shall we?" And with that, he dealt seven cards, face down— six formed a triangle, and the seventh he placed in the triangle's center.

He reached toward the two cards at the bottom. "If I remember correctly, these cards will show us the present." He flipped the first one, revealing a cloaked figure in a small boat, navigating a troubled sea.

"Death?" asked Lourdes.

"No, *the Six of Swords*," Bayless replied. Winston looked more closely at the card to see a cargo of six swords resting in the keep of the ship. "Six souls on a restless journey."

"Then there *are* six of us!" said Tory. "Now we have proof!"

"If you can call this proof," mumbled Winston.

Bayless flipped the second card. A chariot being torn apart by a black horse and a white horse. Bayless looked at the card, and began to sweat just a bit.

"Death?" asked Lourdes.

"*The Charioteer,*" said Bayless. "It's making me uncomfortable, but I don't know why. . . . See, the horses that pull this chariot are very powerful. They have to be stopped or the chariot will be destroyed."

"So what does that mean?" asked Winston.

"Not sure yet."

Bayless went to the next two cards. "These cards will show where your journey must take you."

He anxiously flipped the first to reveal an image of a tower being destroyed by lightning.

"*The Tower.* Does the tower mean anything to you?"

The three kids shook their heads.

Bayless nodded. "It will soon."

He flipped the next card. It showed a dark figure covered in shrouds, in the midst of desolation.

"Death?" asked Lourdes.

"No—*the Hermit.*" Bayless's voice was becoming shaky, filled with both fear and wonder. "This is someone you must face . . . if you get that far."

"What's wrong?" asked Lourdes, as Bayless began to wring his fingers.

"He frightens me." Bayless said, confused. "*The Hermit* shouldn't frighten me . . ."

His eyes darted between the three kids, and he returned to the cards. "Well, we've begun, we have to finish it," he said. Now Winston was beginning to feel as if he didn't want to see the rest.

"This is what you will find at journey's end," Bayless said. "These two cards are your destiny."

He reached for the first card, hesitated for a moment, then flipped both cards simultaneously.

Winston looked at the first, and his heart missed a beat. Lourdes didn't have to say it this time. The masked figure of darkness was unmistakable.

"*Death,*" said Bayless. "And *the Five of Wands.*" The second card showed a man and woman with five glowing torches doing battle with a dragon. "Death will surround you. And those who survive will face a greater challenge."

"What sort of challenge?" whispered Winston.

"If I knew, I would tell you." Bayless quickly flipped the cards back over so he didn't have to see them. "I forgot how much I hated telling fortunes."

"What about the last card?" asked Tory.

Bayless cleared his throat.

"The central card. It binds your past, present and future. History and destiny." He didn't even reach for it. "Maybe you don't want to see this card."

"Turn it," demanded Tory, and so the astronomer-turned-fortune-teller reached for the central card with a shaky hand, grabbed it by the corner, and pulled on it.

The card ripped in half.

It had caught on a splinter of wood in his old desk. Bayless gasped in horror, as he looked at the torn half of the card in his hand.

Winston took the card from him and pulled the torn half from the table, holding the two halves together. The card showed a golden circle, containing a creature: half-man, half-woman. In the four corners were a torch, a star, a sword, and a grail.

"What is this card?" demanded Winston, but Bayless only shook his head and stammered like a crazy man.

"Tell us!"

"Everything." He said. "This card is *the World*."

And their fortune tore it in half.

Bayless stood up, his eyes darting around the observatory. He gasped, a revelation coming to him, and he began to rummage through his papers. "I understand," said Bayless. He was terrified, but at the same time overcome by some excitement that the others were yet to understand.

And there was something else . . . a strange hum that was growing in the room. A vibration that made everything shake.

"What do you understand?" shouted Tory. "Tell us!"

"I'm ready for this," said Bayless. "Everything I've done—everything I've written, everything I've learned—my whole life has been for this." He began piling up books on his desk, pulling them from shelves and talking as if he made perfect sense, which he didn't. "I'll come with you—I'll document every single moment and no one will laugh at me again."

By now the gears and casing of the telescope had begun to rattle and groan with the strange vibration. The three kids stood up, and looked around in terror. Something was very wrong here.

"Listen to me!" shouted Bayless, ripping open the drawers

of his filing cabinet and pulling out piles of papers. "There are things I can tell you; things I've never published because until now they've never made sense. Things you have to know!"

The roar in the observatory was deafening now, an ear-splitting shrieking that sounded almost like voices. But Bayless was too excited to care.

"I know what's happening to you!" proclaimed Bayless.

But before he could get any further, there was a blast of light, and they all began to scream.

Because the room was suddenly filled with monsters.

MICHAEL DID NOT HEAR their screams—he was far away, bolting aimlessly over the fields, cursing the stars that looked down on him, cursing the earth that supported him, until his wanderings brought him in a circle back to the buildings of the university.

A class was letting out, and he hunched in the shadows, watching every pretty girl that passed—and they were all pretty in one way or another to Michael. As the crowd thinned out, one girl was left by a bicycle rack.

Michael stepped out of the shadows. He thought he would just watch her as she rode away. That's all. Just watch.

For days Michael had looked away from girls—he had fought that burning feeling by standing in the cold rain, by screaming into empty fields—but now his resistance was low. He was tired . . . and before he even knew it, he had turned on his peculiar magnetism like a tractor beam.

When the girl heard his footsteps stalking closer, she didn't think anything of it at first. "Did you enjoy the class?" she asked.

Michael just stared at her, enjoying her every move. "I'm not a student," he answered.

She began to get a bit apprehensive, glancing around to see

if any of her friends were still there, but everyone was gone. They were alone.

"You're very pretty." Michael took a step closer, she glanced at him, and in an instant she was caught.

Before Michael could pause for a moment's thought, he was kissing her and she didn't resist for a moment.

Michael broke away.

"No," he said, fighting it, "that's not what I meant to do. . . . What I really need . . . I mean what I really want to do is just . . . talk. That's all."

But she didn't hear him; she was staring into his eyes the way they always did. She spoke, almost giggling, as if this were all part of a dream. "My name's Rebecca," she said. "What's yours?"

"Michael."

She smiled and leaned forward to kiss him again. "Why am I doing this?" she said.

"Full moon," said Michael, although it wasn't. He was burning inside now, the sweat beading on his face.

Rebecca glanced over her shoulder, to make sure that everyone was gone, then took his hand and led him off down a dim, tree-lined path.

As they ran, Rebecca looked to the right and left. Michael knew she was searching for some hidden place where they could get back to what they had started—a place to match that dark hidden place in Rebecca's mind that Michael had already found. She was already falling into that darkness with the thrill of a sky-diver.

They came to a windowless building—the school's physical plant. Steam billowed from the roof, air whistled through vents, and inside a pump rang out a dull toll sending water, gas, and electricity to the many buildings of the campus.

Rebecca pushed Michael up against the door, kissed him, then giggled. "You kiss good," she said.

It was getting out of hand. He knew that he should never have looked at her, but now his worries were drowning in a stormy sea of Rebecca's kisses. Going around the bases was not a good thing for Michael. He had only done it once—in Baltimore, and after what happened there, he swore not to let it happen again. Since then, bunting his way to first had been the name of the game—but suddenly he realized that he was about to swing away.

"You really don't want to do this," said Michael feebly, but even as he said it, he gripped her tighter and felt his own sense of control slipping away.

They leaned into the door, and it squealed open into a cavern smelling brackish and damp, where a water pump pounded and rattled them from head to toe.

Maybe it will be different, thought Michael, *maybe it will be all right,* and he clung to that thought like a parachute, as he slipped into the darkness, like a man leaping from a plane.

MONSTERS!

The shadows Tory Smythe saw leaping around the observatory became permanently carved into her mind. Although it all happened in just a few seconds, she knew exactly what she had seen.

Shadow-black tentacles wrapped around the cradle of the telescope. A clouded face that swarmed with a million hideous insects descended upon the astronomer's desk, and something with cold dark fur brushed past Tory, its breath sickly sweet.

In an instant the telescope was torn from its moorings and came crashing down. The primary focus lens broke free and spun on the ground like a coin, casting patterns of refracted

light around the circular room. Bayless was screaming—
everyone was screaming—then the creatures let out their own
unearthly wail and a blinding explosion knocked them all to
the ground. Something leapt at Tory. She opened her mouth
to scream . . . and it was gone. The beasts were all gone. The
light faded, and she just sat there, hands pressed against her
ears, eyes shut tight, and her face contorted in a silent scream.
She heard the others screaming, though—Winston and
Lourdes—she heard them burst out of the observatory and
race down the hill.

But Tory couldn't move. She had heard old stories of how
looking at some monsters could turn you to stone, and she
wondered if that had happened to her. She cursed herself for
having come here.

I don't believe in monsters, she told herself, but that didn't
make a bit of difference, because she knew what she had seen.

At last she was able to force her eyes open. The ruined
observatory was silent and still. The only light in the room
came from the fading fragments of the telescope lens, which
had exploded and sent glass splintering in all directions.

As she finally got to her feet, Tory realized that whatever
Dr. Bayless was going to tell them was going to remain his
secret. He would be viewing no more stars. He would be telling no more fortunes. Whatever these beasts were, they had
not wanted Bayless to tell what he knew. They had caused the
explosion—they had come to silence him.

She couldn't help but feel responsible for what had happened to the astronomer. She felt pity for the man, but even
more she felt fury that she was again left with more questions
and riddles. It was that fury that overcame her fear, and she
decided she wouldn't run just yet—there were still things she
had to do.

She grabbed whatever was left of the books and papers Bayless had pulled out and shoved them in her pack. She found the seven tarot cards scattered on the floor and took them as well, and then found a canvas tarp in the corner and brought it over to Bayless.

Around the room, the light was getting dimmer as the glowing splinters of the lens faded. The lens had shattered into half a dozen pieces. Five of those pieces were embedded in the walls like glass lightning bolts. The sixth had found a much more specific destination.

As Tory covered Bayless's body, she knew what she had to do—she owed at least that much to the poor man, And so before drawing the canvas over his face, she reached toward the silent astronomer, then took a firm hold of that last shard of crystal and, biting back her terror, pulled it from between Dr. Bayless's eyes.

THEY FOUND MICHAEL AT the edge of the campus, retching his guts out in the middle of the street and had to rush him out of the way of a speeding fire engine.

He knelt there by the curb, heaving and gripping his stomach.

"What the hell is wrong with you?" demanded Winston.

Tory and Lourdes knelt beside him and helped him stand up.

His face was wet from tears and pale—almost green.

"What happened?" asked Lourdes.

Michael didn't answer. Instead he just held his stomach and forced his breathing back under control. Finally he said, "I got lost . . . that's all." And no one dared to question him further.

They turned and headed off in a direction their internal compass told them was west, while behind them, way down the road, the fire truck stopped in front of a physical plant that was billowing black smoke.

9. LIGHT AND SHADOWS

THAT NIGHT THE STORM RETURNED WITH A VENGEANCE EVEN before the streets had a chance to dry. The night that had seemed so steamy quickly turned cold, and the sky let loose an unrelenting assault of sleet. It battered the windshield of the van with such fury that they had to pull off to the side of the road and wait.

Tory studied the map; they were somewhere west of Omaha now, in the middle of nowhere, and it occurred to Tory with an awful shiver that they were always in the middle of nowhere. It seemed from the moment her journey had begun, Tory had slipped into the dark festering world that existed between the walls and beneath the floors of the rest of the world. A rat-ridden place filled with the torn, ruined things that nobody wanted. They were all now residents of this waste-world, and the eerie capriciousness of the weather—never deciding on hot or cold, wet or dry—made the rest of humanity seem further and further away. It seemed to Tory that their lives had slipped into a place so dismal that souls perished and only weeds could take their place.

As the sleet pummeled the van, Winston sat in the back with Lourdes, sewing pieces of fabric onto her clothes so that they would still fit.

"Maybe The Others are dead," Winston dared to whisper at one point. "Maybe they were killed by those monster-things that tried to get us."

Lourdes shook her head and said, "If they were dead, then why do we still feel pulled to the west?"

And Lourdes was right the pull was still there and still strong. Tory, who always rode shotgun, was the official navigator, and when she looked at the map, certain roads and cities seemed to jump off the page at her. Interstate 80, Big Springs, Nebraska, Torrington, Wyoming. They had to go to these places, in hopes of finding traces of the other two who were still missing from their little band. It wasn't much, but it was all they had to go on. *The whole is greater than the sum of the parts,* Tory kept telling herself. *When we're all together, we'll be stronger—and it will all make sense.* She clung to that belief as if it were a lifeline.

Michael had little to say on the matter. Since they had left Omaha, he had become completely withdrawn. He sat silently in the driver's seat in an icy daze. His demeanor had become as hard and bitter as the torrents of ice that brutalized the van.

The moment they got to the van, Tory had begun leafing through the things she had scavenged from the observatory. First she puzzled over the cards. *the Six of Swords and the Charioteer; the Tower and the Hermit; Death, and the Five of Wands.* And the torn world. Then she began to look through the books. Astronomy mostly—textbooks that Bayless had written himself. Page after page yielded nothing relevant to Tory, and now as they sat in the ice storm, she seemed no closer to a solution.

"Something that he said keeps going over and over in my mind," Tory told the others. "He said that his whole life was just preparing him for this . . . for *us.*"

"Then why don't you look at his whole life?"

It was Michael who spoke, and everyone was startled to hear him speak after being silent for so long. "He was a biologist before he was an astronomer," said Michael. "And you've been looking at the wrong books."

Michael then held up the book he had been looking at.

It was a book on parasites.

"Bayless wrote this years before he became an astronomer," said Michael. "It says here in the introduction that when he was a kid his pet dog was just about eaten from the inside out by worms. Since then he was fascinated by parasites—creatures that live off of other creatures."

Then Michael began to read from Bayless's book: *"There are whole universes of life hiding in the dark places where no one dares to explore. They thrive in the hidden expanses we take for granted . . . between the very cells of our body . . . between the walls we call our world."*

Tory gasped. "He said that?"

Michael nodded, and Tory shivered. It was like hearing a man echoing her thoughts from beyond the grave.

Michael passed around the book, and they leafed through it. It was a bizarre collection of diagrams, photos, and case studies, and Bayless seemed to have had a morbid fascination with it all. There was a picture of a tapeworm the size of a garden hose found in the gut of an elephant. There was a barnacle the size of a trash barrel on the back of a whale. There were leeches from the Amazon the size of running shoes.

"This was his specialty before he took up astronomy," said Michael. "The study of parasitic organisms."

A gust of wind rocked the van and a sheet of ice assaulted the windshield like a cascade of ball bearings. Winston asked the question that no one else dared to voice.

"What's it got to do with us?"

Michael couldn't look at him in the face. He turned to look out of the window, but all the windows were fogged with the steam of their breath.

Between the walls of the world, thought Tory. Right now it seemed no world existed beyond the small capsule of the van.

"Something happened to me while you were all still in the observatory," said Michael. "I didn't want to talk about it . . . but I think I'd better . . ."

Everyone leaned closer as Michael began his story.

"I DID GET LOST for a while, just like I said," began Michael. "But then I ended up outside of a lecture hall. There was this girl unchaining her bike. I went up to her, just to talk, you know . . . but before I knew it we were kissing.

"After a while she pulls me into this doorway. The door opens, and we go in—and I know we shouldn't, but by now I don't care, 'cause I'm feeling like nothing else in the world matters.

"But then I think about what happened with that girl, back when I lived in Baltimore—the only time things ever went too far. Thinking about it makes me scared, so I push myself away from this girl. I run clear across the room, and I think it's over . . . but then I look back at her from across the room and that's when I see the most horrible thing I've ever seen in my life. She's surrounded by fire—an unnatural blue-green fire—and it's all over her, but she's not burning . . . and the fire—it has a dozen arms and legs—but worst of all it has eyes. *It's alive!* But all I can do is sit there and watch, too horrified to even scream, as this thing wraps itself around her like a cocoon . . . and she doesn't even know. It's like she's hypnotized.

"Finally the girl goes limp, and the monster turns to me. I try to run, but my feet slip and when I look back, it's moving toward me through the air—and then in a second it's on me and I swear I can feel this monster oozing back inside me, right through the pores of my skin . . . and for the first time I realize that the feeling inside that always drives me crazy . . .

isn't me—it's this thing that's been living here inside me, like a leech, stealing away all my strength.

"When I look up, I see the girl walking toward me. It looks like there's nothing wrong with her—but the room is on fire all around her, real fire, orange and hot, just like what happened with that girl in Baltimore—only that time I never saw the creature, because I didn't rip myself away from it . . . and that time I didn't get the girl out of the fire in time.

"So now, with the fire all around, I pick her up, carry her out before the fire gets us, and as soon as we're outside, she turns to me and smiles, not even noticing anything strange is going on.

"And that's when I realize that she's dead.

"Yeah, she's alive, but she's also dead! That thing . . . it ate her soul and left her body alive!

"She smiles at me and says 'Hi,' like everything's blue skies and sunshine, and I think, *She doesn't even know! Something has just devoured her soul, and she doesn't even know!*

"I couldn't stand it, so I ran from her as fast as I could . . . but only got to the next street before I started puking my guts out. That's when you found me."

ONLY AN ANGRY CHORUS of sleet responded to Michael's terrible tale. No one had anything they could say. No words of consolation. No advice. Everyone's eyes began to sting with cold tears.

Michael bit his tongue to stop his teeth from chattering and wiped the tears from his eyes. "So now I know why we're dying. Those horrible beasts in the observatory didn't just come out of nowhere. They were there all along. They're here now. All four of them."

Someone let out a wail of agony—it must have been

Lourdes—and then tears of anger, terror, but most of all help-lessness, burst out around the van. It was simply too much to take alone, and in an instant all eight of their hands were reaching for the others, longing to make connection once more—even Winston. They clasped hands, the circle of four was closed, and their breath and their heartbeats began to match—panicked and fast. The truth was indeed terrible, but easier to grasp and accept when the circle was closed.

"We're possessed . . . ," said Winston.

"Not possessed, infected," said Tory.

"Infested," offered Michael. "The way people get lice . . . the way dogs get worms. Each of us is infested by some . . . *thing*. They must have found their way inside us years ago, when all the bad stuff started . . . and ever since then, they've been growing."

They looked at each other's faces, for the first time seeing the ravages of the infestation for what they really were. The creature that hid within Lourdes crushed life out of others and turned it into fat. The one clinging to Tory could turn flesh rancid from disease. The one in Winston paralyzed anything it touched and was stealing Winston's life away years at a time. And everyone knew what Michael's did.

"Why us?" said Winston, shaking his head, still not want-ing to believe.

"Because we're star-shards," answered Tory. "It's like that elephant and the giant tapeworm; these monsters can only live and grow inside of *us*." Tory tried to feel the creature within her, but all she could feel was the pain in her face and her joints. "We might have the world's biggest souls . . . but they've become infested by the blackest parasites that ever existed."

"Could be that everyone's got them," suggested Lourdes. ". . . It's just that ours have grown a few million times bigger than normal."

Winston shivered. "Cosmic Killer Leeches," he said. "I wish my father were alive—he could have pulled a cure right out of his pharmacy."

"Yeah," said Michael. "Shampoo twice a day, and drink lots of sulfuric acid." They all laughed at that, and found it strange that they could laugh at all. Perhaps they weren't as hopeless and helpless as they thought.

"We gotta figure out a way to destroy them," said Tory, "before they destroy us."

"Or worse," said Lourdes.

Tory looked at Lourdes, wondering what could possibly be worse than having an invisible parasite rout your soul . . . and then she looked at the central card that Bayless had dealt to them, and shivered. *The torn world . . .*

How powerful were these creatures? How many people in this world could they destroy if they had the chance—and what if the kids lost complete control and gave themselves over to the will of these dark beasts, choosing to feed them by visiting their horrors upon others? To paralyze them. To disease them. To crush them. To devour their souls.

If any one of them chose that path rather than bear the suffering, the devastation left behind would be unimaginable. It would be like tearing the world in half.

They looked at each other, four souls, thinking a single thought.

"My God!" said Tory. *"We have to find the other two!"*

10. THE FALL OF BLACKBURN STREET

DILLON DREAMED HE WAS RIDING ON THE BACK OF A PANTHER—
a great, dark beast bounding into a wild unknown. The power
he felt in the dream made the rest of humanity seem small and
unimportant, and as he rode he saw the weak, guilt-ridden
boy he was before trampled beneath the beast's pounding feet.
Dillon awoke from the dream exhilarated, out of breath, and
knowing that it was not entirely a dream. He wondered why he
had resisted for so long.

His wrecking-hunger had evolved. Now it felt like a creature, burning with primal fury, yet acutely intelligent . . . and
Dillon had learned that riding this beast was far better than letting it ride him.

He imagined Deanna there beside him, riding her own
creature—a powerful pale horse—a terror-mare. Together he
and Deanna would charge their beasts into the wind, and no one
would stop them as they sped down paths of greater and greater
destruction.

Where are you taking me? Dillon would silently ask it, and
although it never answered, Dillon knew that it had a glorious
purpose that he would soon understand.

Deanna, on the other hand, was no longer so entranced by
her situation.

She had watched Dillon change from a teary-eyed boy,
crushed by the weight of his own terrible actions, to a young
man who was getting far too sure of himself.

Yet in spite of that, Deanna knew that he still needed her.

Who else but Deanna could look deep into his eyes and find something inside that, even now, was still good and worthy of love? And if her capacity for love were greater than her capacity for fear, perhaps it would save her in spite of the destruction. Perhaps it would save them both.

Dillon gratefully accepted her love, and, in turn, she accepted his wisdom.

"Forget about the 'Other' ones," he had told her. "They'll only bring us trouble." If Deanna didn't accept this, she would have to face the alternative, and so Deanna pushed The Others out of her mind as they raced headlong into the great northwest.

"We're the strong ones," Dillon had said. "Those Others are nothing compared to us." And it was true. She and Dillon were stronger than all The Others combined.

Then why did she feel so weak?

Dillon had said he was like her good luck charm, but she wasn't exactly wearing him around her neck; it was more like she had climbed into his pocket and hidden there.

Was her soul so frail that all she could do was follow him, borrowing his will for her own? She had been a hostage of her fears, and Dillon had freed her. . . . Did that make her *his* hostage now? She didn't know—but she did know that she would follow him to the ends of the earth . . . which was exactly where she suspected they were headed as they crossed from Wyoming into Idaho.

THE STREETS OF IDAHO Falls were gilded with a million orange leaves. The tall oaks of Blackburn Street had begun to shed summer, day by day, but still kept a dense cloak of yellowing foliage.

Dillon and Deanna arrived late in the afternoon, his arms

around her waist, and her hand wedged in his back pocket, holding each other the way people in love often do. They stood there, in the middle of the quaint residential street, staring at the old homes on either side. Dillon looked at the homes one by one, then turned his head, as if sniffing the air.

"What are you doing?" asked Deanna.

"Getting to know the neighborhood," he answered. "Looking for a place to eat."

Deanna didn't like the sound of that. "Promise me you won't do anything bad here."

Dillon turned to her blinking, as if he didn't know what she meant. "I promise that I won't do anything that isn't absolutely necessary," he said.

A young boy breezed past them on his bike, stopping at the second house on the right. A small license plate on the back of the bike said "Joey." Dillon slipped his hand from Deanna's waist, and he approached the boy, with Deanna following in his wake.

The boy hopped off his bike and strolled toward his front door.

"Hey, Joey," shouted Dillon. "Your brother around?"

Joey turned to look at Dillon, studied him for a moment, then said. "Naah, Jason's still at practice. He'll be home soon, though. . . . You friends of his?"

"Yeah," said Dillon. "I was on the team with him last year."

The boy looked at Dillon doubtfully.

"Jason tells me you're almost as fast as him now," said Dillon. "Hell, you even walk like him!"

Joey beamed at that, but tried to hide it. Any hesitation the boy had was now gone. "You can wait inside if you like."

Deanna turned to Dillon as they neared the porch. "How'd you know he had a brother?" she whispered.

"It was obvious," Dillon whispered back. "He walks like he's copying someone, but not someone who's grown up. . . . He wears hand-me-downs, even though he can afford those brand-new running shoes. . . . He rode up to the house like he's competing in a race. . . . It's all part of a pattern that says he's some jock's kid brother."

Deanna stared at Dillon in amazement, and he just smiled. "C'mon," he said, almost blushing behind his boyish freckles. "You know me pretty well—this stuff shouldn't impress you anymore."

Joey led them into the house. Dillon noted how the boy used keys instead of knocking, how he glanced up the stairs, and how quietly he closed the front door. Dillon took a sniff of the air, and said, "How's your grandfather doing?"

Joey shrugged. "Okay, I guess. Better, now that he's back from the hospital."

Dillon turned to Deanna and winked. Deanna just shook her head. What a show-off!

"Jason'll be back soon, you can wait for him here." Joey left them alone in the kitchen and went back out to fiddle with the chain on his bike. Once Joey was gone, Dillon got down to work. He began to search through drawers and cabinets—he didn't take anything, he just let his eyes pore over everything he saw, observing . . . cataloguing . . . filing the information away.

Deanna had seen him do this the day before, at the farm-house they had stopped at. Dillon had secretly rifled through the drawers, closets—even under sofa cushions. Deanna had asked what he was searching for. "Clues," he said softly.

Now his hands were moving quickly through the kitchen, his mind working with such force that Deanna could swear that she could feel it pulsating like a high-tension wire. He was fascinating to watch.

"Tell me what you're thinking," said Deanna. "I want to know what you know—I want to see what you see."

"Okay," said Dillon. "Five people live here. Parents, two sons, and a grandfather. Mother smokes, father quit. Kids do okay in school." He pointed to a picture on the refrigerator. "This is the older brother and his girlfriend, right? But something's not right there—look at his smile; he's not smiling *for* the picture—he's smiling *at* the person taking the picture."

"So who took the picture?"

"Isn't it obvious?" said Dillon. "The angle, the background, the way the girl's gloating to have snagged the track star? Her *sister* took the picture, and good ol' Jason would rather be dating *her*!"

Deanna just shook her head, marveling.

"Let's check out the parents," said Dillon. He glanced around, until setting his sights on a high knickknack shelf. Then he pulled down a small bronze Statue of Liberty pencil sharpener and held it out for Deanna to examine.

"The parents honeymooned in New York—but look—there's no dust on it, even though there's dust on the rest of the shelf . . . that means someone's taken Miss Liberty down recently, and has been thinking about it. Smells like dishwashing soap. The mother took it down—either she's nostalgic, or she's worried about the marriage for some reason. Let's see what the doorknobs have to say."

"Doorknobs?"

Dillon opened the back door and touched the outside and inside doorknobs, then smelled his hands.

"Men's cologne going out, women's perfume coming in—not his wife's, because I can smell that everywhere else. The husband is seeing another woman. Good chance his wife knows, and divorce is in the air. Will they break up? Let's find out!"

Dillon opened the refrigerator. "He keeps his beer on the same shelf as the milk and the soda—not in the door all by itself." Dillon opened the hallway closet. "Everything in this house is neatly arranged—these people love order and tranquility, right down to giving their sons sound-alike names. *But* Dad's coats are mixed in with Mom's, instead of on their own side: their order is tightly intertwined." Dillon turned and glanced at the back door again. "And his dirty work boots—" he said. "They're inside the house, on a mat; he's considerate enough not to leave them on the wood floor, and she's accepting enough not to make him put them outside."

"So?"

"So if we leave this little family-stew to cook, I can tell that dear old Dad gives up the other woman, and the marriage is saved. Ninety-six percent probability."

"You're incredible!" said Deanna. "Sherlock Holmes couldn't be that exact!"

Dillon shrugged. "It's like looking at a work of art," explained Dillon. "It's just a bunch of paint, but when you look at it, you see the Mona Lisa, right? Well, when I look at all of these things, I see a picture, too. I see who these people were, who they are, and who they're probably going to be."

"What do you see when you look at me?" asked Deanna.

Dillon didn't even try—he just shook his head. "You're like me," he said. "Too complex to figure out."

She smiled at him, and he took her hand. "C'mon," he said, "I know all I need to know about this family . . . let's move on."

As they left, Deanna noticed the way he rolled his neck, and the way sweat was beginning to bead on his forehead.

"The wrecking-hunger . . . it's back again, isn't it?"

"I try not to think about it," he said, and tugged on her arm a little more urgently. "C'mon."

Out back, they saw a man in the next yard patching up a hole in a boat.

"Hi! We're Joey and Jason's cousins," said Dillon to the man.

"Josh and Jennifer," added Deanna with a smirk.

The neighbor nodded a quiet hello. Dillon noticed the circles beneath his eyes, and the ghost of a missing wedding ring on his tan left hand. Dillon listened to the way in which a dog inside the house yowled.

"Sorry to hear about your wife's passing," said Dillon . . .

ON THEY WENT, weaving in and out of homes and yards, pretending to be people they weren't—and no one doubted them because Dillon was so very good at the game. He knew the exact things to say that would make people open up their homes, and their hearts, telling him things they would never usually tell a stranger. It was as if they were hypnotized and didn't know it.

All the while Dillon's sweats had gotten worse, his breath had gotten shorter, and his face was becoming flushed.

In the last home, a woman had offered them iced tea and looked at Dillon with worry in her eyes.

"You sure you don't want me to call a doctor?" she asked, but Dillon shook his head and stumbled into the street.

"He'll be okay," said Deanna, covering. "Asthma—his medicine's back in our cousin's house." Deanna left the house and hurried after Dillon, feeling her own worry explode into fear. More than just fear . . . terror. Her own familiar brand of terror.

At the edge of the street, Dillon leaned against a tree, gritting his teeth and clenching his fists. His breath came in short labored gasps. *Not yet,* he told the hunger that gnawed on the ragged fringe of his soul. It was so powerful now, he knew if he didn't feed it soon, it would turn on him and devour him in an instant. *You have to wait! You have to wait until everything's ready,* he told the hunger. Dillon kept telling himself that he was its master, but all beasts turn on their masters if they're not fed.

By now the sun was low in the sky, casting hazy patterns of light through the trees. Patterns of light, patterns of life— sights, sounds, and an impossible puzzle of relationships between the people on this peaceful street.

Not so impossible. Dillon looked from house to house, jumbling all the patterns in his mind, looking for a common thread . . . and at last he found it. He marveled at the power of the solution he had found. It was like a key to open a great Pandora's box. But it was so *big*—many times bigger than what he had done the day before. Did he dare do it? The wrecking-hunger answered by twisting his gut and bringing him to his knees.

Deanna ran toward him pale and frightened, and held him to keep him from falling to the pavement.

"Tell me what you need," she said. "I can help you if I know."

"You already know," he answered.

Deanna looked away. Yes, she knew. He said he had come here looking for a place to eat. But deep down Deanna knew that he really meant a place to *feed*.

The look on Dillon's face had become so helpless and desperate—so consumed by the hunger, she would have destroyed something herself to save him now.

"Will you let me do it?" asked Dillon. "Will you promise not to hate me?"

"Do it," said Deanna. "Feed it any way you can."

Deanna was shaking now; her eyes darting back and forth

as if death would come swooping at both of them from the sky. His hunger and her fear were so tightly connected, she knew that when the hunger was fed and he was strong once more, she would be strong as well.

Dillon found the strength he needed to get to his feet and stumble off into the road toward the second house on the right, where Jason, Joey's older brother, had just arrived home with his girlfriend.

Deanna watched him go, then turned away as she felt something begin to rise in her own gut—and it wasn't just fear.

Will you let me do it? he had asked. He had never asked so bluntly before, but the question was there every time. He needed her permission. He needed her approval for every monstrous act he committed, and she always gave it—as if in some way she was in control. As if she was the one setting him loose to create chaos.

There were many things she could make herself deny. She could deny the sounds of disaster they left behind, she could convince herself that, beyond all reason, something good would come from all this destruction. But now she could not deny that it was all happening because of her—because she gave Dillon permission. She bit her hand to hold back her own scream.

Across the street, Dillon approached Jason's girlfriend, who was waiting for Jason on the porch. By now anything human had drained out of Dillon's voice, and he spoke in a rough snarl that came deep from his gut. It was the voice of the hunger itself.

"You!" growled Dillon as he approached her.

The girl gasped at the sight of him hobbling closer on his weak legs.

Dillon came right up to her, looked into her eyes, read her soul, and said, *"Ask Jason to tell you the truth."*

One of the girl's wide black pupils suddenly constricted down into a pinpoint in a huge blue eye. "Okay," she said dreamily, "I'll ask him." She turned and headed into the house.

Dillon stumbled across the street, already beginning to feel the tiniest bit better. He found Deanna standing just where he had left her.

"Let's get out of here," said Dillon, but she wasn't budging. Her hands were clenched by her side in tight, anxious fists.

"Tell me what you did to her."

"I thought you didn't want to know," said Dillon.

"I want to know now!"

Dillon turned on her with a vengeance. "I'm trying to protect you!" he shouted. "That's what you want, isn't it? That's what you've always wanted!"

Deanna drew a deep breath and said slowly, forcefully, *"Tell me what you did!"*

Dillon kicked the ground hard. "I planted a seed, like I did at the farmhouse. I just made a suggestion, that's all." Dillon told Deanna what he had said to the girl, and Deanna listened to his words, thinking that there must be more . . . but that was all Dillon said. A suggestion? A mere suggestion was going to satisfy the wrecking-hunger? How could that be?

But it wasn't just any suggestion, was it? It was the *right* suggestion. Dillon had sized things up and knew the exact words that would set powerful forces in motion that would grind these people up.

"I found the girl's button," said Dillon. "Everyone has a button, you just have to find it . . . and then push it."

Deanna shook her head, her hands trembling so violently she felt her fingers might shake themselves off.

"We have to leave now," said Dillon. "I don't want to see it happen."

"But I do!" insisted Deanna. "If I'm a part of this, then I want to know what we've done!"

Dillon tried to pull her away, but she wouldn't go. They would weather this one out, whether he liked it or not. "All right," he said, "but just remember, I tried to keep you from seeing." Since Dillon knew it wasn't safe where they were standing, he climbed a tree and helped Deanna up. From there, they had a bird's-eye view of the entire block.

"It'll start over there," said Dillon, pointing to Joey's house. Sure enough, inside the house two people were arguing. The argument got louder and louder, until the girl burst out the front door in tears . . . just as Jason and Joey's mother came home, holding a bag of groceries.

"You're just like your father!" the girlfriend shouted back at Jason. "Everyone knows the way he sneaks around!"

The mother heard this, and the shock of this news made her drop a bag of groceries. Inside, a furious Jason took out his frustration on his kid brother. In a moment Joey came running out of the house crying, not seeing the groceries spilled on the front walk. He slipped on a can of peas, went flying, and hit his head on the ground. Hard.

His mother screamed.

Dillon turned to Deanna. "Once it starts, it's like a boulder rolling down a hill," he said. "Watch!"

Deanna watched with sick fascination as a delivery boy riding by on a moped turned his head to see why the woman was screaming—and was distracted just long enough to hit a car head-on.

The widowed neighbor man came out to his porch at the sound of the crash, and his neglected dog bolted from the house, ran across the street, freaked at all the noise, and attacked a woman in her garden. The woman's husband, a nervous man, ran inside to get a shotgun to save his wife from the mad dog. But his aim was very bad. And very unlucky.

Then, in a moment, the events began to happen so quickly, the chain of cause and effect was completely lost. One thing led to five things, led to five more things, and in a matter of minutes the twilight was filled with shattering windows, screaming people, and brutal fistfights, until the entire block had disintegrated into a savage frenzy . . . an explosive chain reaction of unlikely, unlucky "coincidences" that had all been started by a single, simple suggestion.

"People are like dominoes," explained Dillon, in the midst of the cataclysm. His voice was eerily calm, as if the people on this street were just numbers he was crunching through an equation. "You can make them all fall down, if you know exactly who to push, and when to push them."

Somewhere a gunshot echoed. There were crashing sounds in many of the homes and, in one of them, somewhere the *whoosh* of igniting flames.

Dillon's hunger was fed with every blast, with every crash and every wail as yet another person fell from sanity. He closed his eyes and felt the life-patterns in the street around him falling like a spiderweb clipped from its branch, until the only pattern that remained was the unrelenting spiral of chaos in every life around him.

Deanna, too, felt her own terror mysteriously fade away into a dizzy numbness.

"I've fed us both, now," said Dillon.

Deanna just looked at him, blankly.

"Haven't you figured it out yet?" he said. "You've got it as bad as I do—only with you it's not a wrecking-hunger; it's a terror-hunger."

Deanna just shook her head, not wanting to hear it, not wanting to think about it.

"It's true, Deanna; you need fear, the same way I need disaster—why do you think you feel better whenever you're around me? It's because you live on the terror I create—and when you can't live on other people's terror, you start feeding on your own."

Deanna closed her eyes and tried to deny it . . . but the more she thought about it, the more true it rang. Didn't she feel her strongest when those around her were in fear? Didn't she draw strength from other people's terror?

"You'll never feel fear again, Deanna," said Dillon, "as long as I can leave people terrified for you."

The streets around them still echoed with the wails of dozens of souls losing their minds to a nightmare.

"Now do you see why we have to be together?" asked Dillon with a tenderness that clashed with the violence on either side of them. "We're like thunder and lightning—you can't have one without the other. Destruction and fear."

He was right. He was right about everything, because every terrified wail seemed to feed something inside her. Was this who they were? Two hideously twisted creatures that lived like vampires, drinking up the misfortune of others? The very thought made her stomach turn.

This is not who I want to be!

She hid her face in shame and disgust.

Heat flashed as a fireball exploded somewhere down the street, and it was over. All that remained were the weak wails and moans, like the moment after a tumbling airplane came to rest. Survivors wandered the streets, some milling about aimlessly, others talking to themselves. The fine lattice of their minds had dissolved like sugar in water. Those who were dead were the lucky ones. The rest were irreconcilably insane.

My God, thought Deanna, *these people had put so much energy into creating their lives* . . . and now all that energy was being released as their lives detonated. That energy had to go somewhere . . . and that was the energy Dillon was feeding on!

She tried to shake the thought away. No! Human beings don't drink that kind of energy . . .

And for the first time, Deanna began to see that there might be something else living inside of Dillon—a creature that was anything but human. *"I have to feed it,"* Dillon often said. He even spoke about his hunger as if it were a living thing.

Was there something like that inside of her as well?

Only now did she begin to realize the dizzying depths of the pit they were falling into. The severity of their actions was beyond comprehension, and it made her wish she could tear off her body and slide into someone else's, just to be away from herself and this hideous destiny.

"You see there?" said Dillon, pointing down the street toward some homes that seemed just beyond the circle of destruction. "Those are the people I saved. I was actually able to save people! The hunger wanted them but I said no." He spoke with the blind innocence of a child and leapt from the tree, bouncing around in the midst of the disaster as if it were a playground. Stronger than ever before, he gazed past the Armageddon to the homes he had "saved."

"See, I kept my promise," he said, helping Deanna from the tree. "I didn't do any more than was absolutely necessary . . . and I did a good thing saving those people, didn't I?"

The thoughts were swimming in Deanna's head now. Nearly fifty people's lives were destroyed, but all Dillon was willing to see were the fifty whose lives weren't. Was this the best they could hope to do— damage control? Was that something to be proud of?

"See how I control it?" he said. "I don't give it any more than it needs—I leave it a little bit hungry—that's how I control it!"

And Deanna could see that Dillon believed this—he believed in his own ability to control this thing like a small child believed no one could see him when he closed his eyes.

Deanna shook her head to drive out Dillon's excuses and rationalizations, but couldn't.

"Deanna, c'mon—you're looking at me like you hate me or something. You don't hate me, do you? You promised you wouldn't."

Did she hate him? Did she find him beyond redemption? She instantly thought back to a python she once saw swallowing a live rabbit. It was awful to watch, but, after all, that's what pythons had to do. If this was how Dillon survived, could she blame him any more than she blamed that python? And wasn't she doing the exact same thing?

Deanna looked into his eyes, trying to find him there. There was intense darkness inside of him now, surrounding him, eating away at him like a vile parasite. So much of him had turned vile, it was hard to find any good left in him, but she continued to search until, through that blackness, she found the glimmer of light hidden deep within. It was that part of Dillon that was decent and kind—still fighting for life inside the blackness, like a star in the void of space. She focused on that shrinking light within Dillon, and to it she said, "I love you."

Dillon smiled, a tear in his eye. "Me too," he said. He touched Deanna's cheek, gently held her around the waist, and set the pace as they strode off of Blackburn Street, even before the first police car arrived. As they walked, Deanna forced her own will deep into Dillon's back pocket, but this time it didn't slip in as easily as it had before.

I LOVE YOU. DILLON let her words echo from one side of his mind to the other. He drew strength from it, and, in a matter of moments, he had successfully forced the evening's unpleasantness out of his mind. These people here—they didn't matter. They weren't real the way he and Deanna were real. The wrecking-hunger told him so.

Dillon's spirits were high as he left town. The night was refreshingly cool, and he felt he could walk all night. He didn't need sleep anymore. Come to think of it, he didn't need food. He had already gorged himself on the fall of Blackburn Street, and it would be at least another day before he felt the hunger again.

He wondered what he would have to do next to satisfy the hunger. Surely it would be an even greater challenge—for each challenge was greater than the one before.

In the back of his mind he idly imagined an endless cascade of dominoes all lined up and ready to fall if the right one were pushed. The thought was enough to make him giggle like a child.

Part IV
Demolition Day

11. BIG BANG

AT 4:30 A.M., MOUNTAIN TIME, LOURDES HIDALGO DECIDED it was time to die.

It had been two days since that night in the ice storm. With little money, and even less time to spare, the four had searched for a trail—any sign of the missing two. Nothing turned up along I-80, and nothing in Big Springs, but in Torrington, Wyoming, they found a newspaper article that led them to a devastated farm. It reeked of something unnatural.

Once they found the farm, they knew they were on the right track, because the presence of the fifth and sixth shards was as strong as a scent on the wind. What they had feared was now confirmed; those other two had lost control and had set off on a mad rampage to feed the parasites that were strangling their souls. Intuition told them that number five was the dangerous one and that number six probably fed on the aftermath of destruction like a vulture fed on a lion's kill.

After that, following their trail was like following the ashen trail of a burning fuse. News reports had led them to the ruined neighborhood in Idaho Falls, which seemed ten times worse than what they found at the farm. They were only a day behind as they headed deeper into Idaho, terrified of what they would find next.

They rested in Boise, finding a cheap hotel for the night. It had been a major effort for Lourdes to haul herself out of the van this time, and each footstep felt like it would be her last.

Like everywhere their journey took them, this hotel was right in the armpit of town, where old decrepit buildings loomed ripe for the wrecking ball.

Lourdes could see one such building from the hotel window, across the expanse of a vacant lot: a concrete warehouse seven stories tall, with slits for windows and a big faded sign painted on the side that said "Dakins Worldwide Storage." The building's few entrances were boarded over, and the abandoned property was fenced in. Apparently Dakins had found better worldwide storage elsewhere.

While the others slept, Lourdes kept a vigil and watched that solitary, lonely building, feeling a strange affinity for it as she pondered the short time remaining to her own life. Few buildings on earth could be as unloved as this one.

In the days since they had banded together, they had witnessed wonders and had watched each other deteriorate. Winston's dignity was the first casualty, for his body had grown so small he couldn't see out of the van's windows when he sat, and he had to eat soft food because all his teeth were receding. Tory, who had been a driving force all along, was slowing down, as her disease turned inward, swelling her joints with painful arthritis . . . and Michael . . . well, rather than allowing his passion to wreak havoc on the soul of every girl he encountered, Michael had turned his mind to a dark lonely place within himself and seldom came out. Brooding and silent, with dark, wan eyes, he looked like he was dying of cancer.

As for Lourdes, there were no mirrors large enough to present her full image. She could feel the weight on her bones growing, building density, like ice on the branches of a tree.

She could feel her heart pounding in her chest, fighting to force blood through clogged arteries. She could feel her bloated self, ready to burst through the shell that contained her, and knew that it could happen at any moment.

So she stayed awake . . . and at 4:30 a.m. one of the many seams on her blouse tore so violently that the blouse itself literally burst in two.

That's when Lourdes decided that it was time to call it quits.

Outside, the rain had let up a bit, and Lourdes could see the warehouse more clearly. There were people milling about the building, and it seemed odd to Lourdes that such a lonely place would be the center of anyone else's attention but hers, so she watched and wondered. In a few moments, things became very clear to her, and she knew exactly what she was going to do.

"MICHAEL, WINSTON, WAKE UP!" Tory shook them both, dragging them out of a deep sleep. "It's Lourdes! She's gone!"

Wearily, the three searched the room and the hallway. Tory looked in the closet. The others looked under the beds—as if Lourdes could possibly fit in any of those places.

That's when Michael happened to glance out the window. Dawn was beginning to break on the distant horizon, and in the faint half-light he could see a huge shape lumbering through a vacant lot toward an old Dakins warehouse a block away.

"Look," he said. "There she is!"

THE FRONT OF THE old warehouse was teeming with activity, but Lourdes approached from the rear and no one saw her. She smiled as she approached. All this time the four of them had been running, unsure of their destination. It was nice, for once, to have a destination.

Her momentum took her through the fence that surrounded the property as if it were paper, and she pushed on through the police line, tearing the ribbon as if it were a finish line. She leaned against the boarded-over door, and her sheer weight forced the door inward, leading her into a dark cavernous space where her labored breathing echoed from distant concrete walls. To the right was a flight of stairs and, without pausing for further thought, she began to heave herself step by step toward the upper floors of the desolate building.

ACTIVITY WAS GROWING AT the front of the warehouse as the three kids followed Lourdes in through the back door.

Once inside they paused to listed and heard the heavy footsteps of Lourdes straining on stairs high above.

"What she gonna do? Climb out on the roof and jump?" said Winston, trying to catch his breath.

The very thought made Michael turn and bound up the stairs as fast as his legs could carry him.

Tory took a moment to look down at her hands. Her knuckles were swollen and they cracked when she bent them. It made her so angry that she squeezed them in a fist, but that only hurt more. She turned to Winston, who was still catching his breath. "Did you ever think you'd be chasing someone through a warehouse at the crack of dawn?" she asked.

"No," said Winston, in a voice that was higher pitched than the day before. "But then I never thought I'd be five years old again either."

It was as they turned to go upstairs that Tory glanced at the great cavern around her. The tiny slits of windows were mostly boarded over, and in the dim half-light, she could see a series of pillars stretching down the empty warehouse, holding up the floors above. There were bulges near the top of a good dozen of those pillars; bulges like tumors growing out of the concrete. And each of those bulges had a tiny, blinking light.

Tory grabbed Winston's arm, and yanked him around. "Winston, tell me you don't see what I see . . ." This time when they looked, not only were the tumors visible on the concrete, but so were the wires. They draped from the dark tumors, snaked across the floor, and all came together in a bundle that made a determined path out the front door.

It didn't take a genius to figure out that the tumors were explosives.

MICHAEL REACHED THE SEVENTH and final floor of the warehouse, before the others had even begun to climb.

"Lourdes?"

She stood at the far end of the vast empty loft. She wobbled a bit and finally collapsed under her own enormous weight. As she hit the ground, the concrete echoed with a boom like the slamming of a heavy vault door, and the dust burst out from beneath her like her very soul dispersing. She didn't move.

Michael, afraid to say anything, for fear that she wouldn't answer, approached with caution, and to his great relief saw that she was still alive.

"You okay?" asked Michael.

"Go away." Lourdes made a mighty effort to turn her head, so Michael could not see her tears. In all the time he had known her, Michael had never seen Lourdes cry like this. She had stoically borne all her hardship with a stiff—if somewhat fat—upper lip, but not now.

Michael sat beside her and wiped the tears away.

"I feel like a beached whale," she said.

"Well," said Michael, "the Pacific Ocean's only three hundred miles away . . ."

Lourdes laughed in spite of herself.

"When I die," she said, "I'm gonna sit on God until he yells uncle." They both laughed again, then a silence fell between them.

"Why did he do this to us, Michael?"

Michael shrugged and thought for a moment. "He didn't *do* it to us, he just didn't stop it."

"That's just as bad," said Lourdes.

Michael lifted her heavy head and began to gently stroke her hair. "Maybe he's a clutch player," said Michael. "And he's just waiting for the right time to make a move."

Winston and Tory finally made it to the top floor.

"We gotta get outta here now!" shouted Winston as he ran with Tory from the stairs. "This building's condemned and it's coming down today. They've already rigged the explosives."

"I know," said Lourdes.

That caught everyone off guard.

Lourdes gritted her teeth and closed her eyes to keep herself from crying. "Maybe the three of you have some time left, but not me. If I have to die today, then I want to go out with a big bang, not a whimper."

"We won't let you do this," said Tory. "Can't you feel how close The Others are? . . . If we just hold on a little longer . . ."

"I don't feel anything anymore," said Lourdes. "All I feel is fat, and I'm tired of feeling it."

Outside there were shouts from the demolition crew.

"That's it!" shouted Winston, the preschooler on the verge of a tantrum. "I don't care how lousy you feel! Get your ass down those stairs!" His voice slipped deeper into his Alabama drawl, which always grew stronger when he got angry.

"I can't," said Lourdes. "I can't move anymore. At all."

They all looked at her there, straining to breathe as she lay on the ground. Winston panicked and rammed into her with what little weight he had. "C'mon, help me!" They all took to pushing against Lourdes, but she wouldn't budge.

"Grab her arms," suggested Tory. They grabbed her arms and legs to pull her, but nothing helped.

"Just go!" shouted Lourdes, through her thick throat. "It's better if you just go!"

They let go of her arms and legs, and just stood there, unable to help her . . . and in that moment of silence Michael made a decision.

"I'm not leaving you," he said, and he sat down next to her.

Winston stared at him incredulously. "You're just gonna sit here and let yourself get blown to smithereens?"

"Face it," said Michael. "None of us has much time left. A day or two at the most . . ."

Tory, grimacing in pain, looked at her swollen knuckles, then at her swollen knees. "Michael's right. We haven't had control over anything for the longest time. . . . Maybe here's something we can control . . ."

Winston turned to her, his eyes filled with terror. "No!"

"If I gotta die," said Tory, "then I want to die with dignity,"

Winston threw up his hands. "I can't believe this! You said it yourself, Tory, The Others are close now—we can find them—we can stop them . . ."

"We lost, Winston," said Michael. "We fought hard, but we lost."

"No!" shouted Winston defiantly. "With our luck, instead of dying proper, our souls'll get blown up again into a thousand cockroaches or something. No! If I gotta die, I ain't going out in flaming glory—I'm going the way I was meant to go!"

Winston grew red in the face as he looked at them. He threw himself on the ground kicking and screaming in a full-fledged tantrum, then finally gave up on his companions. "Fine," he said, tears swelling in his eyes. "We started this together, but if I have to finish it alone, then I will." Then Winston, all three feet of him, stormed across the dusty floor and disappeared down the stairwell.

When he was gone, Michael turned to Tory. "When we die," said Michael, "you think those . . . those awful things will die with us?"

"That's what I'm counting on," said Tory.

Lourdes, without the strength to move her lips anymore, could only rasp her breath in and out.

They held hands, now just a circle of three. "I'm glad," whispered Tory. "I'm glad we all found each other. No matter what, I'll never regret that."

Outside the rain had stopped, the wind had stopped, and the black clouds above waited with guarded anticipation. Far away lightning struck, and every distant rumble echoed within the warehouse, shaking the walls and reminding them of the great thunder that would soon tear out the foundation of their lives. With every rumble, concrete flakes skittered to the ground, like the footfalls of a thousand cockroaches.

WINSTON, WITH THE PHYSIOLOGY of a five-year-old, found his days swinging back and forth between complete exhaustion and uncontrollable energy. Had he been exhausted when they asked him to stay, he might have just curled up, thumb in mouth, and fallen asleep before the big blast came—but Winston was feeling very much alive and did not intend to go quietly. Today was a day to live.

As he leapt down the stairs two at a time, he had to keep reminding himself that he hadn't abandoned the other three. They, in fact, had abandoned him. They had given up. Now he would be alone. He would chase the tail of the other two shards until he could no longer walk, until he could no longer crawl. When his body had withered itself out of existence, he would die knowing he fought to the end. *That* was dying with dignity, not being buried beneath ten tons of shattered concrete.

Winston bounded down the stairs to the first level and was surprised to see, just twenty yards away, a worker in a hard hat, facing away from him. Winston could see he was double-checking the wires, and the realization that there were still a few minutes till the building blew made him reconsider his options.

There was time to save the others! Even if they didn't want to be saved, he could save them. He would run up to the man in the hard hat, he would tell him of the others still upstairs, he would ruin their awful plan.

Winston took a few steps closer, about to shout out, when suddenly a second figure that had been eclipsed from Winston's sight came into view. It was a boy—no older than fifteen, and he was staring straight at the worker. The boy had red hair.

Immediately Winston felt a rush of dizziness that took the wind right out of his lungs. This was wrong. This was very wrong. He ducked behind a pillar and watched.

The worker was frozen, his flashlight at his side, casting a light on the dusty floor. The boy with red hair seemed anxious and sweaty, and very, very intense.

"You've placed the explosives wrong," suggested the boy to the man in the hard hat. *"You should do something about it."*

The worker just stared at him. "Okay," he said dreamily and strolled off into the shadows.

Winston gasped, and the red-haired boy snapped his eyes to Winston.

The second their eyes met, Winston knew *exactly* who this was.

He was the fifth shard.

Winston couldn't break eye contact with the redheaded boy. His gaze riveted Winston to the ground. If there were indeed six shards, then this boy had inherited the largest, most powerful one, and in its shadow had grown the worst parasite. Winston knew he was no match for the force behind those eyes.

The redheaded boy stood stunned by the sight of Winston— but only for a moment. Then he turned and disappeared down a hole in the concrete floor.

Once he was gone, a hundred thoughts flew through Winston's mind fighting for purchase. *Run for your life! No—follow him! No—break the worker out of his trance!* But the one thought that overrode them all was the urge to race back upstairs and tell the others!

He bounded up the stairs, racing past the demolition man, who mindlessly whistled a Beatles tune as he moved a pack of explosives from one end of the building to the other.

ON THE SEVENTH FLOOR, Lourdes, Michael, and Tory waited in silence. They could hear the sounds of morning in full swing. Car horns, diesel engines. The occasional shouts of the demolition workers as they diligently prepared for the morning's spectacle.

Then they heard footsteps racing up the stairs and knew by their lightness that it had to be Winston. He had changed his mind. In the end they would be together. As it was meant to be.

Winston burst through the stairwell.

"We've got to get out of here!" he shouted.

"Winston . . . ," said Michael. "We've made up our minds . . ."

"We're not leaving Lourdes . . . ," said Tory.

"No! You don't understand!" He grabbed Tory by her plagued arms and looked into her eyes. "Tory, you were right! You've been right all along—*The Others are here!*"

Realization slowly dawned in Tory's eyes.

"What?"

But the only answer was a blast louder than thunder that shook the world and sent pulverized concrete dust flying into their faces.

Seven floors below, the foundation of the old Dakins warehouse blew apart, and the building began its freefall journey to the earth.

THE CHINESE TONGS THAT had built the impossible maze of tunnels beneath Boise were long dead, and the opium dens those tunnels once connected were gone and forgotten. Now, more than a hundred years later, Dillon and Deanna traveled those lost passages. Dillon should have found the pattern of twisting, intersecting tunnels easy to figure out, but as he raced wildly to reach Deanna, he found himself lost. He had never been lost before, but what had happened in that old warehouse had thrown him for such a loop, he wasn't thinking straight.

They were here.

The Others.

Somehow they had found him, and he was convinced that they were here to kill him.

At last, down the long dim underground corridor, Dillon saw Deanna, just as the blast went off somewhere above their heads. The explosion was so loud, it sent pain shooting through his ears, and the rumble that followed rattled his teeth. He fell into a puddle of stagnant muck, while behind him concrete dust shot through the tunnel like steam through a pipe.

Then, through the dust blasting into his face, Dillon saw and heard hideous things. Sinewy gray tentacles reaching for him through the dust cloud—blue flaming hands around his neck, sharp claws digging into his chest, fangs, and eyes—so many angry eyes!

It must be my imagination, he thought in a panic. *It can't be real,* yet even so, he felt a tentacle wrap itself around his ankle and dig in. Dillon clawed at the ground to get away, he gripped a stone in the wall, but something stung his hand.

Choking from the concrete dust filling his lungs, Dillon could swear he felt hot breath on his face and heard a sound in his mind louder than the collapsing building.

Knocking.

Many hands knocking on a door—a furious horde demanding to be let in. *Anything!* thought Dillon. *Anything to stop that horrible knocking in his brain.* He opened his mind as easily as opening a door, and the creatures were gone, leaving only the blinding dust in his eyes.

As the dust around him began to settle, Deanna appeared in front of him.

"Dillon! What's happening?" she asked desperately.

Dillon coughed out another lungful of dust. And forced himself not to think about the monster-hallucination. Instead he let himself feel the wrecking-hunger feed on the collapse of the Dakins building. But that was only a first course.

"Listen," said Dillon. "Listen, it's wonderful!" The relief filling him soon grew into joy, and then ecstasy.

The first building had come down far above them, but the

roaring had not stopped. From the right came another rumble, just as loud as the first, and then another, further away, and then another until they couldn't tell where one ended and the next began.

Deanna sank to the ground, shivering as if it were the end of the world. "It's like a war out there," said Deanna.

Dillon beamed a smile far too wide. "Oh, it's much better than that!"

His dim flashlight went out, but that was all right. Dillon didn't want Deanna looking at him right now, because something was beginning to happen to him. He was beginning to change; he could feel it all over.

Dillon closed his eyes, imagining the beast he had learned to ride so well . . . only now when he tried to picture it, he saw a whole team of beasts instead: a wave of dark horses teamed together by a single yoke carrying him along at a breakneck pace.

There in the dark, his flat stomach began to slowly swell, and his many freckles began to bulge into a swarm of angry zits.

IN THE DIM LIGHT of this awful morning, the foreman of the demolition crew could do nothing but watch as his well-orchestrated detonation became a nightmare.

It should not have happened. The way the explosives had been set, the building should have come straight down . . . but it didn't. Instead the entire building keeled over backward and landed on Jefferson Place—an office building across the street that had been evacuated as a precaution. The old office building shifted violently on its foundation, and keeled over to the left . . .

. . . Where stood the Hoff Building—a city landmark.

No one had thought it necessary to evacuate that one.

The Hoff Building took the blow, and for a moment it looked as if it was only going to lose its eastern face. But then it, too, began a slow topple to the left, its domed tower crashing into the Old Boise Post Office.

Dominoes, thought the foreman. *They're going down like dominoes.* It was impossible; it would take a pattern of incredible coincidences for each building to hit the one beside it with just the right force to bring it down as well . . . but the evidence was here before their eyes.

Debris struck the capitol building, which seemed to be all right . . . until the pillars holding up its heavy dome buckled and the dome crashed down and disappeared into the building, hitting bottom with such force that all the windows shattered.

And it was over.

Seven buildings had been demolished.

Beside the foreman, his explosives expert just stood there, rocking back and forth, and happily whistling "Twist and Shout." Another crew member was screaming at the top of his lungs.

They're insane! thought the foreman. *They've completely lost their minds.* And finally, the combination of everything around him was exactly enough to make the foreman snap as well. As he felt his own mind slipping down a well of eternal madness, he realized that the destruction he had just witnessed was somehow not over yet. In fact, it was just beginning. In a moment he started laughing hysterically. And he never stopped.

MICHAEL LIPRANSKI NOW UNDERSTOOD death. It was blind, cold, and dusty. It was filled with a loud ringing in one's ears that didn't go away. Death was oppressive and choking.

These were the thoughts Michael was left with after having died. There were, of course, many questions to come, but the one question that was foremost in his mind was this: Why, if he was dead, did he still feel like coughing?

Michael let out a roaring hacking cough and cleared concrete dust from his lungs. He opened his eyes. They stung, but he forced them open anyway. Around him were three other ghosts . . . or at least they looked like ghosts. They all began to stir, and as they sat up, a heavy layer of white dust fell from them.

"What happened?" asked Winston.

And as they looked around, the answer became clear. They were still on the seventh floor . . . or at least what was left of it. Just a corner really. The rest of the building was gone. So were quite a few other around it. It looked as if downtown Boise had been hit by a small nuclear bomb.

"He did this," said Winston.

"He, who?"

"The Other One . . . the fifth one. I told you I saw him!"

"He saved our lives!" asked Tory

"I don't think he meant to," said Winston.

They looked out at the devastation once more. Lourdes, her death-wish forgotten, stood and walked to the jagged edge where the seventh floor gave way to open air. The rest of the building had shorn away and had turned to rubble. Had they been anywhere else on that floor, they would have been part of the rubble . . . but they weren't anywhere else, they were right here . . . and Lourdes began to wonder idly what sort of intuition had made her collapse in the north corner rather than the south corner, or was luck so incredibly dumb that it didn't even know an easy target?

Tory looked stunned. "I guess it takes more than a few thousand pounds of explosives to get rid of us."

"Lourdes, you're standing!" Michael approached Lourdes

at the jagged edge of the concrete floor. Indeed, she had found the strength to lift her weight again . . . or was there less weight to lift? "Is it my imagination . . . or do you have one less chin?"

The others came closer. The change was almost imperceptible . . . but the others were able to notice.

Tory looked at her hand and flexed her fingers. Her skin was still as awful as before, but the swelling that had come to her joints was fading. Tears came to her eyes, and the salty tears didn't even sting, for her sores were slowly beginning to close.

They looked at each other, afraid to say what they now knew, for fear that speaking it would somehow jinx it. Finally Tory dared to utter the words.

"They're gone . . . ," she whispered. It took a few moments for it to finally hit home. Then, in the midst of the devastation Tory's voice rang out from the top floor of the ruined Dakins building, a clear note of joy in the midst of sorrow.

"We're free!"

THE JAGGED BROKEN WALL provided them with a treacherous path down to the rubble below.

There was chaos around the scene, but not the chaos one might expect. People screaming, crying, wandering like zombies—it was as if the shock wave of this event had driven everyone around it completely insane.

Winston looked around him and fumed. The redheaded boy had created this wave of destruction. The physical wasn't enough for him—he had to destroy the minds of the survivors. It made Winston furious . . . furious at himself for having seen him and not trying to stop him! Not even the knowledge that his own parasite was gone could calm his fury.

Winston approached a policeman sitting on a fire hydrant.

He was staring into the barrel of his own gun with a blank expression. When he saw Winston, he turned to him, pleading.

"Am I in trouble?" asked the officer. "Am I gonna get a whooping?"

Winston reached out and gently pulled the revolver out of the man's hands. The officer buried his head in his hands and cried.

"How did he do this?" asked Winston, as they stumbled their way through the nightmare of insanity.

"How?" said Tory. "How many thousands of people could you have paralyzed if you wanted to? How many plague epidemics could I have started? The only difference between him and us," she said, "is that *we* didn't want to."

About three blocks away from the wreckage, sanity seemed intact. People gawked and chattered and paced, but not with the same mindless chaos that surrounded the site of destruction.

As they left the insanity circle, it was Lourdes who took a moment to look back. In the midst of the rubble, the only thing left standing was the seven-story sliver that had been the corner of the Dakins storage building.

"Clutch player?" Michael suggested with a grin.

"Maybe," said Lourdes. "I was thinking that it looks like a tower. A tower that was struck by lightning."

As the sound of approaching sirens filled the air, Tory turned to the others. "I don't think those *things* died," she told them. "I mean if we're alive, then they're probably alive, too. I think they bailed because they thought they were going to get blown up. The explosion scared them out . . . but that doesn't mean they're gone for good."

Tory touched her face, to make certain that the pain there

was still slipping away. "We still may have to fight those things," she said. "But maybe when the six of us are together—"

"When the six of us are together," said Winston, feeling the weight of the revolver in his pocket, "I'm gonna send that redheaded son-of-a-bitch where he belongs."

12. SHROUD OF DARKNESS

AT THE EDGE OF THE WRECKAGE, A MAN WITH NO MIND stumbled away from his Range Rover. It was just one of many cars left idling in the middle of the road. Deanna and Dillon used it as their ticket out of Boise, and in a moment they were careening wildly northwest.

Deanna, who had never been behind the wheel of a car before, gripped the wheel and taught herself to drive at ninety miles an hour on the straightaway of I-84.

"How many people died?" she demanded. She would not turn her eyes from the road, but out of the corner of her eye she could see Dillon sitting beside her. He seemed completely absorbed in his map, pretending not to hear her.

"*How many?*" she demanded again.

"I don't know," said Dillon. "I can't tell things *that* exactly. Anyway, what's done is done," he said, and spoke no more of it.

Things were changing far too quickly for Deanna to keep up. What had begun for both of them as a cleansing journey, filled with the hope of redemption, had become nothing more than a mad rampage with no end in sight. It made her want to get out and run ... if only she could bear the fear of being on her own. Stepping out of that car and leaving Dillon would have been like stepping out of an airlock into space. She needed him, and she hated that.

She glanced at Dillon as he pored over the Triple-A map. He tossed it behind him and pulled another from the glove compartment.

"I won't keep running like this," said Deanna.

"We're not running, we're going somewhere," he finally admitted.

"Where?"

"I don't know yet . . . ," he snapped; then said a bit more gently, "I'll tell you as soon as I know, I promise."

"We were wrong," said Deanna. "We should find The Others—"

"The Others are dead," he said.

Deanna knew this was a lie. It was the first outright lie he had ever told her.

The road ahead of them was straight and clear, and Deanna dared to take a long look at Dillon. He had changed since she had first seen him in that hospital room. There he had been a tormented but courageous boy who had whisked her from her hospital bed. He had been a valiant, if somewhat disturbed, knight in shining armor. But now his courage had turned rancid. There was no armor, just an aura of darkness flowing around him like a black shroud—as if his body could no longer contain the blackness it held.

It was more than that, though—his body was changing as well. Had he gained weight? Yes, his slender figure had begun to bloat. She could see it in his face and hands—in his fingers, beginning to turn round and porcine. His skin, too, had changed. It began to take on an oily redness marked with whiteheads that were appearing one after another. *He's beginning to look on the outside what he's becoming on the inside,* Deanna thought, and shivered.

"Damn it!" said Dillon, hurling the map behind him. "I need more maps! These don't tell me what I need to know!" He took a deep breath to calm himself, then rubbed his eyes and said, "There's a town—when we get to the Columbia River—a good-sized population."

"Why does the population matter?" Deanna couldn't hide the apprehension in her voice.

"Because it means they'll have a decent library," Dillon answered. "And a decent library will have a decent almanac, and an atlas. A world atlas."

"And?"

Dillon rolled his eyes impatiently as if it were obvious. "And when I see what I have to see, I'll know where we have to go."

She heard him take another deep, relaxing breath, then he gently put his hand on her neck. It felt clammy and uncomfortable. She could feel that aura of darkness. How revolting it felt.

"It's okay," he told her. "Everything's gonna be great."

This too was a lie, but she knew that Dillon believed this one.

"When we get where we're going," Deanna asked, "is this all going to be over? Will it end?"

Dillon nodded. "Yes," he said. "Once we get there . . . everything will end."

BURTON, OREGON. POPULATION 3,255. In the center of town, a harvest festival sent bluegrass music wafting toward Main Street, where all was quiet. The library was empty today, except for Dillon and Deanna.

Dillon piled the large wooden reference table with volume after volume of atlases and almanacs. The librarian was delighted to see a young man so involved in his studies. Deanna, as curious as she was unsettled, helped him pull down heavy volumes describing the people and places of the world. First he stared at the maps—the way roads connected and wound from city to city, state to state, nation to nation. Then he looked at numbers—endless lists of numbers, graphs, and charts. Populations—demographics; people grouped in whatever ways the researchers could find to group them; by race or religion; by economics; by profession; by politics; by every imaginable variable.

"What are you looking for?" Deanna asked. But Dillon was so engrossed in his numbers he didn't even hear her. He was like a computer, taking in thousands of digits, and processing them through some inner program.

Then, one by one Dillon closed the books. The atlas of Europe, and of Asia. The books on Australia and South America. The studies of Africa, the American Almanac . . . until he was left with the map of the northwestern United States. He stared at the map, drawing his eyes further and further northwest, his finger following the tiny capillaries of country roads until he stopped. Dillon's master equation had finally spit out an answer.

"There."

His finger landed in the southwest corner of Washington state. "This is where we have to go."

"What will we find there?" asked Deanna.

"Someone."

"Someone we know?"

Dillon shook his head. "Someone we *will* know. Someone important."

They left, not bothering to shelve the books.

THEIR COURSE OUT OF town took them right past the harvest festival. They had no intention of stopping, but the Rover needed gas. The gas station was right across the road from the festival, where most everyone in Burton was spending this fine day.

Dillon, who was driving now, got out to pump, while Deanna scrounged around the messy car, finding dollar bills and loose change to pay for the gas. It was when she looked out of the window at Dillon that she knew something was wrong. The old-fashioned mechanical pump clanged out gallons and racked up dollars, but Dillon wasn't watching that. Instead, he was looking at the pump just ahead of them, where a tattooed, beer-bellied man stood pumping up his run-down Trans Am. His equally unattractive wife stood beside him.

It seemed that Dillon had caught the wife's attention, and she was staring at him in a trance. Dillon stared right back. Then this woman in high heels and decade-old tight pants stepped over the gas hose and began to approach Dillon, but her husband, sensing something out of the ordinary, held her back.

He scowled at Dillon. "Got a problem?"

Dillon looked away, shook it off, and the episode was over . . . but it lingered in Deanna's mind. There were many strange twists and turns on the roller coaster the two of them had been on, but in some way those other turns were consistent. This seemed to take the coaster wholly off its track. She turned to Dillon again and noticed the beads of sweat beginning to form on his forehead. She knew what that meant, and she began to panic. What happened in Boise should have satisfied his rapacious hunger for a good while. She knew she had to get him out of town, so she quickly paid the attendant in crumpled bills and loose change—but when she turned, Dillon had already disappeared into the crowds of the fair.

IT WAS TWILIGHT NOW. The lights had come up on the Ferris wheel, and the Tilt-a-Whirl spun its merry victims past one another in flashes of neon blue and red.

Deanna searched everywhere for Dillon, in every dark corner, in every crowd, but he seemed to have completely dissolved into the mob.

Finally she spotted him on the midway. He was walking . . . no, wandering, down the hay-strewn path with the aimlessness of a zombie. He was drenched in sweat.

Deanna ran toward him, but stopped when she saw him once more lock eyes with another girl, just as he had with the woman at the gas station. This one was sixteen—maybe seventeen. She ate cotton candy and watched her muscle-bound boyfriend launch rubber frogs into the air with a sledgehammer, trying to win her a prize. The boyfriend grunted as he swung the hammer and didn't seem to notice as the girl dropped her cotton candy, crossed the midway to Dillon, and then, for no apparent reason, leaned forward . . . and kissed him.

Deanna just stood there gawking.

Clearly this girl had never met Dillon before . . . and here she was launching herself into his arms with the same passion that her boyfriend launched his rubber frogs.

Deanna watched as Dillon brought up his arms and pulled this girl closer, kissing her in a powerful way—a way in which he had never kissed Deanna. It was not an embrace of love, or even lust—it was passion turned rancid. It was everything that a kiss should not be.

But it wasn't a kiss, was it? It was more like a bite.

The girl's arms turned white from the tightness of Dillon's grip, and she gave in to his embrace completely. Deanna's mind swarmed with powerful, conflicting emotions—jealousy not the least of them.

Although she never wanted him to steal this kind of kiss from her, she didn't want to see him steal it from anyone else, either.

How could a kiss be so evil—and what had possessed the girl to step into it? It couldn't have been Dillon's looks—not anymore. What once had been an attractive face was now puffy and infected. His dark eyes had become an icy, unnatural turquoise.

Here he was kissing another girl—right there in front of her, and he didn't even care! The sense of betrayal was unbearable.

Dillon squeezed the girl against him, and Deanna could see his dark aura stretch around her—then Deanna saw—no—she *felt* something invisible pass from the girl to Dillon.

The boyfriend, who had just won a pink dinosaur, turned and gawked with blinking idiocy at his girlfriend, kissing this sick-looking kid.

"What the hell is this?" he said.

At last Dillon moved his lips away from the girl's, and she looked into his eyes. This time his touch had not scrambled her thoughts.

The boyfriend stepped in and delivered a right hook that sent Dillon's head snapping to the left. Dillon recovered quickly ... but not the boyfriend. He gasped and looked at his hand, where it had touched Dillon's chin. His knuckles were locked. Not just that, but his whole forearm was locked in a muscle spasm that caused his sinews to bulge like ropes from his elbow to his wrist.

The boyfriend stumbled away, forgetting the girl, staring at his paralyzed arm. As for the girl, she just wandered off wide-eyed, and Deanna sensed that something had been stolen from her—something very important that she would never get back.

Dillon just grinned dumbly.

"Why did you do that?" Deanna demanded, overwhelmed with disgust.

"I don't know ..."

"You really enjoyed it, didn't you?"

"Yes . . . no . . . I don't know." He put his hand to his temples, as if keeping his head from blowing apart. "Deanna, what's happening to me?"

She had no sympathy for him now as she locked eyes with his, and scrutinized him.

"Deanna, don't look at me like that . . ."

Deanna peered deep into his eyes, searching as she always did . . . seeking the glimmer in the darkness. She looked long and hard, through the rank and fetid decay that encased his body and soul . . . and finally Deanna realized that the light in him was gone. The part of Dillon that had shone so brightly in his darkness all this time had been wrapped in so many shrouds of evil that she could not find him anymore.

The moment she realized that, was the moment she knew she had to run—to get as far away as she possibly could. She instantly turned without pause for another thought and abandoned the shell that had once been Dillon Cole, racing into the crowds—but Dillon desperately pursued.

"Deanna!" he screamed. "Don't go!"

She couldn't stop herself from glancing back as he chased her, and what she saw made her run even faster.

Dillon was pushing through the crowds just as she was, and everyone he touched fell from him with hideous afflictions. Some collapsed in paralysis, others lost their minds, others seemed to deflate as if their chests had been crushed inward, and still others turned red and diseased. "Deanna!" he screamed, not even noticing the people he had destroyed.

She broke free of the crowd and scrambled away from the fair, to the top of the hill.

"Deanna, come back!"

When she reached the top of the hill, she dared to look back once more. Dillon was still standing there at the edge of the crowd. He stared at her a moment more . . . and finally with a scowl on his face, he turned and defiantly grabbed the first girl in sight. She came to him like he was a gift from heaven, and he kissed her, stealing her soul away with his kiss. Then he turned and headed back into the crowd.

From the top of the hill, Deanna watched him go, the living darkness now cloaked around him and trailing behind him. He stalked his way to the center of the crowd around the bluegrass band. He looked left, then right, until he finally found The Right Person—a matronly woman clapping her hands happily to the beat. Then Dillon whispered something into her ear.

And the crowd detonated.

From where Deanna stood, she could see how it happened. It began with people becoming irritated, then irritation built into anger, anger into fury, fury into rage, until the entire crowd thrashed in a chaotic screaming tarantella—a dance of destruction, wild and insane, spreading outward like a shock wave. The music stopped and was replaced by wails of anguish and pain. In five minutes the townsfolk had turned into chaotic, murderous fiends, their sanity wiped from their minds by Dillon the destroyer.

Deanna turned and ran, screaming, into the woods.

WOODS ARE A RIPE place for fears, and Deanna's were thriving on the branches and shadows that surrounded her. She had refused to feed on the terror Dillon had unleashed, so now every shape was a threatening demon, every shadow a portent of pain. She stumbled over and over as she raced through the lonely woods, not knowing where she would go.

At last she came to a road and tumbled to the gravel, skinning her knees through her jeans. She sat up on the empty asphalt, breathless, her voice ruined from all her screaming.

Finally a pickup truck swerved to stop in front of her.

A man got out—a middle-aged, family-looking man. There was a boy in the back of the pickup, all dressed up in an Indian outfit.

It seemed normal, and Deanna just wanted to dissolve into this man and his family, forgetting who she was and what was happening.

"I have to get out here," Deanna rasped. "So do you! You have to get away from this town!"

"Now hold on, there," said the man warmly. "Let's just calm down." He looked her over as he stepped from the cab of his pickup. "You've had some fright," he said. "I know just the thing for you."

"Please," begged Deanna, "you don't understand . . ."

"Now just wait a second," he said, with a calm and soothing voice. "I'll be right back." He reached into the back of his pickup and grabbed something, then turned back toward her, revealing what he held. It was a piece of a white picket fence, broken so that the white wood came to a sharp point.

And then Deanna noticed the man's eyes. One pupil was closed down completely, the other wide and wild. This man had already been to the fair.

"We'll take care of you," said the man. "Fix you up real good."

Deanna could now see that the tip of the picket was already covered with blood.

In the pickup, the boy mindlessly sang a single line from a nursery rhyme over and over like a broken record, lazily rolling his head from side to side, as he watched his father throw Deanna to the ground.

"This won't hurt but a bit," the madman said as he raised the picket above his head and pointed it at Deanna's heart.

Deanna would have screamed if she still had a voice.

13. TURNING NORMAL

Tufts of white speckled a rich blue sky on the Idaho–Oregon border. It was a weak legion of clouds that could not even block out the sun.

Michael could not remember blue sky; there were always clouds and storms tormenting the heavens, and when the storms slept, there was always a rumbling fog keeping the sky an everlasting gray.

But not today.

Michael lay on a brushy hillside staring up at the glorious sky. Beneath them lay Huntington, Oregon. They were barely a hundred miles out of Boise, but to Michael, what they left behind in Boise was a million miles away.

"What do they look like?"

Michael turned to see Tory come up beside him.

"That's what you're doing, isn't it? Looking for shapes in the clouds?"

"I was just looking." Michael sat up and glanced down the hill, where the town spread out before them. Changing leaves glimmered in afternoon sunlight turning the town to gold. The air was neither hot nor cold, but temperate. Nice. Normal.

They had spent an entire day and night in and around Boise, spiraling outward from the epicenter of Chaos, searching for *The Others*, or, more specifically, the redheaded boy who was at the core of the nightmare. But they had also wasted time as they reveled in this new feeling of freedom now that the beasts were gone. It had taken until the next morning for them to feel the slightest pull northwest, and they realized he had left town long ago.

Now they had driven into Oregon and, somewhere in the town below, a tireless Winston was searching for signs of ruin, but he was the only one. Here on the hill, Lourdes lay on her back, asleep, with every exhalation breathing out another ounce of fat, and he and Tory just looked at the clouds.

Michael glanced at Tory and smiled.

"What is it?" she asked.

"Your eyelashes," said Michael. "The way you were before, I could never see them." What he didn't tell her was that he never really looked at her face before. It had been so hideous. He could not bear the sight. But now the sores had closed, and bit by bit the swelling was going down.

Tory gingerly touched her face. "There'll be scars. They're always scars from bad skin conditions, you know?"

"Maybe not," offered Michael, wondering about the scars his own condition might leave behind.

Michael lay back down and turned his eyes on the clouds again, his mind finding their shapes. An angel. A unicorn. A tall sailing ship. He had always played this game as a child. He was very good at it.

"Can I tell you something, Tory?"

"Shoot."

"I don't think I'm as brave as the rest of you."

"How do you figure?"

Michael kept his eyes on the drifting clouds. A wind seemed to fill the sail of the tall ship. "Well, take Winston, for example; he feels this in his gut. He knows he has to go out there and take care of this bad kid. And you—you were the strong one, who pulled the rest of us all this way . . . and if it weren't for Lourdes, I would have given up a long time ago . . ."

"I was ready to call it quits lots of times," said Tory.

"How about now?" He turned to Tory, but Tory didn't answer. "I saw that horror in Boise," said Michael. "I know what that other kid is capable of . . . I know what *I* was capable of too . . . but now I've come out of the nightmare, Tory. Maybe there's some blood-sucking Hell-thing driving him to do what he does—but the one that was inside of me is gone! The problem is, it was living in me for so long, I can't remember being any other way. I don't know how to feel about anyone or anything, you know?"

Michael looked away. "Tory . . . I don't have any of the feelings I used to have. Feelings for girls, I mean."

"You mean . . ."

"I mean I don't know what I mean. I don't know *anything*." Michael took a deep breath. "It's like everything inside me has been locked in a vault since I was eleven, and now that same eleven-year-old kid is coming back out. I've got to learn how to *feel* all over again, because right now I don't feel anything either way."

"Well, I don't think it's something you can figure out in one day. If we make it through this, we'll have our whole lives to deal with the regular stuff, but right now we've got other things to think about," reminded Tory. "Our friendly neighborhood Hell-pets are still out there—they can still come back . . ."

"If they're not back already, then maybe they've found a better place to be," said Michael. "Anyway, I don't want to go looking for them under stones. I just want to go home, figure out who I am, and how I'm supposed to feel . . . and then be normal. I don't even care what shade of normal it happens to be. Any kind of normal would suit me just fine."

Michael turned to see Tory dab a tear from her face.

"I don't think we get to be normal," she said. "We're Scorpion Shards, remember?" Then she took his hand. "Come here, I want to show you something. It's sort of a . . . magic trick."

She led him over the hill to a burned-out campsite—a place with torn mattresses and soggy cardboard. It reeked of urine and rot, and it reminded Michael of the type of world they had traveled through to get this far—to get into the light of this pleasant day.

"Find me something disgusting," said Tory. "The most disgusting thing you can find."

There were plenty of disgusting things around to choose from. Michael settled for a sopping rag, so rank it had turned black. It smelled like death on a bad day. He picked it up with his fingernails—just touching the thing made his body shiver in disgust.

"Now give it to me," requested Tory.

Michael held it in her direction. "What are you going to do?"

"You'll see."

She took the disgusting rag and, to Michael's horror, used it to wipe her hands, then, as if that wasn't bad enough, she brought it to her face and wiped her face with it. Michael had to look away. Finally, when she was done, she held the rag back up to Michael.

"Take it," she said.

Michael reluctantly held out his fingertips and grabbed the corner of the rag. The rag was still wet, but that's all it was. A damp rag, perfectly clean, as if it had just been taken out of the washer. Even the smell was gone.

"Kills germs on contact," said Tory. "I'm better than Listerine."

Michael smelled the rag again, amazed. He wiped his own face with it and felt its cool sterile dampness on his face.

"Everyone's got a hidden talent," said Tory. "I suppose ours are a bit more interesting than most. Our talents are less . . . normal."

Tory glanced up at the puffs of clouds blowing across the sky. "An angel," she said. "A unicorn . . . and that one's a schooner ship."

Michael glanced back at the clouds, wondering how on earth she had seen the exact same things he had seen. The reason became clear in an instant, and Michael couldn't believe his eyes.

The clouds had become like soft, white figurines, hovering in the sky. The wind had carefully sculpted the clouds into exactly what Michael had seen them as!

Tory smiled. "You make nice clouds," she said. "Or at least you do when you're head's screwed on straight."

MICHAEL STARED AT HIS clouds for a good ten minutes, but then they were finally torn apart by powerful crosswinds. He tried to create them again, but found he didn't have the concentration. As he watched them dissolve, Michael began to wonder how many of the storms on their trip had been of his own creation.

Meanwhile, Lourdes had woken up and was staring at a dead squirrel . . . only it wasn't dead.

"I was talking to it gently—coaxing it closer," she told Michael. "And then it just keeled over and fell asleep. What could possibly make it do that?"

Michael looked at the silent squirrel, realizing that this could be the first hint of Lourdes's "hidden talent." Then suddenly the squirrel snapped open its eyes and scampered off.

"Isn't that weird?" said Lourdes.

Michael chuckled as he imagined Lourdes surrounded by animals like Snow White . . . but it wasn't about animals, was it? This was just a trick—like Tory's rag, or Michael's sky sculptures. As with all of them, Lourdes's talent had many layers to be discovered, and it took Michael's breath away to think of the possibilities.

"We need to talk," Michael told Lourdes, and she began to look worried.

"About what?"

Michael smiled and gently touched her arm, which was not quite as massive as it had been that same morning. "Good things," he assured her. "Only good things."

Just then Winston came bounding up the hill, out of breath.

"The redheaded kid didn't stop in this town," he announced. "We gotta keep moving." Michael noticed that Winston's pants, which they had cut down to match his diminishing stature, were already an inch above his ankles. Then Michael caught a glimpse of the revolver Winston had taken from that crazy cop in Boise. He kept it with him in his inside jacket pocket.

Michael imagined the days ahead of them now, and the joy he had felt only moments ago began to dissipate as quickly as his clouds in the windswept sky. He knew what they had to do. Stop the destroyer. Stop him at all costs, before he . . . *before he what*? It was hard to imagine anything worse than what they had seen in Boise.

As they gathered their things, Tory came up to Michael once more. "Still thinking of going home?" she asked.

Michael shook his head. "What would you do without me?" he said.

"Stay dry?" suggested Tory. "Keep warm?"

"I promise," said Michael, "no more storms." But even as they turned to go, Michael could feel a cold wind blowing, as nature itself reacted to the growing chill he felt within.

14. FEAR IS AN ICY WIND

THE DRY BRUSH OF EASTERN OREGON SLOWLY BECAME GREEN, then turned into dense woods as I-84 cut a tireless path west. With Michael behind the wheel, the four kids tried every exit off the interstate, in search of anything that didn't seem right. It was a slow and painstaking task, but it gave them the time they needed to talk.

"So now you two are Rain-man and Mrs. Clean?" said Lourdes to Michael and Tory. "I wonder what that makes me— Squirrel-girl?"

"It might not seem like much," said Tory, "but we'll need every skill we have if we're gonna stop this guy."

Tory looked at Winston, anticipating his usual reaction. "I know it's a big stretch," she said to him, "but these talents are for real—you have to believe us!"

Winston looked at her, insulted. "Why shouldn't I believe you?" he said. "It makes sense—I just wish I knew what mine was."

Michael laughed. "Nice stretch, Winston. Maybe you're a bungee cord after all!" Michael jokingly tugged on Winston's arm, as if it would stretch like plastic-man. It didn't of course, and Winston tumbled out of his seat belt.

"Hey watch it!" said Winston, only half angry. "Before I grow some teeth and bite you!"

BURTON, OREGON, WAS SIX miles off the interstate, in a densely forested valley. About a mile down Old Burton Road, Michael stomped on the brakes, and they all tumbled forward.

An object loomed before them—something so bizarre that they could only stare at it, trying to make their minds accept what they were seeing. It was huge and blue, lying half on the road and half off. It looked like a giant metallic Q-tip that had crashed from the heavens and taken down a dozen trees with it.

"Water tower," said Lourdes.

Tory swallowed hard. "I think we found the town where he stopped."

The word "Burton" was still visible on the toppled water tower. Its bulbous tank had ruptured, sending its full load of water flooding the forest around it, turning it into a swamp.

"If I read the sign right," said Michael, "there's more than three thousand people in this town."

He turned to Tory, but Tory turned her eyes away. They were all thinking the same thing. The demolition of downtown Boise, as bad as it was, had only a quarter-mile radius. . . . But if the redheaded kid had found a way to shatter the people of this town . . . it meant that the range of his ability had grown, and the human wreckage would be unimaginable.

The car itself seemed to shudder.

They slowly navigated the gravelly shoulder of the road down the long, slender cylinder that had once held up the water tank. At its ruined base sat a burned-out eighteen-wheeler with a crushed grill.

Across the road, in the drenched undergrowth, a woman sat knitting, wearing nothing but the strands of clashing yarn that draped over her and into the mud.

Lourdes casually pushed down her door lock. It engaged with a dull *thud*. It was echoed by the thud of the other three doors being locked as well. Michael eased onto the gas pedal, and they pressed cautiously forward.

The first homes came into view—lonely homes set back from the road, about a hundred yards apart. In the first house, a shadow leered from an upstairs window, staggering back and forth. On the porch of another home, a woman in a rocking chair let out a ghostly sound.

"We still have three miles to go till we get to the center of town," reminded Tory.

Winston nodded. "It's going to get worse before it gets better."

And it did. A car was parked through a living-room window. Several homes were smoldering ruins . . . then all at once, Michael slammed on the brakes as a local kid no older than them, screaming and bloody, dashed out in front of them. He was stalked by a band of teenagers, as if the prey of some awful hunt.

They watched as the mob disappeared up the hillside.

"I've had nightmares like that," said Tory; then added, "Whoever he is, I hope he wakes up."

Lourdes mumbled something in Spanish and let out a groan of grief. She grabbed Michael's hand; he held Tory's shoulder; she gripped Winston's leg; he reached back until he found Lourdes's wrist, completing the circle of four. They took a deep breath and tried to force out the grim images that assaulted them from outside.

"Nothing can hurt us," said Tory. "Nothing can hurt us when we're like this." But it wasn't true. Yes, they were stronger, but they weren't invincible—and the sum of the horrors outside their car was far greater than the sum of the four of them.

"We shouldn't look at what happened here," said Lourdes. "You should never look when you're passing through Hell." And with that in mind, Michael gritted his teeth until his face began to turn red.

"What are you doing?" asked Winston.

"Making the sky fall," was his answer.

Up above the dense cloud-cover began to ripple. "If I can make myself feel fog on the inside, it'll happen on the outside."

"How do you feel fog?" asked Winston.

"Fog is confusion," said Michael, through clenched teeth. "Just like anger is a lightning storm, and hopelessness is a rain of sleet."

In a moment the clouds descended into the valley, sinking over their windshield until the entire town of Burton was shrouded in fog. Then an icy wind that could only be Michael's fear hit them from behind, whistling past the car, and blowing the fog before them. The wind left a tunnel through the fog that followed the road to the center of town.

DOWNTOWN BURTON HAD BECOME a ghost town. The mad had long since disappeared into the woods—their anguished cries echoing across the valley like a thousand dispossessed souls. Michael slowly drove the van into the heart of havoc, but the fog could not hide everything. Through the mist, shadows of the dead seemed to stretch in all directions off the side of the road. The town's firetruck lay on its side. Shattered window glass crackled beneath the wheels of the van.

At one point Winston got up on his knees and looked out of the window, toward a gas station, which could barely be seen through the fog. "Stop the car!" he said. Michael did, and they all watched as Winston pressed up against the car window, not daring to open it—as if the very air of this town was poisoned. Finally, Winston said, "He was there . . . then he crossed the street . . ." Winston pointed into the fog. "But where did he go from here?"

"Feels like he went straight on through town," said Tory.

"I feel that, too," concurred Lourdes.

They turned to Michael, but his struggle to maintain the fog didn't leave room for him to feel much of anything else.

IN ANOTHER MILE, MAIN Street faded behind them, and Michael lost control of the fog. The wind shifted the haze away through the woods, revealing a narrow country road ahead. They all breathed a sigh of relief, thinking the worst was over . . . until the road took a blind curve and they almost broadsided a pickup truck that sat diagonally across their lane.

Michael hit the brake, sharply turned the wheel, and the van spun out of control, tires squealing, until they spun to a stop, narrowly missing the pickup.

It was the moment the van stopped that they began to feel a sense of *presence* that was so strong it bristled their neck hairs like static electricity.

"He's still here!" said Tory. "Somewhere nearby!"

They quickly unlocked their doors and got out.

Once outside, the smell of smoke was strong and pungent. From the woods they could still hear the distant wails of the wandering mad, chasing each other through the timberland maze.

In front of them, the pickup truck barred their path; beside the truck lay a man, face-down in the mud, very much dead. In his hand he held a bloody fence picket. A crude arrow had caught him right in the jugular.

Michael turned away and leaned against a tree, gasping for breath. "I think I'm gonna puke," he said.

"Don't," said Tory. "We might get hail."

It was Lourdes who was able to get a sense of direction. She turned to the right and pointed to a house about a hundred yards further down the road.

"There . . . ," she said. "I think he's in there."

They took action instantly. Lourdes stalked forward, ready to rely on her bare hands, but Tory had her own ideas. Grimacing, she grabbed the dead man's picket from his stiff hand.

"Maybe if I stake him through the heart, it'll sanitize his soul," she said.

Michael pulled a crowbar from the pickup truck. "Maybe I can use this as a lightning rod," he said.

Winston, still not knowing his hidden talent, reached into his coat and pulled out the revolver, taking off the safety. "No maybe's about what this'll do to him," he said.

The dwelling seemed very innocent as they approached. Just a two-story country house.

"What if he's armed, too?" said Michael. "What if he shoots us?"

"Then we die," said Winston. The thought of dying in this town did not sit well with any of them. It would be better to die anywhere else but here.

The front door was slightly ajar, and they stood there on the porch for a quick moment, then burst in. Tory held her stake high, Michael gripped his crowbar in both hands, the sky already rumbling with his fury, and Winston aimed his gun at anything—*anything* that moved.

Inside the living room, a figure stood silhouetted against a window, holding something large and heavy in its arms.

Winston, his hands shaking, leveled the gun at the figure's head.

The figure stepped closer, Tory and Michael froze, and Winston hesitated.

"Shoot!" shouted Lourdes. "Shoot now!"

Winston almost did, he pulled his finger back on the trigger halfway . . . but then hesitated . . . because there was something he suddenly remembered.

The figure stepped out of the shadows. It was a girl with long, black hair, and slightly Asian eyes.

There are six of us, thought Winston. *Six! . . . and this one was not the destroyer.*

Winston lowered the gun. Michael dropped the crowbar with a clang.

The girl held a young boy in her arms—about seven or eight years old. He wore a toy Indian headband on his head, and he clung to her as she approached them.

The girl glanced at Winston's gun, but didn't seem intimidated by it at all. In fact, she didn't seem frightened by any of them. "Could one of you go into the kitchen and get a towel?" she asked calmly.

There was a foul smell in the air, and from the smell, they knew that the boy in her arms had soiled his pants. Tory put down the picket and hurried to find the towel.

"I've been waiting for you," said the girl. "Dillon said you were dead, but I knew he was lying."

"Dillon? That's his name?" asked Winston. "The guy with red hair?"

"Yes. I'm Deanna."

They introduced themselves as Tory returned with the towel. Then Deanna put the boy down on the sofa, cleaning him the way a mother would clean a baby—with tender care and patience.

"Who's the kid?" asked Michael.

"Just a boy from town," said Deanna. "He doesn't seem to know his name, so I call him Carter, since that was the label on his shirt."

When the boy looked up, they could see how truly terrible his eyes were. One of his pupils had closed down completely, and the other one was open wide and black.

"They all look like that once Dillon is done," explained Deanna. "There's not much we can do for them."

She told them the story of how she met Dillon—the things they had done together, and how she finally broke free. She explained how the boy's father was going to kill her with the bloody picket, but just before he brought the deadly spike down upon her chest, the man was hit by the arrow.

"I got him!" said the boy. "We were playing cowboys and Indians, and I got him good."

Deanna cleaned the boy, and dressed him in oversized pants she found lying around the house. Tory took the soiled towel from Deanna, held it tightly in her hand, and the stench quickly vanished.

"You thought you were going to die, didn't you?" Tory said as Deanna washed up. "You thought you were dying, so the thing living inside you panicked and ran away—the same thing happened to us—they got scared out of us!"

"I saw it," said Deanna, calmly. "It was like a snake. . . . No . . . more like a giant worm."

Everyone else shuddered, but Deanna didn't seem bothered by the memory at all. She seemed rather fearless about the whole thing. "Anyway it vanished through the woods, heading west."

Carter wandered around the living room and found his bow and arrows. He set to work removing the rubber suction-cup darts, and sharpening the wood with a pocket knife, as he had done with the first one. Lourdes went over to watch.

"Do you have a car?" asked Deanna.

"Just down the road," answered Michael.

"We have to get going. . . . I knew you'd be coming, so I stacked some supplies by the door—I know where Dillon is headed."

"Look!" said Tory, and they all turned to catch sight of Lourdes at the other end of the room with Carter. Lourdes had gained the boy's attention now—he had put down his knife and arrow. Together they seemed to be playing some sort of game—a mirroring game, where the boy would copy whatever Lourdes did.

"Lourdes, this is no time to be fooling around!" said Winston.

"Shh!" said Tory, sharply.

Lourdes kept her eye contact with the boy. She raised one arm; so did he. She raised the other arm; so did he. Only this wasn't a game, and he wasn't simply mimicking her, his actions were too perfect, too exact.

"She's controlling him like a marionette!" said Michael, staring in wide-eyed disbelief. "She's controlling every movement of his body!" Each motion Lourdes made was exactly duplicated. She wiggled her fingers; so did he. She rolled her neck; so did he. Was it just the boy's muscles, or did it go beyond that? Could she control his heartbeat? His breathing? His very metabolism? Until yesterday, she couldn't control her own grotesque physiology, but now the physiology of others seemed within her grasp!

Lourdes looked at the boy, and the boy's ruined eyes began to close. He nodded off to sleep.

Lourdes turned to the others. "Did you see that?" she said, just as surprised as the rest of them. "I think I did that!"

They all just stared at the sleeping boy in wonder, realizing that the title of "Squirrel-girl" for Lourdes didn't quite hit the mark.

"Those creatures turned our strengths into weaknesses!" said Tory. It was becoming clearer to each of them now. Michael's ability to affect nature had been used to wreak havoc in the very nature of people around him; Tory's cleansing touch had been turned into a touch of disease; Lourdes's ability to control the metabolism of others had been used to draw the flesh out of their cells and add it to Lourdes's.

Tory turned to Winston. "We can figure out what your strength is now!"

"I already figured," said Winston uneasily. He looked around, then asked Michael to bring down a potted plant from a shelf Winston couldn't reach. Winston put the plant down on a coffee table, took a deep breath, then grasped the stem in his hand and concentrated. Right before everyone's eyes, the plant grew until it had doubled in size and flowers bloomed. Winston smiled. It was the first time any of them had seen him really smile.

"Looks like we got a flower-child," said Michael, with a grin. "What are you gonna do, beat Dillon with a corsage?"

Winston shrugged. "Ain't *my* problem if *you* can't see the possibilities."

"You'll find a good use for it," said Deanna. "Don't worry."

And indeed it seemed that Deanna was not worried. By anything. Her fearlessness was a powerful strength. It gave them focus; it gave them clarity. She told them how Dillon had changed in the end, making it horribly clear where all their beasts had gone—and it seemed likely that Deanna's beast had found him as well.

"He's stronger than all of us," said Tory. "If he can survive with all six of them inside him."

"You said you knew where he was going?" asked Michael.

Deanna nodded, and picked up sleeping Carter, refusing to leave him alone in this awful town, and they all headed back to the car.

"There's still time to stop him, but it will take all of us to do it," said Deanna.

"Stop him . . . from what?" asked Lourdes.

"Don't you know what he wants to do?" she asked, looking at each of them. Only Deanna had the courage to say the words aloud.

"He's going to shatter the world, the same way he shattered this town . . . and once it starts, we won't be able to stop it."

15. RESONANCE

JAGGED SPIRES OF DEAD WOOD STRETCHED THROUGH THE morning mist. Thousands upon thousands of trees had once blanketed the steep hills, stretching toward a distant mountain. . . .

. . . But now every last tree was dead.

Wind, rain, and rot had eaten away their branches, leaving vast acres of wooden monoliths standing in a mulch of peat and heavy gray ash. This forest had died long before Dillon Cole got to it, and the cause of death was still there on the horizon, breathing steam like a fire god asleep.

The sheer power of it, thought Dillon as he drove from life into the miles of death that surrounded the northern face of Mount St. Helens.

The smell of decay within this realm of desolation blended with the rich, dark smell of volcanic ash, creating an aroma that was at once both clean and vile, like the awful smell of a sulfur spring.

As he drove into the volcanic wasteland, fear began to writhe in his gut, but he beat it down. The fear had descended on him shortly after Deanna had left him. Terror had suddenly coiled itself around his gut like a serpent, making him feel paranoid and claustrophobic in the cab of the Range Rover as he left the dying town of Burton. He had fought it down until it wasn't so overpowering, but still the fear kept coming back, urging him to drive faster and more recklessly to his final destination.

The hands that now gripped the steering wheel were not

his hands—at least not the hands that he remembered. These were bloated and swollen—covered with red boils. This body was not his either. His growing gut had burst out of his pants in the middle of the night. He was forced to find a truck stop and confiscate larger clothes from a trucker whose life had come to a sudden and unexpected end. Now Dillon had to roll up the pant legs as well—he swore that he was an inch shorter than the day before. Inside he could feel many, many hungers now, coiled within him, competing for his will, all screaming to be fed.

The wrecking-hunger, however, still screamed the loudest, and its final feeding was all that mattered—a feeding so great that when it was done, there would be nothing left to devour.

Back in the Burton Library, he had studied the maps, the charts, the statistics. He had worked calculations that a super-computer would have shied away from, and he had pulled out an answer, sifting it through a secret sixth sense. The answer he came up with was this: of all the locations in the world from which to set up the ultimate chain reaction, only one rested in North America. The epicenter of destruction was in Washington state, in the shadow of Mount St. Helens. Here, in this secret fulcrum of human existence, Dillon would have to find a human fuse. It would have to be someone with no ties to the outside world and filled with a lonely anger. Someone separate and alone. It would have to be a hermit, whose destiny Dillon could aim with the pinpoint accuracy of a sniper.

Although the calculations that brought him there were complex, the actual plan was simple: Dillon would find his hermit, then find the hermit's weakness and fire him toward a nearby city. In the city, there would be a gathering place—a bar, perhaps—where this man would create a chain of events that would drive everyone there beyond the limit of their sanity. Those who survived would carry the insanity home with them.

At least one would board a plane.

At least ten of the people on that plane would board other planes, and in this way, the seed of destruction would be planted within the minds of thousands of travelers, moving in hundreds of different directions. In a matter of days, people around the world would suddenly be faced by the exact chain of events that would bring them to their breaking points and drive them mad. Millions of patterns collapsing like a house of cards.

In the end, the destruction of mankind would not come as a great nuclear holocaust. It would not come as a meteor splitting the earth in half. It would come from a simple thought whispered in one lonely man's ear. A single thought, which would breed a rage of chaos that would sweep across the globe in a swift chain reaction.

Dillon remembered seeing a film once about a great steel bridge that had violently collapsed, brought down by mere resonance—the simple vibrations of the air around it. Dillon's thought would surely resonate and bring down something far more mighty than a steel bridge. He was the hammer that would fracture every thought mankind had ever had, making civilization crumble to its very foundations.

Dillon pondered how a single thought—the right thought—had always had such power to create. Simple thoughts pushed in the right direction at the right time.

The idea of the wheel; the thought of the written word—simple ideas that had picked up momentum across the globe, swelled like a tidal wave and created civilization. How fitting that a single thought was all it took to bring it crashing down.

The power of such an act could only be surmounted by the

power released when everything fell—power that would feed the wrecking-hunger like it had never before been fed. Just imagining it made Dillon drool, and he longed for the great process to begin.

For an instant the image of his dead parents flitted through his mind.

Are you proud of me now, Mom and Dad?

He didn't wait for an answer. Instead he floored the accelerator, and the engine's powerful roar drowned out the question before it could resonate in his mind.

Part V
Between the Walls

16. THE HERMIT

SLAYTON.

He didn't need a first name.

Most of the time he didn't need a name at all. He'd only drive his rusty pickup down into Cougar every few weeks or so for supplies, paying with ancient, crumpled bills, then he would disappear again down a dirt road that passed from life into death, from green trees into the dead valley in the shadow of the smoking mountain.

He was forty.

His skin was beginning to age, his hair beginning to gray—but inside, his thoughts and ideas, his very perception of the world had never grown beyond age eight or nine.

He was slow.

Not only in the way he thought, but in the way he moved. He had come to accept this as the way of things, and it only bothered him when he was among others, whose thoughts and actions were quicker. For that reason, he didn't care much for people—being around people drained him—made him feel less of a man. So he steered clear of them and made himself the center of his own solitary universe, where things moved at his own speed.

He learned to care for himself at an early age.

He built a shack in the woods, and when the timber company

that owned the land kicked him off, he moved, and built another. And then another. Now, he finally thought he had found a place where no one would bother him—a dead forest gray and bleak that no one wanted. Here they would finally leave him alone.

He drank too much.

A habit he had picked up from his father, years and years ago. When the wind would blow, and the alcohol would swim through his mind, he would swear there were ghosts in the trees, like in stories his ma used to tell. Ghosts and demons were very real to Slayton. And so he was not entirely surprised when the Devil appeared at his door one bleak October evening.

The door creaked open to reveal him standing there. Slayton didn't make a move. He just sat at his table, holding his half-full bottle of whiskey. The other half was already in his head. Slayton knew who it was without him having to say a word.

"You must be Slayton."

"How do you know my name?"

"They told me about you in town."

The Devil did not look quite the way Slayton expected. He was fat and young. A redheaded teenager with an awful complexion.

"I've been looking for you," the Devil said.

"I'll bet you have."

Slayton invited the Devil in, watching him carefully as he moved. Darkness surrounded him like a black hole. Shadow flowed in his wake, rippling like a dark cape. A living fabric of death.

The Devil closed the door behind himself, and suddenly fear and anger began to overtake Slayton—but he bit it back, determined to stand toe to toe with the Devil. Slayton reached up, got a glass and poured some whiskey as the visitor sat down at the table. His darkness ebbed and flowed on the table like waves lapping the shore.

"Drink with me?" asked Slayton.

The Devil-boy shook his head, pushing the glass away.

"What's the matter? Not old enough?" And Slayton let out a rough wheezing laugh at the thought of the Devil being underage. That was a good one!

"No time," said his guest, looking into Slayton's eyes, probing his thoughts. "No time, I'm in a hurry."

Only then did Slayton notice that this Devil-boy across the table was sweating something awful. He was breathing quickly, and shallowly as if he was out of breath—as if he was panicked, but trying to hide it.

"What's yer angle?" asked Slayton.

"Angle?"

"If ya come to take me, how come y'aint done it? Go on get it over with. I ain't got no patience for the likes a you!"

The Devil-boy smiled a crooked, leprous smile. "You have no idea how very important you are," he said. "I wouldn't touch a hair on your head."

"Then what are ya here fer?"

"Dinner," said the Devil.

Slayton shook his head, and the world spun in circles one way and then the other. He took another swig of whiskey and left to see what there was to eat in the kitchen. *What was the Devil likely to eat?* he wondered. *Beef jerky? Saltines?* When he stumbled back out of the kitchen, he saw his visitor searching through his munitions locker, which had been locked.

"You get your nose outta there!" shouted Slayton, but the fat Devil-boy didn't move.

"You collect weapons?" asked the Devil-boy.

"What business is it of yours?"

The Devil-boy swung the door wide to reveal Slayton's cache—a regular arsenal of all types of weaponry from rifle to pistol, from Bowie knife to crossbow. All shiny and clean.

"Most of 'em never been fired," said Slayton. "All loaded, though. You never know when you might need one."

"It's a fine collection," said the Devil-boy. Then he turned to the many items on Slayton's shelves. Old family pictures. Knickknacks from here and there. He brushed his finger across the dusty shelf, and his eyes darted back and forth, looking at everything—first everything on the shelf, then everything in the room. His eyes moved so quickly, Slayton couldn't keep up with him. Those awful blue-green eyes— they were invading him, weren't they? They were violating all of his personal things. Slayton could not stand for this, so he grabbed one of the many weapons stacked in his closet—a rifle—and aimed it at the Devil.

"I don't got no dinner for you," Slayton said. "You'd better go now."

The Devil-boy ignored Slayton. Instead, he tilted his head slightly, as if listening . . . then he sniffed the air . . . and then it was as if something snapped into place. He turned his eyes to Slayton once more and fixed his gaze.

"You loved your mother very much, didn't you," said the Devil. "It's sad she died so young."

"Wh . . . what do you know about it?"

"I know enough. I know your daddy worked the timber-line and was always gone. I know he never gave a rat's ass about you. I know how he and most everyone else called you names . . . but your ma, she defended you against all those cruel people, didn't she?"

Slayton lowered the rifle a bit and nodded slightly.

"She had a special name for you. Something secret—between the two of you. What was it?"

Slayton swallowed hard and lowered the gun to his side. *How does he know this?*

"Little Prince," said Slayton. "Just like the book."

The fat Devil-boy smiled. "When she died, your daddy just left you. How old were you, fifteen?"

"Just turned it," said Slayton. "Then he drunk hisself to death. I was glad, too."

"I know you were." The Devil began to move closer and Slayton couldn't turn his eyes away.

"This is important, Slayton. After your father died, you lived in a city for a year or so, before you moved back into the woods. . . . Tell me the name of the city."

Slayton bit his lower lip to keep it from quivering. *The Devil knows everything, don't he?*

"Come on, Slayton. Tell me the name of the city."

"Tacoma," said Slayton weakly.

"Tacoma!" The Devil smiled in some sort of deep relief. "Listen to me, Slayton," he said. "I'm going to make you the most important man in the world, and all you have to do is listen to me."

"I'm listening," said Slayton, his gaze locked onto the Devil's swimming blue eyes.

Then the Devil got as close as he possibly could to Slayton's ear, without touching him, and whispered in the faintest of voices:

"There's someone in Tacoma . . . who owes you."

It took a moment to register . . . and then the words hit home, ringing as true as a church bell in Slayton's mind. Every fiber of his soul resonated with the thought, until he felt as if his very brain would be rattled apart. *Yes! Someone in Tacoma did owe him.* He didn't know who it was, but whoever it was, Slayton would find him and make him pay!

Even Slayton could sense that this was the start of a grand chain of events that would greatly affect his life and the lives of many, many people.

He was about to turn to his munitions locker.

That's when all hell broke loose.

WINSTON HAD GRASPED THE gun in his pocket for so long, its cold handle had grown warm in his palm. A tip in the nearest town led them to this shack, and now as they kicked in the crooked door, Winston held the revolver out in front of him, afraid to pull the trigger, but also afraid not to. Everything was crucial now. No mistakes could be made.

The room was dim as they burst in, and it was hard to see. The others filed in, creating commotion, getting in the way.

There were two figures in the room, and in a moment he had identified which one was Dillon—but as Winston's eyes adjusted to the dim lamplight, he hesitated. They all hesitated, because they could not believe what they saw.

"Madre de Dios!" cried Lourdes.

Dillon barely looked human—his body had bloated like a balloon, his face was swollen with festering blisters. His eyes were blazing sapphire holes.

Winston could feel the presence of the creature that had laid waste to his own soul in there as well. It was true—all of their monstrosities were now inside of Dillon!

"No!" screamed Dillon. He tried to make a break for it, but the five of them lunged at him, trapping him in a web of ten hands. He twisted free of their grasp and backed into the corner, a terrified, caged animal.

Across the room, the old hermit could only stand there by the open closet door and gawk, while the little boy, Carter, looked in from the cabin's threshold with his awful empty eyes.

"Do it!" Tory shouted to Winston. "Do it now!"

"It's too late!" Dillon screamed. "It doesn't matter now, whatever you do won't matter!"

"Shut up!" shouted Winston.

"It's too late!" cackled Dillon again.

Winston stared at this creature in the dark corner and raised his gun. *The plan, the plan, follow the plan.*

Winston tightened his two-handed grip on the revolver, steadied his shaking hands, then leveled his aim and pulled his trigger.

The roar from the six beasts drowned out any sound the gun could have made.

A flash of light—a flash of darkness—shadowy figures leaping in six different directions—screaming—blue flames—tentacles—horrid fangs! Six dark shadows clinging to the walls screeching and wailing in fury . . .

And in fear.

"They're afraid of us!" shouted Tory. "Look at them!"

The beasts recoiled from the kids in the room, leaping, slithering, flying from wall to wall.

"Don't let them inside you!" shouted Michael. "Fight to keep them out!" Although none of them knew how to do that, they willed themselves to stand firm against the raging, snarling shadows, and the creatures did not dare come near them.

Without a host, the beasts could not survive long in this world. And so they left it.

It was something the kids could not have anticipated. The six hideous leech-things came together in the center of the room, and with a blast that rocked the weak foundations of the tiny cabin, they ripped the world open.

A ragged hole tore in the fabric of space, and the creatures escaped through it, into blind darkness.

The hole! thought Winston, before he even understood what it was. *We're all too close to the—*

Dillon's limp body slipped into the gaping breach—Deanna grabbed him, losing her balance. Winston caught her, and before any of them knew what was happening they had all grabbed hold of one another in a twisted huddle as they lost their footing and slipped into the vortex, from light into darkness.

And for an instant . . . just an instant they felt it:

Wholeness.

The six of them touching.

Complete and invincible.

Perfect and joyous.

An absolute union.

But the feeling ended when the six of them came through the darkness and hit a hard, unearthly ground, crashing apart once more like a fragile pieces of glass.

SLAYTON WATCHED THEM GO.

It had all happened so fast, he wasn't sure what he had seen . . . but then he realized that it didn't matter because

someone owed him in Tacoma.

Nothing mattered but that simple fact. Not the sudden disappearance of the Devil-boy and his devil friends. Not even the hole to Hell that still hung in the middle of the room. Nothing mattered because he had a mission.

Five minutes later, he had loaded most of his weapons into his pickup truck. He hadn't noticed the little boy who stood there watching, until the boy spoke.

"Mister, you playin' a game?" asked the boy, his head lolled to one side like he was half dead.

Slayton didn't have time for questions, or things that got in his way, so he reached into his pickup bed and grabbed a loaded shotgun.

"Are you a cowboy, or an Indian?" asked the boy.

Slayton took aim at the boy. No one would get in his way between here and Tacoma.

17. UNWORLD

Dillon felt his mind, body, and soul ripped apart, then a moment later he was torn from the world.

He never heard the gunshot, but the pain was very real. It exploded in the back of his head where the bullet must have left his skull.

All was still now. Silent. He felt his blood pouring from the back of his head, and he moved his hand toward his forehead, certain that this would be the last action of his life. He would touch his own shattered forehead and then die.

But there was no entry wound.

And in the back of his head, there was no exit wound either. There was only a sharp stone upon which he had fallen, and a gash on the back of his scalp that spilled blood onto sands that were already the color of blood.

Everything was spinning in Dillon's head. He felt an unbearable emptiness. A hollowness. He had been crammed tightly with seething, horrid creatures, but now they were gone, and the emptiness they left behind was strange and terrible. He heard the voices of the other kids around him—the ones who had tried to kill him.

"They're getting away," one of them said.

"We can catch them!"

"Don't just sit there, run!"

He heard feet running off, then saw the black kid who had fired the gun standing over him.

"You dead?" asked the black kid.

"Yes," groaned Dillon.

"Good," said the black kid, and he took off with the others.

Dillon closed his eyes again. And tried to feel something . . . anything. He could feel the blood pulsing in his hands and feet, he could feel the pain in the back of his head, but he couldn't feel anything *inside*. The events of the past few weeks were slowly coming back to him, like the details of a nightmare . . . he remembered Boise, and Idaho Falls, and Burton, and the many other people and places he had carefully destroyed, but with those memories came a fog of numbness. No feeling. No remorse. No sorrow or joy. Nothing. He had no feeling inside him at all. No heart. No soul.

"Dillon?"

He opened his eyes, and there beside him knelt Deanna. She helped him to sit up, and as he shifted, he felt something hard against the small of his back. He reached behind his back and pulled out the gun that should have killed him. Deanna gently took it from him and exposed the barrel.

"Four chambers; three bullets. We fired the empty chamber hoping we could scare them out of you. If it hadn't worked, we still had the three full ones."

Dillon felt weak, feverish. He realized he hadn't eaten for days.

"Where are we?"

His eyes had adjusted to the strange harsh light, and he looked around. The sands were vermillion red, the sky an icy frost blue. A much smaller tear, ten feet in the air above him, marked the passage back to their own world.

And all around them was despair.

Downed airplanes and crushed ships littered the sands. Rusted cars with crusty skeletons lay strewn every few hundred yards like a great garden of death. All the people and things that had ever disappeared without explanation were well accounted for in this unnameable place, having fallen through tears in the fabric of time and space. And yet this was not quite another world—it was an unworld—an unloved, unseen, unattended-to place. A place between.

Dillon turned to see a solitary mountain looming behind them; it seemed as out of place as everything else. At the top of this peak stood what appeared to be a castle carved out of the rock itself.

Dillon's beast was climbing this mountain. So was Deanna's. The other four kids had taken off in various directions across the sands after their demons, but Dillon's and Deanna's were getting away.

And still Dillon felt nothing.

He turned to Deanna.

"Deanna . . . I want you to look at me and tell me what you see."

Deanna looked him over, and tried to hide the grimace on her face. "It's not so good . . . but the weight is already going away, and your skin . . ."

"No," said Dillon. "That's not what I mean."

He gripped her tightly and looked into her eyes. "I mean . . . what do you see . . . when you look at me . . ."

Deanna peered into his eyes, as she always did. He could almost feel her probing inside of him . . . searching . . . and then a tear trickled down her face.

"They've killed me, haven't they?" asked Dillon. "Those monsters left my body and my mind, but they killed my soul . . ."

"No . . . ," said Deanna, smiling gently though her tears. Dillon could now see that these were not tears of sadness; they were tears of joy. "The other day," said Deanna, "I thought you were gone forever, so I ran. . . . But I was wrong. . . . You're still alive, Dillon, body *and* soul."

Deanna leaned forward and kissed his blistered, swollen lips. And for a moment Dillon felt a twinge of feeling coming back to him.

He glanced up at the rift in space just out of their reach, remembering the extent of their situation.

"Slayton," he said weakly. "I launched him toward Tacoma . . ."

Deanna calmly helped him to his feet. "First the beasts," she said. "They're too powerful—they have to be destroyed."

Dillon couldn't keep his eyes off of her. After everything he had done, she still cared for him—and after all the terror, she could face this new challenge with fortitude and peace. "How can you be so strong?" he asked. But Deanna only smiled. *What a wondrous gift,* thought Dillon. *To be so strong. To be so brave.*

He stood on wobbly legs like a dead man refusing to give up the ghost and tapped into Deanna's will, borrowing it for his own. Then they set off toward the mountain to face their demons.

TORY HAD BEEN THE first to realize that these beasts could be destroyed. She knew by the way the beasts moved. They didn't zip across these sands like shadows; they ran, they crawled, they slithered, like beings of flesh and blood. Indeed, in this unworld these beasts were creatures of flesh. That meant they would have weaknesses and could be hunted! The creatures raced off in different directions, and the kids took off after the beast each recognized to be their own.

In this world, Tory's beast appeared to be an amorphous gray blob, continually shifting and changing shape—but as she drew closer she realized it was not a blob, but a swarm. Millions of mutated bacteria—a colony of pestilence—buzzing in perfect formation, like a single being with a million minute bodies all following a single will.

Like a swarm of bees.

It was that thought that made her realize how she might kill it.

The swarm, only a dozen yards away now, took off, darting through strange leafless trees and bulky derelict vessels until reaching the wreck of an old propeller plane. When the swarm disappeared into the side of the plane, Tory knew she'd be climbing into a hive.

The wreckage was filled with rotted airplane seats and skeletons of passengers long dead. Toward the front of the cabin, the beast waited; a buzzing horde that had taken on a new formation complete with arms and legs, roughly in the shape of a human body.

Tory stalked closer, and the buzz in her ears grew as the creature advance, then attacked. Hideous ugly bugs surrounded her, crawling over every inch of her body. They stung and bit; they gnawed and drew blood; they burrowed under her skin. The pain was unbearable, and Tory cried out in horror. She was being eaten alive by these things! She would die right here. With her body burning from the stings of the swarm, she reached deeper and deeper into it, hoping beyond hope that she'd be able to carry out her plan before the swarm killed her. Then, in the center of the buzzing mass, she found what she was looking for. There was a creature hovering there, twice the size of her fist, with a grotesque bulging body, tendrils, and insectile eyes. It seemed half mosquito, half jellyfish. The thing's segmented eyes stared at her in fear and fury, while all around her the swarm continued to bite—raising welts, burrowing into her, fighting to make her their hive.

The colony of disease—this *ugliness*—had once found a

place in Tory, but she had no room for such ugliness anymore. Now as she gripped the queen of the swarm, she pumped all of her anger into her clenched fist and drove out her own revulsion, replacing it with determination. This thing had turned Tory's own unique power against her . . . but now the creature was on the *outside*, and it had no defense against Tory's cleansing touch.

The filthy thing writhed in her grasp, the disease draining from it, its flesh fading from sickly gray to jelly-clear. Its swarm fell to the ground one by one, pattering like a fall of rain, until the queen was alone and unprotected. Without her guardians and without her filth, Tory knew this creature in her fist was nothing. . . . So she hurled the thing to the ground and crushed it beneath the heel of her shoe, the way she would crush any bug that became a nuisance.

MICHAEL CHASED THE BLUE-BURNING beast of many hands toward the shore of a violent sea, where black water lapped like oil upon the vermillion sands.

As he dove on the beast, bringing it down, he felt himself overwhelmed by a tempest of emotions so powerful he thought it would tear him apart. Sorrow, slashed by anger, scalded by desire, and each emotion was so extreme, Michael felt the turbulence alone would destroy him. He flipped the creature around to face him—but it had no face; only eyes. Turquoise, hypnotic eyes, and many burning hands, each stronger than his own.

Then the creature did grow a face around those deep, deep eyes. It was the face of a beautiful girl; somehow a mixture of all the girls he had known and wanted—and its many hands no longer clawed him but caressed him. Those soft hands tingled across his chest and his legs. His arms slipped from around the creature's neck to its shoulders. He felt hands on his head pulling him closer into a powerful embrace, and all his battling emotions were flooded by something more powerful than all the rest. It was the old familiar feeling; the brutal passion that ruled his days and nights.

The beautiful creature pulled Michael into a fiery kiss.

You can't imagine the pleasure I could give you, he felt it say. *All the Joys you could imagine . . . if only you stop resisting . . . if only you feed me . . .*

Michael could feel the intensity of its passion mingling with his own.

Take me back, he felt the creature say. *Invite me back in.*

Michael could feel it trying to slide beneath his skin and dissolve into his blood.

Invite you in? thought Michael. Is that how it had happened in the first place? Did it have to be invited in?

He thought of the girl in Baltimore, and then the one in Omaha. This thing had now become so powerful that it could steal a soul with a kiss. Was he going to invite this thing to rule him?

Michael knew he could not let it happen, so he turned everything off—and was amazed to find that he had the power to do it. He shut down the fear, he closed off his anger, he doused his lust. He made himself feel cold, calm, and unaffected by the grip of this sensual creature that clung to him.

The air around them began to chill and fill with flurries of snow, but there was no icy wind of fear.

The creature wailed, its hands becoming claws again, digging into him, its face melting away into those burning blue eyes. It thrashed as if each snowflake were made of acid, and the snow kept falling heavier by the moment.

Only now did Michael realize that he was killing it—but he didn't allow himself to feel excitement.

Cold. Calm. Unaffected.

Michael pulled away, standing above it, feeling the snow grow stronger; feeling himself feel nothing for this creature.

For all the spirits we destroyed, for all the girls whose souls we invaded together, I leave you cold. I will not be your accomplice. I will not be your slave. My body will not be your vessel. And I will walk away feeling nothing for you.

The snow was like a mountain of sand around his wailing creature now. With a hundred flaming blue hands it tried to free itself, but could not. Michael watched as it sunk into the snow and drowned. The snow itself flowed a bright blue for a few moments as the creature dissolved into it, but then the hot, black waters of the unworld sea crashed upon the glowing mound, melting it. In a moment, nothing was left but a thin blue foam shredded by the dark, churning surf.

LOURDES STRUGGLED WITH HER immense, slow-moving beast, but as strong as her muscles had gotten beneath all that fat, this beast was far stronger. It was like an octopus; a great boneless jet black thing with tentacles as thick as her thighs and a singular, hateful eye.

But the worst was its mouth—a great toothless maw that stretched itself open wide as the tentacles pushed Lourdes toward it. She tried to dig her feet into the sand, but it was no use. It pulled her in and swallowed her whole with a mighty roar.

Lourdes took a last gasp of breath before the mouth closed around her, forcing her into a wet, airless darkness. She pushed her elbows against it, she scraped its gullet with her fingernails, she felt her heart pounding, using up the last of the oxygen in her lungs . . . but she heard the beast's heart beating. She was inside it now, rather than it being inside of her . . . and it dawned on Lourdes that this made all the difference. She fought to stay conscious and concentrated on the sound of the creature's bloated heart, until she saw it in her mind. . . . Then, in the same way she had made Carter and the squirrel sleep, she forced her will into the nervous system of this beast.

And she shut down its heart.

The creature began to thrash as its heart seized into a heavy knot. It violently spat Lourdes out onto the sand, and Lourdes, wet and slimy, but very much alive, gasped for breath, feeling her head spin. She kept the creature under her control, clenching her fists, imagining its heart clenched as tightly, until finally the thing quivered and fell to the ground, its life slipping away with the steamy breath from its swollen mouth. Lourdes watched the hatred in its awful eye vanish into the indifference of death.

WINSTON CHASED HIS BEAST into the looming shadow of a steamer ship that listed dangerously in the sand, its rusted hull wedged between two boulders.

Winston's creature was small—even smaller than he was, and it surprised him. It loped on all fours, with stubbly legs and long arms. Winston could have caught it easily, if his ankle hadn't been twisted in the fall, but now he had to limp after it, grimacing with every step.

In the shadow of the listing steamer, Winston got close enough to grab the beast's furry leg; to Winston's surprise, the creature did not resist. It turned to Winston and gazed into eyes.

This was not the creature Winston imagined. Its eyes were large and friendly; its fur was soft; it's face seemed innocent . . . inquisitive, and it resembled a cross between a monkey and a bear cub.

As Winston looked at it, he felt a sudden urge to hold it

close to him, so he did. It wrapped its furry arms and legs around him.

It felt good. Comfortable. Safe. He felt as if he could take this soft thing beneath his arm, curl up, and fall asleep.

The soft creature did not slide beneath his arm, however. It slid around him, clung to his back, and held him tightly around the neck.

Winston felt its open mouth by his ear. He smelled its breath; it was clean, like a baby's breath.

I can make everything like it was, it whispered to him. *Just like it was before your father died. I can make it all go back, and you can feel the way you used to feel all those years ago.*

The creature's sweet smell and the softness of its fur was enough to comfort his doubt. Enough to paralyze his fear.

Paralyze?

The creature's mouth opened wider and its fangs drove deep into the back of Winston's neck, settling in his spine. He felt his days slipping away again; his life moving backward, his body growing down. Winston roared with anger. He might have once longed for time to take a giant step backward, but not anymore! He grabbed the beast and flung it from him so hard that it hit the side of the rusty old ship with a clang that echoed inside the hollow hull.

The creature was advancing again, long sharp claws on its fingers, fangs in its mouth, but those longing, innocent eyes never changed.

It came at him through the sharp nettles that had grown in the shade of the behemoth boat, moving much faster than Winston.

What am I going to do, beat it with a corsage? The words came slinging back through his mind . . . and then he realized that he could do just that and more! Without an instant to lose, he grabbed the gnarled hardwood stem of the bush before him, painfully gripping the thorns, and pushed life into it.

The ground beneath him began to rumble and undulate. Lines like mole tunnels pushed up the dirt, and shoots of thorn-laden branches sprouted from the ground. The furry creature found its fur caught in a sharp web of growth. It whined and cried and bleated like a lamb, as bright flowers sprung from branches, hiding the sharpness of the thorns.

Winston fought his way through the malevolent shrubs until he found a branch that was close to the creature. He touched that branch, and immediately it sprouted new shoots that wove in and out of the dirt, winding around the creature until it was trapped in a prison of thorns.

The earth around them continued to undulate, as beneath them the roots grew deeper and stronger. The leaning ship creaked on its precarious bed of sand.

The creature bleated and cried, writhing in agony, its fur shredding on the barbs of the new growth.

"Cry all you want," Winston told it. *"But I'm growing up!"*

A heavy root the width of a tree trunk forced up the earth beneath the steamer. The great ship let out a ghastly metallic moan as it was shifted by the massive roots.

Winston began to scramble away, leaving the beast in its thorny prison. He pulled himself across the sand, through the nettles, until he was out from the shadow of the ship.

Another ghastly moan and a heavy rattle.

Winston looked back to see the keel of the steamer finally lose its battle with gravity. The entire ship began to fall to its side and, beneath it, the screaming, bleating beast fought to get free of the thorns, until the mighty ship came down upon it. The ship shook the earth with a colossal rumble, crushing the small, deadly beast under a thousand tons of steel.

. . .

DILLON AND DEANNA HEARD the falling ship, and felt the shock wave shake the mountain beneath them moments later. Stones and pebbles, dislodged by the shaking of the earth, flew down the mountain toward them—but their only concerns now were the creatures climbing thirty yards ahead of them.

From behind, Dillon's appeared half-human, but moved with powerful, otherwordly grace. Its skin was smooth, hairless leaden-gray over bulging muscles; both magnificent and repulsive at the same time—the very sight of it churned Dillon's stomach. Deanna's beast had no grace. It had no arms or legs either; it was a serpentine thing, flat and segmented like a giant worm.

They soon reached a plateau that was too smooth to be natural. It was, in fact, a grand stone court that led to the crumbling palace carved out of the stone, and the creatures disappeared into the dark recesses of this ancient acropolis. This was their home. Their lair.

"Don't be scared," said Deanna, "We'll find them."

Then she disappeared down a corridor that led to the left, and Dillon headed off to the right.

DEANNA KNEW THAT SHE should have been frightened, but she was not. She kept her wits about her as she ascended the stone stairs, passing the crumbling bones of ancient human skeletons as she stepped deeper into darkness. It could have been crouching in any dark corner she passed. It could have been waiting inches above her. She knew that somewhere nearby it was coiled like a cobra, ready to strike.

Her foot touched something. A stone? No—it moved. A rat? Were there rats in this forgotten place? She turned but was faced by more darkness. Webs brushed across her face that were too thick to be made by earth-born spiders.

She smelled it before she saw it—an acrid, dank odor of peat and fungus as it sprang at her from the left. She turned and it struck her shoulder, clamping on with toothless, powerful jaws like a bear trap. She felt its slippery scales coiling around her, its icy body constricting around her chest, cutting off her air and circulation. She lost her balance and rolled down a flight of stone stairs.

At the bottom of the stairs she was able to wrench her hand free, and she grabbed the thing by its neck, tearing its awful jaws from her shoulder. Her eyes had adjusted to the dim light, and she could see it now as she held its flaring head away from her. Its breath was chill and foul, and its face was almost human . . . except that it had no eyes.

Then Deanna realized something. It was in the way it darted left, then right—the way it snapped sightlessly and frantically in the air. Deanna knew that feeling all too well.

You're terrified, aren't you?

The serpent coiled itself tighter around her.

You're terrified that you'll die!

Deanna could sense that although it had a stranglehold on her, it didn't want to kill her. It wanted her to let it inside. To let it come . . . home.

Take me back, it seemed to plead. *Please let me in. . . . I'm sooooo frightened. Don't make me kill you!*

Deanna, on the other hand, felt no fear at all within her. She calmly held its head away so it could not strike. She felt herself growing weak from the lack of air as its body coiled around her chest.

I am not your home, she told it silently. *And I am not afraid of you. So I suppose you'll have to kill me.*

The serpent, more terrified than ever, squeezed her tighter, but Deanna forced herself to her feet and pressed her thumbs firmly against its neck. It, too, began to gasp for air, and as they staggered across the rough stone floor in a lethal dance, it became a simple matter of who was going to strangle who first.

DILLON COLE, STILL FEELING a mere shell of a human being, slowly stalked the halls of the ruined place. Window glass had long since crumbled to sand. Bones of the dead crumbled to dust beneath his feet. He wondered if, perhaps, he would join the minions of the dead in this godforsaken place.

The creature was easy to follow; its large feet left clear footprints on the dusty floor. Dillon followed the steps up, until he came to a great room.

There, between two pillars, sat a regal stone chair, and in that stone chair sat the crumbling remains of a man. His clothes were still intact, but the threads had mildewed and decayed until it was barely recognizable as a tattered royal robe. This palace—this whole mountain—had fallen here from another world, and all that was left of its royal occupants were bones crumbling to dust.

On the other side of the room stood Dillon's beast.

Dark gray flesh, rippling with strong muscles . . . and a familiar face.

Dillon's face.

The creature made no effort to run. Instead it stalked closer, mirroring Dillon's movements, until they stood five feet apart. It made no move to attack, nor did Dillon. Instead, Dillon stared into its eyes, trying to read some pattern there.

As complicated as it was, Dillon could read the pattern of its past. This being had begun as something small and insignificant—a maggot that he had invited into his soul in a moment of weakness. And once there, it had grown, evolved into something larger, then something larger still. Even now it seemed on the verge of a new metamorphosis. Through its translucent skin, Dillon could see a new form taking shape, ready to emerge . . . as soon as it was fed.

Dillon pulled the revolver from his shirt. This time the first three chambers were all full.

A smile appeared on the creature's face. It was a twisted, evil version of Dillon's own smile.

I can destroy you with a single thought. You'll be gone long before the hammer hits the chamber.

Still Dillon tightened his grip on the trigger.

So the creature pushed a single thought into Dillon's mind. *Suffer the weight,* it said to him. *SUFFER THE WEIGHT!*

Dillon's finger froze on the trigger, and from somewhere deep inside he felt all his feelings return to him at once. His crippled soul was called out of hiding, and with it came an eruption from the pit of his stomach that came screaming out of his mouth. All his emotionless memories finally locked in with their meanings, and they surged like bile through his brain.

Remorse!

Sorrow!

Shame, blame, and guilt echoed through his brain like a sonic boom, rattling his mind until he felt himself about to fall into the same chaos that he had created around him. He tried to deny all the things he had done—tried to deny that he had *chosen* this path, but even among shades of gray, the truth was there in black and white: it had been his choice to destroy. It had been his choice to feed the beast.

The sheer weight of his crimes weighed upon him now with such a pressure that he wished that fourth chamber had been full when Winston had pulled the trigger.

But he could right that mistake, couldn't he? The first three chambers were full. He could rid himself of the pain—the horrible guilt.

Suddenly the creature standing before him didn't seem to matter. All that mattered was ending the pain, so he turned the gun around and touched the cold barrel against his own temple.

And then, in front of him, he saw the creature flex its fingers and take a deep breath, waiting to be fed.

To be fed.

Dillon gritted his teeth and with all his might kept his finger from pressing that trigger. Destroying himself would be feeding the creature. It suddenly became clear to Dillon that the only way to deny this creature satisfaction was to bear the pain. And so Dillon did. He accepted the blame for the death and for the insanity. He felt the awful weight on his shoulders . . . and that weight, pressing like a thousand stones, almost killed him right there.

But It didn't.

And instead he was left with just enough strength to turn the gun around again and pull the trigger.

The bullet caught the creature in the shoulder. It wailed in pain and surprise, then grabbed Dillon and hurled him across the room.

Dillon came crashing down on the throne, shattering what was left of its former occupant. Bone fragments splintered into the air and a cloud of dust rose from where Dillon sat.

The creature, bleeding a viscous, dark blood, leapt toward him, and Dillon fired again.

The second blast caught the creature in the stomach.

It doubled over in pain.

Dillon rose from the throne and the creature backed away

toward an open veranda, pulling itself along, limping, leaving a path of its slippery blood.

Dillon stalked after it. Then, at the threshold of the balcony, it turned its eyes to him once more.

Finish it, the beast said, taunting. *Shoot now!*

Something inside Dillon told him to look at the patterns—to check the series of outcomes that firing the bullet could create. But he didn't listen; instead he just leveled the gun and let his anger fly uncontrolled with the firing of the final bullet.

The beast moved its head at the last moment, the bullet barely grazed its ear, and when the beast stepped away, Dillon realized how fully and completely he had been tricked . . . and how much heavier the weight of his soul had suddenly become.

Behind the creature, on the veranda, Deanna was coiled in a death grip with her serpent of fear, when suddenly her arms went limp from the bullet that had grazed the ear of Dillon's beast . . . and then hit her in the chest.

"No!!!!!!!!" Dillon ran to her.

The serpent squealed, uncoiled, and retreated to the corner, quivering, and Dillon caught Deanna's collapsing body.

The dark spirit laughed a healthy, hearty laugh. It flexed its muscles and absorbed this act of destruction. It fed on Deanna's dying breaths.

Deanna gasped for breath in Dillon's arms.

"I'm sorry," he said. "I'm sorry, I'm sorry, I'm sorry." But his words felt impotent and useless. She tried to speak but couldn't. He felt the wound in her chest, which was pouring blood, and saw the light slipping from her eyes.

Deanna gazed at him weakly. "I'm not afraid," she said. "I'm not afraid . . ."

Dillon could see the pattern of death. He could see her mind imploding—feel death beginning to break down her body. He felt her disappearing down that long tunnel.

And then he realized he could stop it.

He concentrated on her wound. He concentrated all his attention. His talent was not only to *see* patterns but to *change* them. Could he close the pattern of a wound the way he could instantly solve a Rubik's Cube? Could he reverse the patterns of chaos and death the same way he could create them?

He put his hand on Deanna's wound, which had stopped pumping blood. He felt the wound ever so slowly beginning to close—

—But then he felt the pattern of her mind collapsing, so he focused on that, keeping her mind from giving in to death—

—But then he felt the pattern of her cells begin to slowly decay, so he turned his attention to keeping her flesh from giving over to the silence of death—

—But her wound had begun to bleed again . . . so he turned his attention to that.

A screaming, tear-filled rage overcame Dillon. This was a task he could not accomplish, no matter how powerful his talent. He did not yet have the skill to prevent Deanna's death. In the end all he could do was hold her in his trembling arms and watch her great light disappear into eternity.

Standing just a few feet away, Dillon's creature fed on Deanna's death and completed its metamorphosis. Its outer skin broke away to reveal a lattice of veins and fine bones that pulled away from its body spreading wide, casting a shadow of a pair of wings, blacker than black, over Dillon and Deanna.

The creature still bled—wounded, but still alive.

Suffer the weight, Dillon, it said to him again. *And every moment you suffer is a moment I grow strong.*

Then it turned from him and leapt off the balcony, soaring

high on its great black wings and leaving a veil of darkness that trailed behind it, followed by Deanna's serpent, which slithered down the rocky slope.

Dillon leaned over Deanna's body and cried, but his tears did no good, and when he had no more tears, he lifted her up and brought her to the throne. He brushed off the dust and fragments of ancient bone, and he gently set her down, wrapping her in the moldering royal robe . . . and as he held the robe, he could see its pattern coming back together in his hands. It was a simple pattern, just a weave of fabric. In a few moments what had been tattered, disintegrating cloth became a rich royal-blue robe of silk.

Order out of chaos.

How could he have been so blind as to let his talent be used to destroy when it could have been used to create?

He held the cloth a moment longer until all its fragments had woven together in his hand and it was as bright and clean as the day it was made. Then he finished wrapping it around Deanna's limp body and closed her unseeing eyes.

He kissed her cold cheek. "I'll come back for you, Deanna," he promised. "I'll bring you back."

Was it possible? Was life out of death something he could ever manage? Could his talent ever be honed to weave back a tapestry of life the way it rewove a tapestry of silk?

He kissed Deanna again and let her go. She seemed to recline regally in the throne, like a queen in repose.

"I love you," he whispered.

He turned and stepped out on the veranda once more, the sorrow almost overtaking him so that he had to hold onto the stone to keep from doubling over. Down below, he could see the others trying to climb back to their world. While way in the distance the winged Spirit of Destruction soared into the icy sky, and the serpentine Spirit of Fear followed in its shadow, like thunder after lightning.

IN THE HEAT OF the red desert, they didn't discuss how they had defeated their foes—instead they focused all their attention on the task at hand. There was a hole fifteen feet off the ground, and it was quickly healing itself closed. They pushed a rusted car beneath the hole, then piled everything from stones to airplane seats to rusted bicycles—anything they could find to get themselves high enough. Then, when their mound was done, Winston laid his hands on a vine, which grew around the mass of loose objects, locking them together in a living mesh.

They only stopped in their task once; the moment they felt one of them die. Then they all took a deep breath and continued stacking, not daring to talk about it.

They had already begun to climb toward the hole when they saw Dillon coming toward them.

"They got away," said Dillon. ". . . And Deanna's dead." The four hesitated, not even wanting to get close to him. It was Tory who finally stepped down.

"We need to know about the hermit on the other side," said Tory. "What can we do to stop him?"

Slayton! He had forgotten about Slayton! He was long gone, somewhere in Tacoma by now, already beginning the great collapse.

"I don't think he can be stopped," said Dillon sadly. "You should have killed me."

But instead, Tory reached her hand out to him. "Hurry, the hole's almost closed."

Up above, Michael and Lourdes had already forced their way through the hole, which was no larger than a basketball now.

"You're gonna let *him* come with us?" Winston shouted down to Tory. "After what he's done? With his leech-freak still out there?"

"He's one of us," was the only answer Tory gave.

Winston threw a bitter gaze at Dillon, and then threw himself into the hole and vanished. When Tory got to the top, she took a moment to look at the desolation here in this infinite "between." Then she pushed her way into the hole, which stretched around her like tight elastic, until she disappeared into darkness.

Dillon hesitated. If the world on the other side of that hole was already starting to fracture, it would soon be more of a Hell than this tormented place they were leaving. But it was *his* world, and *his* responsibility to face what he had done there. So he took a deep breath and grabbed the lip of the hole with both hands, stretching the rend in space as wide as it would go. Then he squeezed his way into a layer of cold, suffocating darkness, and finally he pushed himself through the gap on the other side, into the world of life.

THE WEAPONS LOCKER WAS empty.

This was the first thing Dillon noticed as he fell from the hole to the cold wooden floor of Slayton's shack. The weapons locker was empty, and Slayton was gone.

Dillon squeezed his eyes shut, trying to somehow disappear inside himself, but could not. "You don't know how awful it's going to be," he told the others. "You can't imagine what the world will be like tomorrow . . ."

They all looked at each other, then turned back to Dillon.

"There's something you should see outside," Lourdes said.

It was light now, and the hermit's old pickup was still there, its headlights shining straight at them. Its engine was on—

overheating and billowing steam; radiator fluid soaked the ground.

Two figures were in the light of the headlights: a small boy making rivers in the dirt with the spilled radiator fluid, and Slayton, who was sitting up against the grill. It seemed Tacoma was no longer of any interest to him.

"Was this part of the plan?" Michael asked Dillon.

Clearly it wasn't.

"You were good . . . ," Tory told Dillon. "But I guess there's some things not even you can predict."

Lourdes picked Carter up in her arms, as the five of them stared at Slayton, loaded shotgun still in hand, sitting motionless against the grill of the pickup.

The radiator was leaking because it had been punctured by a steel arrow. The same steel arrow that pinned Slayton's lifeless body to the radiator grill.

"We was playing cowboys and Indians," said Carter, still gripping Slayton's crossbow in his hands. "I won."

Inside the dead hermit's shack a hole in the wall of the world quietly healed itself closed and disappeared with a tiny twinkling of light.

18. THE FIVE OF WANDS

They buried Slayton beside his shack with his own shovel. He had lived forsaken, but was laid to rest with more tender care than he had known in life. They buried his weapons with him and, with each shovel of dirt, they not only buried the man, but also the nightmare they had lived under for so long.

They finished at dawn, and now the forest that had seemed so desolate revealed its own slow recovery in the growing light. Between the gray, lifeless trees, grass and wildflowers had come back to begin the process of life again.

Winston gathered some of the wildflowers, strewed them across the barren grave, then brushed his fingers across them until the grave sprouted into a colorful garden. Then the four of them built a fire to warm themselves, and stood around it, talking of small, unimportant things, which they never before had had the luxury to do.

Only Dillon stayed away, still an outsider.

He had been the first to begin digging the grave, the first to gather wood for the fire, but when nothing was left for him to do, he placed himself in exile. They all were painfully aware of his presence.

"Someone should say something to him," suggested Tory.

Winston gnawed beef jerky on teeth that were still coming in. "I got nothing to say to him," he declared coldly.

They all stole glances at Dillon, who sat alone by the hermit's grave, aimlessly shuffling a worn deck of cards he had found in the shack. He was thinner now, and his face almost cleared up, but there was a burden in that face, so weighty and oppressive, it was hard to look at him.

"What can we say that will make any difference?" wondered Lourdes, and glanced toward Carter, who now busied himself dropping sugar cubes into a bucket of rainwater, watching them dissolve with the same mindless indifference he must have felt when he fired that crossbow. The boy was a living testament to the people and places Dillon had shattered, and nothing any of them could say would change that.

"Any one of us could have ended up like Dillon," said Michael. "I know I almost did."

Michael left the warmth of the fire and was the first to brave the distance to the boy they knew only as The Destroyer.

"SOLITAIRE?" ASKED MICHAEL AS he approached Dillon.

Dillon didn't break the rhythm of his shuffling. "A trick," he answered.

"Can I see it?"

Dillon looked at Michael apprehensively, then handed Michael the cards. "Shuffle them and lay them face up," he said.

Michael sat down, shuffled the cards, then spread them out, showing a random mix of fifty-two cards.

Dillon picked up the deck again and began to shuffle it himself. "I never liked playing cards," said Dillon, "because no matter how much I shuffled the deck, the first card I always turned over was the ace of spades. The death card."

"That's not the death card," said Tory as she came over and sat beside them. "Believe me, I've *seen* the death card, and it's not the ace of spades."

Lourdes came over as well, leaving Winston the only one refusing to talk to Dillon. They watched as Dillon shuffled the deck over and over, and when he was done he handed the deck to Tory. "Flip the first card," he said.

Tory flipped it. It was the ace of spades.

"Cool trick," said Michael.

It was Lourdes who realized the trick hadn't ended. "Why don't you flip the second card?" she suggested.

Tory flipped it; the deuce of spades.

"So?" said Michael.

Tory flipped another card; the three of spades; then the four of spades; then the five. She looked at Dillon warily, then turned the entire deck over and spread the cards face up.

The cards were in perfect order; ace through king, spades through diamonds! They stared, not sure whether to be aghast or amused.

"Pretty good trick, huh?" said Dillon. His eyes betrayed the truth; this was much more than a mere trick.

"So what's the big deal?" asked Michael as he examined the deck.

"Entropy," said Tory.

"Entro-what?"

"Entropy," she repeated. "Newton came up with it—it's one of the basic laws of the universe, just like gravity."

"What is?!" demanded Michael.

Tory rolled her eyes. *"That things go from a state of order to disorder.* You know—mountains erode, glass breaks, food rots—"

"Cards get shuffled," said Lourdes.

"Right," said Tory, "but Dillon here . . . he's breaking that law."

They all stared at him. "Is that true?" asked Lourdes.

Dillon quivered a bit, and said, "Go directly to jail, do not pass 'Go.'"

While Michael chuckled nervously, and Lourdes just stared at the cards, Tory scoured the area for a way to test her theory. She finally settled on Carter, who had long since drowned all his sugar cubes, and was just staring into the bucket of water. She took it from him, and he hardly seemed to notice it was gone.

"The law of entropy say that sugar dissolves in water," said Tory, brining the bucket over to them. "Right?"

Everyone looked into the bucket. The water was clear; not a granule of sugar left.

"Dillon, put out your hands," asked Tory.

Dillon did, and Tory slowly poured the water through his fingers.

What they saw didn't appear spectacular. . . . At first . . . it just seemed . . . well, weird. As soon as Tory began to pour the water, granules of sugar appeared in Dillon's hands, out of the clear water. The water kept spilling through his fingers, and his palms filled with the white powder . . . but it didn't stop there. The grains seemed to be pulling themselves together as Dillon concentrated, and once the water had poured through his fingers and the bucket was completely empty, Dillon was left with not just a handful of sugar . . . *but a handful of sugar cubes.*

They stared at the cubes, stupefied.

"That's awesome!" said Michael. "It's like reversing time!"

"No it's better," suggested Lourdes. "It's reversing *space.*"

Dillon put his handful of sugar cubes down, and they slowly dissolved into the mud.

"What do you do with a talent like that?" wondered Michael.

"What can't you do with it!" said Tory. "It's better than all of our talents put together. . . . It's like . . . creation."

The very thought made Michael pale. A chill wind blew and somewhere in the distance a small cloud began to darken.

"Don't mind Michael," Tory said to Dillon, "he gets a little bit moody."

But it wasn't just a matter of Michael's being moody. He had something else weighing on his mind.

"So what happens now?" asked Michael.

The question had hung heavily in the air since dawn, but had gone unspoken. *What now?* Any urge they had felt to come together had long since faded away, just as the light of the supernova had dimmed in the night sky. If anything, the urge was to drift apart. They all turned to Dillon for an answer—as if somehow he were the one holding them together like crystals of sugar, and they needed his permission to go their separate ways.

"We do," said Dillon, "whatever we want to do."

It was a quiet declaration of independence, but seemed as profound a moment as when the exploding star first filled the night sky.

"I want to go home."

It was Winston who spoke. They all turned to see him there, a fraction of an inch taller than he was just moments before. "I gotta fix things—*change* things, get my life moving," he said, then he wiped a tear from his eye before it had a chance to fall. "And I miss my mom and brother."

No one could look each other in the eye then. Thoughts of home that had been locked away all this time now flooded them.

"By the time I get home," said Lourdes, "they won't even recognize me. . . . It's all gonna be new . . ."

The shifting wind blew cold again. "What if we don't go home?" whispered Michael.

"You will," said Dillon.

Winston crossed his arms. "How the hell do you know?"

Dillon shrugged. "I can see the pattern," he said. He studied the four of them—the way their eyes moved, the way they breathed, the way they impatiently shifted their weight from one leg to the other.

"You'll leave here not sure of anything; not even the ground beneath your feet," he told them. "But the further you get away from this place, the saner it's all going to feel . . . and every place you stop, there'll be people coming out of the woodwork talking to you—wanting to be near you, and not even knowing why. Waiters will tear up your checks—strangers will open up their homes to you; everyone will think you've gotten your lives together, and you'll laugh because you'll know the truth. And each person you come across—they'll take away something they didn't have before—something pure, or joyful, a sense of control, something to grow on. At least one of those people will get on a plane. And then it'll spread to places you've never even heard of."

They stood there aghast. Michael stared at Dillon, slack-jawed. "You can see all that?!"

Then Dillon's straight face resolved into a wide grin. "Sucker!" he said.

Tory burst out with a relieved guffaw, and soon the others were laughing and razzing Michael, as if they hadn't fallen for it as well.

Dillon's grin faded quickly and that solemn melancholy returned to take its place. "You'd better all go," he told them. "You've got a whole country to get across." Then he glanced at Carter. "You can leave him with me."

Somehow it didn't seem fitting to say good-bye, so Tory reached out her hand to Dillon and introduced herself.

"I'm Tory," she said. "Tory Smythe."

Dillon smiled slightly, and shook her hand. "Dillon Benjamin Cole."

The others were quick to follow.

"Michael Lipranski."

"Lourdes Maria Hidalgo-Ruiz."

Winston kept his hands in his pockets, refusing to shake Dillon's hand. "Winston Marcus Pell."

Then the four who had come together turned and headed toward Michael's van, dissolving away from Dillon, the way they would soon dissolve away from each other.

Winston was the last to go. He stood there, a few feet from Dillon, a scowl well-cemented on his face. He looked Dillon over head to toe.

"You know you'll never be forgiven for the things you've done. There ain't enough grace in all the world to cleanse you of that."

Dillon had to agree. "You're probably right."

Winston studied Dillon a few moments longer, and his scowl softened. He shook his head. "I wouldn't want to be you," he said.

Behind them, they heard the others piling into the van. Winston took a step back, but before he turned to leave, he reached out and tapped Dillon on the arm, the closest he could bring himself to a friendly gesture. "Stay clean," said Winston. "Don't let the bugs in."

Dillon nodded, and Winston ran off to join the others. In a moment their minds were far away, their voices growing with joy and anticipation. Then Michael started the engine, and the four great souls ventured forth into the bright morning, ready to embrace their new, old lives.

It wasn't until lunch time that they spared a thought for Dillon again, when a coffee shop waitress told them their lunch was on the house.

. . .

DILLON WATCHED THEM DRIVE down the dirt road away from Slayton's shack. The van's stereo was blasting, and Dillon could tell they were already soaring back into the world of love and life—a place where Dillon could not join them. Once the sound of their engine faded in the distance, Dillon approached Carter.

The boy still sat near Slayton's grave, doing nothing, thinking nothing. Dillon sat down in front of him and looked into the boy's eyes; the large back pupil of the left, the tiny pinpoint of the right.

Dillon gathered all of his attention, pushing out his own fear and confusion. He held this boy by the shoulders and looked through those empty eyes, until he found the impossible jigsaw of a little boy . . . mindless . . . patternless, splintered beyond any hope of repair, and yet Dillon set himself to the task of repairing it.

Dillon sat there ten minutes, twenty minutes, an hour, pushing his own mind into the boy's chaos and stringing a lifetime of thought and meaning. It wasn't as easy as destruction; it was a thousand times harder to re-create what was no longer there, but Dillon forced himself to do it.

When he was done, Dillon felt drained, cold and exhausted—but when he looked into Carter's eyes now, the boy's eyes looked normal. And they began to fill with tears.

"I done bad things," cried the boy, with a mind all too clear. "I kilt people. I done bad, bad things."

"It wasn't you," Dillon told the boy. "It was me."

Dillon took the sobbing boy into his arms and together they cried in the lonely woods. Dillon cried for all the souls he had ruined, for all the pain he had caused . . .

. . . And he cried for Deanna. Losing her was more than he could bear. If she had been here, she could have comforted this boy, touching him with her gift of strength and faith. She could have healed his heart just as Dillon had healed his mind. What a wonderful world this could have been if Deanna could still be in it.

So they both cried, and when neither of them could cry anymore, Dillon put the boy into the Range Rover and got into the driver's seat.

The boy, still sniffling a bit, studied him. "You old enough to drive?" he asked.

Dillon shrugged. "Not really."

The boy put on his seat belt, and Dillon started the car. The boy didn't ask where they were going. Maybe he just didn't want to think about it, or maybe he already knew.

INTERSTATE 84 CROSSED OUT of Washington, then followed the Columbia River east, along the Washington–Oregon border. Just before dark, they turned off the interstate, heading down a country road that wound through a dense forest. Less than a mile down, the road was blocked by a police barricade; only the truly determined would be getting anywhere near the town of Burton, Oregon, for a good long time.

Dillon stopped the car and took a deep breath as he stared at the barricade. In the distance, he could hear ghostly wails of the mad ones still lost in the woods—so many of them, it made Dillon wish he could turn and run, screaming louder than the voices in the woods. But then he remembered how bravely Deanna had faced things at the end. Certainly Dillon could find a fraction of that bravery now.

As they got out of the car, the boy looked at Dillon with trusting eyes, as if Dillon had all the answers in the world.

"Can you make it all better?" asked the boy. "Can you fix everything?"

Could he? There was no pattern Dillon could see that gave him an answer; there was only his will, the boy's hope, and a memory of Deanna's faith in him. But perhaps that's all he needed to begin the mending.

"I don't know," said Dillon. "We'll see."

Then he took the boy's hand, and together they walked toward the barricade of the shattered town.